Coaching the Brain

Everything we do, and sense, happens through our brain. In *Coaching the Brain: Practical Applications of Neuroscience to Coaching,* highly experienced coaches Joseph O'Connor and Andrea Lages ask and answer the question: 'How can we use our knowledge of the brain to help ourselves and others to learn, change, and develop?'

This book will show you how to apply insights from the latest neuroscience research in a practical way, in the fields of personal development, coaching and cognitive therapy. Accessible and practical, it begins with an overview of how the brain works along with an explanation of how our brain changes due to our actions and thoughts, illuminating how these habits can be changed through neuroplasticity. Understanding the neuroscience of goals and mental models helps us to work with and change them, and clarity about emotions and the emotional basis of values can help achieve happiness. Most importantly, neuroscience illuminates how we learn, as well as the power of expectations. The book also explores the key lessons we can take from neuroscience for high performance and leadership. Eminently accessible, this book gives you new tools to help yourself and others create better futures. As a whole, the book will provide you with a deep respect for the depth and complexity of your thinking and emotions.

Coaching the Brain: Practical Applications of Neuroscience to Coaching, with its clarity and practical application, will be essential reading for coaches in practice and in training, as well as leaders, coach supervisors and HR and L&D professionals, and will be a key text for academics and students of coaching and coaching psychology.

Joseph O'Connor is an executive coach and coach trainer, consultant and author of twenty books on coaching, Neuro Linguistic Programming (NLP) and management. He is based in London, UK.

Andrea Lages is an executive coach, consultant, coach trainer and the author of five books on coaching. She is based in the UK and Brazil and works internationally offering coaching and training in English, Portuguese and Spanish.

Joseph and Andrea are founders of the International Coaching Community (ICC), one of the largest and most respected coaching organisations in the world.

"Joseph and Andrea pursue brain-based leadership coaching with flair and precision. I highly recommend their book."
Marshall Goldsmith, Thinkers 50 #1 Executive Coach and only two-time #1 Leadership Thinker in the world

"This highly accessible and practical book takes modern neuroscience research and demonstrates how it is being used today in the fields of personal development, coaching and cognitive therapy. If you are a coach, this book will make you appear brilliant to your clients. Make sure your clients don't read it first; the book has so many instantly applicable techniques, they might improve themselves before you can do your work."
Brian Van der Horst, Founder NLP Institute for Advanced Studies, San Francisco and Paris; Chief Facilitator, Integral Institute, Europe; Consultant at Stanford Research Institute

"A great practical book for coaches and everyone interested in how to apply the new research in neuroscience to change and development."
Adam Harris, Chair, Vistage, Executive coaching; author of *The Check-in Strategy Journal*

"While most coaches focus on working with the minds of their clients, *Coaching the Brain* takes a powerful dive into the field of neuropsychology, showing coaches how the brain works, how coaching can change the brain, and how valuable these changes can be."
Brian Whetten, author of *Yes Yes Hell No! The Little Book for Making Big Decisions*

"*Coaching the Brain* is an enjoyable, informative and practical guide for coaches to help their clients grow, change and improve. Every coach needs to know how the brain functions and how that relates to coaching. This book provides just that. Joseph and Andrea integrate neuroscience with coaching skills to present an easy to understand roadmap of the brain and how to apply it – to help coaches and their clients learn more efficiently, be more creative and be happier."
Robert Dilts, co-founder of NLP University and Generative Coaching; author of *Coach to Awakener*

"A practical and informative look at our deepest, most complex functions. Joseph and Andrea have taken a notoriously confusing topic and, with their gripping writing style, made the amazing topics of neuroscience and psychophysiology accessible to anyone that has an interest in this fascinating area of science. Not only is the topic made accessible but, more importantly, it's made applicable through the artful use of examples, metaphors, and stories. Anyone wishing to understand themselves and others in a deeper, more insightful way should read this book and apply the knowledge it holds. A 'must have' on the bookshelf of all coaches!"

Aaron Garner MSc, Director, EIA Group

Coaching the Brain

Practical Applications of Neuroscience to Coaching

Joseph O'Connor and Andrea Lages

Routledge
Taylor & Francis Group

LONDON AND NEW YORK

First published 2019
by Routledge
2 Park Square, Milton Park, Abingdon, Oxon OX14 4RN

and by Routledge
52 Vanderbilt Avenue, New York, NY 10017

Routledge is an imprint of the Taylor & Francis Group, an informa business

British Library Cataloguing-in-Publication Data
A catalogue record for this book is available from the British Library

Library of Congress Cataloging-in-Publication Data
A catalog record has been requested for this book

ISBN: 978-1-138-30051-4 (hbk)
ISBN: 978-1-138-30052-1 (pbk)
ISBN: 978-0-203-73337-0 (ebk)

Typeset in Times New Roman
by codeMantra

Printed and bound in Great Britain by
TJ International Ltd, Padstow, Cornwall

To our daughter, Amanda

Contents

Abbreviations and orientation

Abbreviations

ACC	Anterior cingulate cortex
ADHD	Attention deficit hyperactivity disorder
dlPFC	Dorsolateral prefrontal cortex
DN	Default network
EEG	Electroencephalogram
fMRI	Functional magnetic resonance imaging
GABA	Gamma aminobutyric acid
HPA axis	Hypothalamus–pituitary–adrenal axis
NA	Nucleus accumbens
OCD	Obsessive compulsive disorder
OFC	Orbital frontal cortex
PET	Positron emission tomography
PFC	Prefrontal cortex
PNS	Parasympathetic nervous system
SNS	Sympathetic nervous system
SPECT	Single-photon emission computed tomography
vmPFC	Ventromedial prefrontal cortex
VTA	Ventral tegmental area

Brain Orientation

Medial	Towards the middle
Lateral	Towards the side
Superior/dorsal	Above/at the top
Inferior/ventral	Below/at the bottom
Posterior/caudal	At the back
Anterior/rostral	At the front
Orbital	Above the orbits of the eyes
Medial	In the middle

Foreword

Believe in coaching- have faith in yourself

Science, beautiful science, has discovered the universe is expanding. If it is expanding, then in the past the galaxies were closer. The further back we go, the closer they were. Once the whole Universe was one point, infinitely compressed and incredibly hot. Fifteen billion years ago there was the 'Big Bang' and the Universe as we know it, began. After the explosion, the initial temperature, of more than a trillion degrees Celsius, began to decrease, and the atoms of matter as we know it originated from the smallest of particles.

At first there was only gases – nor more than the equivalent of a few cups of hydrogen and helium. Then came more complex elements. Stars and galaxies were born; one of them was our sun. Our earth after four billion years gave life a home, and here we are, the latest arrival - *homo sapiens*. Then there was another Big Bang - the 'Brain Big Bang', an explosion of creativity that produced unique human beings with limitless potential and a magnificent brain with the power to direct the entire body. It coordinates the heart rate and the lungs in breathing. It manages our digestion and our clever hands with their opposable thumbs. It is controls how we sleep and think, how and when we taste, touch, see, hear and orgasm.

Now, science is moving towards admitting the existence of mind: an essentially non-organic and non-material superstructure of the brain in intimate and mutual relationship with it. This mind is a versatile instrument. Versatile enough as to accomplish everything that a person wants, everything they longed for since childhood; versatile enough to make dreams become reality.

There is also a subtle part of our mind we are not aware of – the unconscious. There are infinite riches all around, if you open your mental eyes and contemplate the unconscious treasure house within you. There is a gold mine within you, from which you can draw everything you need to lead a glorious existence, filled with joy and abundance. Many people are deeply asleep because they are unaware of this infinite gold mine of intelligence and unlimited talent that is in each one of us.

We live the century of self-knowledge. We know our mind and body is valuable and unique. We have built an increasingly complex and rich world with science and education. Life has never been so universally good, yet the incidence of mental illnesses such as anxiety, depression, and suicide is increasing. How to explain this paradox? This is what Joseph O'Connor and Andrea Lages do here in such coherent way, bringing the best of theoretical and applied neuroscience into coaching to build practical wisdom for a more balanced and healthy life.

With compassion and knowledge, spanning philosophy and neuroscience, this book is a guide for the promotion and expansion of mental health and human well-being. It gives a new perspective on health that is not about disease, but about human potential.

The book strolls through the major themes of current neuroscience: perception, memory, decision making, social and emotional intelligence; it is a unique and passionate tour of the organ that allows us to build our reality: our brain and our mind. This is an indispensable book about an urgent topic: how to reconcile our external material wealth with an internal balanced and happy life.

The English words coaching and coach, originated from the name of the city of Kócs, in Hungary, where four-wheeled coaches were first designed. In the eighteenth century, the university nobles of England went to their classes conducted in their carriages by coachmen called Coachers. By 1830, the term Coach was used at Oxford University as synonymous with 'private tutor', the one who 'carries', 'leads' and 'prepares' students for their examinations. Now, a coach is a guide, a driver, a pathfinder and much more.

This book is an investment for life, both personally or professionally. With artificial intelligence approaching, what will keep us human will be exactly what this book offers: the balance of internal and external skills. Human beings are the only creatures who, thanks to their intellect, can contemplate the universe and show consideration for other forms of life.

The most important thing for us is to believe in ourselves. Without this confidence in our resources, in our intelligence, in our energy, we will not attain the victory to which we aspire. As the Brazilian novelist Clarice Lispector says: 'Discover yourself, and gradually you will discover that it is safer and more rewarding to value yourself.' Or, as the Buddha puts it: 'We are what we think. All that we are arises with our thoughts. With our thoughts we make our world.' Finally, note the words of Swami Vivekananda: 'Choose an idea. Make this idea your life. Think about it, dream about it, live thinking about it. Let brain, muscles, nerves, all parts of your body be filled with that idea. That's the way to success.'

When we have doubts about our talents and potentialities, let us not forget that everything began from one point, we share those same primordial elements, and that the complexity of the Universe arose from the simplest of materials.

Welcome to 21st Century Coaching!

Acary Souza Bulle Oliveira
Affiliated Professor of Neurology, UNIFESP -
Federal University of São Paulo, Brazil

Fabiano Moulin de Moraes
Assistant Professor of Neurology, UNIFESP -
Federal University of São Paulo.

Introduction

In 1918, The great American psychologist William James wrote, 'Nature in her unfathomable designs had mixed us of clay and flame, of brain and mind, that the two things hang indubitably together and determine each other's being but how or why, no mortal may ever know'. This quote is the perfect image for the promise and challenge of neuroscience. We are the flame; bright, flickering, lambent and ever-changing. It is who we feel we are: the conscious 'me' and we protect it. The material clay supports it, unglamorous, but essential. The flame depends on the clay. Our nature is flame and clay. This book is about how they work together. We will be the brightest flame by understanding our material roots – the biology of the mind. Our reason for writing this book is to give a deeper understanding of how the brain works to create experience. To give new tools to help create a more fulfilling reality for yourself and others.

This book applies cognitive neuroscience to coaching. Cognitive neuroscience explores the biological basis of mind, the structure and function of the nervous system and brain, and their relation to behaviour and learning. Coaching is well established as a powerful way to help people change and grow and perform better, especially in a business context. This is a book on the insights, research and perspectives of cognitive neuroscience and how to use them to help people to experience a better life, to fulfil their potential and be happier. This is our job as coaches, and so while this book is written mostly with coaches in mind, these insights can be used in any profession that helps people change and work for the better: training, therapy and leadership for example. This book is for you if you want to understand thinking, feeling, deciding and well-being more deeply.

We started coaching over twenty years ago. Psychology, the study of the flame, was well advanced. Cognitive Neuroscience, the study of how the clay produces the flame of consciousness, was much less developed. Now neuroscience is popular and growing fast, bestowing credibility on everything it touches; research shows even a picture of a brain in a psychology article gives it more credibility in the mind of the reader.

Here, we will focus on the brain; it is the largest, most complex and specialised part of our nervous system. As neuroscience comes to understand the brain better, the brain is proving stranger than we thought. Perhaps stranger than we can ever imagine.

Focusing on the brain, we can learn the most about our thoughts, emotions and behaviour, and how they are generated, shaped and changed. However, We cannot forget the body – our brain needs our body, it evolved as part of us. All our mental faculties are embodied. Lastly, brains do not exist in isolation. Our brain is shaped by others from birth, by our parents, carers, community and culture,

Our brain is involved in everything we do. Everyone who works helping people change and learn needs to know how it works. Coaches work with the client's subjective experience. They ask questions, explore and probe the client's experience and help them to understand their goals and values and move to a more satisfying life. We are not trying to reduce experience to brain functions. We are looking at the brain to see how it creates our experience and then explore that experience again with those insights. Then, we can understand our subjective experience more fully and get practical insights into how to run our lives.

We talk to our clients and listen to their reply. From a neuroscientific point of view, we are communicating with a very small part of the client – the part that is conscious and has access to the language part of the brain. There are many parts that have no voice and need to be heard, and many parts of our thinking and decision-making is not conscious. We don't know what we don't know. We need to understand and communicate with more of the client, to trace the intricacies of thinking and emotion. Seeing how these are woven in the brain gives us a different view that enriches our understanding. We can coach and help our client more effectively. It is a new perspective on experience, another lens we can take to understand ourselves.

Coaching still relies largely on anecdotal evidence of success. Coaching needs to be rooted in research, and neuroscientific research will give it further credibility. Coaches need to know psychology and neuroscience (although not all the anatomical details) to guide their clients' experience in the most helpful way. Neuroscience gives an enhanced roadmap. We foresee that in a few years' time, coaches who do not know basic neuroscience will be at a disadvantage.

The layout of this book

We want this book to be practical, so we have organised it round experience and not brain parts or functions. Coaching applications are in every chapter. There are footnotes with references and interesting spinoffs from the text. Read them as you go, don't leave them to the end.

The first chapter introduces our neuroscientific client – the brain. Complex Latin names are optional, and a degree in anatomy is unnecessary for this (or any other) chapter. It gives a basic understanding of how the brain is organised and what it does.

Chapter 2 deals with neuroplasticity - how the brain changes itself through experience. Your brain adapts to new ideas and new circumstances. It reflects your changing learning, interests and actions by strengthening connections, making new ones or weakening others, letting them decay and vanish.

Chapter 3 covers goals, planning, thinking skills and 'cold cognition'. It covers the neuroscience of goals from planning to action.

In Chapter 4, you will find system 1 and system 2 – how our thinking is often hurried, self-serving and influenced by our surroundings. This is fascinating material on how easily our thinking is led astray.

Chapter 5 deals with emotions and so-called hot cognition – emotional-based thinking. We will explore happiness, emotional profiles, the 'amygdala hijack' and how we can regulate our emotions. Emotions suffuse our thinking like a drop of ink in water, influencing everything we do.

Chapter 6 explores how we make decisions and how we can make better ones. Life is basically a series of decisions, as we weave our way, choosing one path over another, never being able to retrace our steps. Our brain makes simulations of the future, compares them, integrates information and emotion and then chooses. The choices we make leave changes in our brain.

Chapter 7 is about memory – how we are constantly balancing our experiencing self and our remembered self. Memory is not a record of what happened; it is a fresh reconstruction made by the brain every time we remember. Clients tell their tales from their memory. How real are they?

Chapter 8 is about learning, rewards and building habits. How do we learn? Our brain makes predictions and expectations and updates them constantly. We look at the reward circuit, dopamine, addictions and the hedonistic treadmill.

Chapter 9 is on mental models – habits of thinking, mental grooves cut by continuous use. Well-worn brain circuits lead to well-worn thinking and behaviour. Limiting mental models are the biggest obstruction to happiness and achievement. Here, we will see how to jog the client's thinking out of its ruts (and help the client fashion more worthwhile grooves).

Chapter 10 looks at our social brain – relationships and empathy, trust and fairness.

Chapter 11 is about identity – who are you and how does the brain create sense and continuity? Your brain is more like a spin doctor than an objective witness.

The last chapter brings the threads together to see where 'you' are in this. Hopefully, more knowledgeable and successful than when you started the book.

When we write of generic coaches or clients, we will write without gender, using the pronoun, 'they', to avoid clumsy sentence construction.

We write about what excites us. It has been more than five years since we wrote our last book, and this field has emerged since then. Now, we can share this exciting field with you. We hope you enjoy and benefit from it.

Acknowledgements

There are many who contributed to this book. We want to thank David Eagleman who first inspired us in neuroscience and who is a model of excellent, accessible writing about the field.

Also our editor at Routledge, Susannah Frearson for having faith in the idea. Thank you to Anna Lages, who drew many of the diagrams illustrating this book. Our clients have provided us with many insights, and we tell some of their stories in these pages. Our special thanks to Doctor Acary Souza Bulle Oliveira and Doctor Fabiano Moulin de Moraes for writing the Foreword. Thanks to Warren Zevon, Iron and Wine and J.S. Bach for providing great music to think and write to. We think they would have enjoyed a jamming session together.

Finally, our daughter Amanda, who always asks the best questions.

Joseph O'Connor and Andrea Lages
June 2018

Chapter 1

Clay and flame

The brain is the soul's fragile dwelling place.

William Shakespeare

Prologue

In December 2016, when we were in New York on holiday, we both had a single-photon emission computed tomography (SPECT) scan. We were not ill; we wanted to take a closer look at how the brain worked and decided to start with the most available one – our own. A SPECT scan is an unusual experience. You stay still, moving as little as possible for about thirty minutes while three high-resolution rotating cameras circle your head and take pictures of your brain. These pictures are combined to make three-dimensional colour scans. SPECT scans don't just show the structure of the brain, but they also show how it works – which areas work well, which areas are working hard (perhaps too hard) and which areas are not working hard enough.

How does it do this? The more blood flow, the more gamma rays are picked up by the camera. Areas with the most blood flow show up as most colourful. Areas with the least blood flow have the least radiation and are darker in the scans. We did two scans. One for the brain in resting state. The other the next day while we worked on a computerised test that demanded focus and concentration. The final scans look quite spectacular, rather like a picture of the earth from space, where the cities are brightly lit and stand out from the vast swathes of land with little or no light. The scans show the pattern – the lighter, the more activity; darker for those parts not so active. The contrast between the scans at rest and when concentrating shows what areas are working and how intensely.

Why did we do this? For the same reason, people take personality tests, intelligence tests or enneagrams – to discover more about ourselves. I (Joseph) looked at my scans afterwards with a sense of wonder. Here was a perspective I have never taken before, a new window on my world: how my brain is powering my thoughts, moods, feelings, dreams and nightmares. And the scans showed my brain was more active in the resting state than in the focus state. (That is not as bad as it sounds, the brain never rests; it is always up to something.)

These scans are only part of the story. There were interviews and questionnaires about lifestyle, goals, health, spiritual interests, sleeping patterns, social life and diet. The brain is involved in all of these, and all of these affect the brain. Finally, a doctor helped us interpret the results, put the scans in perspective and make recommendations. More of this anon. We had plenty of questions. If coaching changes people, it changes their brain. How?

We had started on a fascinating path that led (among other things) to this book.

Your brain

This book is driven by two questions:

How does our brain create the world we experience?
How can we use that knowledge to help ourselves and our clients to learn, change and be happier?

It has been said that if the brain were simple enough to be understood, it would not be sophisticated enough to meet the challenge of understanding itself. How can one and a half kilogram of pinkish, off-white matter, with the consistency of soft butter, create Beethoven's Ninth Symphony, the Taj Mahal, the Internet, supersonic air travel, CRISPR, Pokémon Go and spray-on hair?

We can't answer that, but in this book, we will gaze down the glittering corridors of our brain to explore how it creates our wants, needs, habits, beliefs, joys and fears.

We will explore questions like:

How do we get angry at ourselves, argue with ourselves and deceive ourselves? (And exactly who is deceiving who?)
How do we create and change habits?
Faced with myriad possibilities, how do we decide what to do?
What does it mean to trust someone?
How does our brain weave all the disparate pieces together to create such a seamless experience of the world?
There are answers in those glittering corridors that can help us with these questions.
This book brings neuroscience to help us understand our goals, values and beliefs as we experience them. Then, we can better understand ourselves and others, and lead a richer, more fulfilled life.

Your brain is incredibly complex. It is made up of 100 billion neurons or nerve cells (give or take a few), each with between 1,000 and 10,000 synapses, or connections, to other cells. The number of possible connections is greater than the number of particles in the known universe (roughly ten followed by seventy-nine zeroes). Your brain contains about 100,000 miles of blood vessels and does not feel pain or pleasure, although it generates the pain and pleasure you feel in the rest of your body. No brain – no pain. Everything we know about the world is through the brain. It controls your heartbeat, breathing, sleeping, waking, sexual energy and appetite. It directs and influences your thoughts, moods, memories, decisions and actions. The world of sight, sound, touch, taste and smell is put together seamlessly by the brain for our attention and entertainment. The amount of work that goes on behind the scenes to present this amazing *son et lumiere* show is hidden from us. Whatever is really out there, the world we perceive is created in our brain through billions of nerve cells, interweaving trillions of electrical and chemical signals, and then projecting the result 'out there' in a multisensory pageant. The world is how it is because we are who we are. We only perceive what our brain allows us to perceive.

We have the illusion that we control our decisions, and that we are the masters of our destiny. However, most of our thinking, feelings, decisions and actions are not under our conscious control. Our brain is like a magician – it hides things from us and foregrounds others. 'It' is the master of illusion, misdirecting our attention to create the reality we think we perceive.[1] As we go on through this book, we will see what this means in practice.

We must never forget our brain is embodied. It doesn't command the body like a puppet master commands a marionette. It is an integral part of the body.[2] Nor does it have a monopoly on nerve tissue. The heart has over 40,000 neurons. The gut has 100 million neurons, and dozens of neurotransmitters, earning it the title of 'The second brain'.[3] And there is often a friendly rivalry between the two brains.

Metaphors of the brain

There are still many myths about the brain that should be laid to rest. The prime example is that the brain is a glorified computer.[4] If the brain was a computer, it would work the same regardless of weather, emotional mood, surroundings and who turned it on. It would remember everything perfectly. (And it would crash if it tried to do two things at once, and the person would have to be rebooted.) But it doesn't. It is affected by emotions, what other people are doing, and it has off days. The brain has no CPU – it operates more like a collection of independent apps forced into the same place. Sometimes they cooperate, sometimes compete and often interfere with each other.

Another widespread myth is that we only use a small percentage of our brain. We use all our brain most of the time and most of our brain all the time. Even when sleeping, the brain is active, often more active than when we are awake. The ten percent myth is useful to remind us that we have more potential than we think and can probably do better than we are doing, but this is the field of motivational psychology, not neuroscience.

Finally, there is also the enduring myth that the left side of the brain is the seat of rationality, like a university library, built on logic and order. The right side of the brain is zany and artistic; a college party with lots of music and everyone having a good time. There is the tiniest sliver of truth in this which we will explore later. Each hemisphere is good at some things, not so good at others, but they cooperate well. (For example, the parts dealing with language tend to be mostly in the left hemisphere.) There is revelry in the library and rationality in the party.

Coaching and neuroscience

Neuroscience is the study of the structure and function of the nervous system and brain and their relation to behaviour and learning. Cognitive neuroscience is the biology of mind, the connection between our nervous system and our thinking and behaviour. The brain is the principal part of the nervous system, and here, we will focus on how the brain works and the applications for coaching.

Neuroscience gives an extra vital perspective in coaching. It does not explain our behaviour directly but helps us unravel how we construct our subjective world. Everyone constructs their reality from their experience, and every person's reality is unique. Our experience is processed by our brain. Our world, so rich, colourful, musical and diverse, is created in the dark in an alien language of electrochemical signals between our brain cells. The webs of associations and meanings we make from experience are paralleled in the webs of nerve connections we make in our brain. This does not lessen the richness of our experience, but we can look 'under the bonnet' to see how it is created. Knowing how it is created we can create better realities.

Coaching helps people change. What does that mean in practice? Change is a movement from a present state to a desired state. In our trainings, we like to simplify coaching by exploring three questions.

First, where are we now?

To move from this, you need to understand it, especially the constraints and habits that keep you in place. You need to focus your attention. Neuroscience can tell us a great deal about attention and how to use it. Have you ever tried to keep your attention focused on one thing? A quick experiment (try it now) will show you how fickle and distractible our attention is. Sit back in your chair and take ten deep breaths, counting each one.

Do it anyway, you will feel better even if it does not prove a point.
Then repeat three times.
Concentrate only on your breath.
How far did you get without your mind wandering?
To get past the first set of ten is pretty good.
Focus and concentration are very desirable skills.
How can we focus our attention and avoid distractions?

Second, where do we want to be?

What do you want to create? How do you want your life to be different? Neuroscience can show us how we formulate goals, how emotion helps us decide what to do, and how working memory underpins the whole process.

Third, what is in the way?

If change were easy, no one would need a coach. There may be external obstacles, but most of the time what stops us are habits of thinking that are insufficient to solve the problem. A habit is something we do or think that was once rewarding but is no longer. It is driven by an outside stimulus, and the neural pathway runs all by itself; repeated use has made it fast and unconscious. The gossamer threads of repetition have coalesced into an iron chain. Habits are our friend when we want to stay the same, but when we want to change, habits become the enemy. The unthinking ease of the habit makes it hard to shift. Habits of thinking lead to habits of action. Habits of thinking are the automatic paths we follow without any reflection. Understanding our brain helps us in two ways. First, we will see that thinking is very easily influenced by our surroundings and other people, much more so than we think. Knowing how that happens gives us a chance to counter it. Second, understanding how the brain builds habits shows the best way to dismantle them and build new ones.

Why change now? When is the right time for a change? Sometimes, a sudden shock has brought something to the surface, or an issue has been cooking too long and now we are smelling the smoke. We change when it is important, so our values are involved. While goals and planning can be coldly cognitive, values are warmly emotional; they move us to action. Neuroscience gives us many insights into how the emotional centers in the brain ('hot cognition') work together with the more reasonable parts ('cold cognition') to plan, decide priorities and act on them.

At the heart of change is learning. How do we learn? We learn from our experiences, and we change our actions and thinking in response to our experience. We change because something new looks more valuable and rewarding. How do we attach value and reward to experiences? This is a field where neuroscience has a lot to say; the brain has a reward system fuelled by the neurotransmitter dopamine. We had better understand how this works if we want to understand value, reward and the experience of wanting. Wanting is not the same as liking. You can want something but not enjoy it, like that extra piece of cheesecake that turns to ashes in your mouth after the first guilty bite. Wanting and liking are governed by different brain systems, and they do not always agree.

Coaching ends with action – a strategy to take us from present state to desired state. We need to sequence and align our actions. We need to stop ourselves from doing some things and motivate ourselves to do others. We need to think long term and short term, coordinate memories and keep focus. Welcome to the world of the prefrontal cortex (PFC) sitting behind your forehead, the so-called CEO of the brain. However, the CEO is not completely in charge. Fear may override our plan. We plan a good presentation but get so anxious we make a mess of it at the crucial time. The PFC can tell us not to be stupid but is sometimes powerless against the small almond-shaped structure deep in the brain that manages fear – the amygdala. The amygdala is the main player in our emotional circuit. When any emotion overrides intelligent action, we experience the truth that we are not one person, but a busy collection of different parts all with their own agenda. Understanding how the brain operates in practice will help us tame the turbulent team and be more congruent and effective.

We live in a social world. Coaching is usually done one to one, but the client brings the imprints of their family, significant others, culture and society into the session. The brain is studied as if it were isolated, but we are born into a social world. Society predates us and will be there when we have gone. We are born into language and culture and a dynamic world. We grow up as individuals and forget how much we owe to others. Your brain has no *material* links to any other brains, but the material connections in the brain are formed through experience with others and by the culture you internalise. The field of Social Cognitive Neuroscience (SCN)[5] – how the brain is shaped by others – is growing. No brain is isolated; other people constantly stimulate and change our thinking, emotions and decisions. Other people are the greatest mystery. We have known from an early age that they are like us, but independent. We cannot know for sure what they are thinking, and yet we routinely work miracles of mind reading, predicting other peoples' intentions correctly. How do we connect with others and empathise with them with each brain isolated in a different skull? This is another question neuroscience can help to answer, so coaches can put the answers into practice.

In short, studying the brain gives us insight into the mind – the coaches' playground.

We do not need to know detailed anatomy and nomenclature of the brain. We want the broad strokes of how this incredibly complex system works with applications for coaches (Figure 1.1).

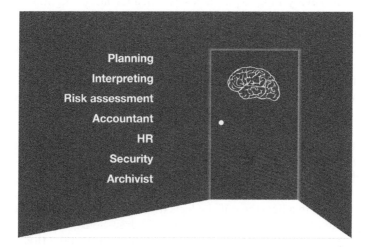

Figure 1.1 The team in the closed room.

Coaching the brain

Indulge us for a moment in a thought experiment. Imagine you are called into a multinational company to coach their top team of directors. The Human Resources (HR) manager has been rather reticent about the team and the nature of your task, but it pays very well; the company is reputed to be one of the wealthiest, pervasive and most secretive in the world. The top management team is something of a mystery; no one really knows who runs the company. You are shown into the waiting room and told that the team is in the next room behind a closed door. However, before you can start, she tells you there are some unusual conditions in your coaching contract.

First, you will not meet any of the team face to face. Second, only the CEO will communicate with you directly. His name is Peter Bach, and he will speak for the others. All the team will consult together, but you will not hear their conversation, only the result. You think this is odd, but you agree, and you ask for information about the other members of the team, as you will neither see nor hear them.

'Well', says the HR manager, Most of the team don't speak your language, so there are two translators, Vera Score and John Broker. Vera will translate what you say to them and John will translate the CEO back to you telling you what the team thinks.

'How good are they at their job?' you ask.

'Depends', replies the manager, 'Usually they are OK, but they have their off days. And I must warn you', she goes on, 'The team does tend to embellish everything to put themselves in a favourable light. Remember that when you listen to John's translation. He doesn't exactly lie, but he can be economical with the truth'.

While you digest this, she says, 'Then there is the CFO Victor Strickland; he is very focused on whether your advice will give a return'.

'A word of warning about Victor', the manager continues, He needs to see a clear profit from the session. He tends to discount anything that is too far in the future. Also, he likes new ideas. If he has heard it before, he is not impressed regardless of the merit of the idea.

You frown and settle deeper into the chair facing the closed door of the boardroom.

'Who else is in there?' you ask.

'Della is Risk Assessment; don't get on the wrong side of her – she will stop the session in a heartbeat if she feels threatened. She works closely with the head of Security and Surveillance, Andrew Solo'.

You begin to wonder if you made the right decision to take this job. She pauses for a moment and stares into the distance. 'Mary Island is an important member of the team, she gets people to wake up and focus on the issue. They can be a bit disorganised without her. And then there is Jan Sanctum, our organiser and fixer *extraordinaire*. Everything has to run by him, he knows the best person to deal with every issue'.

The HR manager continues, We mustn't forget the Global Human Resources manager Richard Border, he is great at getting on with people, make sure you connect with him. Also, we have our Head of data processing, Mary Steed, who keeps a record of every meeting. If anyone gets lost, they refer to her record.

'A word about Mary', says the manager leaning close. 'She tends to edit all the time and every time she pulls out a file, she changes it before putting it back. So, you had better take your own notes too'.

'Is that all of them?' you ask.

'That is all I know about', says the manager, 'There may be others'.

Welcome to coaching the brain. We will explore the ways to make a success of coaching this strange team, located in everyone's head.[6]

The material brain

First, a quick brain tour to get our bearings. There is a glossary at the end of this book. The brain is an incredibly complex system; we will keep the description as simple as possible, but no simpler. Neuroscience cannot yet provide a complete and tidy description of how the brain works and perhaps never will. While it is tempting to allocate mental faculties to places in the brain, it is not possible. Some parts are specialised but need back up from many other parts to operate. A part of the brain may be necessary but not sufficient for a function. For example, we need the hippocampus to remember; if you remove parts of the hippocampus, the result is a profound amnesia. But injuring other parts of the brain can also lead to memory disturbances, and long-term memory traces seem to be stored in the frontal cortex. So, when we say a part of the brain 'has' a function, we really mean that this part plays a major role and we can't do without it, but other parts are needed for full function. Most parts have several functions and contribute to different systems. (For example, the hippocampus is also involved in planning, learning and appropriate expression of emotion.) There is a lot of built-in redundancy.

With that caveat, on with the orientation.[7] The brain fills the top part of your skull and is divided into two halves, or hemispheres, that are mirror images of each other. They are connected by a large bundle of nerve fibres known as the corpus callosum. The largest part (eighty percent of the brain's total weight) is the cerebrum or cerebral cortex.[8] This fills the front and top part of the skull like the foam casing in a bicycle helmet and is divided into four parts. The first is the frontal lobe (behind the forehead and eyes). This deals with planning, executive decisions and rational thought. It also controls our wayward impulses, so they never get translated into actions. As you might expect, it is very well connected to other brain areas (Figure 1.2).

The parietal lobe (behind the frontal lobe) deals with sensation. The sensations from external world and from inside the body are mapped onto this

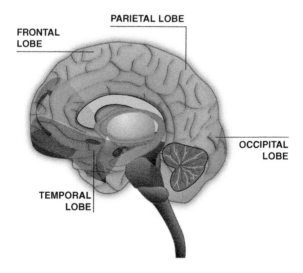

Figure 1.2 Cerebral cortex.

part of the cortex. The temporal lobe (underneath the parietal and frontal lobes) deals mostly with hearing and memory. The occipital lobe (at the back) deals with vision.

Imagine your brain like a clenched fist with knuckles pointing forward. Looking down, the frontal lobes are the knuckles, the temporal lobes are the fleshy sides of the hand, the parietal lobe is the back of the hand near the knuckles and the occipital lobe is the back of the hand near the wrist.[9]

The structures underneath the cortex are known as subcortical and handle basic processes that keep us alive, as well as emotions, pain and pleasure. The thalamus is a small but important structure. There is one in each hemisphere, and it acts as a relay station, coordinating signals and passing them on to other parts of the brain. Protruding from the lower back of the cerebral cortex is the cerebellum ('little brain'). The cerebellum also has two hemispheres and coordinates movement, posture and balance. Down from the cerebellum and connecting the brain with the spinal cord are parts that run our basic life systems like breathing, temperature regulation and blood circulation (Figure 1.3).

Other important structures are located under the cerebral cortex and not visible. The hippocampus (one in each hemisphere) is where our memories are formed. The amygdala (again one in each hemisphere) is the key part of the brain for processing emotion and emotional memories, especially fear. The basal ganglia are a series of small structures at the bottom of the brain. They are involved in seeking pleasure and reward and controlling movement (Figure 1.4).

Finally, there are two areas that give us the gift of producing and understanding language. They are remarkably small for managing such a hugely important part of our lives. Broca's area is usually in the left hemisphere of the frontal cortex and processes the production of language. Injury in this

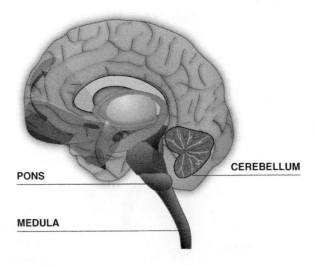

PONS

CEREBELLUM

MEDULA

Figure 1.3 Cerebellum.

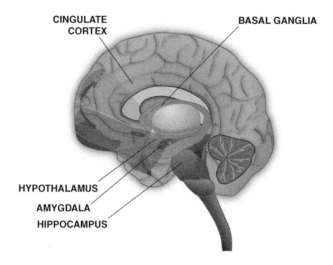

CINGULATE CORTEX

BASAL GANGLIA

HYPOTHALAMUS

AMYGDALA

HIPPOCAMPUS

Figure 1.4 Subcortical structures.

area leads to the loss of ability to communicate in comprehensible sentences. Wernicke's area is an area on the left side of the temporal lobe. Damage here leaves people unable to understand written or spoken language.

How the brain communicates

How does the brain communicate with itself and to the rest of the body? The brain is made up of nerve cells (or neurons) that transmit information in the form of electrochemical signals.[10] They take information from other neurons, and then pass it on (or stop it from being passed on). Neurons have a cell body, with many hair-like projections that become thinner and more delicate as they extend further away. These are called dendrites, and they receive input from other neurons. Neurons also have a long extending filament called an axon which passes the information on to the next neuron at speeds of up to 200 miles an hour. There are small gaps between the axon of one cell and the dendrites of the next cell called synapses. A signal must jump the synapse to continue. The process is like using a telephone. The signal (your friend's voice) comes down the telephone and jumps the gap to your ear through the air. In nerve cells, the signal is transmitted across the synapse mainly by chemicals called neurotransmitters that are made in the synapse. The neurotransmitters allow the signal to flow to the next neuron. No neurotransmitter – no onward signal. There are more than 100 neurotransmitters. Dopamine, serotonin and gamma-aminobutyric acid (GABA) are the most important ones, and we will meet them and their effects later. Now, we are on more familiar terms with the team in the closed room. The next step is to see how it changes itself.

Notes

1   We know this last sentence does not make sense. How can 'It' create an illusion of an 'I' and then indulge in a game of epistemological hide and seek? Language cannot express this properly. No one has been able to figure out how the brain gives rise to our conscious feeling of ourselves as free agents. Throughout this book, we will see how the brain functions, but how this jumps the gap into becoming our subjective experience is not clear and may never be clear. Who lights the candle? We know the brain is necessary but not sufficient for conscious awareness.

2   For a very good account of embodiment, see Claxton, G., *Intelligence in the flesh*. Yale University Press (2015).

3   Gershon, M. (1999). *The second brain*. Harper Collins. A fascinating study by one of the leading neuroscientists in this area.

4   When computers were first made in the 1940s, they were called 'electronic brains', not because they were like brains, but because people thought they would be able to do what brains did. As computers got faster and better, they did some things better than brains (like playing Chess and Go) but lagged far behind human brains in their ability to recognise faces, understand sarcasm and control fast, fluid and graceful movements, something we do every day without breaking sweat. Even when playing Chess and Go, computers win by crunching huge numbers of possibilities and selecting the best one, which is not the way humans play. Neural network computers, which are modelled more on how nerve cells are connected, have not been very successful. They take a long time to train and need a lot of data to do things a human toddler can do in a few seconds (e.g. recognise facial expressions).

5   Lieberman, M. D. (2007). Social cognitive neuroscience: a review of core processes. *Annual Review Psychology, 58*, 259–289.

6   When you want to know which team member represents which part of the brain, look at the end of Appendix 1.

7   There are several apps that give a good three-dimensional (3D) picture and description of the brain. 3D brain by the Cold Spring Harbour Laboratory DNA Learning Centre is particularly thorough.

8   You may notice most of the names of brain structures are Latin. They were named by early anatomists according to the convention at the time. This makes them sound mysterious and scientific, but also hard to remember.

9   The cingulate cortex (represented by the underside of the fingers in our fist) lines the cerebral cortex and is involved in error detection (an extremely important function), processing pain and focusing attention.

10   The brain also contains glial cells that seem to provide a kind of supportive packing round the neurons.

Bibliography

Claxton, G. (2015). *Intelligence in the flesh*. New Have, CT: Yale University Press.

Gershon, M. (1999). *The second brain*. New York: Harper Collins.

Lieberman, M. D. (2007). Social cognitive neuroscience: a review of core processes. *Annual Review of Psychology, 58*, 259–289.

Chapter 2

Thinking about change – neuroplasticity

Neuroplasticity

Coaching changes people. Change in behaviour and thinking must mean change in the brain too. When you take a new job, most of your routines change. When you learn a new language or move to another country, you think differently. All this is reflected in changes in the brain; new circuits are created, like new roads to new mental towns and villages. Old highways are abandoned, and populated areas become deserted.

Neuroplasticity is the process by which the brain changes itself in response to new thoughts, experiences and actions. The brain is not like a collection of statues; it is like a busy crowd, jostling, talking, making new friends and shedding others. Some people leave, some people join. Neuroplasticity is the basis of all our learning and our ability to change, so it is fitting we deal with it first.

Neuroplasticity comes in three forms – the formation of new neurons, the formation of new synapses and the strengthening of existing synapses. A newborn baby's brain has nearly the same number of neurons as an adult brain. By the age of two, their brain has reached 80 percent of the adult size. This infant brain forms two million synapses a second as it grows – an incredible feat. The world is new for an infant, they learn from everything indiscriminately, because they do not know yet what useful and worth knowing, so nature plays safe and takes in everything.

What is significant and worth learning gets clearer as time passes. (Mummy does not like it when I yell – worth remembering.) Other things do not matter. (Sometimes people wear blue hats – not important.) Many neural connections are lost, and those that remain get strengthened. The more frequently pathways are used, the stronger they get. Other paths are unused and fall into disrepair. By adolescence we have lost billions of synapses, and those that remain are strong and well connected. The adult brain is formed throughout our teens and there, it was thought, the story ended.[1] Then, in the mid-1990s, the work of Elizabeth Gould and Fernando Nottebohm[2] overturned this orthodoxy. Gould demonstrated that animals made new brain cells throughout life. Nottebohm's research showed that song birds made new brain cells to sing their songs. (Intriguingly, this only happens to birds in their natural habitat, not when they were raised in cages.) But these were animal experiments. Then, work by Eriksson in 1998 showed that new neurons are produced in the hippocampus of the adult human brain.[3] Slowly, the metaphor of the brain changed from a static hard disk to a self-renewing organism.

Making connections – synaptic plasticity

Changes in the synapses is known as synaptic neuroplasticity. Synaptic neuroplasticity is how we build habits and gain skill, whether it is to learn tennis, touch type or smoke cigarettes. A synapse is strengthened when the neurons on both sides are active at the same time, making the signal more likely to be transmitted across the gap. The neuron before the synapse (the presynaptic neuron) must reliably fire before the neuron after the synapse (the postsynaptic neuron), so the signal keeps flowing. The process is known as long-term potentiation. This was captured succinctly by what is known as Hebb's law: 'What fires together, wires together'. Donald Hebb was a Canadian psychologist who did pioneering work on neural networks in the mid-twentieth century.[4] 'Neurons that fire apart, wire apart' puts it another way.

Competitive neuroplasticity

Not only can synapses be created, destroyed, strengthened and weakened, but neurons themselves can be taken over and reused. Neurons are not narrow specialists, but versatile workers that can switch jobs if necessary. The brain is much more adaptable than we thought. It is even opportunistic – if some nerve cells are not being used, they can be taken over and used for another purpose, like finding your unused spare bedroom has been turned into a second kitchen when you were not looking. This is known as competitive neuroplasticity, and there are plenty of fascinating examples.

We know that blindness causes other senses like touch and hearing become more acute to compensate. This is the result of synaptic neuroplasticity – hearing and touch are used more, so the connections are strengthened and increased. Competitive neuroplasticity does more. Unused neurons are taken up and used for other things. When someone is blind, the part of the brain that normally processes the input from the eyes (mainly the occipital lobe at the back of the brain) gets nothing. But it does not stay idle. It starts to process inputs from other senses, such as touch and hearing.[5]

We think we sense the external world and feel parts of our body, but it all takes place in the brain. The brain is a series of endless dark corridors alive with electrical and chemical signals. All input whether it is sight, sound, touch or taste must be converted into this strange universal language of the brain and then processed into something we sense. Eric Weihenmayer has been blind from the age of thirteen. In 2001, he became the first blind person to climb Mount Everest. He climbs with a grid of hundreds of tiny electrodes on his tongue called a brain port. The grid translates video into electrical impulses which the tongue decodes into visual patterns of distance, shape and size. The information does not have to come from the eyes because we do not see with our eyes. We see with our brain. It takes the input from the eyes and creates what we experience as sight. The brain can create pictures all by itself in the occipital lobe even without external input and project them outwards as hallucinations. The same process applies to hearing; the brain creates what we experience as sound by decoding the input from the ears. It can also produce auditory hallucinations in the temporal lobe. We feel with our brain. It decodes the touch sensations from our skin. We can also have touch hallucinations – feeling something that is not there. Stimulating cells in the motor cortex of the brain causes the person to feel the sensation in the corresponding part of the body.[6]

Thinking and neuroplasticity

The brain changes itself in response to what we do in a dynamic world. Repeated actions lead to changes in the brain, for example, playing the guitar will enlarge and strengthen parts of the primary motor cortex that control the fingers. Other areas will also enlarge and show more activity, including the corpus callosum.[7]

Can thoughts change the brain? The brain is a physical, palpable part of our body. It weighs a couple of pounds. Thoughts are intangible, weightless, whether they are Nobel Prize-winning insights or about what to have for breakfast. All are equally insubstantial. And yet thoughts can change the brain; they can reorganise neurons and synapses. The brain's language is electrochemical messages passing along axons and triggering neurons. These messages are the result of both physical actions *and* thinking. The brain expresses them both in the same way.

There is plenty of evidence. One experiment (Pascual-Leone 1995)[8] took people who had never played the piano and divided them into two groups. The first group mentally practised a musical sequence for two hours a day for five days. The second group physically played the passage for the same amount of time. Both groups had their brains mapped during the experiment. Both groups could play the sequence, and both had similar brain maps. Both groups played well by the third day. The mental practice had formed the same maps in the motor cortex as the physical practice.

Thinking changes the brain, and then the changed brain influences our future thinking. What we repeatedly think about gets easier to think. This is how we build thinking habits that empower us or keep us limited; the mental equivalents of our physical habits. The thoughts we entertain on a regular basis go from being our guests to our lodgers to perhaps, eventually our masters.

The parable of the two wolves puts it more poetically. An old man was telling his grandson about the battle that goes on inside everyone. 'The battle', he said, 'is between two wolves that we all have inside us'. 'One is bad. It is greedy, arrogant, and full of self-pity and resentment'. 'The other is good', he continues, 'It is peaceful, loving and kind'. The man falls silent. The boy thought for a moment and then asked, 'Which wolf wins?' The man replied, 'The one you feed'.

Coaching applications

All neuroscientific research shows the brain is a dynamic and sensitive system responding to what we see, hear, feel and do. A habit makes a brain map, and every time you repeat it, the map and connections get strengthened and elaborated. The connections get faster (Merzenich and Jenkins 1993).[9] Habits are learned and unlearned; skills are won and lost. What we repeat gets stronger, what we neglect grows weaker.

As the Chinese saying puts it, *'Habits begin as cobwebs, but end as chains'*.

Coaching helps clients learn new skills and change limiting habits of thinking for more empowering ones. To know how this works in the brain is incredibly helpful. Many clients feel trapped by habits. They may believe that some habits cannot be changed. 'You can't teach an old dog new tricks', sums it up. A coach may struggle to change that belief. Now we have research that tells us our brain is not a sluggish, unchangeable collection of cells but a self-renewing, system. The realisation is liberating. Change becomes possible, even inevitable. We recreate ourselves a little differently every day by what we do and what we think. Coaches can become the enablers of self-directed neuroplasticity. The client decides the change, makes the change and sticks with it. They are reorganising their brain with the help of the coach.

The dark side of neuroplasticity

The experience of being caught in habits, of finding ourselves doing the same old thing and thinking the same old thoughts, even when we do not want to – this is the dark side of neuroplasticity. Our brains give space to those things we habitually do – the thumb for the compulsive texter, the fingers for the violinist, the palate for the wine sommelier. The connections for habitual thoughts are strengthened, making them smoother and easier to access. The thoughts may be healthy and helpful or damaging and self-destructive, the process is the same. The brain does not judge which habits are good or bad. Once entrenched, they are equally difficult to shift. Habits form when we are not looking. 'Just one more time won't hurt' is a dangerous mantra. The chains of habit can be too light to be felt until they are too heavy to be broken. So, the first lesson for coaches is to treat habits with great respect. We want neuroplasticity to work for us, not against us.

Modern technology and social media work in this way. Search engines and social media analyse your searches and deliver based on what you liked in the past. The algorithms work by assuming you are the same as when you last used them. They can, if we let them, filter what we see in terms of where we have been, not where we want to go. The connections you make and the digital paths you travel are strengthened and served up to you again and again. The result is a digital filter bubble that you do not notice because you never see it from the outside. We tend to assume that a search engine will search for what we want, but they search for what they think we want based on what we have searched for in the past. The brain creates its own filter bubble unless we are careful, always doing and thinking what is familiar already.

We recommend novelty, and we ask executives to explore a new interest every three months. It must be completely outside their normal interests. It could be radio astronomy, Romanian folk music or the history of the New York subway, it does not matter. It is important to break out of the filter bubble. They always report getting some interesting new ideas and perspectives. A new interest looks at the subject in a new way and suggests new ways of looking at old tasks. Whether they drop the interest later does not matter. What matters is opening some new pathways in the brain.

Here's another implication from the dark side of neuroplasticity. The brain follows the path of least resistance. The signals flow through the pathways more travelled. This limits creativity. For example, put the book down for a few moments and think of a beach by the sea ....

OK, what came into your mind?
A glorious sun in the sky sparkling on the waves?
Fine white sand that trickles through the fingers?
Lapping waves?
Perhaps a palm tree, hammocks, beer on ice?
Maybe you live in a city by the sea like Rio de Janeiro, you may think about
    your favourite beach ...
Clichés! These are familiar ideas.

There is nothing wrong with them. We are just making the point that your first thoughts are likely to be clichés. To think creatively you need to deliberately leave the well-trodden paths. You have to stop the easy answer. The first answer out of the mouth of a client is likely to be habitual thinking on the issue. Push for a second and third. Leonardo da Vinci would distrust his first solution to a problem, even if it looked promising, and would always dig deeper. Coaches need to push their clients to be more like Leonardo. Do not take the first answer, push the client for something better.

Habits

Nearly all coaching involves a change of habits. A client wants to be a better listener? They need to stop their habit of listening and create a different habit. A client wants to go to the gym regularly? They have a habit of doing something else (maybe relaxing or watching TV) and they want to change it. To change a habit of thinking, you need to act differently, and to change a habit of acting, you need to think differently.
Here is the formula.

First, the client needs to be aware of the habit. The insidious part of habits is they run without awareness. Clients often need reminders or structures to 'wake them up'. These can be tailored to the client. It might be a new picture on the desk, a new screen saver or a new colour pen to use in the meeting. Anything to interrupt the usual behaviour. Begin with a very easy version of the new habit. For example, if it is to write, start with one sentence a day. If it is to get fit, a few push backs against the wall; if listening, just take ten seconds to listen to the sounds around you wherever you are. What normally happens is that the client will do more than they are asked to do – much better than trying to do too much and falling short. Gradually, they can increase the time and quantity. Eventually, the new neural circuits will be strongly in place. One of the main reasons people do not follow through with new habits is they want them all at once, but this is not how the brain works, it works one step at a time. Change is easier when it works with the brain rather than against it.

We also encourage our clients to take an inventory of their habits in the area they are working on – some will need to be changed, but some will be helpful.

What do they habitually do?
What do they habitually think?
What are the typical phrases they use to describe their problems?
In neuroscientific terms, what are their habitual connections?
Once a client has a sense of these habits, they can answer this question:
'What habits do I want to keep, and what habits do I want to change?'

This is a powerful question. There will be habits that are making the client's desired change more difficult. Equally, there will be habits that are help-ful. The idea of change seems so powerful and desirable that we sometimes forget that we need a basis of stability to launch ourselves from. Habits give stability; they are not always the enemy. Successful change is knowing which habits to change and which to keep.

Attention

What else can a neuroscientifically literate coach do to help clients change? (Forgive the clumsy phrase, which means 'a coach who knows about how the brain operates and can help clients with research-based practices on how to succeed'.) They can help a client pay attention.

'Pay attention!' The favourite phrase of parents and teachers to rudely jolt us from our daydreams. We know that paying attention means focusing. Our teachers wanted our attention outwards, not inwards on our thoughts and sensations. (When we are focusing inwards, we are probably running on the default network of the brain – those parts of the brain most active when we are 'doing nothing' and not concerned with goal-driven action.)

There are two ways our attention can be directed. One is voluntary or top down from the prefrontal cortex (PFC). It is goal driven. You are paying voluntary attention now as you read this book. The other type of attention is reflexive or bottom up. This is driven by a stimulus you cannot ignore. For example, your focus on this book would be interrupted if you smelled smoke or had a sudden pain.

Voluntary attention is under your control. It is the *quality* of attention that drives the neuroplastic changes. The main brain regions involved in paying voluntary attention are parts of the frontal lobes, the insula, the parietal lobes and the thalamus. When we pay attention, dopamine is released, and this neurotransmitter is associated with alertness and a positive attitude. Dopamine also helps to consolidate memories more quickly.[10] Research consistently shows that neuroplastic changes are greatest when we pay voluntary attention.[11]

This makes sense. Joseph played the guitar for many years, and it was very clear, for himself and his students, that thirty minutes of practice with careful attention was worth hours of 'going through the motions'. Paying attention is even more important if we are trying to carve a new habit and dismantle an old one. Voluntary attention stops us slipping into the grooves of the old habit. We often suggest executives practise voluntary attention by asking them to practise the skills they want in the most difficult circumstances. We made them practise presentations in different ways: with notes, without notes. Blindfolded. Wearing ear phones playing their favourite (and least favourite) music. Sometimes, we keep interrupting them with questions. We once asked a trainer who wanted to improve their presentation skills to talk to the waves from the top of a cliff (at a safe distance of course). We do this not because we are sadists but to force them to pay attention to what they are doing. When they do the real presentation, it will be easy by comparison. Mindfulness or meditation practice also helps to build attention.

It also has many other neuroscientific benefits. We will be revisiting meditation a lot as we explore more about the brain.

It can be challenging to pay attention. Our work environment seems designed for attention deficit disorder, bouncing from one thing to another, at-
tempting to multitask, 'paying attention' to a colleague while surreptitiously
checking the cell phone, simultaneously juggling our mental calendar to fit
in all the meetings. The brain cannot multitask. It switches very quickly between tasks,[12] giving us the illusion of doing several things at once. It is possible to get faster at switching, but it is more difficult and less efficient than
concentrating on one task at a time. Multitasking gives worse results than
giving each task your full attention. Finally, multitasking does not build any
neuroplastic connections because there is no willed, sustained attention.

This suggests two coaching interventions.

First, explain to clients the evidence about multitasking and encourage
them to focus on one thing at a time, even if only for a short time. Second,
encourage them to redesign their work environment. The more they can cut
down on competing, simultaneous demands on their attention, the better
work they will do. They can cut down on demands for attention. Changing
the environment is often easier and more effective than changing yourself.
Coaching tends to look for resources and solutions inside the client. Clients
want to develop new personal qualities and think differently about their
challenges. This is fine but can miss an opportunity. When a client gets more
control of their context and environment, they may not need to work so
hard. Sometimes, a business will search for special talent to do a job, rather
than design the job so it is easier to do. The more a client can take control of their environment, the better they function. So, rather than building
more resilience to cope with a difficult work environment, start by trying to
change the environment, at least in small ways. This is not cheating. Some
clients think they 'should' be able to cope and see the environment as unchangeable. The brain knows nothing about 'should'. It works with what is.
The brain is very influenced by context, far more than we think, as we shall
see in later chapters. We have had clients close their doors, redesign their office, put up 'Do Not Disturb' notices to stop interruptions and distractions
in order to have difficult conversations with their peers. The results have
been remarkable. Sometimes you do not need to change yourself if you can
change the environment.

Practice

Repetition consolidates neural pathways and memory, so we need to repeat
(with focused attention), to get neuroplastic changes. There is no hard or fast
rule about how many times you need to repeat or how long it will take. It
will depend on what the skill is, how complex it is and the balance of memory and physical action involved. It also depends on what level of expertise you are aiming for. Short periods of concentrated practice undoubtedly

strengthen neural pathways. They lead to quick gains, but equally, to quick forgetting. This accords with the psychological research that shows we have a natural 'forgetting curve' unless we repeatedly practise and consolidate the information. Permanent changes take more work over a longer period.

What about mental rehearsal? Mental rehearsal does help (it activates the same motor networks as the real action) but is not enough. The reason for this is interesting. We learn from feedback only if we cannot predict it in advance. If you know what will happen, the brain does not learn. There is no feedback from the outside world in mental rehearsal; everything is created inside your head, so it has limited value. It is useful for reinforcing physical sporting skills giving a more fluid basic movement (e.g. a tennis backhand), but even then, with no outside feedback the perfectly executed backhand can still miss the real ball the opponent fires towards you. Do not rely on mental rehearsal.

Skill at the highest level takes a long time to develop. The neuroscience of expertise is an emerging field.[13] To date, the 'ten thousand hours' rule applies. This was originally proposed by Anders Ericsson[14] and became widely known through the book 'Outliers' by Malcolm Gladwell.[15] To excel at any complex skill, whether it be playing the piano, teaching, playing videogames, writing or managing a company you need to devote upwards of 10,000 hours of practice. This averages about twenty hours a week for ten years. And not just any old practice. The practice needs to be disciplined, attentive and with feedback built in (and here coaching can help a great deal). It needs to be interesting. Monotony is the enemy of attention and therefore of neuroplasticity. Talent is no explanation of expertise; it is just a label we give to people who are very good. Even so-called prodigies, such as Mozart, Tiger Woods or the Beatles who became world class in their chosen profession early, put in the hours needed if you look at their lives in more detail.[16]

Physical exercise

Coaching is assumed to happen above the neck. However, the brain is embodied, so physical exercise makes a difference. All the research points towards the importance of physical exercise for good brain function. The exercise does not need to Olympic weightlifting. Walking running, cycling or any cardiovascular exercise stimulates the production of a compound called BDNF. BDNF stands for brain-derived neurotrophic factor, and its name reflects what it does. BDNF comes from the brain and grows neurons. It is released when neurons fire together. It helps to strengthen their connection, so they can fire together consistently in future.[17] It is also used in producing myelin, the fatty, insulating sheath surrounding neurons that speeds up the signals.

Sleep

Finally, and perhaps surprisingly, sleep. Sleep is extremely important for the brain. Sleep, mindfulness and physical exercise are a trio we cannot escape in exploring brain-based coaching. The importance of sleep is just being appreciated in learning, memory, creativity and health.[18] We know that sleep consolidates memory, and we will look at this in more detail later. Sleep deprivation lowers BDNF levels[19] although it is not clear whether sleep deprivation alone does this or stress that leads to both sleep deprivation and lowered BDNF levels. Whichever way the causal arrow goes, stress and sleep deprivation deplete BDNF and neuroplasticity. Our learning and memory suffer.

Successful practice needs attention and sleep. Brain scanning of subjects learning to play the piano showed that after sleep, movements were transferred to 'automatic pilot' and playing was easier the following morning. Stage two sleep was responsible, which is the last two hours of an eight-hour slumber.[20] In 2015, the International Olympic Committee published a statement about the critical need for sleep in athletic development. Creative thinking, presentation skills or any such activity, relying as they do on memory and good brain function, will also need sleep. It's ironic that in our need to do more and do it faster, we are skipping sleep, which is exactly what is needed to work more effectively.

Neuroplasticity is the link between the insubstantial world of thought and the material world of nerve cells. Somehow clay and flame blend, so they influence each other. Neuroplasticity makes everything easier and more effortless, whether it is playing the guitar, making a presentation, meditating, picking your nose or shouting at your kids. Understanding how it works is the key to learning and stopping habits. A coach is the enabler of the clients' self-directed neuroplasticity (Table 2.1).

Table 2.1 Neuroplasticity – summary

Neuroplasticity
Neuroplasticity is the process by which the brain changes itself in response to new thoughts and actions.
Neuroplasticity happens through one or a combination of the following:
• the formation of new neurons • the formation of new synapses • the strengthening of existing synapses.
Synaptic plasticity involves changes in the synapses.
Long-term potentiation is when a synapse is strengthened
Hebb's law captures the idea of neuroplasticity: 'What fires together, wires together'.
Competitive neuroplasticity is when neurons are taken and reused for another, often completely different function.
Neuroplasticity is the basis of habits, learning and change.
Thought as well as actions can result in neuroplastic changes to the brain.
The dark side of neuroplasticity is that it makes any action or thought process easier and automatic, not just the ones we want.

Notes

1   Doing more than is necessary, and then pruning it back in the light of what you
    need is a good way to learn in many fields. We used this method to write this
    book. We are not even sure if this footnote will survive the pruning.
2   Nottebohm, F., Stokes, T. M., & Leonard, C. M. (1976). Central control of song in
    the canary, v Serinus Canarius. *Journal of Comparative Neurology, 165* (4), 457–486.
3   Eriksson, P. S., Perfilieva, E., Björk-Eriksson, T., Alborn, A. M., Nordborg, C.,
    Peterson, D. A., & Gage, F. H. (1998). Neurogenesis in the adult human hip-
    pocampus. *Nature Medicine, 4* (11), 1313–1317.
4   Donald, H. (1949). *The organisation of behaviour.* John Wiley.
        To be exact, Hebb's law is a paraphrase of a sentence by Siegrid Lowel, pro-
    fessor of Systems Neuroscience at the University of Göttingen: 'Neurons wire
    together if they fire together'. However, Hebb's Law is catchier and gives credit
    where credit is due.
5   Pascual-Leone and his colleagues at Harvard Medical School set up an exper-
    iment to explore this. Volunteers are blindfolded and taught Braille. After five
    days, they were able to understand Braille better than the control group who
    were taught Braille but not blindfolded. Functional magnetic resonance imag-
    ing (fMRI) scans on the blindfolded volunteers showed their visual cortex was
    activated. They were using what were specialised 'visual' neurons for processing
    touch. In five days, the brain was already reorganising itself. Unfortunately, the
    effect disappeared quickly too – after twenty hours without blindfolds, brain
    activation went back to normal.
        See: Merabet, L. B., Hamilton, R., Schlaug, G., Swisher, J. D., Kiriakopoulos,
    E. T., Pitskel, N. B., ... Pascual-Leone, A. (2008). Rapid and reversible recruit-
    ment of early visual cortex for touch. *PLoS One, 3* (8), e3046.
6   The Neuroscientist Vilayanur Ramachandran has done pioneering work with
    people who have lost a limb through surgery or accident. In one study, he found
    that a man whose forearm was recently amputated, 'felt' his arm touched when
    touched on the cheek. This is possible because the area corresponding to the
    face is right next to the area for the arm in the brain's sensory cortex. The nerves
    from the face had taken over the area formerly devoted to the arm, which were
    idle because they had no longer had input.
        Reorganisation of neurons in the brain also explains 'phantom limb' pain.
    Some patients who have amputations feel pain in the limb that is gone. This is
    because the nerve cells in the brain that used to receive input from the limb are
    'stuck' registering pain signals from the time the limb was damaged. Surround-
    ing regions cannot take over this area because it is still active. Ramachandran
    devised an ingenious way to trick the brain into thinking there was new input,
    hoping the nerve cells in the brain would respond and new sensations would
    replace the pain. Ramachandran made a box with mirrors. The patient put his
    undamaged arm inside the box, so he could view a reflected image of this arm
    in the place of the missing one. When he moved the healthy arm, the reflection
    looked like the missing arm was moving, fooling the brain. This therapy has
    been remarkable successful in helping to alleviate phantom limb pain. (This
    idea was used as a plot device in an episode, titled 'The Tyrant' in the fourth
    season of the TV medical drama 'House'.)
        See: Ramachandran, V. S., Rogers-Ramachandran, D., & Cobb, S. (1995).
    Touching the phantom limb. *Nature, 377* (6549), 489.
        Chan, B. L., Witt, R., Charrow, A. P., Magee, A., Howard, R., Pasquina,
    P. F., ... Tsao, J. W. (2007). Mirror therapy for phantom limb pain. *New England
    Journal of Medicine, 357* (21), 2206–2207.

Ramachandran, V., & Blakeslee, S. (1998). *Phantoms in the brain*. William Morrow.

7 Münte, T. F., Altenmüller, E., & Jäncke, L. (2002). The musician's brain as a model of neuroplasticity. *Nature Reviews Neuroscience, 3* (6), 473–478.

8 Pascual-Leone, A., Nguyet, D., Cohen, L. G., Brasil-Neto, J. P., Cammarota, A., & Hallett, M. (1995). Modulation of muscle responses evoked by transcranial magnetic stimulation during the acquisition of new fine motor skills. *Journal of Neurophysiology, 74* (3), 1037–1045

9 Merzenich, M. M., & Jenkins, W. M. (1993). Reorganization of cortical representations of the hand following alterations of skin inputs induced by nerve injury, skin island transfers, and experience. *Journal of Hand Therapy, 6* (2), 89–104.

10 Sawaguchi, T., & Goldman-Rakic, P. S. (1991). D1 dopamine receptors in prefrontal cortex: Involvement in working memory. *Science, 251* (4996), 947–951.

11 Antal, A., Terney, D., Poreisz, C., & Paulus, W. (2007). Towards unravelling task-related modulations of neuroplastic changes induced in the human motor cortex. *European Journal of Neuroscience, 26* (9), 2687–2691.

12 Dux, P. E., Tombu, M. N., Harrison, S., Rogers, B. P., Tong, F., & Marois, R. (2009). Training improves multitasking performance by increasing the speed of information processing in human prefrontal cortex. *Neuron, 63* (1), 127–138.

13 Bilalić, M. (2017). *The neuroscience of expertise*. Cambridge: Cambridge University Press.

14 Ericsson, K. A. (2006). The influence of experience and deliberate practice on the development of superior expert performance. *The Cambridge Handbook of Expertise and Expert Performance, 38*, 685–705.

15 Gladwell, M. (2008). *Outliers: The story of success*. UK: Hachette.

16 Colvin, G. (2008). *Talent is overrated*. Penguin Books.

17 Heyman, E., Gamelin, F. X., Goekint, M., Piscitelli, F., Roelands, B., Leclair, E., … Meeusen, R. (2012). Intense exercise increases circulating endocannabinoid and BDNF levels in humans – possible implications for reward and depression. *Psychoneuroendocrinology, 37* (6), 844–851.

18 See *Why we sleep* by Matthew Walker (Allen Lane 2017) for a superb summing up of current research.

19 Lucassen, P. J., Meerlo, P., Naylor, A. S., Van Dam, A. M., Dayer, A. G., Fuchs, E., … Czeh, B. (2010). Regulation of adult neurogenesis by stress, sleep disruption, exercise and inflammation: implications for depression and antidepressant action. *European Neuropsychopharmacology, 20* (1), 1–17.

20 Walker, M. (2017). *Why we sleep*. Allen Lane.

Bibliography

Antal, A., Terney, D., Poreisz, C., & Paulus, W. (2007). Towards unravelling task-related modulations of neuroplastic changes induced in the human motor cortex. *European Journal of Neuroscience, 26*(9), 2687–2691.

Bilalić, M. (2017). *The neuroscience of expertise*. Cambridge: Cambridge University Press.

Chan, B. L., Witt, R., Charrow, A. P., Magee, A., Howard, R., Pasquina, P. F., … Tsao, J. W. (2007). Mirror therapy for phantom limb pain. *New England Journal of Medicine, 357*(21), 2206–2207.

Colvin, G. (2008). *Talent is overrated*. New York: Penguin Books.

Dux, P. E., Tombu, M. N., Harrison, S., Rogers, B. P., Tong, F., & Marois, R. (2009). Training improves multitasking performance by increasing the speed of information processing in human prefrontal cortex. *Neuron, 63*(1), 127–138.

Ericsson, K. A. (2006). The influence of experience and deliberate practice on the development of superior expert performance. *The Cambridge Handbook of Expertise and Expert Performance, 38*, 685–705.

Eriksson, P. S., Perfilieva, E., Björk-Eriksson, T., Alborn, A. M., Nordborg, C., Peterson, D. A., & Gage, F. H. (1998). Neurogenesis in the adult human hippocampus. *Nature Medicine, 4*(11), 1313–1317.

Gladwell, M. (2008). *Outliers: the story of success*. New York: Hachette

Hebb, D. (1949). *The organisation of behaviour*, New York: John Wiley.

Heyman, E., Gamelin, F. X., Goekint, M., Piscitelli, F., Roelands, B., Leclair, E., … Meeusen, R. (2012). Intense exercise increases circulating endocannabinoid and BDNF levels in humans – possible implications for reward and depression. *Psychoneuroendocrinology, 37*(6), 844–851.

Lucassen, P. J., Meerlo, P., Naylor, A. S., Van Dam, A. M., Dayer, A. G., Fuchs, E., … Czeh, B. (2010). Regulation of adult neurogenesis by stress, sleep disruption, exercise and inflammation: Implications for depression and antidepressant action. *European Neuropsychopharmacology, 20*(1), 1–17.

Merabet, L. B., Hamilton, R., Schlaug, G., Swisher, J. D., Kiriakopoulos, E. T., Pitskel, N. B., … Pascual-Leone, A. (2008). Rapid and reversible recruitment of early visual cortex for touch. *PLoS One, 3*(8), e3046.

Merzenich, M. M., & Jenkins, W. M. (1993). Reorganization of cortical representations of the hand following alterations of skin inputs induced by nerve injury, skin island transfers, and experience. *Journal of Hand Therapy, 6*(2), 89–104.

Münte, T. F., Altenmüller, E., & Jäncke, L. (2002). The musician's brain as a model of neuroplasticity. *Nature Reviews Neuroscience, 3*(6), 473–478.

Nottebohm, F., Tegner, M. S., & Christiana, M. L. (1976). Central control of song in the canary, v Serinus Canarius. *Journal of Comparative Neurology, 165*(4), 457–486.

Pascual-Leone, A., Nguyet, D., Cohen, L. G., Brasil-Neto, J. P., Cammarota, A., & Hallett, M. (1995). Modulation of muscle responses evoked by transcranial magnetic stimulation during the acquisition of new fine motor skills. *Journal of Neurophysiology, 74*(3), 1037–1045.

Ramachandran, V., & Blakeslee, S. (1998). *Phantoms in the brain*. New York: William Morrow.

Ramachandran, V. S., Rogers-Ramachandran, D., & Cobb, S. (1995). Touching the phantom limb. *Nature, 377*(6549), 489.

Sawaguchi, T., & Goldman-Rakic, P. S. (1991). D1 dopamine receptors in prefrontal cortex: Involvement in working memory. *Science, 251*(4996), 947–951.

Walker, M. (2017). *Why we sleep*. London: Allen Lane.

Chapter 3

Thinking and feeling – the neuroscience of goals

Plato compared the human mind to a chariot drawn by two horses – one intellect and the other emotion. (The white horse was intellect, and the black horse was emotion. Nothing changes; emotion is still seen as the bad ride.) The charioteer, the conscious self, was forever battling to get them to run harmoniously. This conflict between them has haunted our thinking ever since. Emotion seems to disrupt thought and impair judgement. But maybe the chariot needs both horses to move at all.

Thinking (cognition) is defined as knowing, reasoning and judgement; it deals with facts, information and deductions. It is often language based. Cognition is the calm, reflective lake of thought. Emotions are feelings about thoughts and experiences; they affect our body, and they move us. They are hot streams that make the lake more turbulent. The resulting river of thought is mostly lukewarm but with sporadic bursts of steam and regular chill currents. Whatever the temperature, we are immersed in our thinking. From the brain's point of view, it's just activity in different areas. Some of it we experience as emotion, some as thinking.

The words 'thinking' and 'feeling' are different, but our experience is always a mixture of both. There is no thinking without feeling and no feeling without thinking. A few weeks ago, we were making plans about moving to a new house: contacting movers, writing to solicitors, making financial calculations. The goal and plans were clear, but there are plenty of feelings too: happiness at the thought of living in our new house, annoyance at the slowness of our solicitor, anxiety about the money issues, uncertainty about which mover to choose. There were memories too. The good and bad times in our old house. All was driven by one goal: to move to another city.

Thinking is a complex activity, involving many parts of the brain. The prefrontal cortex (PFC) is directly involved in cognitive control, planning and executive functions. It is active in goal setting, decision-making and action planning. It is self-appointed CEO of the brain, and like a good CEO, takes input from other members of the team. The PFC generates thoughts, and it inhibits distracting thoughts. The PFC is the master of inhibition. This ability to inhibit impulses, distractions and irrelevant thoughts is crucial to focused thinking. When the PFC does not inhibit well, the result will be attention deficit hyperactivity disorder (ADHD). There are degrees and different types of ADHD, but all come with a proneness to distraction and an inability to focus. The main treatments for severe ADHD are stimulants, which seems counter-intuitive when the answer should surely be less stimulation, not more. The stimulants work by rousing the PFC to do its work of inhibiting the myriad parts of the brain from jostling and claiming your attention.[1]

The dorsal (upper) part of the PFC (dPFC) is associated with 'cold' cognition – planning and rule-governed action. The dPFC also monitors actions for social appropriateness. A client with a highly functioning dPFC would be excellent at planning and execution and less prone to emotional influences on these plans. The lower (or ventral) part of the PFC consists of the orbitofrontal cortex (OFC) and ventromedial PFC (VmPFC) and is associated with 'warmer' thinking, emotional memory and socially acceptable behaviours. This part of the PFC is active when we are emotionally involved with others. It is also active when we take a moral or ethical perspective. A client with a highly functioning VmPFC would have very good control over their impulses and their social behaviours. The OFC (put your finger on the bridge of your nose between your eyes – you are pointing right at it) has a critical role in integrating emotion in decision-making and bringing together the hot and cold streams of thinking, so we apply moral rules and appropriate behaviour in a rational way. Ideally, dorsal and ventral systems work together. Planning and logic are tempered with emotion; a person is neither too rule bound nor too impulse driven. The two horses run together.

The OFC is also crucial for reversal learning – when something that was rewarding changes and becomes neutral or bad. One client we remember used to enjoy talking with a fellow manager, until suddenly that manager became critical and sarcastic. What was a pleasure became a pain. He struggled to understand why, but the immediate issue was to adjust to the new situation, and that is where the OFC comes in. It helps us change track and not continue to flog a dead horse. Without reversal learning, people keep doing something that hurts them, even as they realise it is hurting them (Figure 3.1).

We faced a question when we were planning this book: what to cover first: emotion or cognition? Or a huge chapter covering both at once? We decided to run cognition first, hoping the whole picture will be clear when both are clarified separately.

So, our first stop is cognition and goal planning.

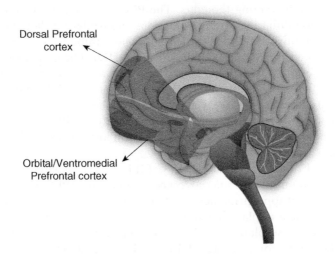

Dorsal Prefrontal cortex

Orbital/Ventromedial Prefrontal cortex

Figure 3.1 Hot and cold cognition.

The neuroscience of goals

What do you want? This simple question powers our actions; it is the fundamental coaching question. What starts as a thought, ends in an action. The brain uses the same neurotransmitter, dopamine, to modulate both the feeling of wanting something (through the reward pathway and the PFC) and the ability to act (through the basal ganglia, a group of structures deep in the brain that control movement). Goal-oriented action is so natural to us, and it is hard to imagine what life would be like without it.[2]

How do we decide what to do? We choose what we think is valuable and rewarding. We want it and then try to get it. Sometimes, the reward is alluring (sex with a desired partner, chocolate cake or the shiny new gadget) and the craving is strong. Other times, the reward is more abstract (self-esteem, freedom or reputation) and the wanting more cerebral. Whatever it is, we plan to get it; we imagine possible futures, anticipate obstacles and adjust our actions constantly towards the desired state. The path to success can mean effort, pain and sacrifice. In the end, we might not even like what we achieve. Wanting and liking are not governed by the same circuits in the brain. Sometimes, we think we want something, but what we really want is the feeling we think we will have when we have achieved the goal.

We must maintain our focus on the goal in the face of setbacks. Whether we get the goal or not, the journey involves creativity, planning and visualisation. It needs the ability to focus over time and to ignore distractions. Old habits must go, and new ones formed. We look over the past and into the future to see obstacles and resources and form a plan of action. Many brain areas need to be coordinated. How does this work in practice? There are three main processes in goal-oriented behaviour: creating, sustaining and completing.

Creating

The main function of the brain is to calculate the future. The brain is not a passive lump of tissue waiting to respond to what happens 'out there'. It is continually trying to make sense of experience, bringing up memories and trying to predict the future. The best way to predict the future is to create it.

The brain generates expectations from experience and then uses incoming information to modify them. We do not see what is 'out there'. We see what is 'in here' modified by what we perceive 'out there' (and we perceive a very small part of what is out there anyway, and much of that gets lost in the processing). If you doubt this, go to YouTube and watch videos where a person in a gorilla suit strolls across the screen and people do not see it (selective attention).[3] Or see the video where people change appearance, and others do not notice (change blindness).[4] These tricks work because the brain creates first what it expects to see and does not always pay attention to what is out there. Our brain is creating all the time, we are natural creators.

But we don't feel like creators, quite the opposite. We feel like puppets at the mercy of people and events out there. Creating is a brain state and an attitude to the world. There are two fundamental stances we can take to the world. One is to be a creator. A creator makes possibilities and feels powerful. The other is to be a victim. A victim reacts to events and feels helpless. We believe that this is a central distinction for coaches, and all successful coaching helps the client to be more of a creator of their life – as well as to pay attention to the feedback from out there.

A creator feels that they have influence to change themselves and the world. A victim feels that they have little choice and are at the mercy of outside events. A creator sees the outside world as feedback; a victim sees it as coercion. A creator knows that they cannot control events, but they can control their reaction to events, so no event is intrinsically bad or good. What matters is how they think about it and what they do with it. A creator takes responsibility. A victim blames others.

We talked in the previous chapter about top-down and bottom-up processing. Top-down processing is driven by our plans and goals. Top-down processing allows us to be creators. Bottom-up processing comes from the bottom – our attention is captured by the stimulus. Bottom-up processing is sometimes very important – we need to pay attention to pain, danger, hunger and thirst, for example. Bottom-up processing is there to help us survive. When survival is at stake, the brain does not compromise and bottom-up processing wins. However, if our attention is constantly captured by outside events that are not life threatening, then we are dancing to someone else's music. Habitual bottom-up processing for mundane events will turn us into victims.

Constantly reacting to events on the outside is stressful. When feel threatened, the hypothalamus–pituitary–adrenal (HPA) axis swings into action.[5] The adrenal glands are stimulated to release the stress hormone cortisol. The stress response is useful, and it energises us. Cortisol has an unfair reputation; it is not bad for you. It stimulates you and gets you prepared for a challenge. You need cortisol. However, too much cortisol over too long a time is bad for the body and leads to the symptoms of stress – high blood pressure, mood swings and poor sleep.

Every day, we can take a victim, reactive position or a creator active attitude. Here is one example from a client who was trying to have a better relationship with his spouse. One morning he described how she snapped at him over some trivial issue. Bottom-up attention would react to the hurtful remark at its face value. That would lead to anxiety, perhaps irritation or anger at the unfairness of it all. That could lead to a cutting remark in return and soon a full-blown quarrel. Our client, however, decided for top-down attention. He noticed his reaction and accepted it but did not act on it. He wanted a better relationship with his partner, so this was an opportunity to find out what was bothering her. He created a different meaning for the conversation. Once he had accepted the situation, he could look at it dispassionately, he had choices and could be creative. Reacting can never be creative.

To be creative is to be in the moment, dealing what is there, rather than going by past habits. A habit no longer demands attention – it runs by itself; there is no longer a reward attached. It is automatic, running down a path carved by neuroplasticity. Habit-driven actions and goal-directed actions compete in the brain, and the OFC is the part that decides which path to follow – creation or reactivity. The OFC is the judge as to whether we follow habit or reflect on what we want in the situation.[6]

To stop habitual action, the PFC must inhibit the response. Then, the way is open to be creative. Creativity is a playground, but the first step is always inhibition – stopping the habitual thought or response so that there is a space for new thinking.[7] Patients with damage to the PFC, react to their surroundings, in pre-programmed ways without considering the context. This has been called 'utilisation behaviour' – behaviour that reacts to the environment. The actions are often bizarre. For example, a patient in a hospital in Paris, when confronted with a hammer, a nail and a picture in the doctor's office, set about putting the picture on the wall, for no apparent reason.[8] Patients with PFC damage often depend on and react to stimuli from the outside, and even then, their actions may not be appropriate.

A different future

First, the OFC will decide whether to follow habit – that is, make the future the image of the past – or to create a different future. A different future means creating goals. The PFC then inhibits habits and distractions, and the creative process begins.

The first skill needed is abstraction thinking. Our thinking develops as we age from the concrete operational thinking of the child to the more abstract nuanced thinking of the older child and adult. Children deal with concrete objects – chairs, milk, cookies, teddy bears, bicycles. Next, they learn to group these into abstract categories – furniture, food, toys, means of transport. Once we can group objects into categories and deal with these abstractions, our thinking is free to combine and manipulate thoughts in ways that are impossible with concrete thinking. The PFC is the place where we process abstractions and the ability develops as the brain matures.[9] When we can think in abstractions, we can set goals like better relationships, better leadership skills and so on, and we can set 'being' goals – becoming a better person.

The second skill is the ability to travel in time. This sets us free from the present single point of time to range over past and future. Goal creation needs the ability to look to the past, learn from it and gather resources from it and project into the future, while acting in the present.

We know the suprachiasmatic nucleus in the hypothalamus is a kind of pacemaker in the brain. It controls circadian rhythms of sleep, body temperature, memory and performance. When your body timer does not match the clock in the country you are in, you are jet lagged. Not much is known about we measure longer time frames. The PFC, basal ganglia and hippocampus are probably involved,[10] but exactly how it works is still a mystery.

Think back to something you did last year ... and then year before.
How can you know one memory happened before another?
The brain must somehow 'tag' memories with a time stamp, although the
    further back we go, the less sure we become of the order and the years
    melt into each other.

Here are some useful coaching questions to help the client at the goal creation stage:

What do you want to create?
How do you want this to be different?
When you have made the change, how will your life be?
Describe your new life ....
What will be true for you when you get this goal?
What puzzle is this goal the answer to?

Sustaining

While writing this book, we wanted to move to a new house out of London. Our daughter was changing school, and we wanted to be closer to the school. We created an idea of the sort of house we wanted and the area we wanted it and the kind of life we wanted to live. It was abstract, optimistic and was built partly from our memories of what we enjoyed in the past. We needed information about the area, so we spent many weekends touring the area and getting a feel for it. Then, we could make an action plan. It was difficult to create a fresh picture – the temptation was to try to have everything we had before, but in a different place. This is the 'expat' trap – like an expat living abroad who still eats English food, speaks English to the locals, has a ring of expat friends and for all intents and purposes lives how they would live in England (but with better weather).

Creating needs to be followed by planning and action. This must be sustained sometimes over long periods. To work towards the goal, we need to keep track of progress and work out the next step. For this, we need working memory. Working memory is where we store and work with information in the short term (no more than a few minutes). It is 'The blackboard of the mind'. On this work space, we pull up long-term memories, move them around, park them, link them to the present and project into the future. Working memory is crucial to planning and maintaining focus on the goal. The dorsolateral PFC (dlPFC) is the place where stored knowledge (originally from the hippocampus and the PFC) is integrated with our present perceptions. The dlPFC also inhibits distractions to working memory – the smell of coffee or the tempting chime of the phone telling us we have another message. Holding ideas in working memory and being able to consider them at length without jumping to a solution is the hallmark of a fluid intelligence with abstract, creative thinking, pattern recognition and problem-solving. The anterior cingulate cortex (ACC) monitors the whole process. Its job is to find errors and then feedback to the PFC. ACC activity is higher whenever we detect mistakes or incongruence.[11]

Goal creation and sustaining is not only cognitive. Emotions colour our thinking at every turn. They might interfere – PFC processing is interrupted by signals from the amygdala if we feel anxious or afraid. Values are involved, and memories carry emotion. The OFC integrates the hot and cold pathways, evaluating the emotional tone of the ideas. Values and emotions guide our decisions as we go along. Values are what is important to us in that situation and are linked with emotion in the limbic system. They represent what we find rewarding.

Completing

Goals are like Russian dolls, one nests inside another and completing one leads to another. Long-term goals divide into sequences of shorter goals.

Goal planning is iterative, and we apply the same thinking to each of the subgoals, while keeping the main goal in mind. In our example, find a solicitor, arrange funding, find an estate agent, find a house to buy, find a buyer for our house, make the sale and finally move out of the old and into the new.

We cannot control what happens, and every step of the way is a cocreation involving yourself, other people and random events. Sometimes it works out, and sometimes it does not. When it doesn't, the ACC is alerted, and the sequence starts again.

Destination and journey

Goals must be rewarding, otherwise, why bother? One reward is from achieving the goal – getting to the destination. The other reward is in the journey. It is immensely satisfying to have finished this book and deliver the manuscript, but more rewarding is the learning from writing it. When we think about goals, it seems the destination *is* the reward, but that is an illusion. Our brain evolved over tens of thousands of years and during most of that time, rewards and values were simple: food, shelter and sex, and all as soon as possible, because life was short and uncertain. Now our goals can be more abstract and long term. Long-term goals like skill acquisition, self-development, leadership or good relationships are very complex. They can twist, change and transform as we go. Success is not about you alone, plenty of other people need to be involved. Even when you get what you want, it may not be what you expect, and you may not feel what you thought you would feel.

We have had several clients who have laboriously climbed the career ladder, triumphantly placed the foot on the top rung, and looking round, are appalled that the view is nothing like they imagined it. So, the path had better be rewarding; otherwise, goal achievement can be a great disappointment.

Here is the best example. Suppose you want to climb Mount Everest. You will be at the top (if you make it), for thirty minutes at most; that thirty minutes will be wonderful, but then you have got to start down. The climb and descent will take weeks. Preparation will take months. Climbing Mount Everest is a journey, and the whole journey needs to be rewarding and worthwhile. The view from the top is the cherry on the cake. Whatever the goal we spend much more time on the journey than at the destination. The thrill of the summit never lasts, and we look round for another summit to conquer. The journey needs to be rewarding so that even if you do not reach the destination, you can still feel that it was worthwhile.

A journey needs long-term focus and perseverance. This is linked to the neurotransmitter dopamine that we shall meet in chapter eight. Suffice to say, dopamine is the neurotransmitter that dominates the reward pathways of the brain making us want and seek out those things we see as rewarding. It acts on the PFC to give us the feeling of motivation, energy and desiring. The PFC has many dopamine receptors, and motivation comes from dopamine pathways in the PFC being activated. To be motivating, goals must be rewarding – they must be linked with values. The value must not only be in the achievement but also in the journey. No link with values – no dopamine. No dopamine – no motivation. No motivation – no action. (Dopamine is also the primary neurotransmitter that activates the basal ganglia to act.) When clients complain of lack of 'motivation' what they are saying neuroscientifically is: 'This goal does not appear to be rewarding enough and valuable enough to activate my mesolimbic dopamine pathways, so I am experiencing a lack of energy and drive to take action to get this goal'. Answer – connect the goal to their values and therefore to dopamine. As dopamine levels increase in the PFC, so motivation increases.[12]

Flexibility is needed as well as focus and perseverance. Circumstances change, and plans must be rethought. The OFC is involved with reversal learning – when what was rewarding, ceases to be so. The ACC is also called into play. First, it is activated when we use a longer time frame. ACC damage restricts the view to only the immediate past. Second, it is activated more by actions we can control. When a client does not believe that they have much influence, the ACC may not be activated to the same degree and they may restrict their time horizon. A coach must keep the client in their zone of influence – where they can have direct impact on what happens.

Coaching applications

Now to bring the themes together using the example of our own foray into house buying and selling.

Using stored knowledge (dPFC and hippocampus)

We had experiences before in buying a house but not in selling and buying at the same time. We did have experience of finding the funds to buy, so that was useful. However, much of our previous experience did not apply as the market conditions were quite different now.

Where we had neither knowledge nor experience, we contacted experts, estate agents, nd solicitors for dealing with the legal process.

Here are the two important things we learned:

- It was tempting to follow the obvious and familiar steps.
  Many times, it paid off to take a second look.
- We 'outsourced our PFC' to trustworthy professionals as much as we could.

It was tempting but futile to try to control the whole process. We controlled what we could and paid others to attempt to control what we could not.

Useful questions were as follows:

What do I know about this already?
How much of this knowledge applies now?
How are circumstances different now?
Who or what can help me and how do I find them?

Motivation and reward (dopamine, PFC and the limbic system)

There were strong values leading us to the move.
We wanted to move to the country, we valued the lifestyle there.
We wanted to be close to our daughter's school.
The main values for moving were a sense of space, peace and a beautiful area.
There were many good things about where we lived, but we knew we would lose some things in a new place. It took ten months to complete the move. There were many times we felt cramped, anxious and argumentative, and each time we tried to remember why we were moving.

Some useful questions were as follows:

What is important about this?
How do I feel about this?
Is my next action in line with what is important about this?
Do I still want this?
What small reward can I give myself for getting this far?

Error detection (ACC)

Many times the process seemed becalmed, and it was hard not to get anxious. One event tested us to the limit. We had just lost one buyer and had three new prospects lined up to view our house. At four o'clock on a Monday morning, Joseph was woken by the sound of running water. He jumped up in alarm and went into the bathroom on the first floor which was directly over the kitchen below. The floor was awash from a broken pipe. He stopped the water flow and then went downstairs to the kitchen prepared for the worst – and was not disappointed. The kitchen looked like a water bomb had hit it, the plaster ceiling had collapsed and was in soggy pieces all over the floor. A ton of builder's debris that had been stashed between the floors had come down with the ceiling. This was a catastrophe. We felt like the ceiling had fallen on our dreams. There was nothing to do but clean up, cancel the viewings and ring the necessary electricians, plumbers and decorators needed to put the kitchen back in order. This took over two weeks. In the end, there may have even been a benefit. The kitchen got a complete redecoration, and in its new white and shiny incarnation, was more attractive to buyers than its former shabby self.

Some useful questions at this stage:

What are the risks?
What could go wrong?
What can I do to mitigate these threats?
How much influence do I have?
How do I get back on track?

Reversal learning and flexibility (OFC)

Plenty of examples here. At some stages, we had to press the estate agents and our buyer. There were times when we wanted to press but held back, because it was not going to help. Most of the time we left the process to the solicitor, but other times we had to step in and take charge of the process. The kitchen ceiling incident put everything on hold. Instead of seeking buyers, we had to put them off for two weeks.

Some useful questions:

What actions do I have to keep doing throughout?
What actions do I need to review that may not be serving me well now?
What actions do I need to rethink or stop due to this change in circumstances?

Action (basal ganglia)

Actions flow easily if the planning has been good. You can construct a whole action plan step by step, but always be aware that reality is always more complicated, and you will have to change and adapt. There is a military saying: 'No strategy survives the first contact with the enemy'. Or as we would put it, 'No action plan survives the collapse of the kitchen ceiling'. But there is always another action plan.

The question is simple:

What is my next action step?

Table 3.1 The neuroscience of goals – summary

Skill	Brain system
Planning	dlPFC
Creativity	PFC (inhibition)
Top-down processing	PFC
Abstraction	PFC
Wanting	Dopamine
Working memory	Hippocampus
Time horizon	ACC
Error detection	ACC
Focus	Mesocortical dopamine pathway
Motivation	Dopamine
Values	Limbic system
Long-term memory	Hippocampus and PFC
Integration of emotion and cognition	OFC
Reversal learning	OFC
Decision-making	OFC
Flexibility	OFC
Action step	Basal ganglia

There are many types of goals, we have concentrated on 'doing' goals, but there are also 'being' goals – self-development goals. These are more personal, but the brain deals with them in the same way. Creating, sustaining and completing a goal is a complex process; there are so many simultaneous systems working. Our brain is brilliant at managing this. It is not so good at gathering and evaluating information – the subject of the next chapter.

Notes

1 Treatment for ADD and ADHD can also involve drugs to help with motivation and perseverance by stimulating the dopamine pathways (e.g. Adderall). Drugs that modulate dopamine pathways are necessarily addictive, and this is a major drawback of these treatments.
2 We can know what a goalless life is like by seeing what happens when the brain areas that control goal setting fail. This is very rare. The literature describes one patient who was referred to a neurology clinic because he did not care about anything. He would start actions but not complete them (e.g. a game of tennis but then forget to keep track of the score). He could not support himself financially and borrowed money incessantly. He was intelligent; he knew something was amiss but did not seem to care about himself, his future or his happiness. He could not plan coherently. Tests revealed a large tumour had invaded his left PFC and other parts of the frontal lobe. The prognosis was very bad, but the patient did not want to do anything about it. He had lost the ability and energy to direct his life in the way he wanted. See Knight, R. T., Grabowecky, M. F., & Scabini, D. (1995). Role of human prefrontal cortex in attention control. *Advances in Neurology, 66*, 21–36.
3 https://www.youtube.com/watch?v=vJG698U2Mvo

4   https://www.youtube.com/watch?v=VkrrVozZR2c
5   The hypothalamus releases corticotropin-releasing factor (CRF). This stimulates the pituitary gland to release adrenocorticotropic hormone (ACTH). This, in turn, stimulates the adrenal cortex to release cortisol for several hours.
6   Gremel, C. M., Chancey, J. H., Atwood, B. K., Luo, G., Neve, R., Rama krishnan, C., ... Costa, R. M. (2016). Endocannabinoid modulation of orbito-striatal circuits gates habit formation. *Neuron, 90* (6), 1312–1324.
7   Neuroscience and creativity is a fascinating topic but not one that we can cover in detail here. Many studies have been done using neuroimaging to explore brain function while subjects are engaged in solving various puzzles. Inevitably, the more complex the problem, the more systems of the brain are involved, and the results can be difficult to interpret. Simple puzzles give simpler results, but creativity is much more than the ability to solve puzzles.
    If you want to follow up on this, see:
    Abraham, A., Pieritz, K., Thybusch, K., Rutter, B., Kröger, S., Schweckendiek, J., ... Hermann, C. (2012). Creativity and the brain: Uncovering the neural signature of conceptual expansion. *Neuropsychologia, 50* (8), 1906–1917
    Amabile, T. M., Conti, R., Coon, H., Lazenby, J., & Herron M. (1996). Assessing the work environment for creativity. *Academy of Management Journal, 39* (5), 1154–1184.
    Sawyer, K. (2011). The cognitive neuroscience of creativity: A critical review. *Creativity Research Journal, 23* (2), 137–154.
8   Lhermitte, F. (1983). 'Utilization behaviour' and its relation to lesions of the frontal lobes. *Brain, 106* (2), 237–255.
9   The lateral part of the PFC behind the nose has been identified as being involved in the ability to think in abstractions. This develops during adolescence. See Dumontheil, I. (2014). Development of abstract thinking during childhood and adolescence: the role of rostrolateral prefrontal cortex. *Developmental Cognitive Neuroscience, 10*, 57–76.
10 Grondin, S. (2010). Timing and time perception: a review of recent behavioural and neuroscience findings and theoretical directions. *Attention, Perception, & Psychophysics, 72* (3), 561–582.
11 Carter, C. S., Braver, T. S., Barch, D. M., Botvinick, M. M., Noll, D., & Cohen, J. D. (1998). Anterior cingulate cortex, error detection, and the online monitoring of performance. *Science, 280* (5364), 747–749.
12 But only up to a point. Too much dopamine makes performance go down, especially in tasks which need flexibility. High levels of dopamine result in a dogged single-mindedness without flexibility.

Bibliography

Abraham, A., Pieritz, K., Thybusch, K., Rutter, B., Kröger, S., Schweckendiek, J., ... Hermann, C. (2012). Creativity and the brain: Uncovering the neural signature of conceptual expansion. *Neuropsychologia, 50*(8), 1906–1917.

Amabile, T. M., Conti, R., Coon, H., Lazenby, J., & Herron, M. (1996). Assessing the work environment for creativity. *Academy of Management Journal, 39*(5), 1154–1184.

Carter, C. S., Braver, T. S., Barch, D. M., Botvinick, M. M., Noll, D., & Cohen, J. D. (1998). Anterior cingulate cortex, error detection, and the online monitoring of performance. *Science, 280*(5364), 747–749.

Dumontheil, I. (2014). Development of abstract thinking during childhood and adolescence: The role of rostrolateral prefrontal cortex. *Developmental Cognitive Neuroscience, 10*, 57–76.

Gremel, C. M., Chancey, J. H., Atwood, B. K., Luo, G., Neve, R., Ramakrishnan, C., … Costa, R. M. (2016). Endocannabinoid modulation of orbitostriatal circuits gates habit formation. *Neuron, 90*(6), 1312–1324.

Grondin, S. (2010). Timing and time perception: A review of recent behavioural and neuroscience findings and theoretical directions. *Attention, Perception, & Psychophysics, 72*(3), 561–582.

Knight, R. T., Grabowecky, M. F., & Scabini, D. (1995). Role of human prefrontal cortex in attention control. *Advances in Neurology, 66*, 21–36.

Lhermitte, F. (1983). 'Utilization behaviour' and its relation to lesions of the frontal lobes. *Brain, 106*(2), 237–255.

Sawyer, K. (2011). The cognitive neuroscience of creativity: A critical review. *Creativity Research Journal, 23*(2), 137–154.

https://www.youtube.com/watch?v=vJG698U2Mvo

https://www.youtube.com/watch?v=VkrrVozZR2c

Chapter 4

Thinking – tricks and traps

Coaches ask questions to stimulate new thinking and springboard questions from the answer. The questions untangle the problem and help clients think in new ways. Coaching is mostly cognitive. We take pride in our thinking abilities. Here's the bad news. The brain's thinking skills are erratic. It is far from an objective, logical, thinking machine. Our usual way of thinking distorts, simplifies and downright mangles the information we get. The good news is that when we understand how it works, we can think better. This chapter will set out the traps that can warp our thinking without our knowledge.

Two ways of thinking

We have two systems of thinking. The first is fast, automatic and mostly unconscious. It jumps to conclusions based on general rules of thumb; many of these rules are hardwired by evolution. They give quick, easy answers suited to simpler times. We tend to use it for everyday decisions, but it is unreliable and influenced by our circumstances – where we are and who we are with. We rely on it at our peril for complex decisions. This is 'thinking without thinking', with no pause to reflect. This is generally known as 'fast thinking' or (rather unimaginatively) 'system 1', from the work of Daniel Kahneman in Behavioural Economics.[1] We tend to justify our quick answers because we have little or no reflective access to our thinking.[2] We are bad at 'thinking about thinking'. System 1 thinking activates the insula, the anterior cingulate cortex and parts of the limbic system.

System 2 is slow, conscious and reflective. It is much more reliable but … it demands effort and inhibiting that fast, obvious (but often wrong) answer from system 1. System 2 uses abstract, decontextualised thinking and is needed for important decisions – taking in information, carefully considering it, seeking out what is missing without being swayed by the what is happening here and now. System 2 uses the neocortex, especially the prefrontal cortex (PFC) and parietal cortex.

What about intuition? System 1 is not intuition. We see intuition as system 2 working beneath the surface and backed up by a lot of experience. Some people can make very good judgements from very little information, (so-called thin slicing).[3] They often call it intuition, but it is fast appraisal built on extensive knowledge (Figures 4.1 and 4.2).

Our thinking is a mixture of system 1 and system 2. However, it needs special effort to inhibit system 1 and use system 2. System 1 thinking comes from being 'cognitive misers'.[4] We want to spend as little effort as possible. We are all cognitive misers, hoarding resources, quick to use system 1. No judgement for doing this; it is the brain's default process.

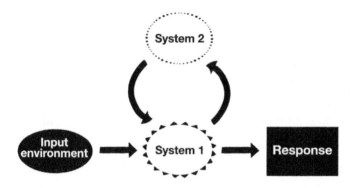

Figure 4.1 Systems 1 and 2.

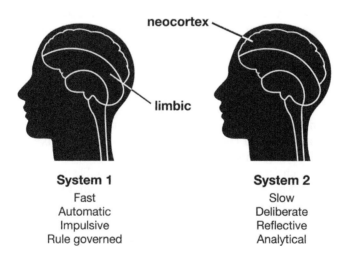

Figure 4.2 Decision-making: systems 1 and 2 processing.

Clients first answer to a question is usually from system 1 thinking. We generally disregard a client's first answer, especially if it comes quickly. We call it a 'top of the head' answer.

So, we follow up a quick answer with questions like:

'That's your first thought. What's your second?'
'Tell me something you don't know'. (This one needs rapport but is very effective.)
'Is that your best thinking about this?'
'Just reflect a little more and then tell me what you think'.

We use the same approach when we have a nightmare client who seems to have all the answers, with a ready riposte for every question. They give the impression they have thought of everything. These are trapped in system 1,

System 1 in action

System 1 is unreliable in three ways.

First, it uses hardwired cognitive shortcuts (heuristics) and applies them indiscriminately. For example, we tend to think tall, good-looking people are more capable and more trustworthy.[5] We judge this in less than a tenth of a second from facial appearance.[6] This can lead to big mistakes.[7]

Second, system 1 is biased to *believe* – it understands by believing, not by analysis and reflection.

Third, and most important, system 1 is influenced by the situation and gives answers based on immediate context rather than general principles. System 1 is heavily influenced by context in the here and now. System 2 looks to the past, present and future. It considers the there and then as well as the here and now.

Here are the main biases of system 1.

Loss aversion

We hate losing more than we love winning. A guaranteed gain (even small) is more appealing than a risk of losing. If already losing (like investing in shares that are losing value), we are more likely to gamble and risk a bigger loss if it gives a chance of regaining our money (double or quits).[8] The loss does not have to be tangible like money; it can be anything we value like respect, love, well-being or freedom. People play double or quits with all of these.

The 'status quo bias' is a variation of loss aversion. System 1 favours the status quo because a change is seen as a loss. Never mind all the other good things that may come from a change, a sense of losing something can be enough to tip the balance in favour of the current situation. This bias explains why many clients who say they want to change, do not. Clients always come to coaching wanting to change, but they have not thought about what they lose in the process. They may resist changing even if the cost is small.

When Joseph was considering moving from London to Brazil a few years ago, he hesitated, he kept thinking of what he would *lose*. Andrea made a simple verbal reframe, saying instead to think about what he would *leave*.[9] 'Leaving' is something you control. 'Losing' is something that happens to you that you cannot control. Leaving implies things are still there where you left them, and you can come and reclaim them. Losing implies they are gone for good. This thought helped Joseph a lot at the time and has helped many clients since.

Another variation on this theme is the 'sunken costs' fallacy. Have you ever looked forward to seeing a film, concert or play? You anticipate a great night out. The lights go down, the performance starts and within five minutes you know it's a disaster. You are confronted with a choice: to get up and leave, or to sit through to the end in the vain hope it will improve. If you stay to the end, then you are caught in the sunken costs fallacy. You have already lost time and money (and that does not feel good) and you do not want to admit it. Yet it does not make sense to stay. Why waste more time? You will never get back what you have already lost. This same dynamic keeps clients in bad relationships, bad friendships and bad investments. We have had clients struggling on with a project that is clearly doomed, but loss aversion stops them from calling it a day.

What are the applications for coaching?

First, knowledge is power. Tell the client about system 1 and loss aversion. Second, explore the client's present state in detail, it may be less valuable than it appears. Third, notice how the client talks about decisions in terms of loss or gain.

Finally, be careful how you frame alternatives. Make sure the client is clear on both the losses and the gains of any course of action.

When there are losses, encourage the client to look at them objectively. Some things must be let go to move to better alternatives. You can also use the loss/leave reframe.

Attention bias

System 1 directs our attention. We look for familiar things, especially in strange, new settings. The familiar attracts our attention. Oddly enough, we do not have to consciously know they are familiar for this to happen. You are likely to judge a person more attractive if you have seen a picture of them before, even if you do not remember seeing it.[10] Research also shows people are more likely to judge a statement as true if they have heard it before, even when they swear they have never heard it before.[11]

We also look for what we expect. Expectations are our attempts to predict the future, and we are heavily invested in being good forecasters. We look for evidence, however flimsy, to prove we are right. We expect people to act in certain ways and often don't notice if they act differently. This is called attentional blindness; we don't see what we don't expect, especially if we have been instructed to look for something else. The famous example is the video of the 'gorilla in the room'. The video shows a group of students in different coloured shirts passing a ball to each other. Your task is to count the number of passes. In the middle of the video, somebody wearing a gorilla suit strolls across the screen, pauses in the middle, beats their chest and exits stage right. A large percentage of people who watch this video for the first time will not 'see' the gorilla, even though eye tracking software shows they looked directly at it.[12] They are amazed when they look again and wonder how they could have missed it.

An even funnier twist on this experiment was done at Western Washington University. A clown with a big red nose in bright purple and yellow clothes pedalled a unicycle round the student campus. A survey of 150 students afterwards found only fifty percent of people walking on their own saw the clown. (A smaller percentage of people in groups noticed the clown and only twenty-five percent of students using a cell phone saw the clown. Modern technology reinforces attentional blindness.)

Confirmation bias

Confirmation bias is variation of attention bias.

We notice and remember those things that confirm our ideas.

We often see what we want to see. There are volumes of research on this from 1998.[13] We notice facts that confirm our beliefs, and we ignore or discount facts that go against our ideas. This means we tend to be overconfident in our ideas and can happily continue with beliefs that fly in the face of the facts. We had a client who had collected a diary of evidence on the incompetence of his immediate boss. He fully believed the person was useless at their job. Every day brought him new evidence. In one coaching session, he said he was prepared to set aside his belief and have an open mind for a week. We told him to spend the week collecting a diary of the times he saw his boss doing a good job. The resulting diary was as detailed as the first and surprised the client. His boss was human – some good days and some bad days. Confirmation bias leads people to interpret events in line with their preconceived ideas and therefore to be more set in their ideas.

Now for a puzzle.

Look at the four cards below. Each has a picture of a bird or a tiger on one side and a rose or a nest on the other (Figure 4.3).

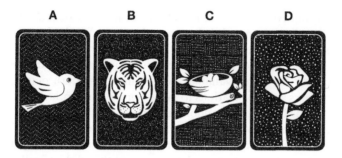

Figure 4.3 Confirmation bias.

Here is the rule: all cards with a bird on one side have a nest on the other.
What two cards would you turn over to confirm the rule?
Think before reading on.

Most people say turn over card A with the bird. This is correct. If there is not a nest on the other side, then the rule is broken.

The second common answer is to turn over card C, showing the nest (which should show a bird on the other side). But ... this is the system 1 answer. If the picture on the other side is a bird this will only confirm the hypothesis. It will not tell you if it is true (because there is no rule stopping the tiger card from having a nest on the other side). You need to turn over card D showing the rose, because if that has a bird on the back, then it disproves the hypothesis.

This little game shows a deeper point. Even with nothing at stake, we tend to look for evidence confirming ideas, rather than evidence to challenge them.[14] No wonder confirmation bias is so powerful. System 1 understands statements by trying to make them true (confirming them). System 2 understands statements by trying to make them false (testing them). 'The exception proves the rule' must be the stupidest saying ever coined. An exception *disproves* the rule and means there is a deeper rule to find.

Clients need to be aware of their confirmation bias. Confirmation bias is not stupidity; it is just the default way the brain works.. Coaches do well to ask clients for evidence that disproves their idea or observation. Ask for counterexamples, questions that challenge the client's assumptions. If the client is correct, is which case, looking counterexamples will not hurt them.

Availability bias

We pay attention to what is available. We are swayed by our own experience and what we know, even if it is not representative. Thinking of travelling by airplane? Our mind turns to two air crashes in the last couple of months, so decide maybe to take the train. Air crashes are high-profile disasters, they get reported and we remember them (bad things make the news, which tends to bias thinking even more). We forget the millions of safe journeys by air in the same time frame; they did not make the news. We don't know what we don't know and often we don't bother to find out either.

We notice coincidences and give them more importance than they deserve simply because they are available. The brain is a pattern detector, always looking for links and associations to make sense of the world even when there aren't any.[15] The brain hates randomness; it is always trying to make meaning of events. A client calls just as we were thinking about them. Coincidence? Certainly. We remember that time because it was unusual but forget the thousands of times we thought about that client and they did not call. The world is full coincidences that system 1 makes into patterns. 'Bad luck happens in threes' is a piece of folk wisdom and will be true ... as long as you wait for the third instance.

A variation of availability bias is the 'survivor bias'. We overestimate the chances of success because the winners make the headlines and those are the stories that make the news and we remember. History is written by the victors. We do not hear about the failures. We hear of big companies and how they started from humble beginnings and think that we can do the same. Maybe we can but don't forget all the hundreds of companies that tried the same idea and failed. Study the failures too and find out what they did wrong. Look in the cemeteries as well as on the pedestals for guidance.

Keep the survivor bias in mind when coaching a client through an important project. It is great for them to be confident and inspired by success stories, but they still need to think carefully about their strategies and not blindly follow a path just because it led to success for someone else. We are always cautious when I client says something like 'I know this can work because my friend John did it'. OK, but how many others tried it and it did not work? What were the critical factors that allowed his friend John to succeed when so many others failed?

Outcome bias

System 1 evaluates decisions by the result rather than by the process.
Look at the following sentences:

All living things need water.
Trees need water.
Therefore trees are living.

Looks OK, right? Perfectly logical.
Now look at this one:

All flowers need oxygen
Elephants need oxygen
Therefore, elephants are flowers.

Really?? Clearly wrong, but notice the logic of the argument is the same as the first example.

The logic is wrong. The first proposition should read:

All living things need water.
Trees are living.
Therefore trees need water.

You don't spot the wrong argument in the first example because – it gives an answer you agree with. We tend to jump to conclusions we agree with (system 1), rather than checking the logic behind the conclusion (system 2).

Good decisions come from a good decision-making *process*. Even tossing a coin will be right half the time. Results are influenced by many things, most of which are out of control.

Like the elephant example above, a successful result may be generated by a terrible process. For example, a coach claims to have a foolproof method for getting coaching clients. Let's suppose he gets eighty coaches to try it. In fact, the method is poor; it only works for one in every four. So, sixty get no benefit, but twenty do well. He then asks the twenty who were successful to invest in his next great idea. The Law of Averages says ten (50%) will do well. So he takes these ten to try out his next great idea. Each time he works only with his success stories. After a few more iterations, he will end up with a handful of individuals who have done well every time. These will be the people he will give as references for his great ideas. They are known as 'success monkeys'.[16] They will swear by his method and tell everyone how well it works. (It doesn't work. They were lucky.)

Fundamental attribution error

This one causes a lot of trouble. It means we credit results to people and discount the *circumstances*. We routinely underestimate the influence of the context on peoples' behaviour. It is easy to see why. We know our own intentions very well. When we judge others, we assume they are the same and what they do is driven by their intentions. We do not take the situation into account. (But we are very quick to explain our bad results by the pressures of circumstance.) In practice, this means we judge people too readily and assume they act consistently across all situations. Trustworthiness and capability are very context dependent, but we tend to attribute those qualities to the people, not to their behaviour in a situation. We label people as 'trustworthy' or 'untrustworthy', when, in fact, it is not so simple. Most people are trustworthy in certain situations and cannot be trusted in others. This means we may trust people in circumstances where they should not be trusted and hire people who are not competent for the work we want to give them.

We vastly overestimate our own expertise, influence and knowledge. This is sometimes known as the 'Lake Wobegon effect' (a term coined by Professor David Myers about a fictional town) where 'all the women are strong, all the men are good looking and all the children are above average'. Surveys show that most people think they are above average[17] in any skill you ask. (Who would admit to being below average intelligence?) Bear this in mind when you ask clients about their skills.

The more we study Neuroscience, the more we realise the power of context. Leadership studies are a good example. There are libraries of books about the qualities of leaders and how possession of these qualities will make you a good leader. System 1 likes stories to be simple and personal and forgets that it is person plus context that makes success. You must be in the right place at the right time. Sheer dogged perseverance, showing up regularly is one of the most underestimated qualities of success. There is a growing body of research on situational leadership showing that a leader does not have to be a charismatic inspiring individual, but they do have to represent their followers against the opposition.[18]

When clients know about this system 1 bias, they will be more realistic about their skills and the skills of others. They will assess results as a combination of the person and the situation. They will provide the best circumstances for others and focus on the best place and time for their own actions. And they will be not be fooled so often and be more effective in what they do.

Correlation or cause?

System 1 jumps to conclusions, especially about cause and effect. The brain looks for patterns, and cause-effect is a very important pattern, because you can predict the effect if you know the cause. Effect always follows cause … but … that does not mean that whatever follows something is caused by it? People wash their hands before eating but washing hands does not make them eat. When two things are found together, it does not mean one is the cause of the other. Usually, a third factor causes both. The beaches where the most amount of ice cream is sold also has the highest incidence of sunburn. Ice cream and sunburn are not connected, but both connect to large numbers of hot holidaymakers. Correlation does not mean causation. In other words, if two things happen together, it does not follow that one caused the other. There may be no connection at all.

There is a very close correlation between cheese consumption and death from becoming tangled in your bedclothes. The more cheese you eat, the higher the chance of death by tangulation.[19] The correlation is nearly ninety-five percent, which is statistically impressive.

What could explain this unexpected menace of eating cheese in bed?

Well, eating too much cheese might somehow cause you to die in bed. (Perhaps threshing around in a cheese-induced nightmare might get you strangled by your bedclothes.) Another equally unlikely explanation is that dangerous bedclothes lead to late night cheese cravings. Or, perhaps some other factor is causing both. (Too much wine?) Most likely, it is a complete coincidence and an illustration that if you carefully select your data you can make a case for almost anything.[20] Politicians, take note.

Logical thinking

We can think logically, but it takes effort. Logic is an unfeeling set of rules and the brain is not well adapted to them. Logic does not depend on context. Below is the cognitive reflection test originally introduced by Shane Frederick.[21] There are three simple questions, and they may be familiar, but many people get them wrong because they jump to system 1 conclusions without thinking.

1   A bat and a ball cost $1.10 in total. The bat costs $1.00 more than the ball. How much does the ball cost?
2   If it takes five machines five minutes to make five widgets, how long would it take 100 machines to make 100 widgets?
3   In a lake, there is a patch of lily pads. Every day, the patch doubles in size. If it takes forty-six days for the patch to cover half the lake, how long would it take for the patch to cover all the lake?

Answers in the footnote.[22]

Next, the infamous 'Monty Hall' puzzle.

Imagine you are in a TV game show facing three closed doors.

You are told there is a valuable prize behind one door (10,000 dollars), but there is nothing behind the other two doors. You pick a door, let's call it door A.

The game show host opens one of the other two doors (door B) to reveal – an empty space.

That leaves you with two unopened doors; one being your original choice (door A) and one which is unknown (door C).

Now the host asks you to choose a door. Do you stay with your original choice (door A) or change to the other door (door C) to get the best chance of the prize?

Think about it for a moment.

System 1 quickly declares that you have a one in three chance of any door having the prize. So, it makes no difference whether you change or not. So, most people stick to their original choice. (Also, the status quo bias operates here, and so does loss aversion. Suppose you changed doors and found out the prize was behind your first choice and you lost it? That would be unbearable.)

Then, system 1 has another thought. You are now choosing between two doors, one with nothing and one with prize. You have a fifty-fifty chance, so, it does not matter which door, you choose, so you might as well stick with door A. (Status quo and loss aversion still operate.)

In fact, surprisingly, if you switch doors and pick door C, you will win two thirds of the time. We won't go into the statistical explanation here, but if you don't believe it, you can play the game simulation and see for yourself.[23]

The practical lesson from the Monty Hall puzzle is the more information you have, the better decision you can make. *New information changes the problem*. At the beginning, you have no information, so the chance is one in three of being right. The second time, you have more information (a *bad* option has gone). So, you are in a better position to choose.

Practical applications for coaches

Knowing how system 1 works makes coaching easier and more effective. First, take the client's first answer as work in progress and not definitive. It is likely to be a 'top of the head' system 1 answer. Always ask for deeper, better thinking.

Second, distrust any statement a client makes that begins with words like 'Obviously ...' or 'Clearly ...'. Things are obvious and clear to system 1. Third, be very suspicious when the client comes with examples concerning

System one summary

System 1 pattern	Description
Cognitive miser	Use least amount of effort for thinking
Loss aversion	Hate losing more than love winning.
Status quo bias	Preference for current situation
Sunken costs	Reluctance to write off resources that have been invested.
Attention bias	Paying attention to the familiar and expected
Confirmation bias	Paying attention to evidence that confirms what you believe already. Tendency to look for confirming evidence rather than counterexamples.
Availability bias	Tendency to use only facts that are easily available. Leads to giving significance to coincidences
Survivor bias	Tendency to only pay attention to success stories and ignore difficulties.
Outcome bias	paying attention to the result rather than the process.
Fundamental attribution bias	Assuming people are solely responsible for their results and the context does not matter. Assuming people are consistent in every situation.
Lake Wobegon Effect	Overestimating one's own skill.
Cause and correlation confusion	Assuming events that happen in sequence or together are a cause and effect.

their insights into a situation. These may be confirmation bias. Ask the client for counterexamples. If they cannot come up with a counterexample, ask them to find one before the next session.

Another application is to start building an action plan from the goal backwards to the present. The present is full of beliefs and biases that can get in the way of a good action plan. The future is a blank slate, so put the desired goal in the future and then work backwards. This will minimise bias. Don't ask the client what they will do first. Ask the client to imagine they have achieved the goal and what they had to do immediately before to achieve it. When they have that step, ask them what they did before to achieve that. Keep working backwards like that until you reach the present. This always gets a better action plan than working from present to future (Table 4.1).

The power of context – priming

Priming is the effect of the immediate environment on our thinking. Our thoughts are 'primed', that is, set up and directed by the situation to a much greater extent than we imagine. Here are some examples that may surprise you.

First, in an experiment dubbed, 'The Florida Effect', experimenters took two groups of college students and gave each a word association test. The control group were given a test with random words. The second group thought they were getting a random test, but they were not. Their test was primed with many words associated with age and infirmity. (Florida figured in the test as it is the favourite United States retirement state, examples of other words were forgetful, bald, grey.) The students were filmed walking down the corridor after they had finished the test. The students primed with the 'elderly' words walked back significantly slower than the control group. None of them believed that the words had any impact on their behaviour. In another similar experiment, one group was given a word test primed with words associated with rudeness and a second group was given a test containing words associated with politeness. Both groups were then interviewed. The group primed with the 'rude' words interrupted the interviewer significantly more times and more quickly than the second group. The priming did not alter their judgement about the interviewer (they did not think he was rude), but it did alter their behaviour.[24]

It is sobering to think that something inconsequential can alter our behaviour without us being aware of it. In another experiment,[25] participants did better at the Trivial Pursuits game after being primed by words relating to intelligence. They did worse when primed by words relating to stupidity. It seems the longer people are primed, the more pronounced the effect.

Our brain makes simple interpretations of the surroundings and takes metaphors literally. This leads to another priming effect. We say people are 'warm' or 'cold' meaning they are friendly or aloof. The PFC takes these as metaphors, but other parts of the brain who have no access to language take them literally. In one experiment,[26] participants who briefly held a cup of hot coffee (as opposed to iced coffee) judged the interviewer as a 'warmer', that is, more caring and generous person than those who held the iced coffee. How can physical feelings of warmth activate ideas of personal caring? The brain deals in electrical signals, not in concepts, and both physical and psychological information about temperature is processed by the insula. The insula is active when we experience changes in temperature and when we are touched. It is also activated by experiences of trust, empathy, social embarrassment and shame.

What about emotional distance? We talk about 'close' friends, and 'distant' relatives. We use distance as a metaphor for emotional relationship. Perhaps, priming happens here too?

It does. A 2008 study[27] primed participants with ideas of closeness or distance. Those primed with the idea of distance were less emotionally affected by scenes of violence and reported enjoying embarrassing scenes more than the other group. Priming ideas of distance also reduced the emotional attachment to family and home environment. We could not find studies of the parts of the brain activated when measuring distance and feeling emotional closeness. Priming suggests that there is a link.

Priming has huge implications. Just for coaching, it matters what we read, who we are with and what we do before an important meeting, conversation, or presentation. It also matters what a client was doing immediately before a coaching session. The effect may be insignificant in everyday life, but it can make a big difference in important decisions and meetings.

Anchoring

We are primed by information. We are affected by information available, *even if it has no relation to the problem at hand.* The brain still tries to apply it.

For example, do you think the great pyramid of Gaza is taller or shorter than 100 metres?

What is your best guess of its height?
Write down your answer.
Now if we ask you: do you think the great pyramid of Gaza is taller or shorter than 50 feet?
How tall do you think it is?
Would you give a different answer?

The odds are you would give a smaller estimate than before, because you are influenced by the *information given in the question.* This effect is known as anchoring. Anchoring is a variation of the availability bias. The brain uses the information that is available. Remember, system 1 understands statements by trying to make them true. Anchoring happens everywhere. It is a headache for pollsters who try to get peoples' unbiased opinions. It is one of the strongest weapons in marketing and sales. View any suggested price as an anchor. It is a crucial part of how the coach should frame their questions

Random words and numbers can be anchors, even when you know they are random. Consider the research with experienced judges who were considering imposing a prison sentence on a lady convicted of shoplifting[28]. Unknown to them, they were asked to roll a dice that was loaded – it came up either with a three or a nine. Then, they were asked if they would impose a sentence in months more than or less than the number they rolled. The average sentence imposed by the judges who rolled a nine was eight months. The average of those who rolled a three was five months. What relevance does the roll of a dice have to a prison sentence? None. And yet it did in practice.

Before you think you would not be taken in by priming and anchoring, remember the Lake Wobegon effect.

Framing and questions

Priming has many implications for coaching. The most important is framing questions. Clients think about questions differently and give different answers depending how the questions are framed.

Focus on gain or loss?
Situation or personal characteristic?
Cause or effect?
Process or result?

This is subtler than avoiding leading questions. Leading questions are obvious ('How bad is the situation … really?' or 'What else hasn't she told you?'). Leading questions attempt to put an idea in your mind. Priming does it without trying.

Questions that start with 'Why?' attract system 1 answers. 'Why did you do that?' asks for an explanation and plays into the confirmation bias. Our brain grabs the invitation to spin a story that makes sense. A 'why' question can also elicit history. ('I did it because of these things in the past …'.) The client can give a chain of events, leading up to action as an explanation) They fall into the correlation/cause trap.

The intention of a 'why' question is usually to get what was important about the situation, so a better question is, 'What is important to you about X?'

Closed questions *always* prime the answer. They frame the question as follows: 'There are only two answers to this question, yes or no, and you need to come up with one of them'. This subtly leads the client in the direction of what the coach thinks, because the coach has limited the possible responses. Clients hardly ever challenge closed questions, because they do not have spare cognitive capacity to look at the *form* of the question. We tell our clients whenever we ask them a closed question, they should point this out rather than answer the question. We want them to think about the question, not just their answers. The more limited the client's possible responses, the more likely the answer will come from system 1.

The so-called TED model of questions is a good way to keep questions open and unbiased. TED stands for 'tell', 'example' and 'describe'.

TED questions are as follows:

'Tell me more …',
'Give me an example …' and
'Describe the situation …'.

System 2

How do we get clients to engage system 2?

First, explain the two systems. Neuroscience gives a client a liberating perspective. They get to know their brain better, tricks and all. System 1 is not 'bad'; there is no blame. Sometimes it works fine and we all use it. Once clients understand, they are primed to watch for system 1 thinking. Part of their PFC is on the lookout, and their thinking will never be the same again. Second, challenge any glib 'top of the head' answers. Push them for their best thinking.

Third, use system 2 yourself in the sessions. Tell the client about it and tell them the coaching session is a haven for system 2. Show the client how system 2 thinking works and its power – deeper, more reflective and not tied to context.

Fourth, ask clients about the context of important decisions or conversations.

Where were they?
Who was there?
What was said?
What happened before?
Context matters. Priming is powerful because we do not notice it.

Fifth, encourage them to surround themselves with good priming, especially before important decisions and conversations.

What company do they keep?
Can they avoid any acquaintances who drag down their energy?
Where do they go and what do they do when they are making important
    decisions?

Six, ask for counterexamples.

System 1 understands by believing.
System 2 understands by doubting and testing.
System 1 starts by assuming information is true.
System 2 starts by assuming information is a starting point to test and build on.
System 2 thinking needs *time*. Time is in short supply these days, especially in business. Executives take pride in being able to talk on the telephone, issue orders to their team, while signing papers with the hand that is not holding their cell phone.

The brain cannot multitask; it does one thing at a time. Multitasking is also more tiring; it increases cognitive load, and cognitive load makes it harder to use system 2.[29]

Finally, do not make decisions when tired or stressed, as this also hinders system 2. Executives pride themselves on quick decision-making, and sometimes a quick decision is needed. Yet, quick decisions are heavily influenced by system 1. So, be clear about which decisions are complex and important and allow time for system 2. A coaching session is a gift of time to think more deeply.

Notes

1   Daniel Kahneman, a Nobel Laureate in Economics, virtually invented the field of behavioural economics with his colleague, Amos Tversky. Economics was dominated for many years by the assumption that peoples' economic behaviour was perfectly rational. The interactions between these completely rational people produced the messiness of macroeconomics. Economic theory was normative – it defined how people <u>ought</u> to make decisions. Kahneman proposed a descriptive decision theory – how they <u>actually</u> made decisions. He showed in detail how our economic behaviour was not rational, that people were very bad at predicting probabilities, calculating risk and making good economic decisions. They use limited information and ways of thinking that are quick – and wrong. It is dangerous to assume people act consistently in a rational way. See Kahneman, D. (2011). *Thinking, fast and slow.* Macmillan.
2   Nisbett, R. E., & Wilson, T. D. (1977). Telling more than we can know: Verbal reports on mental processes. *Psychological Review, 84* (3), 231.
3   See 'Blink' by Malcolm Gladwell (Penguin books 2005). Gladwell coined the phrase 'thin slicing' for the ability to make an accurate judgement from little data. However, his examples are judgements made by experts, who have huge experience in the field and whose intuition is well educated.
4   Fiske, S. T., & Taylor, S. E. (2013). *Social cognition: From brains to culture.* Sage. This is a good book integrating psychology with neuroscience.
5   Dion, K. K. (1986). Stereotyping based on physical attractiveness: Issues and conceptual perspectives. In C. P. Herman, M. P. Zanna, & E. T. Higgins (Eds.), *Physical appearance, stigma and social behavior: The Ontario Symposium* (Vol. 3, pp. 7–21). Hillsdale, NJ: Erlbaum.

Also: Feingold, A. (1992). Good-looking people are not what we think. *Psychological Bulletin, 111* (2), 304.

6   Willis, J., & Todorov, A. (2006). First impressions: Making up your mind after a 100-ms exposure to a face. *Psychological Science, 17* (7), 592–598.

7   Malcolm Gladwell in Blink refers to this as the 'Warren Harding Error' in honour of the very attractive man who was elected president of the United States in 1921 but is generally rated one of the worst presidents in history because of his poor judgements.

8   In one study, participants were given fifty dollars and then asked to choose between two options: keep thirty dollars or gamble on a coin toss. Heads meant they keep all fifty, and tails meant they lose all fifty. In this scenario, most people were risk averse with forty-three percent deciding to take the gamble. Then, they were asked to choose between losing twenty dollars or gambling with an equal chance of losing all or keeping all fifty. Now, over sixty percent opted to gamble, despite the two scenarios being identical. The word 'loss' is very powerful.

9   Read the full story in: Joseph O'Connor and Andrea Lages, Coaching with NLP, HarperCollins 2002.

10 Tom, G., Nelson, C., Srzentic, T., & King, R. (2007). Mere exposure and the endowment effect on consumer decision making. *The Journal of Psychology, 141* (2), 117–125.

11 Hasher, L., Goldstein, D., & Toppino, T. (1977). Frequency and the conference of referential validity. *Journal of Verbal Learning and Verbal Behaviour, 16* (1), 107–112.

12 Go to https://www.youtube.com/watch?v=vJG698U2Mvo for the original test and
    https://www.youtube.com/watch?v=UtKt8YF7dgQ for an amusing twist on the original.
    https://www.youtube.com/watch?v=FWSxSQsspiQ for another amazing example of our inability to pay attention and to continue to see what we expect rather than what is there.

13 Nickerson, R. S. (1998). Confirmation bias: A ubiquitous phenomenon in many guises. *Review of General Psychology, 2* (2), 175.

14 It is true that this is a trivial game, but research shows that our brains are drawn towards evidence that confirms an idea in most areas. There are some areas where we do better, usually when people need to be tested for eligibility (e.g. getting a passport) See Cheng, P. W., & Holyoak, K. J. (1985). Pragmatic reasoning schemas. *Cognitive Psychology, 17* (4), 391–416.

15 A condition known as apophenia – tendency to see patterns where none exist.

16 From the oft-quoted idea that if you have millions of monkeys all typing away on a keyboard for infinite amount of time, one of them will write 'Hamlet'.

17 For example, when asked about their driving ability, most people will say they are above average, while conceding that others may not agree with them.

18 Haslam, S. A., Reicher, S. D., & Platow, M. J. (2010). *The new psychology of leadership: Identity, influence and power.* Psychology Press.

19 See the website www.tylervigen.com for this and other equally bizarre correlations.

20 See the excellent book by Dan Ariely: 'A field guide to Lies and Statistics' (Viking 2016) for a clear treatment of the myriad ways we can deceive ourselves with statistics.

21 Frederick, S. (2005). Cognitive reflection and decision making. *The Journal of Economic Perspectives, 19* (4), 25–42.

22 1. Five cents. 2. Five minutes 3. Forty-seven days.

23 There is a very good explanation on the website
    https://betterexplained.com/articles/understanding-the-monty-hall-problem/
    (accessed 4 January 2018). This site has a game simulation where you can try
    different strategies and see how it works.
24 Bargh, J. A., Chen, M., & Burrows, L. (1996). Automaticity of social behavior:
    Direct effects of trait construct and stereotype activation on action. *Journal of
    Personality and Social Psychology, 71* (2), 230.
25 Dijksterhuis, A., & Van Knippenberg, A. (1998). The relation between percep-
    tion and behavior, or how to win a game of trivial pursuit. *Journal of Personality
    and Social Psychology, 74* (4), 865.
26 Williams, L. E., & Bargh, J. A. (2008a). Experiencing physical warmth promotes
    interpersonal warmth. *Science, 322* (5901), 606–607.
27 Williams, L. E., & Bargh, J. A. (2008b). Keeping one's distance: The influence
    of spatial distance cues on affect and evaluation. *Psychological Science, 19* (3),
    302–308.
28 Englich, Birte, Thomas Mussweiler, and Fritz Strack. "Playing dice with crim-
    inal sentences: The influence of irrelevant anchors on experts' judicial decision
    making." *Personality and Social Psychology Bulletin* 32.2 (2006): 188-200.
29 Gilbert, D. T., Krull, D. S., & Malone, P. S. (1990). Unbelieving the unbelievable:
    Some problems in the rejection of false information. *Journal of Personality and
    Social Psychology, 59* (4), 601.

Bibliography

Ariely, D. (2016). *A field guide to lies and statistics.* Viking.
Bargh, J. A., Chen, M., & Burrows, L. (1996). Automaticity of social behavior:
    Direct effects of trait construct and stereotype activation on action. *Journal of
    Personality and Social Psychology, 71*(2), 230.
Cheng, P. W., & Holyoak, K. J. (1985). Pragmatic reasoning schemas. *Cognitive Psy-
    chology, 17*(4), 391–416.
Dijksterhuis, A., & Van Knippenberg, A. (1998). The relation between perception
    and behavior, or how to win a game of trivial pursuit. *Journal of Personality and
    Social Psychology, 74*(4), 865
Dion, K. K. (1986). Stereotyping based on physical attractiveness: Issues and con-
    ceptual perspectives. In C. P. Herman, M. P. Zanna, & E. T. Higgins (Eds.),
    Physical appearance, stigma and social behavior: The Ontario Symposium Vol. 3,
    (pp. 7–21). Hillsdale, NJ: Erlbaum.
Also: Feingold, A. (1992). Good-looking people are not what we think. *Psychologi-
    cal Bulletin, 111*(2), 304.
Englich, B., Mussweiler, T., & Strack, F. (2006). "Playing dice with criminal sen-
    tences: The influence of irrelevant anchors on experts' judicial decision making."
    Personality and Social Psychology Bulletin, 32(2), 188–200.
Fiske, S. T., & Taylor, S. E. (2013). *Social cognition: From brains to culture.* Sage.
    (This is a good book integrating psychology with neuroscience).
Frederick, S. (2005). Cognitive reflection and decision making. *The Journal of Eco-
    nomic Perspectives, 19*(4), 25–42.
Gilbert, D. T., Krull, D. S., & Malone, P. S. (1990). Unbelieving the unbelievable:
    Some problems in the rejection of false information. *Journal of Personality and
    Social Psychology, 59*(4), 601.

Gladwell, M. (2005). *Blink*. Penguin books 2005.

Hasher, L., Goldstein, D., & Toppino, T. (1977). Frequency and the conference of referential validity. *Journal of Verbal Learning and Verbal Behaviour, 16*(1), 107–112.

Haslam, S. A., Reicher, S. D., & Platow, M. J. (2010). *The new psychology of leadership: Identity, influence and power*. Psychology Press.

Kahneman, D. (2011). *Thinking, fast and slow*. Macmillan.

Nickerson, R. S. (1998). Confirmation bias: A ubiquitous phenomenon in many guises. *Review of General Psychology, 2*(2), 175.

Nisbett, R. E., & Wilson, T. D. (1977). Telling more than we can know: Verbal reports on mental processes. *Psychological Review, 84*(3), 231.

O'Connor, J., & Lages, A. (2002). *Coaching with NLP*. London, England: HarperCollins.

Tom, G., Nelson, C., Srzentic, T., & King, R. (2007). Mere exposure and the endowment effect on consumer decision making. *The Journal of Psychology, 141*(2), 117–125.

Williams, L. E., & Bargh, J. A. (2008a). Experiencing physical warmth promotes interpersonal warmth. *Science, 322*(5901), 606–607.

Williams, L. E., & Bargh, J. A. (2008b). Keeping one's distance: The influence of spatial distance cues on affect and evaluation. *Psychological Science, 19*(3), 302–308.

Willis, J., & Todorov, A. (2006). First impressions: Making up your mind after a 100-ms exposure to a face. *Psychological Science, 17*(7), 592–598.

https://www.youtube.com/watch?v=vJG698U2Mvo

https://www.youtube.com/watch?v=UtKt8YF7dgQ

https://www.youtube.com/watch?v=FWSxSQsspiQ

www.tylervigen.com

https://betterexplained.com/articles/understanding-the-monty-hall-problem/

Chapter 5

Feeling and emotion

Cognition and emotion may be two separate words, but we do not experience them separately. Words cut reality into neat packages, but the brain is not neat; it is a messy, massively interconnected system. Our experience is a complex mixture of cognition, emotion, motivation and desire, each colouring the other. As the philosopher *Friedrich Nietzsche wrote*, 'One ought to hold on to one's heart; for if one lets it go, one soon loses control of the head too'.

What is an emotion? A feeling and response to events or our interpretation of events.[1] Emotions, as the name suggests, move us.[2] We react because we care, they are personal. They may change our heart rate, blood pressure, skin colour and breathing. They propel us to action – shouting, running, crying, fighting. They come quickly, and we can't control them (but we can control what we do with them).

Imagine someone touches your body. The sense receptors in your skin will convey that signal to the brain. Your motor cortex will localise it and you become aware of the feeling. That sensation has no emotional component – yet. Then, your brain gets to work on that feeling and compulsively tries to give it a meaning. Emotion follows from that.

What was the touch?

An insect? Ugh! *Disgust*. Brush it away.

A stranger? *Surprise*. Why are they touching me? Is it by accident? Are they trying to get my attention?

What sort of stranger? Are they dangerous? *Fear*.

Huh, that disturbed me, I was trying to read this book. *Anger*.

Or is it someone I love reaching out and touching me tenderly to get my attention? *Happiness*.

Our brain leaps into action.

From feeling to interpretation, from interpretation to judgement and emotion.

The neuroscience of emotion

Many brain structures are part of the emotional circuit. The emotional centres are subcortical – below the cerebral cortex. The system includes the amygdala, hypothalamus, thalamus, cingulate gyrus and hippocampus and is often called the limbic system. Parts of the orbital frontal cortex (OFC) are also important integrating emotional experiences. The emotional system evolved before the prefrontal cortex (PFC) in a world with no electricity, laws, money or cell phones. It answers to the basics of living, eating and reproducing; without fulfilling these needs, humans would not have survived to develop executive thinking and invent electricity, money or cell phones.

There is no scientific agreement as to the number of emotions,[3] but most psychologists agree on the basic ones: anger, sadness, happiness, disgust and fear. Emotions are strong signals that we cannot override, and some (like fear) signify a threat to our health and well-being. Emotions (and the body changes that go with them) happen very quickly (within a fifth of a second) and are not under conscious control.

From the brain's point of view, there are no 'positive' or 'negative' emotions, only signals and reactions to different events. Positive and negative are judgements we place on the feeling. All emotions are there for a reason and help us function (Figure 5.1).

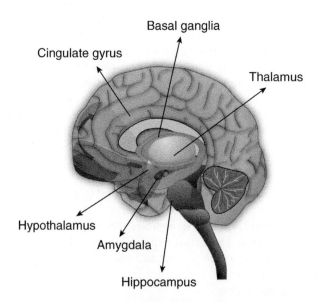

Figure 5.1 Emotional system of the brain.

The amygdala

The amygdala is the most important structure in the emotional system. There are two (but no one uses the ugly plural form 'amygdalae'), one in each hemisphere, deep in the medial temporal lobe. It is one of the most connected structures in the brain. The amygdala is involved in deciding what an event means and what to do about it. The amygdala prioritises our survival and is always on the lookout for threats. Therefore, it mainly responds to fearful experiences, all the way from life-threatening events, to threats to our values, reputation, well-being and self-esteem. People with damage to the amygdala cannot process fear. They cannot identify facial expressions of fear, although they can identify all the other emotional expressions. They also lack the experience of fear. They understand the idea, and they just don't feel it. While this sounds wonderful, it is very dangerous, because they do not recognise or deal well with dangerous situations.[4]

The amygdala's job is to be vigilant for threats. When the amygdala gives warning, the PFC will evaluate the threat. For example, what if someone grabs at us at night? We get a jolt of fear orchestrated by the amygdala. ('With good reason' agrees the PFC.) Other times, reason may disagree. For example, turbulence during air travel. Many people feel afraid, bouncing around at thirty-five thousand feet. The PFC murmurs reassuringly, 'Nothing to worry about, you are perfectly safe. Look, the flight attendants aren't worried. The plane is built to shake with turbulence. Turbulence can't bring down airplanes. Relax'. Here, the amygdala may pay no attention, and we continue to grip the sides of our seat.

There are two separate pathways to the amygdala. One goes directly (and quickly) through the thalamus. This is known as the low road. Simultaneously, the thalamus sends the information to the sensory cortex and other parts of the brain, including the PFC, for analysis. The result of the analysis is then sent to the amygdala. This is known as the high road. The low road is twenty times faster than the high road. If you are alone at night and see unexpected movement in the darkness, you will get an immediate jolt of anxiety (low road), but after a moment, you see it is just the shadow of the moon in the trees (high road). The anxiety loses its edge but does not go away completely until the physiological changes in the body (adrenaline release, increase in heart rate and breathing that prepared you to fight or flee) have dissipated.

We need to evaluate the threat to see how important it is. This is the job of the medial PFC. The more active the medial PFC, the less responsive the amygdala. Mindfulness practices (which we will consider later) strengthen this feedback loop. Coaching can also engage the client's medial PFC to realistically evaluate threats and deal with them effectively.

Our goals and motivations affect amygdala activity. For example, if your business proposal is rejected, your amygdala will be more active if you desperately need to earn money. It will be less active if you do not need the money. The amygdala also responds to risk – the riskier the decision, the more active the amygdala, possibly because of our greater anticipation of loss. Also, people who take more risks tend to have a larger amygdala and less connections between the amygdala and the medial PFC,[5] presumably because the PFC is not so effective in evaluating risk.

The amygdala responds to facial expressions of happiness, anger and sadness, but it responds most of all to facial expressions of fear. Someone looking frightened means danger nearby, so our amygdala reacts. Remarkably, it responds even when we are not aware of seeing the fearful expression. Studies show the amygdala is activated just as strongly when the fear expression is flashed subliminally, masked by a neutral face, as when it is shown normally.[6]

There are probably some hardwired fear responses for the amygdala. Approaching death, pain and paralysis are good contenders. We fear anything that can kill us, hurt us or paralyse us (snakes meet all three criteria, which is perhaps why they are so widely feared). We learn to fear some things (Joseph has trouble with heights, Andrea has no trouble with them. Andrea hates spiders, Joseph does not see what the fuss is about), probably because of bad past experiences. The amygdala can be taught to fear some things, for example, if your partner's silence is usually a prelude to a quarrel, you may feel anxious when they are silent, even if no quarrel follows. One has been associated with the other – this is conditioned learning. This conditioned fear can happen even if you do not remember the events. A classic example was a patient with Korsakoff's syndrome (she had no short-term memory), who was treated by the Swiss psychologist Edouard Claparede. She did not remember or recognise the doctor or any medical staff from day to day. One day, Claparede hid a pin in his hand and shook her hand to introduce himself. She jumped at the pain, but because of her condition, she had forgotten the incident the next day. Nevertheless, when he extended his hand to introduce himself the following day, she refused to take it. When asked why, she said that surely, 'everyone had the right to withdraw their hand'. Her temporal lobe memory system was damaged, so she did not consciously remember the pain or threat.[7] However, the amygdala had learned that there was a danger (painful pinprick) and made its voice heard. She had to justify withdrawing her hand, so the PFC made up an excuse on the amygdala's behalf.

Amygdala hijack

The amygdala has more roles. It enhances memory – we remember emotional experiences more clearly. It is also involved in some way with monitoring social networks. The volume of the amygdala correlates with the size and complexity of a person's social networks.[8]

The amygdala evaluates whether people look trustworthy and friendly.[9] We judge how friendly and how far people can be trusted by paying attention to their eyes. The amygdala is part of the system that orients our attention automatically to other peoples' eyes when we need to make judgements about their intentions.

An active amygdala turns your attention to self-defence. Under threat, it will shut down the PFC and the possibility of open, creative thinking. This is known as an 'amygdala hijack'. Threats can be real and physical – unfriendly animals, enemies, dangerous situations. This system can be triggered by lack of respect, threatening voice tone, overwork, threats of job loss or not enough 'likes' for our Facebook posts. These pose a threat to our well-being and self-esteem but not to life and limb. The fight–flight–freeze responses that are useful with real dangers are useless in social situations where the threat is not physical, but the amygdala still alerts us and the sympathetic nervous system springs into action to send adrenaline and cortisol through our body.

Some people are more resilient than others; they bounce back from adversity more quickly. It seems the better the connections of the PFC with the amygdala, the more resilience.[10] The PFC damps down the active amygdala, thinking through the situation, reframing and planning. But there is a downside to high resilience. Highly resilient people recover more quickly and so can appear unfeeling to others. This can make them appear unsympathetic and emotionally unavailable.

Coaches can help a client recognise an amygdala hijack and what triggers it. They can help clients avoid triggers whether they are social media updates or negative people. When anxious or afraid, it is obvious that we will not make good decisions, but even a slight amygdala hijack stops clear thinking. No one should make an important decision without full possession of their amygdala. On the other side, coaches walk a fine line between challenge and threat. A coach has got to challenge the client out of habitual patterns but go too far and turn it into a hijack.

Good and bad emotions?

There are no bad or good emotions. Fear seems like a 'bad' emotion. It is not pleasant to feel and is associated with bad things happening, but it is there for a purpose. It prepares us to meet danger. Fear flags up a threat that needs our immediate attention and action. The three 'Fs' – fight, flight or freeze – are the responses evolution gives us, and they persist in sophisticated forms. A client who feels threatened may argue with you (fight), discontinue the session or stonewall (flight) or get stuck and be unable to think (freeze). If any of these happens, then there is probably an amygdala hijack.

Anger gives us energy and pushes us to get what we want and push past obstructions. Disgust warns us of something bad. Basically, disgust is triggered by bad food. Food that smells bad can make you ill. The upper lip lifts in the disgusted expression to block the nostrils against the smell. Now, we can be disgusted by people's actions, political opinions or taste in clothes. Sadness is a response to loss and mobilises help from others. Offering comfort is a universal human response to a person who is sad.

Surprise is a gateway emotion; it widens the eyes and orients the attention to what is happening (good or bad). It lasts less than a second. Be wary of anyone who looks surprised for longer than that they are faking. Happiness, nice as it feels, is a luxury from evolution's point of view; it is not necessary for survival. It may have evolved as a way of showing pleasure to others and bonding with them.

Emotions come in two types: towards and away. From a biological point of view, the most important choice is whether to move towards something, because it benefits you, or away from it, because it can harm you. Approaching and withdrawing are basic human reactions, and emotions are feelings propelling us towards or away from something. Sadness, disgust and fear are emotions of withdrawal, they make us avoid or move away from whatever prompted them. Happiness and (strange as it may seem) anger are approach emotions, propelling us towards what provoked it, either to embrace it (happiness), or overcome it (anger). The PFC is structured so the left PFC predominantly processes approach emotions and the right PFC processes away from emotions. The first research suggested that the left PFC processes happiness and the right PFC processes sadness,[11] but further experiments showed the left PFC processes anger as well as happiness. This PFC division seems to be universal. Even newborn babies have this division. When babies taste something bitter, they had more activation in the right PFC and more left PFC activation when they tasted something sweet.[12] Distressed babies have a higher baseline activity in the right PFC. Depressed adults have a less active left PFC than normal.[13]

Serotonin

Serotonin is one of the major neurotransmitters in the brain and regulates mood and emotional state. How it does this is not well understood. What we do know is that drugs that increase levels of serotonin in the brain are very effective at combatting depression.[14] Serotonin is involved all over the brain and seems to increase emotional resilience mainly by making people less sensitive to rejection. It is also involved in mechanisms for reducing pain. Serotonin is not just about stopping pain, drugs like ecstasy also activate the serotonin system in the brain and that makes you feel good. Serotonin also influences our circadian rhythm and our natural resting cycle; it gets converted into melatonin which directly influences our sleep cycle.

The brain has only 100,000 neurons producing serotonin, and these are mostly in one small area of the midbrain known as raphe nuclei; this area projects to many parts of the brain. Ninety percent of serotonin is made in the gut, not in the brain. Poor diet is the greatest enemy of serotonin. It has been called the 'happiness hormone', but it is not really a hormone, and although it affects your mood, high serotonin does not equal happiness.

Happiness

Everyone who comes to coaching wants to be happy. Coaches usually ask them what will make them happy, but rarely do we explore what happiness means to them. It seems self-evident. Isn't happiness extroversion, parties and spontaneous expressions of delight? That is one way it can show itself, but there are many others. Happiness can mean anything from a momentary smile over a passing pleasure, to a deep and abiding feeling of contentment about yourself and your life. It is hard to measure, except by self-reports. There is no machine we can attach to the brain to measure its overall level of happiness.

The question, 'Are you happy?' is not simple. Happiness can have two very different meanings. One is the happiness we experience in the moment as the 'experiencing self'. The experiencing self answers the question, 'How happy are you, *right now?*' Then, there is the happiness of the 'remembered self' – how satisfied we feel over time and we calculate it by looking back on our memories. The remembered self answers the question, 'How happy are you in general?' These two measures can be quite different. Your experiencing self may be having a good time, but your remembered self can discount this and report you are unhappy because your life is not going well.

There is a Zen story attributed to D.T. Suzuki that brings out the two selves.

One day a man was walking through the wilderness and disturbed a vicious tiger. He ran away with the tiger in hot pursuit, but came to the edge of a high cliff. Desperate to save himself, he climbed down a vine and dangled over the yawning precipice. As he hung there, two mice came out from a hole in the cliff and began gnawing on the vine .... Suddenly, the man noticed a wild strawberry growing on the vine. He plucked it and popped it in his mouth. It was delicious!

The experiencing self is happy. The remembered self was petrified.

Most metrics about happiness measure the happiness of the remembered self. The remembered self is the one who can convince you that you were never happy in a relationship, if that relationship breaks down badly. The divorce courts are full of testimonies from the remembered self of how bad the relationship was. The remembering self has its own narrative. We can also experience the emotion of happiness in the moment by going back and reliving some great moments courtesy of the remembered self.

When we coach, we make that distinction between happiness in the moment (experiencing self) and satisfaction with life (remembering self). We define happiness as feeling good about yourself and your life and being able to take pleasure from them.

How happy we feel in general has a strong genetic component.[15] Some people are naturally happier than others. Happiness also depends on good fortune, outside our control. Winning the lottery will boost the level of self-reported happiness in the short term, but then it settles down to its previous level.[16] Misfortune, illness, poverty and bad circumstances will bring down the happiness level, but remarkably, within a short time it climbs back to its former level. Clients think achieving their goals will make them happy. They are usually right. But … this feeling will be short-lived (for reasons we shall see later). They then return to their baseline happiness level and look for the next thing to make them happier. 'Pursuing happiness' is a strange phrase that implies you are chasing something you have not got, an idea guaranteed to make you unhappy. We are incredibly adaptable to changing circumstances, although in general, we are not very good at knowing what will make us happy in a sustainable way.

Some people can make the glow of a good experience last all day, while it fades quickly for others. Being able to sustain positive emotions is part of happiness, and this depends on the activity of the reward circuit (nucleus accumbens and ventral striatum). The more activity here, the more positive outlook. To sustain positive emotions, the left PFC needs strong connections with these areas. Long-term planning and visualising future rewards is a good way to strengthen this link. Another (and counter-intuitive) way to strengthen the link is to give up immediate pleasures. Many PFC connections to the pleasure centres are inhibitory. So, being able to take immediate pleasure but then deliberately forgoing it strengthens the connection. This works well with health goals (giving up those tasty but unhealthy snacks). A third way is to focus on positive aspects of yourself and others. We often ask clients to write down their strengths. We ask them to thank others at every opportunity and to compliment others (appropriately of course). Clients are surprised how often they take others for granted and how quick they are to find fault and correct others. Thanking and complimenting others makes both parties happier.

Happiness (a frequent sense of well-being and contentment) is associated with good health. In one research study,[17] people were given stressful tasks and had their cortisol (stress hormone) levels and fibrinogen (inflammatory markers in the blood) levels measured. High levels of these are linked with cardiovascular disease and diabetes. The people who rated themselves least happy had much higher levels of both, not only at the time of the experiment but also three years later.

Coaching deals with happiness in the sense of a constant level of well-being rather than the emotion in the moment. It helps the experiencing self to be happy in the moment, and the remembering self to accumulate enough happy memories to feel satisfied about life, and this comes from understanding and dealing with their own emotions and the emotions of others.

Emotional expression

Emotions happen very fast and we cannot control them. The feeling is generated in less than one fifth of a second. Our conscious mind catches up a little later, but by that time your face has given you away because the emotional circuits of the brain control the muscles of your face. All you can do is adjust your expression into something socially appropriate. These emotional expressions that flit across the face too quickly for conscious control are called micro expressions, and they show genuine feelings.

You can know what someone is feeling, but you cannot know what caused it. Suppose you tell your friend a sad story and you spot a fleeting smile on their face. This does not mean that they find the story amusing. Your story may have reminded them of an unrelated funny incident. Emotions cannot be faked as easily as words, but they do not replace words. They don't show what you *really* think, they show what you *also* think. The brain is a collection of modules – remember the team in the closed room. You can get two different yet equally truthful messages at the same time from different members.

Emotions appear very quickly, but then they can linger on, like party guests who hang on when you want to tidy up and go to bed. The mood lingers. Not intensely, but enough to colour your view of the world. This is called the refractory period and is a form of emotional priming. We see things through emotionally tinted glasses in the refractory period. For example, suppose you finish an infuriating phone call to customer service about your broadband service. Their script was irritating, and you don't believe they wish you a great day. You stomp upstairs, noticing an ugly tear in the carpet. Looking out the window, you see it is raining. Ugh! You are going out later and the traffic will be bad .... And that reminds you, the car needs a service, but at a different garage. The last one was terrible. Anger can prime your thinking for several minutes. Now imagine a successful call. You would not have noticed the carpet, and the rain would be a just rain. Your brain rummages for memories that match your mood in the refractory period. Do not make important decisions in the refractory period of fear, disgust or anger.

The trolley dilemma

Decisions are often a struggle between the head and the heart – 'hot' and 'cold' cognition. Here is a thought experiment to that brings this out. It was originally developed as a legal puzzle by the philosopher Philippa Foot in 1967.[18]

Imagine you are standing beside a railway track. Suddenly a trolley appears travelling towards you. Behind you there are five people working on the track, oblivious to the approaching danger. The trolley is going too fast to stop in time and the people are too far away to hear a warning shout.

You have no way of warning them in time. Fortunately, you see a lever beside you that will divert the trolley down a side track before it reaches the five workers. Unfortunately, there is one person working on this side track, and if you divert the train by pulling the lever, it will kill him instead.

What do you do?
And why?

(This is the limit of the information; no trick solutions work here.)

Think for a moment before reading on (Figure 5.2).

There are two possible answers. What is interesting is why people opt for one of the answers. Most people opt to pull the switch, although their reasons may be different. One person may pull the lever for utilitarian motives – one death is preferable to five. Another may pull the lever to save lives and let God (or chance) take care of what happens after that. Functional magnetic resonance imaging (fMRI) scans of people facing this choice typically show activity in the anterior cingulate cortex, areas of the parietal lobe and the dorsolateral areas of the PFC. This is cold cognition. The brain treats this impersonal moral puzzle in the same way it treats a maths problem. We know this because cognitive load (giving people other tasks to do at the same time) interferes with this decision, increasing reaction time.[19]

Now imagine you are on a bridge above the track. You see the train approach. The same five workers are on the track below and will be killed

Figure 5.2 Trolley dilemma.

unless you intervene. You can't reach the lever in time. However, standing next to you on the bridge is a very large man wearing a bulky backpack and he is leaning over the parapet to get a better look. You see that a well-timed shove will send him tumbling onto the track, where his size and weight together with the backpack will be enough to derail the trolley before it reaches the five workers. Once again, you can act to save five lives. But the man with the backpack will be killed.

Do you push him or not?

(Again, no hidden information and you do not know the man.)

This looks like the same issue; one man dies for the sake of five. But is it? In the first scenario, your action is impersonal, you pull a lever. In the second, you must physically push a real person. Most people say it is morally wrong to push the man. The same people who would be willing to pull the lever will not push the man. A majority also say it is morally wrong *not* to push the man. When moral principles conflict, then you must make a personal, ethical choice.

This experiment brings up many questions.

Suppose children were on the track?

Suppose your friends or family were on the track?

Does it matter who the man with the backpack is?

A friend?

A family member?

A Nobel Prize winner?

fMRI scans of volunteers facing this second dilemma show activity in the motor area of the brain (imagining the push) and more activity in the regions of the brain that process emotion, especially the posterior cingulate gyrus.[20] Cognitive load does not increase reaction time in these personal moral dilemmas, showing this is not a logical puzzle any more.

Does your mood affect your decision? In the first scenario, positive mood made no difference to the reaction times nor the decisions people made. (In one trial, to induce a positive mood, the test group was shown an excerpt from 'Saturday Night Live' before making the decision. The control group was spared this.)[21] Rational judgement is not influenced by mood. However, a positive mood *increased* the odds of a person pushing the man off the bridge in the second scenario. The researchers proposed that a positive mood offset the feeling of repulsion of pushing the man off the bridge, and so made the cold decision easier. It is possible (but not researched in this paper) that if volunteers had seen morally disgusting scenes before making the decision, it would have had the opposite effect. This research shows the complex play between emotion and cognition, as well as emotional priming in our decision-making.

The brain's emotional system is drawn in by the personal contact and direct action. Our dorsolateral PFC (dlPFC) may argue it is the same problem, but it is not. When we physically interact with people, especially if we know them, emotions influence our decisions.[22]

This is relevant for coaching clients who work in family-run companies. For example, when a husband and wife or brother and sister control the company. Other members of their extended family work in the company, perhaps in accounting or manufacturing and sales. What happens when a family member makes a costly mistake? Cold cognition says get rid of them and hire someone who will do a better job, and this is what would happen in impersonal organisations. In family-run companies, the situation is different. The rational choice is to fire the person. The emotional circuits argue against this. This can lead to deadlock; the dysfunctional family worker stays on and perhaps creates more havoc. When we work with clients who are faced with this decision, we explain how emotion and reason are giving different messages and we explore values. What is important to them in this situation? We go into the consequences of keeping or firing the family member. We explore the circumstances where they would keep the family member, and those where they would let them go. We also help the client to see the situation from the perspectives of the other family members involved. Whatever the client decides, they will be clear on the consequences from multiple perspectives and they know they can live with the decision both emotionally and rationally.

Values

Emotional energy powers our values. Values are what are important to us; they channel our emotional energy and engage us physically. Values are how the brain's emotional circuits show themselves in language an action. There are millions of possible goals; life can always be better. Of these, we select a few to act on.

How?
We feel they are important.

Values are always embodied – we feel them, and they lead to action. When we ask clients, what is important to them about a goal, we look for animation, movement, skin colour change, change in breathing and change in voice tone. All these show activity in the sympathetic nervous system. Without them, the words are insubstantial. Values are paradoxical; they go by the most abstract of names: love, freedom, happiness respect. Yet they engage us viscerally. We take enormous efforts to live them, and some people are willing to die for them.

Values and the emotion that accompanies them is the opposite of 'shoulds'. Except in moral or legal matters, when a client says they 'should' do something, 'should' means they do not want to do it. It means there is some *extrinsic* value, imposed by others, but not completely endorsed by the client. They feel a pressure. They may act, but there is little enthusiasm and often an internal battle. The client needs to explore what they want and feel the emotions involved. Then they leave the session clear what they are going to do and are congruent about doing it.

Emotional intelligence

Intelligence used to be purely cognitive (IQ tests, keeping emotion out of it). Now emotional intelligence is the norm. Emotional intelligence is the ability to recognise our own emotions and the emotions of others and to use this to guide our actions to help ourselves and others to be happier and more effective. This means balancing the PFC and emotional centres and mixing the hot and cold streams from the dlPFC and ventrolateral PFC (vlPFC) into a comfortable temperature by integrating them in the OFC.

To manage our own emotions, we first need to be aware of them.
To manage other peoples' emotions, we need to be aware of them.

This gives us an emotional intelligence grid (Figure 5.3).

	Awareness	Management
Self	self awareness	self regulation
Others	sensitivity to others	concern for others

Figure 5.3 Emotional intelligence grid.

Self-awareness

How aware are we of our emotions? The key structure in the brain for self-awareness seems to be the insula, located between the frontal and temporal lobes. It connects to the amygdala, the anterior cingulate cortex and the cortical areas in the frontal, temporal and parietal lobes that are involved in attention and memory. It evaluates emotional stimuli and seems to integrate all the body sensations into a body feeling.[23] The insula is also active when we take risks, probably because of its link to the amygdala. The riskier the decision, the more active the insula.[24]

Not everyone is self-aware to the same degree, and this may reflect the activity of the insula. On one extreme, the hypochondriac is hypersensitive to every passing pain. On the other hand, some soldier on through high stress, unaware of the signals from their body until their health breaks down.

Self-awareness suffers if signals from the body are blocked in any way. Botox smooths wrinkles by paralysing muscles in the face; they cannot move when we feel an emotion. The crow's feet will not form with a happy smile, the eyes will not narrow with anger and the inside eyebrows will not raise with sadness. The mind body link goes both ways – emotion changes the face, and the brain takes that physiological feedback as emotional information. No muscle movement, no feedback. The insula does not get the signals and the Botoxed person will much less aware of their emotions. You won't know if someone with Botox is angry, sad or surprised, but neither will they.

How can we help clients to be more self-aware? Mindfulness meditation is the best way. Practising moment-to-moment non-judgemental awareness opens awareness to bodily feelings. A coach can also arrange a reminder for clients to be more self-aware. This can be a picture, a cell phone prompt, anything that reminds the client to stop for a moment, breathe and pay attention to what they are feeling.

Occasionally, a client may be too self-aware – sensitive to touch and with feelings and body sensations clamouring for attention. Mindfulness meditation will help here too. It calms the amygdala and reduces uncomfortable self-awareness.[25] Mindfulness meditation is one of the most helpful practises for coach and client. It has many benefits which we will sum up in the last chapter.

Managing your emotions

Many clients have problems managing their emotions. Some worry without good reason. Others are too impulsive, have trouble controlling their temper or feel angry and irritated at small things. We have coached many executives who want to stop alienating people with their bad moods and angry outbursts. We have found three interventions that are helpful.

First explore with the client what happens when they have an emotional outburst (anger for example). There will be a trigger for the anger. It might be an employee's action, a piece of bad news or something someone says. They will have learned this trigger somewhere in their life. The amygdala and emotional system leaps into action. In less than half a second, the brain has started all the familiar signs of anger. Their lips will tighten, their eyes will narrow, the blood will go to the muscles of the arms and legs, the chin may be pushed out and the fists may start to clench. They cannot stop these. However, there is a small window of choice just after that. That is when the PFC can decide whether to let the emotion run its course or kerb it. The client knows they can't stop the initial feeling, but they have a choice about whether they act on it. A deep breath gives them a pause to think. Doing this regularly will make it a habit, courtesy of neuroplasticity.

Next, the client can explore their emotional profile. Every brain is different. Some people have a 'tropical storm' profile. They blow up abruptly, but then the storm quickly subsides. Other people simmer for hours before exploding, and it may take longer to die down again (Figure 5.4).

Most people are somewhere between. We ask clients to draw a graph of their anger pattern. Then, we ask them to share it with their partner or a good friend and ask for feedback. Not surprisingly, partners often correct the graph to something more realistic.

Now the third and final step – managing the emotion. There are many strategies. One is to avoid the situation. Some clients think this is 'cheating', but it is the best strategy whenever possible. If it is impossible, mental rehearsal can help. The client visualises the situation in advance and sees themselves staying calm and everything resolving well in their mind's eye. As we know, mental rehearsal has limited value, but it is better than nothing. Mindfulness practice before a difficult meeting can also help. Research showed participants who practised this technique felt less negative emotions

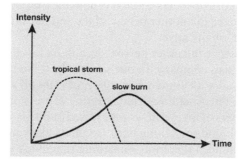

Figure 5.4 Profiles of anger.

and had reduced amygdala activity, together with increased activity in PFC brain regions that control attention.[26]

Distraction works by withdrawing attention from the annoying event. So, looking at the wallpaper or indulging in a pleasant daydream can help, but this is not usually a viable strategy in a meeting.

The most effective strategy is reappraisal or reframing. Thinking about the situation in a different way changes the meaning, and alters the emotion, making it easier to deal with. An annoying colleague can become a challenge and a test of resilience and leadership rather than an infuriating interruption. Reappraisal activates the ventromedial and lateral PFC and diminishes amygdala activity.[27] All the current research shows the amygdala and other subcortical regions of the brain can be influenced by the PFC. The amygdala has a nuanced activity, affected by the person's goals at the time. If you are relaxed, the amygdala will not be so active. Reappraisal will diminish the impact of any disturbance.

Suppressing the emotion does not work. This uses a more primitive brain mechanism. Experiments shows that suppression *increases* the activity of the amygdala, making people more aroused for a longer time after the upsetting experience.[28] Suppression also leads to a less complete memory of the situation.

Knowing other people's emotions

How do we know what other people are feeling? Nearly all adults can understand another's state of mind. 'Theory of mind' develops in children by the age of seven – they realise other people have a mind like their own – but different. So, if we would be upset, then we can predict other people are likely to be as well. This is cognitive empathy.

Emotional empathy is a step further. We feel something of what others are feeling. This happens because of mirror neurons. A mirror neuron is a neuron that fires not only when you perform an action but also when you see the same action carried out by another. We will look at mirror neurons later in more detail as part of our social brain. It is possible that we imitate the slight muscle changes we see in another person's face and our brain interprets that as feeling the emotion ourselves.

We can also observe the other person. Joseph had a client who was a director of a Colombian company. In one session, he talked about an outdoor barbecue he enjoyed with some work colleagues. By all accounts, this was a happy occasion, but Joseph noticed a fleeting expression of sadness as he talked (inside corners of his eyebrows were raised), and his voice lost strength. He was sad. Joseph said something like, 'It sounds like you had a good time, and yet … I have an idea there was something that made you sad …what do you think?' This is an open invitation to connect with the emotion and talk in more depth – but only if he wanted to. The client was thoughtful for a few moments and then talked about a conversation with a colleague at the barbecue when he felt sad about the state of the company and helpless to do anything about it. We explored that feeling in the session, and it led to many insights, who may not have broached that subject without the invitation to his emotional self. Emotions show on a client's face, but we do not know why they are there or what gives rise to them. When in doubt, ask.

Managing others' emotions

A coach does not usually have to deal with strong expressions of emotion, although it is more likely in some cultures than others. To manage others' emotions, you first need to manage your own. Stay calm and do not get pulled into the show. Emotions feed off each other and a situation can quickly escalate if you respond in kind. (This is fine if the emotion is a happy one.) With sadness or anger, the coach needs to pull the client back, before the emotion becomes too much. This is best done by interrupting the session, taking a break and then inviting them to reflect dispassionately on the memory. If the client is sad from an insight in the session, then stay present and sympathetic and pass the paper handkerchiefs. When the client is ready to talk again, you are there for them.

Hopefully, a client will not get angry with the coach in a session, if they do, then the coach has mismanaged the meeting. Break off the session and resume at another time, where the first item on the agenda will be how and why the client got angry. In the meantime, the coach should do some soul searching of their own.

Emotions touch every part of our life. They are the bright warm streams of our interior life, giving depth and meaning to our thoughts and experiences. Our happiness, well-being, and who we trust are based on emotion. They influence our decisions, and that is the subject of our next chapter.

Notes

1 They are different from sensations, which are bodily feelings (which may be pleasant, painful or neutral).
2 There is a huge neuroscientific, psychological and academic literature about emotion with very little consensus. There are many theories. The James-Lange hypothesis asserts that emotions are simply interpretations of our body's reaction (I feel hot, my eyes are glaring, and my fists are clenched – therefore, I am angry). In this view, you cannot feel an emotion without a bodily reaction. Appraisal theories assert that an emotion is a reaction to how we evaluate events on different levels. Emotions are both. Whatever the scholarly explanation, we all know emotions first hand, when we experience them. We also recognise them (even if belatedly) in others.
3 The debate is still on as to whether there are universal emotions, felt by everyone in all cultures. It seems likely there are, if only the basic ones tied to survival, like fear, anger and disgust. Paul Ekman's lifetime work was identifying facial

expression that go with emotions irrespective of culture. It seems likely that human beings everywhere have the same universal expressions for seven emotions. These seven emotions are fear, anger, sadness, disgust, surprise, happiness and contempt. Other emotions (e.g. shame, joy) also are trying to break into this list. See Ekman, P. (2007). *Emotions revealed*. Henry Holt & Co.

4 For a real-life study, see: Feinstein, J. S., Adolphs, R., Damasio, A., & Tranel, D. (2011). The human amygdala and the induction and experience of fear. *Current Biology, 21* (1), 34–38.

5 Jung, W. H., Lee, S., Lerman, C., & Kable, J. W. (2018). Amygdala functional and structural connectivity predicts individual risk tolerance. *Neuron.* doi:10.1016/j.neuron.2018.03.019.

6 Whalen, P. J., Rauch, S. L., Etcoff, N. L., McInerney, S. C., Lee, M. B., & Jenike, M. A. (1998). Masked presentations of emotional facial expressions modulate amygdala activity without explicit knowledge. *Journal of Neuroscience, 18* (1), 411–418.

7 The full story is in 'The Emotional Brain' by Joseph Le Doux, Published by Phoenix Books, 1998

8 Bickart, K. C., Wright, C. I., Dautoff, R. J., Dickerson, B. C., & Barrett, L. F. (2011). Amygdala volume and social network size in humans. *Nature Neuroscience, 14* (2), 163–164.

9 Adolphs, R., Tranel, D., & Denburg, N. (2000). Impaired emotional declarative memory following unilateral amygdala damage. *Learning & Memory, 7* (3), 180–186.

10 Kim, M. J., & Whalen, P. J. (2009). The structural integrity of an amygdala–prefrontal pathway predicts trait anxiety. *Journal of Neuroscience, 29* (37), 11614–11618.

11 This was discovered through the WADA test – where neurosurgeons inject an anaesthetic into the carotid artery on one side of the neck in preparation for surgery. This procedure paralyses half of the brain and shows the surgeon which side the language faculties are located. It turned out that patients who had their right hemisphere paralysed (so they were functioning with the left hemisphere only) became uncontrollably happy, laughing for no reason. Those whose left hemisphere was paralysed became sad and depressed, again for no apparent reason.

12 Fox, N. A., & Davidson, R. J. (1986). Taste-elicited changes in facial signs of emotion and the asymmetry of brain electrical activity in human new-borns. *Neuropsychologia, 24* (3), 417–422.

13 Henriques, J. B., & Davidson, R. J. (1991). Left frontal hypoactivation in depression. *Journal of Abnormal Psychology, 100* (4), 535.

14 These drugs are known as selective serotonin reuptake inhibitors or SSRIs and Prozac is the most well-known one. They block serotonin being taken up at the synapses and so increase the level in the brain, although how this helps depression is not clear.

15 Martin Seligman, the author, neuroscientist and founder of Positive Psychology has a formula to measure happiness. $H = S + C + V$. H stands for your level of happiness at any time. S is your set range – some have a wider range than others. It is genetically set. C stands for outside circumstances, which are outside your control. V is what you can do voluntarily; that is under your control. Given this formula, good circumstances (C) can make us happy, but the only leverage is what we do (V).

16 There is plenty of research on lottery winners showing this. For example, see Gardner, J., & Oswald, A. J. (2007). Money and mental wellbeing: A longitudinal study of medium-sized lottery wins. *Journal of Health Economics, 26* (1), 49–60.

There is also literature on the influence of income levels on happiness. As you might expect, raising your base income makes you happier in the short term, but not in the long term, and there is little correlation between reported levels of happiness and levels of income. See Easterlin, R. A. (1995). Will raising the incomes of all increase the happiness of all? *Journal of Economic Behaviour & Organization, 27* (1), 35–47.

17 Steptoe, A., Wardle, J., & Marmot, M. (2005). Positive affect and health-related neuroendocrine, cardiovascular, and inflammatory processes. *Proceedings of the National academy of Sciences of the United States of America, 102* (18), 6508–6512. Cited in Davidson, Richard, (2012) with Sharon Begley, *The emotional life of your brain.* Hodder and Stoughton

18 Foot, P., (1967). The Problem of abortion and the doctrine of double effect. *Oxford Review, 5* (5), 15.

19 Greene, J. D., Morelli, S. A., Lowenberg, K., Nystrom, L. E., & Cohen, J. D. (2008). Cognitive load selectively interferes with utilitarian moral judgment. *Cognition, 107* (3), 1144–1154.

20 Greene, J. D., Sommerville, R. B., Nystrom, L. E., Darley, J. M., & Cohen, J. D. (2001). An fMRI investigation of emotional engagement in moral judgment. *Science, 293* (5537), 2105–2108.

21 Valdesolo, P., & DeSteno, D. (2006). Manipulations of emotional context shape moral judgment. *Psychological Science, 17* (6), 476–477.

22 Greene, J. D., Nystrom, L. E., Engell, A. D., Darley, J. M., & Cohen, J. D. (2004). The neural bases of cognitive conflict and control in moral judgment. *Neuron, 44* (2), 389–400.

23 Craig, A. D., & Craig, A. D. (2009). How do you feel now? The anterior insula and human awareness. *Nature Reviews Neuroscience, 10* (1), 59–70.

24 Xue, G., Lu, Z., Levin, I. P., & Bechara, A. (2010). The impact of prior risk experiences on subsequent risky decision-making: The role of the insula. *Neuroimage, 50* (2), 709–716.

25 Davidson, Richard, (2012) with Sharon Begley, *The emotional life of your brain.* Hodder and Stoughton

26 Goldin, P., & Gross, J. (2010). Effects of mindfulness-based stress reduction (MBSR) on emotion regulation in social anxiety disorder. *Emotion, 10* (1), 83.

27 Goldin, P. R., McRae, K., Ramel, W., & Gross, J. J. (2008). The neural bases of emotion regulation: Reappraisal and suppression of negative emotion. *Biological Psychiatry, 63* (6), 577–586.

28 Gross, J. J. (1998). Antecedent-and response-focused emotion regulation: divergent consequences for experience, expression, and physiology. *Journal of Personality and Social Psychology, 74* (1), 224.

Bibliography

Adolphs, R., Tranel, D., & Denburg, N. (2000). Impaired emotional declarative memory following unilateral amygdala damage. *Learning & Memory, 7*(3), 180–186.

Bickart, K. C., Wright, C. I., Dautoff, R. J., Dickerson, B. C., & Barrett, L. F. (2011). Amygdala volume and social network size in humans. *Nature Neuroscience, 14*(2), 163–164.

Craig, A. D., & Craig, A. D. (2009). How do you feel--now? The anterior insula and human awareness. *Nature Reviews Neuroscience, 10*(1), 59–70.

Davidson, R., & Sharon B. (2012). *The emotional life of your brain.* Hodder and Stoughton

Easterlin, R. A. (1995). Will raising the incomes of all increase the happiness of all? *Journal of Economic Behaviour & Organization, 27*(1), 35–47.

Ekman, P. (2007). *Emotions revealed.* Henry Holt & Co.

Feinstein, J. S., Adolphs, R., Damasio, A., & Tranel, D. (2011). The human amygdala and the induction and experience of fear. *Current Biology, 21*(1), 34–38.

Foot, P. (1967). The Problem of abortion and the doctrine of double effect. *Oxford Review, 5*(5), 15.

Fox, N. A., & Davidson, R. J. (1986). Taste-elicited changes in facial signs of emotion and the asymmetry of brain electrical activity in human new-borns. *Neuropsychologia, 24*(3), 417–422.

Gardner, J., & Oswald, A. J. (2007). Money and mental wellbeing: A longitudinal study of medium-sized lottery wins. *Journal of Health Economics, 26*(1), 49–60.

Goldin, P., & Gross, J., (2010). Effects of mindfulness-based stress reduction (MBSR) on emotion regulation in social anxiety disorder. *Emotion, 10*(1), 83.

Goldin, P. R., McRae, K., Ramel, W., & Gross, J. J. (2008). The neural bases of emotion regulation: reappraisal and suppression of negative emotion. *Biological Psychiatry, 63*(6), 577–586.

Greene, J. D., Morelli, S. A., Lowenberg, K., Nystrom, L. E., & Cohen, J. D. (2008). Cognitive load selectively interferes with utilitarian moral judgment. *Cognition, 107*(3), 1144–1154.

Greene, J. D., Nystrom, L. E., Engell, A. D., Darley, J. M., & Cohen, J. D. (2004). The neural bases of cognitive conflict and control in moral judgment. *Neuron, 44*(2), 389–400.

Greene, J. D., Sommerville, R. B., Nystrom, L. E., Darley, J. M., & Cohen, J. D. (2001). An fMRI investigation of emotional engagement in moral judgment. *Science, 293*(5537), 2105–2108.

Gross, J. J. (1998). Antecedent-and response-focused emotion regulation: Divergent consequences for experience, expression, and physiology. *Journal of Personality and Social Psychology, 74*(1), 224.

Henriques, J. B., & Davidson, R. J. (1991). Left frontal hypoactivation in depression. *Journal of abnormal Psychology, 100*(4), 535.

Kim, M. J., & Whalen, P. J. (2009). The structural integrity of an amygdala–prefrontal pathway predicts trait anxiety. *Journal of Neuroscience, 29*(37), 11614–11618.

Jung, W. H., Lee, S., Lerman, C., & Kable, J. W. (2018). Amygdala functional and structural connectivity predicts individual risk tolerance. *Neuron,* doi:10.1016/j.neuron.2018.03.019

Le Doux, J. (1998). *The emotional brain.* Phoenix books.

Steptoe, A., Wardle, J., & Marmot, M. (2005). Positive affect and health-related neuroendocrine, cardiovascular, and inflammatory processes. *Proceedings of the National academy of Sciences of the United States of America, 102*(18), 6508–6512.

Valdesolo, P., & DeSteno, D. (2006). Manipulations of emotional context shape moral judgment. *Psychological Science, 17*(6), 476–477.

Whalen, P. J., Rauch, S. L., Etcoff, N. L., McInerney, S. C., Lee, M. B., & Jenike, M. A. (1998). Masked presentations of emotional facial expressions modulate amygdala activity without explicit knowledge. *Journal of Neuroscience, 18*(1), 411–418.

Xue, G., Lu, Z., Levin, I. P., & Bechara, A. (2010). The impact of prior risk experiences on subsequent risky decision-making: The role of the insula. *Neuroimage, 50*(2), 709–716.

Chapter 6

Decisions, decisions

From the moment we wake and our eyes flutter open, our brain starts making decisions.

Do I hit the snooze button?

What do I wear today?

What shall I have for breakfast?

Am I prepared for that meeting?

We decide – we choose one path rather than another, based on the options we see.

Some decisions are easy. (Do I have breakfast today?)

Other decisions are more difficult, both sides have merit.

(Do I go to the gym today?)

Some decisions can affect your future significantly.

(Do I take this new job or stay in the old one?)

Others are trivial.

(Do I wear the red or blue socks today?)

Decisions can be made by habit or choice. A habitual decision is prompted by context. The neural pathway in the brain is triggered; the action proceeds without thought. The prefrontal cortex (PFC) is not involved in a habitual decision. Once upon a time, this decision was associated with a reward, but no longer. Repetition created the neuroplastic changes that made it automatic.

Some of these automatic decisions are useful; we do not want to have to think about them every time. For example, 'Do I stop at a red traffic light or not?'

Other habitual decisions are not so good. Do I smoke another cigarette? That would be a bad choice – if it were a choice rather than a habit.

A decision through choice is when you evaluate the reward and decide accordingly. The PFC is involved.

The neuroscience of decision-making

We make decisions and choose a course of action based on the likely reward. There are basic rewards like food, shelter and sex. There are secondary rewards like money, status, power and reputation, and all these are values. Acting from our values is rewarding; there are questions to be answered before you decide:

Probability – how likely is the reward?
Payoff – how significant is it?
Effort – how much effort will it take and what is the cost?
Timing – how long will it take?

There have been studies with functional magnetic resonance imaging (fMRI) and blood oxygenation level dependent (BOLD) to see the parts of the brain associated with deciding and the value of rewards.[1] Positive values are associated with the ventromedial prefrontal cortex (vmPFC) and parts of the striatum. Striatum activity also goes with the amount of effort involved. Both areas are also active when the goal is achieved. Other regions that are activated in decision-making include the insula, dorsomedial prefrontal cortex (dmPFC) and the thalamus. The orbital frontal cortex (OFC) is most active when there is a high payoff – a significant reward. The ventrolateral prefrontal cortex (vlPFC) is activated more by short-term value (like the calorie-filled second slice of pie), and the dorsal PFC was inhibitory – exercising control and reining in impulsiveness.[2] You will remember that the vlPFC was associated with hot, emotional thinking and the dorsal PFC with colder calculations. Self-control probably depends on the extent the dorsal PFC influences the immediate value signal from the vlPFC.

Should I stay, or should I go – exploit or explore?

The most difficult decisions usually involve whether to continue with what you have or try a change. For example, whether to stay in your present job or strike out and find a better one. Another example: whether to stay in an unsatisfactory relationship or to give it up and find another. In each case, you must give up what you have for an uncertain return. It could be better – or worse. You know the present – but not the future. Sometimes, the present is difficult, and you wonder how much you can stand before enough is enough. You must juggle the decision variables. One way to think about it is whether to stay (exploit) the present situation or to leave and find a new one (explore).

The brain has been making this type of decision for thousands of years to find food and water. Do I stay in the area and try to exploit it or move further afield in the hope of better pickings? Foraging animals and humans obey a basic principle called the marginal value theorem.[3] This proposes an animal exploits the environment until the success rate falls below the average for the whole area. Once that happens, it leaves to explore. Applying this to jobs and relationships means we judge the average job satisfaction and pay or the average satisfaction in a relationship. Of course, this is a very difficult and personal call. You will be very influenced by the people you know; there is no external standard to apply. Once your satisfaction drops below this level, it is time to explore. The decision is a complex one; people have different thresholds of what they will tolerate. The value of the present is weighed against what could be gained and the time and effort needed. Risk taking, need for novelty, as well as the value of security, and the type of person all come into play. fMRI studies show certain cells in the anterior cingulate cortex (ACC) fire when a decision has been made for a change.[4] We know that the ACC is involved in risk assessment.

The most important factors will be as follows:

- How good the situation is perceived in the present (present reward).
- Perceived cost of change (time, effort, money, reputation and emotions).
- Perceived anticipated future reward (and how likely it is to materialise).

The next diagram sums it up.

Divisions 1 and 4 are the difficult options (Table 6.1).

Coaching in these situations will explore several questions:

How much do you value the present situation?
How rewarding is the present situation?
How satisfied are you with the present situation?
What are the advantages of the present situation?
What are the disadvantages of the present situation?
What are the costs of leaving? (effort, money, discomfort, reputation, etc.)
What is the probability you would be better off if you made the change?

Table 6.1 Reward in the present against cost of change

1 High reward in present and low cost of change: Stay but keep options open. (Unless future reward is both higher and very likely – then change.)	2 High reward in present and high cost of change: Stay.
3 Low reward in present and low cost of change: Change.	4 Low reward in present and high cost of change: Uncertain. Work to either raise present reward or lower cost of change. Balance against the likelihood and degree of future reward.

What would have to happen in the present situation to increase its value and
    your satisfaction?
What could be made better about the possible future situation?
Can you keep benefits of the present situation while making the change?

Somatic marking

Our 'cold' cognitive circuits have the job to provide us with the best set of
options. We would like to think that we decide logically on a cost-benefit
analysis, but the brain does not work that way. We decide emotionally.
Throughout life emotions get attached to knowledge and experience. Every
memory has emotional weight. Even facts have emotional weight depending
on where we learned them, who we learned them from and how we learned
them. When we decide, the brain reviews those facts and experiences together with the associated emotions. It puts them all in the balance, weighs
them against each other and inclines to the most positive (or the least negative). This is known as the somatic marker hypothesis, developed by the
neuroscientist and writer Antonio Damasio[5] at the University of Iowa.

Damasio was treating a patient, known as Elliott, after surgery for a brain
tumour. The surgery was successful and removed part of the vmPFC.[6] This
is part of the OFC which connects the brain structures dealing with emotion (primarily the amygdala, insula and cingulate cortex) with the PFC.
After the surgery, Elliott could think and solve problems as usual. What
he could not do was decide between options. He could not prioritise his
thinking. He and other patients with OFC damage had lost the ability to
make judgements based on value. He started to make many poor decisions.
This seemed surprising at the time. The OFC is concerned with emotions,
which were presumed to disrupt good, logical decision-making. But consider this – intellectual thinking is slow and mostly linguistic. Everyday
decisions we make need to be done quickly and we need to feel satisfied
with them. To debate logically what to have for dinner would be – illogical.
Feelings happen quickly and carry a lot of information. The body gives us
an emotional summary of the situation. We *feel* the data, even in complex
difficult decisions.

Gambling with emotions

Damasio tested his hypothesis with a fun experiment known as the Iowa
gambling test.[7] Participants draw cards from four different decks on a computer program. Some cards win money, and some lose money, but participants do not know which ones in advance. Their goal is to win as much
money as possible. The game is set up so that two decks are good; choosing
from them will gain money in the long run. Two are bad; consistently choosing from them will lose money. However, the bad decks were attractive at the

beginning because they paid highly, the losses happened only when they re-peatedly chose from those decks. Galvanic skin response (GSR), a measure of stress, was measured while they played the game.

What happened? Normal subjects started to show stress in the GSR when considering 'bad' decks after only ten trials. They were not aware that the decks were bad, but some part of their brain had picked it up, and the emo-tional reaction was showing in the GSR. The conscious mind did not catch up until about twenty-five trials, when they started to avoid the bad decks. Emotional judgements came well in advance of conscious awareness. Sub-jects with damage to the OFC, however, continued to pick from the 'bad' decks. What is more, they kept doing it even when they knew they are losing money. Another experiment[8] where the pattern was revealed from the start showed participants with OFC damage did as well as healthy participants. So, the OFC is sensitive to *changing* patterns of reward and punishment. This is called reversal learning; in other words, when the world ceases to reward you for something, stop doing it.

Previous research[9] had found that the OFC has distinct areas. Punishment activates the lateral OFC. Rewards activate the medial OFC. The amount of activation depends on the intensity of the reward or punishment. So, OFC damage would prevent someone balancing reward against punishment and making a reasonable decision.

People with OFC damage do not show regret. Regret is the feeling you get when you compare what you did with an alternative that would have turned out better. Regret tends to make people more risk averse (which shows up in the brain as greater activity in the OFC). Damage to the OFC stops re-gret, presumably because the subject cannot make the comparison between what they did and a better alternative. The OFC has many inputs – touch, taste, smell, information about facial expressions – and it has links with the amygdala – anticipation of punishment produces fear – and to many parts of the brain. It is the crucial brain part for decision-making – comparing emotions and evaluating rewards and punishments.

Coaching applications

When clients are paralysed and cannot decide, it is usually because of con-flicting emotions, experienced as a clash of values. For example, a client of ours was considering leaving his job after five years. The company had been good to him. They had promoted him and promised a salary rise to go with the promotion. However, after two years, his pay was unchanged. He felt betrayed. He felt angry and dishonoured. He wanted to speak up. He felt the company took him for granted because he was close to retirement. On the other hand, he wanted to retire as financially well off as possible. If he quit now, he would lose his present salary and have an infinitesimal chance of finding a well-paid job so close to retirement. His retirement would not be so happy and prosperous. His children were in college abroad, and he wanted to be able to visit them regularly. He felt stuck. On the one hand: honesty and honour. On the other hand: financial stability and family. The hands were evenly balanced. Both paths were good in some ways and bad in others. Coaching can help to clarify such a situation, letting the client take as many perspectives as possible. Whatever happens do NOT rush into an action plan.

Somatic marker model for decision-making

Here is our process for resolving values decisions – the 'somatic marker model'.

1   Priming
    Look out for any priming influences that might influence your thinking.
    Where are you?
    Who have you talked with?
    What made an impact on you in the last hour?
2   Emotional state
    Check your emotional state. (Refractory period? Amygdala hijack?)
    Are you calm with your thoughts flowing well?
3   Goals
    Clarify the situation as much as possible. Tease out any different goals and establish a main goal. In the process, you will cover the usual important qualities in a goal – the time frame, fitting for other people, positively expressed and within the power of the client to achieve. In the example above, the main goal was, 'To retire in the best circumstances from family, emotional and financial points of view'. There were other subgoals, and the values in the goal (emotion, finances and family) were at odds with each other.
4   Values
    Get the associated values. These were honesty, honour, financial stability and family.
5   Obstacles
    Explore obstacles. What are the difficulties in the situation?
    What are the complicating factors?
    Here, it was the unwillingness of the business management to discuss salary issues openly and a lack of a coherent view of the future.
6   Resources
    Explore resources – what or who can help? In our example, some resources were his personal financial advisor, some friends and family and his immediate boss in the business.
    What is the cost in time, money and effort in using these resources?

7 Options
   Lay out the possible decisions.
   In the example, there are several.

   • to confront management about a salary increase or not.
   • to continue with the company if they refuse.
   • to leave the company if they refuse.

   Leaving cannot be a hollow threat; he must be prepared to act on it.
   There was a range of possible leaving times stretching over the next two
   years, when he planned to retire and leave anyway.
8 Consequences
   Explore the consequences of the decisions.
   What is the worst outcome for each decision?
   How likely are those outcomes?
   What is the best outcome for each decision?
   How likely are they?
   We can express this in a grid (Table 6.2).

Consequences of Decision

Decision A	Decision B
Worst outcome	Worst outcome
Likelihood of the worst outcome	Likelihood of the worst outcome
Best outcome	Best outcome
Likelihood of the best outcome	Likelihood of the best outcome

9 Somatic marking
   Imagine you went for A and it turned out well.
   How do you feel about that right now?
   Usually, we judge decisions with 20/20 hindsight. We think it was a good
   decision if it turned out well (outcome bias) and a bad one if it turned
   out badly. But *right now*, at the moment of deciding, we do not know.
   What we need to know is the emotional balance *now* for each option.
10 Test the other possible decisions with the same questions as in step 9.
11 At this stage, you will have a wide view of the situation, and a good idea
   of the feeling for each option and will be inclined towards one.
   Then, we ask this question:
   'If you make this decision in the way you favour (let's say option A),
   what would have to be true for it to turn out in the best possible way?'
   You have already explored the best possible consequences in step 8.
   This question shows you what needs to happen to get those consequences.
   Then, you can build an action plan to create these favourable circumstances.

12   At the end of this process, the client will be clear about:
  • the goal
  • the values
  • the options
  • the consequences of the options
  • Which option they favour
  • What needs to happen for this option to work in the best way
  • An action plan to prepare the ground for the best consequences.

Meta values

Meta values are the values the client wants to be true overall, regardless of the decision and the consequences. Our client above talked about integrity, honesty and calmness. While we do not always get what we want, we can act true to our values and hold our head up whatever happens, knowing we have given it our best shot and have been true to what is important. (This is important – it is easy to be happy about *a good outcome from the decision*.) But we want to go further, to make peace with *whatever* happens. Whatever happens, we know we have done our best. There are no guarantees it will turn out well. Even if it turns out badly, there is no guarantee that the other options would not have been worse.We all suffer from the illusion of control – we think we are in control of events – we are not. This illusion of control gives rise to both blame and guilt. If events are controllable then if they go wrong then someone must be to blame – other people (blame) or our self (guilt). Once we realise we do not have control, we just do our best - and blame and guilt evaporate.

Social pressures on decision-making

We have seen how the simple rules and cognitive biases of system one can distort our decision-making. There are also social pressures we find hard to resist. Our brain may be ours alone, but how it works is moulded by relationships with society and culture. Small wonder it is subject to social pressures. These have been well described by the psychologist Robert Cialdini.[10] The psychology of persuasion is widely used in selling, negotiation and persuasion, at best to influence and at worst, to manipulate others.

Authority

Society says respect authority, starting with your parents. Society runs on authority. The idea of hierarchy – some people have the right to tell others what to do – is deeply embedded in our thinking. Companies are built on this principle, however flat they say they are. Anyone who works in a company will be beholden to someone else. The CEO will answer to the shareholders. In the last analysis, authority is based on trust. We trust our parents to look after us when we are small. We trust our teachers to have skill and knowledge. Legitimate authority comes with the built-in premise – this person knows what they are doing. Therefore, when someone shows authority, we tend to assume they have the skills that go with it. We are primed to trust them. We tend to believe first and think later. Unfortunately, authority and competence do not necessarily go together.

What we forget is that except in rare instances, authority is *contextual*. It operates in context, and in some areas, it will not apply. It is fine to do what your manager tells you at work, but you would not take their fashion advice. We obey the cabin crew in an airplane; they have authority on an aircraft. Outside the airport, there is no reason to obey them or believe what they say; they are just as likely to be wrong as anyone else. But we are primed to obey people with authority out of context. A uniform is very persuasive.

We are well primed to respect authority and forget about context, so the trappings of authority, uniforms, degrees and titles (real or assumed) make a person appear more trustworthy in every context (fundamental attribution error). When a client cites research, authority and references as part of their decision process, always explore whether these authorities are suitable and know what they are talking about. Authority out of context should be at the very least questioned, and maybe disregarded.

Rapport

We are influenced by people we like. No surprise here. But should they sway our decisions just because we like them? They may not like us. Also, our likes are influenced by unconscious priming and bias. For example, meeting someone at an event that you enjoy, primes you to like that person. The liking gets transferred from context to person. We tend to like people who are like us. Sharing values and interests gives a bond and we are more likely to listen to what they say. But just because we like them, does that make them right?

There is another trap to rapport. We may like someone because they remind us of someone else.. If that someone else was a friend, then the liking for the friend will be transferred to the new person. The emotional tone of the memory attaches itself to the new person. We also (of course) like people who pay us compliments. People may pay us compliments without having our best interests at heart.

We are also drawn to physically attractive people. Attractiveness is, well, attractive. Attractive people are viewed as more competent and more trustworthy in many areas.[11] Logically, physical attractiveness is nothing to do with trustworthiness but knowing how the brain makes these leaps of logic on the wings of emotion, you are probably not surprised. Good-looking people present a better 'image', and therefore, others want to be associated with them. (Attractive people do better in legal battles – they are found guilty less often and, if sentenced, tend to receive a lighter sentence than people deemed less attractive.)[12]

So, the truth is we are likely to be influenced in our decisions by people we like, by people we think are like us and by attractive people, regardless of how competent they are.

Consistency

Our brain likes predictability and works hard to keep the world consistent through confirmation bias. We want to present a consistent face to the world. This makes us trustworthy and others value that. We try to be consistent with our actions in the past. It is easier to keep the same position, use the same criteria and make the same kind of decisions – to go with the status quo bias. We have a self-image built by our PFC, and it has a strong influence on what we do. Therefore, when we need to decide we look to precedent first, what we have done in the past. Other people will expect us to be consistent, and there is a pressure to take the same decision again. Anything else is tantamount to admitting you were wrong in the past.

The coach can point out that consistency is not the same as trustworthiness. Trust comes from the ability to apply value and principles to different situations and act consistently with those. Consistency for its own sake is a poor reason. Consistency shades into habits, which shades into unthinking compliance. Every decision is new, and consistency is no reason to choose one way rather than another.

Reciprocity

When someone does us a favour (even if unasked), we feel a sense of obligation. We feel in debt. Reciprocity is generally a positive principle; we could not have a social life without it, the things we do and the gifts we give to others are the social bonds that link us. We have a very keen sense of fairness and justice; it seems that a part of our brain keeps track of what we give and receive.[13] It is the basis of law and morality. The sunny side of reciprocity shows our innate sense of fairness. Living with others is a balance of giving and taking, and those that take and do not give soon become unpopular (like a drinking partner who never pays for their round in the bar but always accepts a drink when offered). Most people feel uncomfortable to be always on the receiving end (except the drinking partner). Giving in return is natural. It is also uncomfortable to keep giving and getting nothing back, even when we insist we do not want anything. We still expect at least to be offered something. Cooperation is deeply built into our genes and our brains.

Research shows that a gift that is cheap and unasked for, tends to influence people to buy something much more expensive.[14] (Hence, the cheap pens or mugs that comes with an invitation to sponsor a worthy cause.) So again, we need to be aware of context. Just because someone does you a favour, especially if it was unasked, does not mean you automatically have to return it and certainly not if the return favour is going to be disproportionately greater and more significant than the first favour. Do not let another's generosity affect an important decision. Treat every decision on its own merits. This principle is a good one and is behind the many rules that constrain people in public life from accepting gifts from others.

Scarcity

Have you ever seen signs advertising a sale that say, 'Last day!' or 'Only a few remaining!'? Does that make you sit up a little with added interest? Marketers know that scarcity gives extra value. First, it suggests that lots of other people have bought the item before (building in the principle of social proof – see below), and second, it generates that irrational fear that you will miss out. This has its own acronym in the social media age: FOMO.[15]

There are good reasons for this principle. In our evolutionary past, important resources were scarce; we had to fight for them. Food, drink and shelter were at a premium; you couldn't just pop down to the supermarket and get another if you missed out. So, it makes sense to grab what is there at the time. Why wait? It might not be there later.

Fast forward tens of thousands of years. Those same resources are not scarce at all. The important necessities of life are abundant for most people. Our brain, wired for more difficult times, still sounds a warning. A hint of scarcity makes us interested; it can even override the fact we did not want the item in the first place. (Have you ever bought something in a sale because it had a big discount? Or because it was a limited edition? Would you have bought it otherwise? Scarcity has little to do with value. System 2 knows if you would not buy it when plentiful, then why buy it when it is scarce?

The implication for decision-making is obvious. Do not be pressured by your brain to do something simply because it is scarce. The same principle holds if a special offer is time limited. This makes it scarce in a different way – it will disappear soon. Only take scarcity into account if you are truly undecided, in which case, the safest decision is to take it if the opportunity is good and is time limited.[16]

Social proof

Social proof is safety in numbers. Here's the logic: if many people decide that way, then it must be good. Not only that, but maybe you are being antisocial by not deciding the same way. Finally, even if you are wrong, you will be in good (and numerous) company. No one will blame you because they all did the same. The risk is reduced.

Social proof is an important part of decision-making; we are swayed by others' opinions. We look at reviews, feedback and decide based on what others think. This principle is important in social media – when something gets a lot of likes, it is hard not to join in, even if you don't like it. Recommendations are worth money.

Social proof is useful; we do need to take other people's decisions into account. However, remember the principles of good feedback. Quality counts as well as quantity. When someone you respect with an excellent track record decides one way, then that counts more than hundreds of others who know little about the matter. Expert reviews are worth more than dozens of others. Better to buy the shares that Warren Buffet buys, rather than the shares that thousands of ordinary investors buy.

Endorsements and genuine references are important in evaluating a course of action, but there are other factors. Some classic research on social proof was done by Solomon Asch in 1951.[17] In his experiment, a group of eight students was shown a paper with a straight line drawn on it. Then, they were given three more lines of different lengths and asked which one was closest to the length of the first. The answer was always obvious. As in so many psychological experiments, however, things were not what they seemed. All but one of the students was stooges. There was only one genuine participant, who was told they were part of an experiment in visual perception. All the students could see what answer the others were giving. Most of the time, the seven stooges gave the correct answer. But, every so often on cue, they would give a wrong answer. Now imagine you are the genuine participant. Your fellows, who you have no reason to suspect, are in league against you, and all agree on an answer that looks completely wrong to you. What do you do?

The results were interesting. On average, one third of the genuine participants agreed with the wrong answer. This experiment has been discussed a dissected over the years and is still controversial. The pressure of social proof does seem to play a part, as well as group conformity. There is pressure to fit into a group you feel part of. It is also true that nothing important hung on the decision, as ethical rules forbid experiments where there is anything very significant at stake. Still, it remains a warning of the pressures of conformity.

Now with social media, social proof comes down to likes and online recommendations. However, as we know, both can be bought and easily manipulated. Online social proof is even less reliable than the offline variety.

Do not decide just because many others have decided the same way, unless they are real people you respect and who have gathered the same information you have gathered.

Decision fatigue

When we take a lot of decisions, the quality of the decision decreases with time. This is an example of 'ego depletion' – an experience we can all relate to – continuous mental effort becomes harder as time goes on. A good sleep is needed to reset our brain. What causes ego depletion is not clear, but there seems to be a parallel with physical effort. The mind tires, but unlike the body, it does not 'feel' tired. And therein lies the danger. Our decisions deteriorate, but we do not notice.

The classic study on decision fatigue was done in 2011 with a parole board in an Israeli prison.[18] Prisoners came before the board to have their request for parole evaluated. Ideally, a parole board is objective and decides on the merits of each case, and indeed that was their intention. They heard cases throughout the day. Each day was divided into three sessions with a food break between each. At the beginning of each session, sixty-five percent of prisoners received a favourable decision – early release on parole. As the session wore on this percentage dropped to almost zero but picked up back to sixty-five percent immediately after the next food break. The overriding factor in who got parole was the time of day when their case was considered, not the merits of the case.

This is surprising but understandable from what we know. Thinking and critical decision-making takes effort, and if you are tired, system 1 takes over. System 1 with its status quo and risk averse biases goes with the safest decision – to deny parole. (It also has the merit of keeping options open – the prisoner could be released at another hearing, whereas a decision for release once made is hard to overturn.)

What are the most tiring type of decisions?

Those that are important with a high emotional component. They seem to tax the emotional centres of the brain as the OFC strives to balance values, one against the other. The bigger the risks, the more tiring. Time pressure also adds to the stress and the fatigue of decision-making. The more factors to consider, the more difficult and the more tiring. This taxes the working memory. Choice is great, but too much choice can be stressful. To decide between two jobs, a thorough analysis and a balance of values will give a choice you can feel satisfied with. With dozens of possible jobs to consider, there is far more work involved, and the eventual choice is much less certain. This is the paradox of choice.[19]

Too many choices can lead to paralysis and anxiety about fear of missing out (FOMO). Barry Schwartz in his book, *The Paradox of Choice*, writes about 'Maximizers' and 'Satisficers', terms originally coined by the psychologist Herbert Simon in the 1950s.[20] These clumsy words capture an important idea. A 'Maximizer' is someone who tries to make the very best decision every time, and this means looking at all the options. 'Maximizers' are going to suffer from colossal decision fatigue. A 'Satisficer' has values but does not need to make the very best choice every time. This is a better strategy (From the brain's perspective).

The coaching implications of decision fatigue are obvious. Tell clients about decision fatigue as a well-researched phenomenon. Some clients, especially top executives, will be deciding all day and pride themselves on their decision-making capability. So, do not question their competence, point out the physical parallel. A superb runner cannot continue running all day, they would collapse. Decision-making for the brain is the equivalent of physical effort for the body. Help clients make friends with their brain and know its limitations, as well as its strengths. Get the most important decisions done at the beginning of the day. They need frequent breaks to refresh their neurotransmitters.

Coaches can benefit from their own advice to. Take extra care with your clients just before lunch, after a long morning. Better still, do not schedule too many clients in the day. You cannot do them justice. Plan the coaching day with sufficient breaks.

Everyone makes choices (that means deciding) throughout the day and they add up. There are many ways to simplify life, so the less important choices are not a burden. Barack Obama, President of the United States for eight years with arguably the most difficult job in the world, seemed to know about decision fatigue. He automated as many unimportant decisions as possible. For example, he kept a very small number of suits that he could choose to wear each day. He wasted no mental energy on what to wear each morning – he had limited his choice in advance. He also had a good strategy for communicating decisions, one that we often recommend to clients. He liked to have memos that required a decision delivered to him with three checkboxes at the bottom. They read 'Yes', 'No' and 'Let's discuss'.

Delay discounting – I want it now!

What else makes decisions difficult? Time. Having to wait for the results. We want the world and we want it now. Something of the small child remains in all of us, the child who experiences one hour as an insufferably long time. Children tend to divide time into two types – now and not now. Given the choice, now is always the more attractive proposition, something credit card companies exploit very well. They sell you the ability to buy now – but at a very high interest rate.

Wanting things quickly is natural. Take it now, or it may disappear, we have already met the pressure of scarcity. Tomorrow is an uncertain, unfulfilled promise. Evolution has stacked the cards on the side of now. The reward system of our brains (the ventral tegmental area [VTA] and the nucleus accumbens [NAC]) responds to an immediate return. What drives us most strongly are the four Fs: fleeing, fighting, feeding and having sex. The first two can save your life and the second two make your life worth living.

These brook no delay. In neurological terms, they have the highest discount – in other words, they are the hardest to defer.

Delay discounting, not wanting to wait, puts pressure on decisions, favouring those that give immediate results. Not only that, but punishments and unhealthy consequences are banished to an uncertain future. The price we may pay in the future is faint and insubstantial compared to the rewards of the present. To put aside a present reward (e.g. a second piece of cheesecake), in favour of a future reward (feeling more healthy), takes some effort, and your PFC must convince you that the future reward is either more valuable (e.g. appreciation from your partner), bigger (I can have a bigger piece at the weekend) or is a bad idea and leads to bad consequences (unpleasant full feeling and self-loathing at overeating again). Cheesecake now is not always a bad decision, but cheesecake now – *every time* – is not good.

Leaving aside moral problems, how can we help clients with the appeal of
   the present?
Take the easy promotion now or wait for a better one?
Take a luxury holiday or invest the money?
Eat that chocolate cake now or hold on for the healthy future?

Exercise is another common example. Exercise takes time and effort right now and the penalties of a sedentary existence are comfortably far away.

First, let clients know the problem is not about willpower or laziness. Those are unhelpful value judgements. They do not mean anything. This is a conflict between different parts of the brain. The 'hot emotional system' centred on the amygdala and basal ganglia, linking with the reward system in the VTA and NAC, pulls one way. The 'cool system' centred on the dlPFC weighing up consequences over time pulls the other way.[21]

Second, it can help to bring the future into the present. For example, if the issue is to eat the cheesecake now, the NAC and the VTA may outvote the dlPFC. But the dlPFC has something they do not have – a range over time. So, it can make the argument, 'OK, it will taste great now. And before you eat it, check in with how you will feel in half an hour if you do eat it now …'. This brings the bad consequences into the present. If the feeling is uncomfortable, bloated and guilty, then this may sway the argument in favour of the PFC. We use this principle all the time with clients in decision-making. We ask them to project themselves, days, months, years ahead, and imagine how they will feel if they decided in the way they are favouring. It is a sort of 'time collapse strategy' where the feeling of the consequences collapses into the present to balance the equation. It can be very helpful for clients who feel pressured to take a quick, rewarding, but perhaps unwise decision.

An example. Joseph was coaching a manager who was considering changing jobs. Her existing job was highly paid, responsible and secure. Her problem was the next six months. She had just been appointed the leader of a project she hated. Although she did not think she was the best person for the job, she believed she could deliver. She said she was facing six months of Hell. The alternative was to leave and start her own company, something she always wanted to do, but this was considerably riskier, paid less and had less security.

This sort of decision has no right answer; the client needs to explore their values. Here, one key element was the six-month delay. Is that a long or short time? It depends on what you compare it with.[22] How does six months compare with the rest of her working life? Her age was another factor. The decision for a fifty-year-old would be different than for a twenty-year-old. Many other factors influenced her decision as well: family, friends and co-workers. When she was able to step outside the time pressure, she could evaluate more clearly. Joseph asked her how she would feel in six months' time if she completed the project. He then asked her how she would feel in six months' time if she left the company now. Her orbital PFC integrated all the factors and came up with a decision that made her smile.

The Ulysses contract

Another way of helping clients with the lure of the immediate requires a trip into Greek mythology. Ulysses was King of the Greek kingdom of Ithaca 3,000 years ago, in the time of the Trojan wars. As catalogued by the Greek historian, Homer, the Greeks defeated the Trojans (by way of the famous Trojan Horse subterfuge), and Ulysses and his men set out on the long and dangerous voyage home. They had to pass the small islands of Sirenium Scopuli. According to legend, these were the home of the sirens – women of unearthly beauty. These women sang irresistible melodies, luring sailors close to the islands, where their ships were wrecked on the rocks and the bewitched sailors would happily drown.

Ulysses wanted to see and hear the sirens and still go home alive to his wife. He made a plan. He knew he would be under a spell and 'not himself', so he ordered his crew to tie him securely to the mast and not to release him, whatever he said or did, until they were past the islands. The crew filled their ears with beeswax, so they could not hear the siren song. Ulysses was able to see and hear what no one else had lived to report. Hence, the 'Ulysses contract': a contract between your present self and your future self. Ulysses' present self knew that his future self would not be able to resist the siren song. He ensured his future self could not make the crazy decision that would doom the whole ship. He decided while still rational, to take care of his future self who would be irresistible tempted. 'You' can control your present self to some extent; your future self is another matter.[23]

Coaches can use this idea in many ways. First, they are an accountability partner for the client. The coach works with the client to get their agreement and commitment to action and holds them to it. The coach sides with the client's best self in the present and holds them accountable for their future agreements and action steps. The coach stands in for Ulysses' crew. The client outsources accountability to the coach, knowing the weakness of their own future self. We all like to think that our future self will think and act the same as our present self in the face of temptation, but we cannot count on it. Our future self has a mind of its own, and reminders may not work, the 'mind' they 're-mind' us of is past. The client knows that they are accountable outside themselves, so they borrow the coach's dlPFC, realising their own may not be so resistant when the session ends. The siren calls come from outside temptations as well as habitual thinking.

We have used this principle to help clients avoid difficult situations. One client liked to help others. He would nearly always say 'yes' to any proposal or extra work his co-workers would suggest. He genuinely felt happy helping others, but they were taking advantage, and he realised it needed to stop. His willingness to agree, his habit to agree and the pressure from others made it difficult. Andrea made an agreement with him, that every time someone asked him for help, he would say, 'Let me think about that'. He would then weigh up all the factors and give them an answer later. It allowed him to genuinely sort the good proposals from the bad and to assess each request on its merits. Then, he would report back on each proposal and what he did in the next coaching session.

Why does a client keep agreements with the coach? Why are they willing to outsource accountability? Why not fall into the habit? Why not put off that difficult telephone conversation? ('Just this once …'.) Because they care about the coaching agreement. The relationship of trust and respect between coach and client is crucial. The coach cannot be an accountability partner if the client does not care.

Good decisions

It's a wonder we make any good decisions at all with the many things that can stand in our way.

First, there is the influence of emotions in the moment. Anger, fear, sadness can skew our decision-making from the beginning. Strong emotions will shut down parts of the PFC needed to get a balanced view. The amygdala hijack is the extreme example. Even when the main emotion is past, the refractory period influences our thinking. It takes time to cool down, and during that time, you will tend to interpret events through that emotional lens.

Next comes system 1 with its simplifications, shortcuts and mistakes.

How a decision is framed in terms of loss or gain influences us.

Then, there is the influence of the environment: priming and anchoring.

There are the social factors: authority, liking, scarcity, consistency, reciprocity and social proof.

More bad news is that our memory is not as reliable as we assume, and we rely on memory for many decisions. Memories are also influenced by priming and framing. Memories are not pulled pristine and untouched from an archive. They are reconstructed by our brain every time we remember, and the process of remembering subtly changes them. Sometimes, we fabricate memories and fill in the gaps to create a coherent story and then think that was what really happened.

Finally, decision fatigue can erode our good intentions, and delay discounting sings its siren song in favour of the now (Figure 6.1).

We are still optimistic. Know your enemies. When you know a trap is there, you can avoid it. All the above could and probably will influence your decision at some time, and for many decisions, it will not matter very much. That's life. However, when you have an important decision to make, then you need to be careful.

Use the somatic marker model for important decisions, with that important first step:

Emotional factors	System one	Context	Memory	Others
Amygdala hijack	Loss aversion	Priming	Fabrication	Decision fatigue
Refractory period	Cognitive miser	Framing	Unreliability	Delay discounting
	Attention bias	Anchoring	Priming	
	Confirmation bias		Scripts	
	Availability			
	Outcome bias			
	Fundamental attribution error			
	Correlation/ causality			

Figure 6.1 Factors affecting decision-making.

Check where you are now and how you feel while you think about the decision.

Be aware of possible priming. Look carefully at how the alternatives are framed.

Our decisions change ourselves and our situation, hopefully, to something better. We want the future to be more rewarding than the past, our greatest strength and our greatest weakness is that we are rarely satisfied. The present is a springboard to a better future. In other words, we want the future to be more rewarding than the present.

Notes

1 Bartra, O., McGuire, J. T., & Kable, J. W. (2013). The valuation system: A coordinate-based meta-analysis of BOLD fMRI experiments examining neural correlates of subjective value. *Neuroimage, 76*, 412–427.
2 Hare, T. A., Camerer, C. F., & Rangel, A. (2009). Self-control in decision-making involves modulation of the VmPFC valuation system. *Science, 324* (5927), 646–648.
3 Charnov, E. L. (1976). Optimal foraging, the marginal value theorem. *Theoretical Population Biology, 9* (2), 129–136.
4 Rushworth, M. F., Kolling, N., Sallet, J., & Mars, R. B. (2012). Valuation and decision-making in frontal cortex: One or many serial or parallel systems? *Current Opinion in Neurobiology, 22* (6), 946–955.
5 Antonio Damasio has written many books on the neuroscience of emotions and consciousness. See: *The Feeling of What Happens* (2000) Vintage books.
6 Saver, J. L., & Damasio, A. R. (1991). Preserved access and processing of social knowledge in a patient with acquired sociopathy due to ventromedial frontal damage. *Neuropsychologia, 29* (12), 1241–1249.
7 Bechara, A., & Damasio, A. R. (2005). The somatic marker hypothesis: A neural theory of economic decision. *Games and Economic Behavior, 52* (2), 336–372.
8 Fellows, L. K., & Farah, M. J. (2005). Dissociable elements of human foresight: A role for the ventromedial frontal lobes in framing the future, but not in discounting future rewards. *Neuropsychologia, 43* (8), 1214–1221.
9 Rolls, E. T., Everitt, B. J., & Roberts, A. (1996). The orbitofrontal cortex. *Philosophical Transactions of the Royal Society of London B: Biological Sciences, 351* (1346), 1433–1444.
10 Cialdini, R. B., & Cialdini, R. B. (2007). *Influence: The psychology of persuasion* (pp. 173–174). New York, NY: Collins.
11 Hosoda, M., Stone-Romero, E. F., & Coats, G. (2003). The effects of physical attractiveness on job-related outcomes: A meta-analysis of experimental studies. *Personnel Psychology, 56* (2), 431–462.
12 Mazzella, R., & Feingold, A. (1994). The effects of physical attractiveness, race, socioeconomic status, and gender of defendants and victims on judgments of mock jurors: A meta-analysis. *Journal of Applied Social Psychology, 24* (15), 1315–1338.
13 Cosmides, L., & Tooby, J. (2000). *87 the cognitive neuroscience of social reasoning.* New York, NY: Vintage books.
14 Cialdini, R. B., & Cialdini, R. B. (2007). *Influence: The psychology of persuasion* (pp. 173–174). New York, NY: Collins.
15 Fear of missing out. Now has its own T shirts and explanatory books – better get one while they last.

16 Marketers use this ploy in many creative ways. There are the 'final tours' of rock bands that happen every year, and many presentations are deliberately booked for a small hall, so that it can sell out quickly, creating the idea of scarcity for next time.

17 Asch, S. E., & Guetzkow, H. (1951). Effects of group pressure upon the modification and distortion of judgments. *Groups, Leadership, and Men*, 222–236.

18 Danziger, S., Levav, J., & Avnaim-Pesso, L. (2011). Extraneous factors in judicial decisions. *Proceedings of the National Academy of Sciences, 108* (17), 6889–6892.

19 The Paradox of Choice is the title of a book by Barry Schwartz published in 2003 by HarperCollins. Schwartz argued that while choice is generally good thing, too much choice can be paralysing and can lead to unnecessary regret and anxiety over the choices you did not make.

20 See https://en.wikipedia.org/wiki/Herbert_A._Simon for an account of Simon's career (Accessed 31st March 2018).

21 McClure, S. M., Laibson, D. I., Loewenstein, G., & Cohen, J. D. (2004). Separate neural systems value immediate and delayed monetary rewards. *Science, 306* (5695), 503–507.

22 In the book, *Thinking Fast and Slow*, Kahneman and Tversky ask you to choose between having 100 dollars now or 110 dollars a week from now. What would you take? Most people take the money now; why wait a week for another paltry ten dollars? But what if you were offered $100 in a year's time or $110 if you wait fifty-three weeks? Most people tend to wait the extra week, despite the fact the payoff is the same as in the first example. We don't know at what number of weeks the preference changes, but we suspect it is quite low – maybe two or three weeks. How long would you wait for an extra ten dollars?

23 There is a website www.sticKK.com where you choose your goal, for example – losing weight, going to the gym or writing a book. You agree that if you fail, you will pay a sum of money to an organisation of your choice. As an extra incentive, you can opt to donate it to an organisation you despise. This is a kind of reverse Ulysses contract – where your present self knows the weakness of your future self and engineers a punishment for your future self if they do not keep the contract.

Bibliography

Asch, S. E., & Guetzkow, H. (1951). Effects of group pressure upon the modification and distortion of judgments. *Groups, Leadership, and Men*, 222–236.

Bartra, O., McGuire, J. T., & Kable, J. W. (2013). The valuation system: A coordinate-based meta-analysis of BOLD fMRI experiments examining neural correlates of subjective value. *Neuroimage, 76*, 412–427.

Bechara, A., & Damasio, A. R. (2005). The somatic marker hypothesis: A neural theory of economic decision. *Games and Economic Behavior, 52*(2), 336–372.

Charnov, E. L. (1976). Optimal foraging, the marginal value theorem. *Theoretical Population Biology, 9*(2), 129–136.

Cialdini, R. B., & Cialdini, R. B. (2007). *Influence: The psychology of persuasion* (pp. 173–174). New York, NY: Collins.

Cosmides, L., & Tooby, J. (2000). *87 the cognitive neuroscience of social reasoning. Damasio, Antonio, the feeling of what happens.* New York, NY: Vintage books.

Danziger, S., Levav, J., & Avnaim-Pesso, L. (2011). Extraneous factors in judicial decisions. *Proceedings of the National Academy of Sciences, 108*(17), 6889–6892.

Fellows, L. K., & Farah, M. J. (2005). Dissociable elements of human foresight: A role for the ventromedial frontal lobes in framing the future, but not in discounting future rewards. *Neuropsychologia, 43*(8), 1214–1221.

Hare, T. A., Camerer, C. F., & Rangel, A. (2009). Self-control in decision-making involves modulation of the VmPFC valuation system. *Science, 324*(5927), 646–648.

Hosoda, M., Stone-Romero, E. F., & Coats, G. (2003). The effects of physical attractiveness on job-related outcomes: A meta-analysis of experimental studies. *Personnel Psychology, 56*(2), 431–462.

Kahneman, D. (2011). *Thinking, fast and slow*. Macmillan.

Mazzella, R., & Feingold, A. (1994). The effects of physical attractiveness, race, socioeconomic status, and gender of defendants and victims on judgments of mock jurors: A meta-analysis. *Journal of Applied Social Psychology, 24*(15), 1315–1338.

McClure, S. M., Laibson, D. I., Loewenstein, G., & Cohen, J. D. (2004). Separate neural systems value immediate and delayed monetary rewards. *Science, 306*(5695), 503–507.

Rolls, E. T., Everitt, B. J., & Roberts, A. (1996). The orbitofrontal cortex. *Philosophical Transactions of the Royal Society of London B: Biological Sciences, 351*(1346), 1433–1444.

Rushworth, M. F., Kolling, N., Sallet, J., & Mars, R. B. (2012). Valuation and decision-making in frontal cortex: One or many serial or parallel systems? *Current Opinion in Neurobiology, 22*(6), 946–955.

Saver, J. L., & Damasio, A. R. (1991). Preserved access and processing of social knowledge in a patient with acquired sociopathy due to ventromedial frontal damage. *Neuropsychologia, 29*(12), 1241–1249.

Schwartz, B. (2003). *The paradox of choice*. HarperCollins.

https://en.wikipedia.org/wiki/Herbert_A._Simon

www.sticKK.com

Chapter 7

Memory – into the rose garden

The two selves

Which would you prefer – a fantastic holiday for free, doing whatever you want with whoever you want, no expenses spared, or the normal holiday you have planned?

Who would not pick the first option? But there is a catch – you will remember nothing about the first holiday; when it is over, your memory of it will be erased. It will be as if it had never happened. Now which option do you prefer?

This riddle highlights the difference between your experiencing self and your remembered self. The experiencing self knows the present moment; it is in the 'now'. The remembered self knows your history and plans your future. The remembered self is the raconteur who recalls experiences and weaves them into the story of your life. We often confuse these two selves, when we think about happiness. The experiencing self can be happy in the present moment; the remembered self can be happy about life, regardless of how they feel in the moment. Whenever we coach clients who want to be happy, we explain this distinction to them.

We had a client who was leaving his job and told us about the three years he had been in the company. He passed quickly over most of it, saying he was happy, and everything went well. Then, he described the last three months – how his new boss had made his life hell. It culminated in a huge quarrel with his boss and his team, and he resigned. He said, 'My time there was a nightmare, the last three months ruined it'. Logically, this does not make sense. The happy times were still happy, the past cannot be changed – but his memory of it can. The bad time cast a shadow over the whole three years.

We regularly confuse experience with memory. The divorce courts hear this confusion all the time, as partners describe their time together through the bitterness of their current feelings for each other. Memory is not straightforward. We do not record everything and file it away for future reference. We select experience from the flowing river of the present moment. We grab a handful of water and put it in a memory box and construct our story – what sort of person we are, what we like and how happy we are.

The remembered self operates with three rules.

First, duration does not count. However long the time, it counts as one block. The first part and the last parts make book ends and do figure more prominently. Second, only the most intense moments count. Our brain does not remember averages; the most intense experiences, good or bad colour the whole experience. Third, the ending of the experience will shade the whole memory. If it ends badly, it is labelled as a bad experience. If it ends well, it is a good experience. One experiment[1] carried out by Daniel Kahneman had subjects putting their hand in a bath of iced water. This was painful. In one scenario, they held their hand in for sixty seconds. In the second scenario, they did the same and then kept it there another thirty seconds with the water warmed slightly by one degree. A significant majority of the subjects said they would prefer to repeat the second scenario rather than the first. The second ended better. Rationally this makes no sense, why opt for thirty seconds more discomfort? Our remembered self is not reasonable.

The remembered self can even try to control the future. We plan our future based on anticipated memories, not actual experiences. We do things based on how we think we will feel at the end of it, rather than how we feel doing it. So, the remembered self sacrifices the present for the future. The experiencing self will forgo the future for the present. Somehow, we need to keep a balance.

The client presents their remembered self. The remembered self is the one that makes decisions. When we make choices, we look back on our experience: the highs and the lows. Then, we make choices on what we remember, not what happened. A two-week vacation where nothing much happened seems better in retrospect than an excellent vacation with the last few days marred by terrible weather and hotel mistakes. We do not choose between experiences, but between memories of experiences. Every moment is precious, it is the only time you can experience happiness – and nearly all are forgotten, mixed together, marinated and served up by the remembered self.

Memory

Memory is far more than a store of the past. It is one of our most precious faculties. Mnemosyne, the goddess of memory in Roman mythology, was the daughter of Heaven and the goddess of time. She invented language and was the mother of the Muses – the goddesses of poetry, theatre, song and dance. Quite a job description.

Who are you? You define yourself through memory. You wake in the morning and everything about you crystallises in a few seconds. You know who you are, and you know what happened yesterday and all the other yesterdays. You feel a continuity of being. You never question if you are the same person who went to sleep the night before.

Think of a wonderful experience you had in the past. How do you know it was wonderful? You would have had to compare it with other experiences that were not so wonderful to know. Do you act congruently with your values? You need to remember your values and your actions to check. How do you know if you can trust someone if you have no memory of previous experiences with them? Without memory the world would be unpredictable and uncertain, as it was when you were a child. You need to experience, learn from experience and remember the experience to understand the world. Memory is captured learning, stabilised and available. To shape the future, you need the past.

The neuroscience of memory

How do we remember, how does the brain construct and store memories for the remembering self? Neuroscientists learned a great deal from a man named Henry Molaison.[2] When he was nine, Henry was knocked over by a cyclist and hit his head. After that, he suffered epileptic fits which became increasingly severe, and until at the age of twenty-seven, he was having up to ten blackouts a week. The epilepsy seemed to originate in the medial temporal lobe, and William Scoville, a prominent neurosurgeon, decided the only option was to remove the inner part of the medial temporal lobe on both sides of the brain. This included the hippocampus, a delicate structure, deep inside the temporal lobe. The operation was a success – it cured the fits. It did not change his personality; he remained a normal, intelligent, sociable person. However, he lost memories for the two years before the surgery, although he could remember his life before that. Worse, after the surgery, his memory was limited to a few minutes. He could not convert any experience from short-term memory to long-term memory. You could have a perfectly normal conversation with him, but an hour later, he would remember neither you nor the conversation. He remembered himself as he looked before the surgery. His self-image was of a thirty-year-old. Every day he would look in the mirror and expect to see a thirty-year-old and be shocked at the reflection. His life as he knew it, stopped at the operation, after that, it was one day at a time, each disconnected from the last.[3]

The study of Henry Molaison revealed some of the mysteries of human memory. Memory is a distinct brain process and not directly connected to other abilities. The brain stores and processes our experience in different ways; the result is different types of memory.

First is *sensory memory*. This is the trace of the immediate past, like an echo of a sound or the flash of an image. These are held for a very short time. Sensory memory allows you to repeat what someone just said to you when you are not paying attention (a very useful skill to have during a boring meeting). Sensory memories are stored as a short-term neural trace in the sensory area involved (occipital lobe for visual information, temporal lobe for auditory information).

Next is *short-term memory*. This lasts for up to a few minutes. We pay attention and the brain makes a trace. Short-term memory is complex and involves many different brain regions including the PFC. Information held in the short-term memory decays quickly. Short-term memory is also open to interference, with new information displacing the old, especially if the new information is important.

One type of short-term memory is *working memory*. This stores the information we need right now. As we compose this section of the book, we are keeping different concepts and associations and stories in working memory to put them down as we write. Working memory allows you to hold what the client said while framing your next question. Working memory lasts about twenty seconds at a time and slips away unless refreshed. It is limited to the famous 'seven plus or minus two' chunks of information at any time,[4] and while the number of chunks is limited, the size of the chunk and how they are organised is not. Henry Molaison's working memory was not affected by his surgery.

Long-term memory is everything we 'remember'. It can go back days, months or years. The hippocampus is the brain structure that converts short-term into long-term memories. The hippocampus is found deep in the medial temporal lobe. It has many connections, both to the subcortical portions of the brain and the prefrontal cortex. The brain does not store memories in the hippocampus but seems to move them into the cerebral cortex gradually. Long-term memories are dispersed across the brain. There is no 'long-term memory store'. Visual memories are stored in the occipital lobe (the visual cortex), and auditory memories in the temporal lobe. Reimagining an event is like reexperiencing the event, because the same circuits are activated. Visual memories activate visual circuits, and auditory memories activate auditory circuits.

The hippocampus was one of the first areas to show neuroplasticity of the adult brain. London taxi drivers showed an increase in volume of their hippocampus when they memorised the labyrinthine roads of London for an examination called 'The Knowledge'.[5] The hippocampus also processes spatial information; it contains neurons that code location as well as events and facts. In prehistoric times, *where* something happened could be as important as what happened, so perhaps the hippocampus developed in the brain for navigation, with the rest of the memory function being a happy by-product. Memory strategies that imagine information stored in imaginary locations can help to improve memory.[6]

The stages of memory

We are talking about 'memories' as if they are real things, but memory is a process. It is changed connections between neurons or a shift in strengths between synapses. In a sense, there is no 'memory', only the act of remembering or retrieval. We shall see that this act of remembering can change the 'memory' each time.

Anything that reaches long-term memory must go through three major stages. Miss any one of the stages and there will be no memory.

The first stage is *coding*. Information coming into the brain from the senses creating memory traces. fMRI studies show the hippocampus is active when new information is acquired and so are regions of the frontal cortex. Coding involves changes in the strength of synapses in these brain areas and the making of new synapses through neuroplasticity. The memory traces are stored as changed synaptic connections. Alcohol interferes with the coding process, which is why a heavy drinker can wake up the next morning and not remember what happened.

Surprising events tend to be more strongly coded. Surprise is an emotion that orients our attention and marks the event as significant. Surprise is not positive nor negative; it always segues into another emotion, usually happiness, fear or anger.

The brain has an another, independent process for coding memories using the amygdala, as we saw in the chapter on emotions. So, if you are involved in an emotionally intense situation such as a fight, a car accident or something similar, not only will your hippocampus lay down the memory as usual, but so will the amygdala. You get two memories of the same event, one normal and the other emotionally charged. This extra memory pathway is why time seems to slow down when we are having intense, frightening experiences. The brain does not speed up, but the memories laid down are richer and fuller and seem to, therefore, take a longer time.[7]

Amygdala memories are more vivid and impactful (they are often called 'flashbulb memories'), but they are not more accurate. This was shown in an interesting study of memories of 9/11 Twin Towers tragedy.[8] Most people remember where they were and what they were doing at the time – one of the defining moments of a generation. Researchers interviewed several hundred people a week after the attack, asking what they remembered. A year later, they interviewed them and asked questions again. Assuming the first replies were the most accurate; the replies a year later were only sixty percent consistent with the answers given in the first survey. Another survey two years later showed the same result. Memory of the facts was least affected. (Ninety percent consistent after one year and eighty percent consistent after three years.) The personal memories of where they were and what they were doing at the time were much less consistent. Worst were memories of emotions at the time. Later replies about emotional memories matched the original report only forty percent of the time. Yet these memories were the ones they were most confident about. They gave a confidence rating of four out of five. Confidence in a memory does not mean it is accurate.

The second stage is *consolidation and storage*. This stabilises the memory. Consolidation seems to happen in two phases. There is a fast, initial process, determined by the medial temporal lobes, especially the hippocampus, followed by a slower process that cements the memory in place permanently.

How the slower consolidation happens is not clear, but we know sleep is essential for the process. The hippocampus works with the neocortex and the information is slowly transferred and replaced by an enduring trace in the neocortex. Once in long-term memory we can retrieve it, given a suitable reminder.

Both disrupted sleep and chronic stress disrupt memory consolidation. Physical and mental stress trigger the release of the stress hormone cortisol through the hypothalamus–pituitary–adrenal (HPA) pathway. Cortisol binds to some areas of the hippocampus and disrupts consolidation. One study showed a fourteen percent reduction in volume of the hippocampus for people who experience chronic high stress, compared with non-stressed individuals.[9] Depression also seems to affect memory, as it decreases the volume of the hippocampus.[10]

Head injuries or trauma can block consolidation. Joseph was hit by a car when he was twelve. He remembers stepping out onto the road and being in hospital afterwards, but not the accident itself. He did not lose consciousness. The accident itself was most impactful (in more than one way), strongly coded, but not well consolidated.

Sleep

In Chapter 1, we saw how sleep is important in consolidating muscle memory and enabling neuroplasticity. It will be no surprise to discover it plays a major part in the consolidation of every sort of memory. This is not a new idea. The Roman Historian Quintilian wrote two thousand years ago: 'It is a curious fact ... that the interval of a single night will greatly increase the strength of the memory ... things that cannot be recalled on the spot are easily coordinated the next day ...'.

The link between sleep and memory consolidation was established in scientific terms in 1924,[11] and those results have been replicated many times since, showing memory retention increasing by forty percent after sleep. During non-rapid eye movement (NREM) deep sleep, the short-term memories that are stored in and around the hippocampus are transferred to long term and more secure sites in the cerebral cortex. This is not indiscriminate. Somehow, the brain seems to attach markers, like stickers, to learning we make during the day, marking it as important. During NREM sleep, the brain then seems able to choose the marked information, transfer and strengthen it.[12] Without deep sleep, memories are not transferred and remain frail and easily destroyed and replaced. Rapid eye movement (REM) sleep seems to take these consolidated memories and integrate them, perhaps by madly juggling them in the form that appear as dreams in our mental theatres. It is strange that many people will stage an 'all-nighter', going without sleep, to cram and remember before an examination or presentation – precisely the opposite of what they should be doing.

Retrieval

Retrieval is the third aspect of memory. It is the only way we know we remember – we somehow reactivate the neural network where the memory is stored and up it pops again.[13] We take remembering for granted, but it is an incredible process. It involves accessing the original experience and bringing it back to our conscious mind. We may visualise it, describe it and even feel the emotions we felt at the time. Functional magnetic resonance imaging (fMRI) studies show the hippocampus and parts of the cingulate cortex are active in memory retrieval. The hippocampus only seems to be activated when recalling episodic memory – our personal experiences. Other parts of the temporal lobe become active when remembering familiar events or objects. This suggests that there are different forms of memory for different sorts of events.

We still do not know how the retrieval process works. One theory suggests that different objects may be coded onto single neurons. These so-called grandmother cells encode a single memory, perhaps one for your maternal grandmother and one for your paternal grandmother, hence the name. This cannot be the whole story; otherwise, if the grandmother cell dies, you would not be able to recognise her. Also, how does the cell adapt to recognising your grandmother in disguise, or as she ages? Nevertheless, there have been some results that show that in some circumstances, single cells can hold a single memory. In one experiment, subjects with intercranial electrodes were presented with pictures of celebrities, famous buildings and familiar animals.[14] The researchers found that one cell only responded to a picture of Bill Clinton, another to the Beatles, a third to pictures of Jennifer Aniston. The 'Jennifer Aniston cell' became a celebrity cell and got a lot of research attention. It responded to pictures of the actress, but oddly, not to pictures of her with Brad Pitt. It did respond to pictures of her with Lisa Kudrow, so perhaps the cell was part of a 'Friends' network or represent a concept and not a specific person.

The 'Jennifer Aniston cell' plays into the popular metaphor that long-term memory is like a hard disk where data is stored, retrieved, inspected and returned, unchanged and uncorrupted. But our brain is not a computer and memory is nothing like a hard disk. Remembering personal experience is a creative act that reconstructs the memory each time you retrieve it. What is put back is slightly different from what was taken out. This was shown in some fascinating experiments by Joseph LeDoux and colleagues.[15] They taught rats to associate a loud noise with a small electric shock. The rats would cringe at the sound, expecting the shock. When the experimenters injected a chemical that stopped new proteins being formed in the brain (memory needs proteins to make the new connections), the rats lost the association. The rats could not create the fearful memory, so the shock was unexpected. The researchers went further and wondered what would happen if the injection was made during the act of remembering the shock. They took rats that were afraid of the sound and injected the chemical at the exact moment when the rats were remembering what the sound meant (a shock). The result was surprising – blocking the act of remembering *made the original memory disappear*. The rats did not make the association any more. Granted, this experiment was with rats, but humans have the same memory mechanisms. Other research showed that when a fearful memory is activated, new proteins need to be made in the amygdala for it to be re-consolidated. Remembering is creative and the reconsolidated memory is not quite the same as the original trace. The brain that remembers is not the brain that coded the memory, and the memory must be updated.[16] Memory is a process, not a repository and a personal memory is only as good as the last time you remembered it.

Coaches change memories. Clients remember people, situations, thoughts and feelings and present them to the coach. They tell their story composed of many memories. Coaches take this story, question it, reframe it, make new distinctions and offer new perspectives. As a result, the story changes and the memory that the client leaves with is subtly (or sometimes drastically) different from the one they had when they came in. A client may complain about their boss shouting at them. They have a clear memory, and it means the boss is a jerk. Coach and client discuss the situation, how the boss speaks normally, the overall situation and the client's mood at the time. The client may leave with a memory of an office emergency, the boss being upset, raising his voice and then returning to normal. This gets refiled under a heading of 'Office emergency' rather than 'The boss is a jerk'.

Semantic memory

We store different sorts of information. For example, Joseph remembers facts and information and can easily trace associations between ideas to books and conversations, occasionally with an eidetic image of the page where he first read the information. But he cannot remember where or when he read the book. Joseph is good at what is called semantic memory – the storehouse/ dictionary of general knowledge we all acquire and learn through experience and education. The capital of Brazil, the number of neurons in the brain, where and when coaching began and so on. Semantic memory has no context – just facts. Where and when you learned it is irrelevant. Semantic memories can be wrong – we may have been lied to or we may have misunderstood or the memory was otherwise distorted. Semantic memory is stable; remembering Paris is the capital of France is not going to change that memory, but a memory of what you did in Paris will shift a little every time you recall it.

Semantic knowledge is mostly linguistic: stored in words. Some words are more abstract than others. Education, respect, happiness, communication, argument and presentation for example. Words like this represent values and important concepts, and we all have some semantic memory for their meaning. However, the more abstract the word, the more it will be fleshed out and given emotional tone and meaning by the personal experiences of our episodic memory. These words are given meaning by experience. When a client uses them, their culture, upbringing and experience will give these words a different meaning to the one you have. In these cases, semantic memory is not enough. We need to ask questions to find out what these words mean to the client. Clients do not have the same dictionary as the coach to decipher their words.

Our knowledge has expanded exponentially; we create gigabytes of data every second in the world wide web. Most of our scientific knowledge has come in the last couple of hundred years. We no longer store it in our brain.[17] We no longer even try to remember it. The Internet together with the search engines is an infinite semantic memory repository.[18] In many ways, we have outsourced our semantic memory to Google.

Episodic memory

Episodic memory, or narrative memory, is memory of personal experiences. It always includes context – where and when and who else was there. Andrea has good episodic memory; she has strong visual memories of incidents in her life exactly where and when they occurred. Episodic memory depends on the hippocampus and other structures in the medial temporal lobe. These do not mature until the age of eighteen months, so we do not recall our experiences as infants. Significant events will have a semantic and an episodic memory. For example, we know the facts about the fall of the twin towers in New York on 9/11 (semantic), and we can say where we think we were and what we were doing when we heard that news (episodic).

Episodic memory is the most prone to distortion and forgetting. Digital cameras, YouTube and Instagram have stepped in to fill the breach, although these 'memories' are usually highly manipulated to give an impression.[19]

Script memory

Episodic memory is often confused with script memory. Script memory is not really a memory at all; it is a bundle of many different but similar episodic memories into one general idea of what 'usually' happens. Script memories have no context. If you had to describe what you had for breakfast twenty days ago, you would probably bring up a script memory of breakfast: what you usually have. What you actually had for breakfast (if you had a way of knowing that) might match the script, or it might be different. To make a script memory, you need the ability to form episodic memories, and the ability to generalise several similar instances into one type. We develop script memories about the age of four.

Script memory gives generalisations and bolsters the client's assumptions. A judgement, generalisation or complaint usually comes from script memory.

Coaches work with episodic memories of real events and not scripts. Beware of scripts. Good questions to get episodic memory are 'Give me an example' and 'Tell me some details'. These help clients to remember what happened and not what could have happened. Another way to access episodic memory is to ask about the emotions at the time. You can also ask how that example differs from what normally happens. This will separate the script from the real event.

You can tell the difference between script memory and episodic memory by the language. Script memory will be in the present tense 'I do this ...' even when the event was in the past. A script often uses the conditional tense: 'I would do this ...' Episodic memory is usually described in the past tense with specifics, 'I did this ...' Episodic memory will have plenty of detail and context.

Implicit memory

Implicit memory holds habitual actions. These memories are hard to describe in language; memory is embodied in the doing. (Try and explain how to ride a bicycle.) Implicit memory covers motor skills like walking (which we all learned by trial and error), tennis, driving, playing the guitar and so on.[20] These motor skills involve a different system: the basal ganglia that controls movement primarily through the neurotransmitter dopamine. Conditioned reflexes are another type of implicit memory, as are non-addictive habits. We perform them mostly unconsciously and find it difficult to give an account of how we do them. Even something as mundane as picking up a cup of tea (as we do all the time while writing), takes an incredibly complex coordination of hand, eye and balance.

Reminders and cues

Remembering is not only the strength of the coding or the amount of consolidation. It needs a cue. Sometimes, when people say they have a bad memory, they mean that they have not set up a good enough system of reminders to help them pull out the information they need.

Reminders come in two kinds – the random and the planned. Random reminders happen all the time. We go into a restaurant and the smell reminds us of another place, maybe many years ago. We read a sentence in a book, and it reminds us of another book. We visit a building and memories of what we did there come flooding back. We do not control random cues; they happen if something in the present links with a wider system or stored memories in our PFC, and this brings back other memories, like the twitch on the edge of a spider's web is transmitted to every corner.

Planned cues are what we need to set up when we want to remember and there are many ways to set these up. Some can be external. We can ask others to remind us. (Do not blame them if they forget.) Notes and pictures also work. Context-dependent memory uses the place to remind you. (Walk into a familiar building and the memories come flooding back.) A memory is not just one event but is linked to many associations and cues, all of which can help reconstruct the memory.[21] State-dependent memory is when the cue is your psychological state. Put yourself back in the same mood to access memories of what you did in that mood.

The best cues to help reconstruct a memory are associations linked with the memory. One way is to attach new information to something you already know. On the neural level, memories are formed by strengthening synapses and making connections between neurons. The stronger the connection between neurons, the stronger the memory. When we remember things we have already learned, it activates those existing connections. When the new information is added, it increases the activity, makes the connection stronger, makes the old memory stronger and makes it more likely the new information will be stored with it. The network is already 'hot' to receive the new information. Actors use this method to remember lines; they attach their next line to a cue that links with the last line spoken.

Coaches use reminders to help clients remember action steps. A structure is a specially designed cue to remind the client to do some action or think differently. A structure deals with the common problem where a client wants to remember to do things differently, but in the heat of the moment, just when that new action is needed, they forget. Habitual thinking takes over and they do what they have been doing, instead of what they want to do. Coach and client can build a reminder, tailored to that situation and the best ones link with existing ideas and interests so they join a 'hot' network. For example, Joseph had a client who wanted to improve her balance of life in future years. She felt some parts of her work were taking over too much of her time. She had an interest in painting, so her reminder and action step was to paint a mandala in the form of a cross and put it above her desk. She had talked about integrating two opposing trends and had mentioned the metaphor of a cross, so that structure fitted very well. Coaches should never take the responsibility of reminding the client. The client must be accountable for themselves.

Priming and memory

We discussed how priming works in a previous chapter. Our brain is influenced by context without consciously realising ('The Florida Effect'). Our memories can also be primed. We retain and forget information without realising, and this can lead to some strange effects.

Our memory is primed and influenced by what happened recently. We cannot help ourselves; our brain is 'primed', prepared like a pump to pump out what we are familiar with.[22] For example, if we asked you make a word by filling in the missing letters from H-P-O------S, you are much more likely to make the word 'hippocampus' than 'hippopotamus'. (Even though there are the wrong number of letters to spell 'hippocampus') If this book was an African Safari guidebook, then you would be primed for 'Hippopotamus'. This is a trivial example, but the principle is important. What book do you read before an important meeting or crucial conversation? How is it priming you? When primed with certain words, you will recognise similar ones faster afterwards. Amnesiac patients, who were shown priming words and then tested, were able to recognise and complete the words faster, even though they have no conscious memory of seeing the words before.[23] Priming shows that some types of memory operate as a separate memory system and do not depend on conscious recall. The priming material acts as a kind of cue that bypasses our awareness.

Priming can be good – it can lead to quicker responses because of previous exposure to the material; it can help us connect with what we need in the moment. Priming can also work against us. It can distract. Here is an example. Look round the room now and make a mental note of everything you see that is coloured *green*. Take about twenty seconds. In the next footnote, I will give you a test on your memory. Finished? Now go to this footnote.[24]

Priming orients the brain in advance, and this can lead to mistakes. For example, look at this list of words for about half a minute (Table 7.1).

Memory Priming

Orange	Melon	Raspberry	Menu
Black	Bells	Pie	Currant
Grass	Squash	Mojito	Ford
Pepper	Apple	Grape	Tomato
Core	Bush	Screwdriver	Five
Pineapple	Martini	High	Plum
Avocado	Lime	Olive	Emerald

Now go to the footnote[25] where there is a short memory test. Do this before reading on.

Most people think at least two words and often four were on the first list that were not. The reason was you were primed by certain words to expect ones in the same category. For example, 'lime', 'avocado', 'grass' and 'emerald' are on the original list. They are all green, and prime you for green, but the word 'green' is not there. (There was also an indirect priming for green from the previous test.) Unless you have an excellent memory, you are not going to remember all twenty-four words. This little trick shows how memory can mislead us. Sometimes, we think we remember events or facts, not because they happened, but because they fit into the context so well, they 'should' have happened. So, we reconstruct the memory incorrectly based on priming.

Priming is the basis of many magic and mentalism tricks. Here is an example that works best two or four people.

Choose an even number between ten and fifty.

Got one? Now go to the footnote.[26]

Priming by questions

A series of classic experiments by Elizabeth Loftus[27] showed how memory is primed by the way a question is asked. In the first study, a group of students were shown a video of two cars colliding. They were then divided into five groups and asked to estimate the speed of the cars. One group was asked 'How fast do you think the cars were going when they smashed each other?'

The second group was asked, 'How fast do you think the cars were going when they collided?'

The third group was asked, 'How fast do you think the cars were going when they bumped into each other?'

The fourth group was asked, 'How fast do you think the cars were going when hit each other?'

The fifth group was asked, 'How fast do you think the cars were going when they contacted each other?'

The first group primed by the word 'smashed' estimated an average of nearly forty-one miles per hour. The fifth group, primed with the word 'contacted', gave an average estimate of thirty-two miles per hour. The other groups gave estimates between. Everyone saw the same video. The form of the question changed the answer.

Loftus and colleagues made a further study. One group of volunteers were shown a video of the car accident and asked to estimate how fast the cars were going when they 'hit' each other. Another group were asked about the speed when the cars 'smashed' into each other. One week later, without seeing the video again, both groups were asked if they saw broken glass at the scene of the accident. Those who were originally asked about the cars 'smashing into each other' were more than twice as likely to report broken glass at the accident scene. There was no broken glass at the accident scene. It seems priming made them remember something that was not there.[28]

These studies had huge implications for testimony in court and cast doubt on the trustworthiness of eyewitness testimony. Witnesses rarely lie, they honestly believe in their account, but it is easy to see how lawyers can phrase questions to prime the witness response.

An interesting semantic point came from this research.[29] One group were asked if they 'saw *the* broken headlight'. The other group were asked if they 'saw *a* broken headlight'. The first group were twice as likely to report they saw it. The first question primes and suggests there was one, even though there was not.

Think about the following questions and see if you detect a difference.

1 'Did you interview the potential client?'
2 'Did you interview a potential client?'

The first question implies a potential client exists and asks whether you interviewed them. It primes you to remember a particular client. The second question does not prime you in the same way; the client is not specific. This distinction exists in many languages.

We have no clear model yet how the brain integrates and stores language. There are extensive connections in the left hemisphere connecting the temporal lobes (which processes hearing) and the frontal lobes, particularly Broca's area (which processes concepts). It seems our brain has a mental lexicon – a store of words and concepts, what they mean, how they combine to form sentences together with their spellings and sound patterns. This distinction between 'the client' and 'a client' may be an organisational principle of how we learn and store words.[30] This clearly has implications for coaches and anyone who asks questions trying to get honest and accurate answers. Language has great power to guide and prime thinking. A coach's assumptions about the client or the problem can leak into the way they ask questions and prime the answer.

Forgetting

Forgetting is normal and happens naturally as memories degrade over time. Some things make forgetting more likely. If a memory is not coded well (e.g. alcohol interferes with the coding process), then it is less likely to be consolidated and stored.

The better the memory is consolidated and stored, the less likely it is to be forgotten. Repetition helps consolidation. The first research into forgetting was by Ebbinghaus in 1885 showing people forgot half of what they learn in two hours and eighty percent of it after two days.[31] His research used three-letter nonsense syllables, but the general principle still holds: the longer the time lapse without repetition and therefore consolidation, the more is forgotten.

The brain is not built to store everything. Forgetting is normal and a blessing. Our top-down control from the prefrontal cortex in the form of overarching goals and values influences what we pay attention to and what we remember. Emotionally, important events are saved, and repetition helps consolidate the memory. We also see connections between events or make connections that help us to remember.

Even long-term memories naturally degrade in time. Even if they are well coded and consolidated, they may not be easily retrieved without the cues to reconstruct them. Sometimes, we want to forget, usually because the memory is emotionally unpleasant, but purposeful forgetting is difficult. Once a memory is consolidated, you must retrieve it to know what to forget, and every retrieval strengthens the synapse and prevents forgetting. The synapses do not go back to their original form. Perhaps one day, there will be a drug that will interfere in protein formation of a memory, and if it is injected at just the right moment, like LeDoux's rats, we will forget. No doubt drug companies are working on this as we write.

Coaching applications

Knowing how memory works and how we encode, consolidate and retrieve is very valuable. Sometimes, a client wants to improve their memory, usually as part of another project (e.g. an examination, meeting or writing assignment). Improving memory sounds easy, but remembering involves many aspects. First the coding. The memory trace needs to be well coded by the hippocampus and temporal lobe at the time.

Organising the material, chunking it into clear sections and making associations between them helps coding. The better organised, the better coded. Well coded, it is more likely to be well consolidated and retrieved. Memory palaces are one way of chunking – it organises the material. Another way of chunking is to find shared categories and commonalities among the things you need to remember. Short short-term memory is limited to seven plus or minus two 'chunks' of information, but the size of the chunk is not limited.

You can use priming to your advantage by reading about people with good memories. A study in 1998 primed a group by giving them a talk about intelligence and then giving them a general knowledge quiz. Then, they primed a second group with a reading on soccer hooligans. This group did less well on the same test.[32] (Soccer hooligans may have excellent memories, but they are not known for their intelligence.)

To summarise principles of a good memory:

1   No alcohol.
2   Pay attention.
3   Be in a good state of mind.
4   Have a calm amygdala.
5   Organise and chunk the material.
6   Prime yourself well.

Consolidation is needed to stabilise the memory. We know sleep is essential for this. Also, repetition helps consolidate the memory. Evolution has taught the brain that repeated events are likely to be important for survival. Repetition gives a pattern, and the brain is always on the lookout for patterns. When you make a top-down decision to purposefully repeat something, your brain pays attention.

How frequently and how long to repeat? This is the crucial question for every examination candidate. There are many systems and they generally agree that the intervals between repetitions should gradually get longer, perhaps doubling every time. One repetition after two hours, another after four hours, a third the next day, then the day after, then two days after that. The exact spacings and method depend on the material, but five repetitions in a short time are nowhere near as good as five repetitions spread over three days. The spread over days also helps sleep to work its magic of consolidation.

Not everything is equally easy to remember, so the difficult parts need more repeating. The things you keep forgetting are the things you need to spend the most time consolidating. This means repeating from the beginning every time is not effective. When Joseph started to play the guitar, he used to practice his pieces from the beginning every time. After a week, the beginning was wonderful. The end was reasonable, and there were plenty of mistakes in between. He changed his strategy, spending more than fifty percent of the time on the difficult passages. He remembered the piece better and the performance was much better.

Here is what helps consolidation and storage:

1   Sleep
2   Repetition at increasing intervals
3   Sleep
4   Strategic repetition – repeat the difficult parts more often
5   Sleep

Coaches want clients to remember accurately, and they can help by asking for associations and extra details, especially questions about context. This avoids the danger of getting a script memory. Very few coaching clients deliberately lie but remembering is a delicate process; the memory may be distorted. There may be bits added (confabulation) or missed out (deletion); memory is fallible, and confidence in the memory does not guarantee its accuracy (often the reverse). Clients will, of course, present themselves in the best light and they often put a little self-serving spin on the memory.

Distraction and interruption can disturb memory. A coach is not going to deliberately interrupt the client and divert their attention (hopefully). However, they may distract clients without meaning to. Many clients reconstruct memories visually, by looking up or defocusing. When this happens, the coach needs to keep still and not let their movements interfere with the mental picture the client is trying to build.

We know that priming can bias memory, so coaches must be careful with their questions. The questions the coach asks will influence what the client remembers; they need to choose their words carefully and respect the power of priming.

Knowing how memory works will also help coaches to make the best reminders and structures.

Finally, remember 'The interpreter': that part of the brain that tries to make sense of all the information, looking for patterns, causes and effects, trying to make order out of the chaos of experience. When something does not quite fit, the interpreter will smooth it out in our favour. It makes us the heroes of our own story. All memories have holes, and the interpreter will fill in the holes in a way that makes sense, and this is normal.

Knowing how our brain deals with memory undermines some widespread mental models. Our memory is not so accurate, exact and trustworthy as we think. When we know how memory works, the power of priming, and the allure of scripts we can avoid the traps and make the best of it.

Remembering is a creative process, we are creative even when we recall fixed past events. We can change memories, give them another meaning. Without that power, coaching would not work. The coach is the amanuensis of the remembered self, recording it faithfully and then using the magic of questions, to help the client reconstruct their memories and therefore themselves.

Notes

1 Kahneman, D., Fredrickson, B. L., Schreiber, C. A., & Redelmeier, D. A. (1993). When more pain is preferred to less: Adding a better end. *Psychological science, 4*(6), 401–405.
2 Henry Molaison (or H.M. as he was referred to when he was alive) was one of the most famous patients in neuroscientific history. He is another sad example of a person who helped us understand the brain, at the cost of a traumatic injury. He was born in 1926 and died in 2008.
3 Several films have tried to dramatise this experience of complete retrograde amnesia that Henry Molaison suffered. 'The Curious case of Benjamin Button' and 'Memento', perhaps come closest. Also, the novel 'Hyperion', by Dan Simmons, has one of the characters suffering from 'Merlin's sickness'. This causes them to age backwards, each morning they wake up one day younger than the day before with no memory of the previous day.
4 First proposed by Miller in 1956, this model still holds today. The size of the chunk, however, is whatever you can make it.
   Miller, G. A. (1956). The magical number seven, plus or minus two: Some limits on our capacity for processing information. *Psychological Review, 63*(2), 81.
5 Maguire, E. A., Gadian, D. G., Johnsrude, I. S., Good, C. D., Ashburner, J., Frackowiak, R. S., & Frith, C. D. (2000). Navigation-related structural change in the hippocampi of taxi drivers. *Proceedings of the National Academy of Sciences, 97*(8), 4398–4403.
6 The memory palace strategy has been known to the Greeks and Romans from the eighth century BC. It involves visualising an imaginary house and placing things you want to remember in specific locations. It helps to imagine walking through the house retrieving ideas, visualising the place and hearing the sounds. There are several useful books on memory strategies.
   Your memory, how it works and how to improve it. By Kenneth Higbee, Perseus Books 2001.
   See also the book by Joshua Foer, *Moonwalking with Einstein*, published by Penguin Books in 2011. Joshua Foer is a journalist who became interested in

memory training. After a year of study, he reached the finals of the US memory championships. He competed with others in tasks like memorising the sequence of two decks of playing cards in five minutes. He writes entertainingly about the bizarre world where people memorise huge strings of random numbers. Reading his book, I was reminded of the quip by Oscar Wilde (I think), about an elephant riding a bicycle, 'The only thing more astonishing than an elephant riding a bicycle is that someone would try to teach them'.

7   Neuroscientist David Eagleman explored this phenomenon of 'time warp' in a series of experiments where volunteers (of course) were dropped 150 feet in three seconds, with a top speed of seventy miles per hour into a special safety net. People estimated their own fall to have taken a longer than the falls of other people. By having them look at a special chronometer while they dropped, Eagleman showed that time only appeared to slow. Slowing time for real is the domain of science fiction, in a long tradition from Alfred Bester in his 1957 novel, 'Tiger, Tiger' to the Matrix film trilogy, 1999–2003.

8   Hirst, W., Phelps, E. A., Buckner, R. L., Budson, A. E., Cuc, A., Gabrieli, J. D., ... Vaidya, C. J. (2009). Long-term memory for the terrorist attack of September 11: Flashbulb memories, event memories, and the factors that influence their retention. *Journal of Experimental Psychology: General, 138*(2), 161. See also the website http://911memory.nyu.edu/ (Accessed 24th April 2018).

9   Bremner, J. D., Randall, P., Vermetten, E., Staib, L., Bronen, R. A., Mazure, C., ... Charney, D. S. (1997). Magnetic resonance imaging-based measurement of hippocampal volume in posttraumatic stress disorder related to childhood physical and sexual abuse – A preliminary report. *Biological Psychiatry, 41*(1), 23–32.

10 Bremner, J. D., Narayan, M., Anderson, E. R., Staib, L. H., Miller, H. L., & Charney, D. S. (2000). Hippocampal volume reduction in major depression. *American Journal of Psychiatry, 157*(1), 115–118.

11 Jenkins, J. G., & Dallenbach, K. M. (1924). Obliviscence during sleep and waking. *The American Journal of Psychology, 35*(4), 605–612.

12 Stickgold, R., & Walker, M. P. (2013). Sleep-dependent memory triage: Evolving generalization through selective processing. *Nature Neuroscience, 16*(2), 139.

13 Neuroscientists do not yet understand how memory is stored and then reaccessed so specifically. We can remember a specific event complete with feeling in amazing detail from long ago. One interesting theory is that memory storage relates to the protein cytoplasmic polyadenylation element binding (CPEB, *if you must know)* that changes its configuration under the influence of the neurotransmitters serotonin and dopamine. Once activated, it marks dendrites and synapses as a specific memory that can be reactivated again with the neurotransmitters.
    See: *In Search of Memory*, by Eric Kandel, W. Norton 2006 for an accessible account, by the neuroscientist who did this research.

14 Quiroga, R. Q., Reddy, L., Kreiman, G., Koch, C., & Fried, I. (2005). Invariant visual representation by single neurons in the human brain. *Nature, 435*(7045), 1102.

15 Nader, K., Schafe, G. E., & LeDoux, J. E. (2000). The labile nature of consolidation theory. *Nature Reviews. Neuroscience, 1*(3), 216.

16 Nader, K., Schafe, G. E., & Le Doux, J. E. (2000). Fear memories require protein synthesis in the amygdala for reconsolidation after retrieval. *Nature, 406*(6797), 722.

17 As Sean Connery famously said as Professor Jones in the film *Indiana Jones and the Last Crusade*, 'I wrote it down, so *I wouldn't have to remember it'*.

18 We have invented better and better external memory systems. Systems of writing probably started round 7,000 BC, and it became possible for the first time to

make an independent record of an event apart from the human memory. Gradually, as writing systems improved and languages developed, it became possible to record history and pass it on between generations independently of the storyteller. Until the printing press started around 1,450, writing was slow and laborious, so only very important information was recorded. With the printing press, suddenly it was faster and easier to access information outside our brain. Now with cloud storage, Google and millions of websites, we do not have to remember facts. Google accesses our semantic memory. Perhaps, this will lead to a decline in the ability to remember, because we do not need to.

19   We may be outsourcing our episodic memory to Instagram, YouTube and digital photography.

20   Henry Molaison's procedural memory was not affected by the surgery. He could still learn skills; he would get better at them over time, although he would not remember learning them. This would have been a strange experience – to improve but apparently never practise.

21   Context-dependent memory often works against us. New ideas in the coaching session may be hard to access at work. New skills learned in a training away from work are easily lost back in the familiar work context. Skills and information are learned in a context and are easiest remembered in that context. Scuba divers are taught safety drills and repeat them under water where they will need them, not on land.

22   A short overview can be found in: Tulving, E., & Schacter, D. L. (1990). Priming and human memory systems. *Science, 247*(4940), 301–306.

23   Graf, P., & Schacter, D. L. (1985). Implicit and explicit memory for new associations in normal and amnesic subjects. *Journal of Experimental Psychology: Learning, Memory, and Cognition, 11*(3), 501.

24   Now, make a list of everything you saw that is *blue*.
   Not so easy – because you have been primed to look for green quite explicitly. To remember blue, you must rethink and rescan your memory and ignore what you noticed previously. It also shows the power of attention. By paying attention to one thing, others become invisible. Look round again and notice how many blue-coloured objects you missed.

25   How many of the following words were in the text you just read?
   Write down the ones you remember and then return to the text.

Core	Green
Pineapple	Apple
Grape	Carter
Raspberry	Menu
Pie	Currant
Cocktail	Screwdriver
Orange	Tomato
Bells	Pear
Squash	Five

26   Your number is twenty-four (or maybe forty-two) if the priming worked ('works for between two or four people' and 'twenty-four words' and 'two words on the list'). Maybe you spotted the priming. Next time you see a mentalist look out for priming. Their every word and gesture is significant.

27   Loftus, E. F., & Palmer, J. C. (1996). Eyewitness testimony. *Introducing Psychological Research*. Macmillan Education UK, 305–309.

28   This research has been challenged claiming the subjects were university students and not an average population. Second, they were watching videos with little emotional involvement. If they were involved in, or witnessed a real accident, the

emotional response may affect the memory and make the result different. From what we know, strong emotion would probably distort the memory still further.

29 Loftus, E. F., & Zanni, G. (1975). Eyewitness testimony: The influence of the wording of a question. *Bulletin of the Psychonomic Society, 5*(1), 86–88.

30 These small words like 'he', 'she', 'a', 'the', 'from', 'to' and so on are the social water in which the specific nouns and verbs float. To see how important they are and how the brain processes them, read *'The Secret Life of Pronouns'*, by James Pennebaker, Bloomsbury Press, 2011.

31 Averell, L., & Heathcote, A. (2011). The form of the forgetting curve and the fate of memories. *Journal of Mathematical Psychology, 55*(1), 25–35.

32 Dijksterhuis, A., & Van Knippenberg, A. (1998). The relation between perception and behavior, or how to win a game of trivial pursuit. *Journal of Personality and Social Psychology, 74*(4), 865.

Bibliography

Averell, L., & Heathcote, A. (2011). The form of the forgetting curve and the fate of memories. *Journal of Mathematical Psychology, 55*(1), 25–35.

Bester, A. (1991). *Tiger, Tiger.* New York, NY: New American Library.

Bremner, J. D., Narayan, M., Anderson, E. R., Staib, L. H., Miller, H. L., & Charney, D. S. (2000). Hippocampal volume reduction in major depression. *American Journal of Psychiatry, 157*(1), 115–118.

Bremner, J. D., Randall, P., Vermetten, E., Staib, L., Bronen, R. A., Mazure, C., ... Charney, D. S. (1997). Magnetic resonance imaging-based measurement of hippocampal volume in posttraumatic stress disorder related to childhood physical and sexual abuse – A preliminary report. *Biological psychiatry, 41*(1), 23–32.

Dijksterhuis, A., & Van Knippenberg, A. (1998).The relation between perception and behavior, or how to win a game of trivial pursuit. *Journal of Personality and Social Psychology, 74*(4), 865.

Foer, J. (2011). *Moonwalking with Einstein.* London, England: Penguin Books.

Graf, P., & Schacter, D. L. (1985). Implicit and explicit memory for new associations in normal and amnesic subjects. *Journal of Experimental Psychology: Learning, Memory, and Cognition, 11*(3), 501.

Higbee, K. (2001). *Your memory, how it works and how to improve it.* New York, NY: Perseus books.

Hirst, W., Phelps, E. A., Buckner, R. L., Budson, A. E., Cuc, A., Gabrieli, J. D., ... Vaidya, C. J. (2009). Long-term memory for the terrorist attack of September 11: Flashbulb memories, event memories, and the factors that influence their retention. *Journal of Experimental Psychology: General, 138*(2), 161–176.

Jenkins, J. G., & Dallenbach, K. M. (1924). Obliviscence during sleep and waking. *The American Journal of Psychology, 35*(4), 605–612.

Kahneman, D., Fredrickson, B. L., Schreiber, C. A., & Redelmeier, D. A. (1993). When more pain is preferred to less: Adding a better end. *Psychological science, 4*(6), 401–405.

Kandel, E. (2006). *In search of memory.* New York, NY: W. Norton.

Loftus, E. F., & Palmer, J. C. (1996). Eyewitness testimony. *Introducing Psychological Research.* Macmillan Education UK, 305–309.

Loftus, E. F., & Zanni, G. (1975). Eyewitness testimony: The influence of the wording of a question. *Bulletin of the Psychonomic Society, 5*(1), 86–88.

Maguire, E. A., Gadian, D. G., Johnsrude, I. S., Good, C. D., Ashburner, J., Frackowiak, R. S., & Frith, C. D. (2000). Navigation-related structural change in the hippocampi of taxi drivers. *Proceedings of the National Academy of Sciences, 97*(8), 4398–4403.

Miller, G. A. (1956). The magical number seven, plus or minus two: Some limits on our capacity for processing information. *Psychological Review, 63*(2), 81.

Nader, K., Schafe, G. E., & LeDoux, J. E. (2000a). Fear memories require protein synthesis in the amygdala for reconsolidation after retrieval. *Nature, 406*(6797), 722.

Nader, K., Schafe, G. E., & LeDoux, J. E. (2000b). The labile nature of consolidation theory. *Nature Reviews. Neuroscience, 1*(3), 216.

Pennebaker, J. (2011). *The secret life of pronouns.* London, England: Bloomsbury Press.

Quiroga, R. Q., Reddy, L., Kreiman, G., Koch, C., & Fried, I. (2005). Invariant visual representation by single neurons in the human brain. *Nature, 435*(7045), 1102.

Simmons, D. (1989). *Hyperion.* New York, NY: Doubleday.

Stickgold, R., & Walker, M. P. (2013). Sleep-dependent memory triage: Evolving generalization through selective processing. *Nature Neuroscience, 16*(2), 139.

Tulving, E., & Schacter, D. L. (1990). Priming and human memory systems. *Science, 247*(4940), 301–306.

http://911memory.nyu.edu/

Chapter 8

Learning and reward – the past in your future

Why does a client come for coaching? They want change. They want to build different lives, better lives. A coach helps the client learn from their experience , so they can create different future experiences and continue to learn. Learning is at the heart of all growth and change.

Learning

Learning is changing our thinking and/or behaviour based on the consequences of our actions. When our previous actions are rewarding, we keep doing them. When previous actions are not rewarding, in other words they do not get us what we want, we try something different. Our brain is specialised for learning. The brain does not have goals and values. You do. The brain has neurons and neurotransmitters. How the brain uses these to learn is fascinating. Learning for the brain is the creation of new neural pathways and synapses that lead to more rewarding outcomes. These get reinforced, making new habits of thinking and action. To find out how these new pathways are created, we first need to visit Ivan Pavlov and his famous dogs.

Ivan Pavlov won the Nobel Prize in 1904 for his work on learning and classical conditioning. He was researching digestion at the time so the insights on learning were a fortunate by-product. He was studying how dogs salivate to the sight and smell of food. He noticed that they would salivate at the sound of a bell that signalled feeding time. They salivated at the bell, even if he did not feed them afterwards. The dogs had learned that the bell was a reliable prediction that food was on its way.[1] Their salivation reflex had 'backed up' to the bell ringing. The bell didn't cause the food, but it predicted the food.[2] This is called classical conditioning – where a stimulus gets associated with a response because the stimulus is taken as a good prediction.

Classical conditioning is the simplest type of learning. The dogs were trying to predict the future. Over time, they learned the bell reliably predicted the food, so they drooled. Learning is updating our predictions through experience, so we can react in the right way and predict more reliably in future. Every moment, we base our actions on our expectations of what will happen. For example, I am typing this paragraph and I expect when I hit a key, the letter will appear on the screen. I am so certain, I do not bother to look. But, I then find out that the 'i', 'e' and 'h' keys are not reliable. So typ a sntnc lk ts and t s vry annoyng. Tm to larn.

When we act on our expectations one of three things can happen.

First, our expectations may be correct. We have no need to change, and there is no learning. This is the case as long as the keys worked as I predicted.

Second, events may not work out the way we expect, and we are disappointed. This is called a negative prediction error; a sign the prediction needs updating, and we learn from this. In this case, when the keys did not work, I tried different ways of hitting them. I learned that if I hit the keys too hard, they do not work. I must hit the keys very gently and the letters come out. So, my fingers start caressing the keys instead of attacking them.

Third, we get an unexpected reward. Something surprisingly good happens. We take notice, we would like it to happen again and we learn from it. This is known as a positive prediction error, because the result is in our favour. In this case, I found striking the keys more gently also helped me to type faster.

Here is a professional example. You get a new client and you ask them a series of structured questions. They get a lot of insight as a result. You did not expect this; normally, these questions are nothing special. You are delighted – a positive prediction error. You analyse the questions and try them on a second client. They also have a significant insight. You refine your set of questions and find that they very often lead to client insight. Excellent! You have learned something about powerful questions. After a while you expect these questions to help the client – and they do. You use them regularly with good effect. One day, you have a new client who is completely unresponsive to these questions. Now you pay attention, and this is a negative prediction error. You are not getting the reward you expected. You need to learn to refine the questions further. To learn, we need to keep track of our predictions and update them when they do not work. We learn by acting on a negative or a positive prediction error. The brain does this through the neurotransmitter dopamine.

Dopamine and learning

Let us introduce you to dopamine, one of the main neurotransmitters in the brain. It is everybody's favourite neurotransmitter, linked as it is to action, learning, motivation, focus and pleasure. It is an excitatory neurotransmitter; it increases the chances the signal will jump to the next neuron so it will fire. Dopamine makes things happen. Nearly, all dopamine is made in two places in the brain. The first is the substantia nigra[3] (SN), part of the basal ganglia, which controls movement. Dopamine neurons also project into another part of the basal ganglia called the dorsal striatum.[4] Dopamine is also produced by a small area in the midbrain, close to the basal ganglia called the ventral tegmental area (VTA).

These dopamine-producing neurons follow two paths, and both are important. The first is called the mesolimbic pathway or the 'reward pathway'.[5] Dopamine is released when we have a rewarding experience, like listening to good music, seeing the picture of a loved one, eating good food, having sex and winning a football match. However, the *pleasure* we get from the experience is mostly due to chemicals called opioids that are released in the brain at the time. The reward pathway travels to the nucleus accumbens (NA) which is part of the ventral striatum[6] and onwards to the amygdala, hippocampus and anterior cingulate cortex (ACC).

The second pathway is called the mesocortical pathway and runs to the frontal lobe of the neocortex, including the orbital frontal cortex (OFC). The neocortex needs to know what is happening to make plans to get what you want.

Dopamine is also the main neurotransmitter used in the basal ganglia, the small structures at the base of the brain that control movement. Dopamine is the fuel for goal seeking and action.

You feel tired, you want a cup of coffee and the basal ganglia propel you to the kitchen and the coffee maker.[7] Thought leads to action – which affects the world and ourselves. Sir Charles Sherrington, the neurologist and Nobel Laureate wrote, 'Life's aim is an act not a thought'.

So, dopamine is involved in most of the important brain pathways: the amygdala that processes emotions, the basal ganglia that control movement, the OFC that integrates thinking and emotion, the ACC that controls impulsive behaviour and monitors decision-making and finally the hippocampus that is the major component of memory. The dopamine system connects memory, emotion and decision-making. Release of dopamine makes us feel energised and motivated. It does not decide what happens, but it does control how quickly and strongly it happens. It keeps us persevering in difficult situations. Low dopamine can lead to a lack of energy, like a mild depression. Too much dopamine can lead to anxiety and has been linked with schizophrenia.

Dopamine is behind the feeling of *wanting* (known as 'incentive salience' in the psychological literature). This is shown by studies of mice that have been bred to have more dopamine than usual. These mice show signs of craving, they move towards food quicker and more directly than normal mice but don't seem to enjoy the food any more than the normals (as far as we can judge their facial expressions).[8]

We cannot reduce behaviour to neurotransmitters, but dopamine has profound effects on personality. Dopamine levels are strongly influenced by genetics. Some people have naturally high levels, others have lower levels. People differ in how easily they utilise dopamine. There are at least four types of dopamine receptor, and some people may be born with more dopamine receptors than others. There are also differences in how efficiently they break dopamine down for reuse.[9] Some people seem to have more need for novel experiences; they seek out excitement and extreme sports, perhaps because they use dopamine less efficiently, so seek to boost the level with novelty and thrills. Others are happy to read a book on the beach with a cold beer; they may have naturally more dopamine or use it more efficiently. Self-knowledge includes knowing and respecting how dopamine works for you.[10]

Dopamine and expectations

The current research shows the brain uses dopamine to signal expectations. Dopamine is released when we expect something rewarding; it makes you pay attention. It tells you, 'This is going to be good!' When the experience meets our expectations, then the dopamine level stays at the same level. If the experience is better than expected, more dopamine is released, signifying a positive prediction error. We feel good, the reward circuits are tickled, especially the nucleus accumbens. If the experience does not meet our expectations, then dopamine levels drop, signifying a negative prediction error. We feel disappointed, even if the experience was a pleasant one. A new experience also produces a higher dopamine level. Novelty is unpredictable. It is exciting. The brain does not know where to set the level of dopamine. To sum up, *the dopamine signal is the difference between what you expected and what you got*. The brain learns, by measuring the prediction error using dopamine.[11]

Here's an example from our exciting lives. We train and consult in many countries and have become all too familiar with the inside of airplanes. Several years ago, we used to travel economy class. Not knowing the comforts of business class (apart from the quick look to the left as we boarded the aircraft), our experience of air travel was based on the delights of economy class. This does not differ much between airlines, and our expectations were fixed. Flying was mostly uncomfortable (especially long-haul flights). Our dopamine signal flatlined.

Then, our business improved, and we began flying business class. More comfortable, better food and less stress when checking in. Our first flight in business class produced a large dopamine signal (although we did not think about it in those terms). After the fifth flight, business class was no longer special. It had become the norm. Dopamine levelled out.

Then, a few years ago, we were upgraded from business to first class for a long-haul trip. We had never flown first class before and our expectations were high. The first-class cabin in that airplane was a big disappointment; hardly better than the business class we knew. Our dopamine level plummeted, even though it was still comfortable. We avoided that airline for a long time afterwards. (Unfair, but dopamine is not reasonable.)

Then, we flew business class in an Asian airline (which shall remain nameless as we are not being paid for product placement). It was significantly better than the business class of any other airlines we had used. Dopamine levels soared at first, but after flying a few times on that airline, their service became the new normal. Then, Joseph was lucky enough to be upgraded to first class on one flight on an Airbus 380. Dopamine reached a new high. Great comfort, space, food, service and even the opportunity to take a shower at 35,000 feet. Normal business class was left in the dust. Each new and better experience made the others fade by comparison. The danger is not appreciating what you have, because it does not measure up to what you expected or are used to. The thrill of a new pleasurable experience (i.e., dopamine rush) can never be recaptured in the same way by repeating that experience.

How dopamine controls the delicate balance of expectation and reward was first discovered by a researcher Wolfram Schultz,[12,13] now professor of Neuroscience at Cambridge University. He studied how the dopamine neurons of monkeys responded to rewards in a series of experiments. The monkeys were shown a flashing light, and a few seconds later, they were given a drink of fruit juice. Monkeys like juice, and the dopamine cells in the VTA showed a lot of activity. This was a positive prediction error; the monkeys got an unexpected reward after the light. After many repetitions, the response of the dopamine cells to the juice went down. Schultz reasoned that it was because the monkeys expected the juice after the light, so no prediction error and no extra dopamine. The juice was as tasty as ever.

The most interesting result was the dopamine cells fired up when the light came on. The dopamine response had backed up from the reward to the cue for the reward, just like Pavlov's dogs' salivation had backed up to the sound of the bell. If Pavlov could have tested the dopamine levels in the dogs, he would probably have found their dopamine response shifting to the bell. The dopamine signal backs up to a consistent cue. An everyday example would be coming home from work and seeing a welcoming light shining from your window. You are not yet home, but the sight is a consistent signal that you are going to be there shortly and that makes you feel good.

Schultz made a second experiment. The monkeys saw the light (in a manner of speaking) but did not get any juice. As the monkeys caught on to what was happening, the dopamine response to the light went down. This is the negative prediction error – the expected reward did not materialise, so less dopamine. After a while, there was no change in the dopamine cells at all – everything was back to normal, no light, no juice, no dopamine. The degree of dopamine activity is not about the size of the reward, but how far it meets expectations. The activity of the dopamine-producing cells is the prediction error – the difference between the obtained reward and the expected reward.

This explains how a reward may not be appreciated. Imagine a manager getting an end of year bonus. They are used to it, they expect it and they think they deserve it; there is nothing special about it – no extra dopamine. If they do not get it, however, dopamine levels will drop, and they may feel disappointed and aggrieved. Ingratitude is low dopamine. When you expect a reward and think you deserve it, dopamine will not increase when you get it but will drop if you do not. It is the expectation that matters, not the reward.[14]

Prediction error explains why we are never satisfied. As we work towards a goal, dopamine keeps us motivated and wanting it. Once we have the goal, dopamine levels go down. The new exciting goal has become the new normal, and we look for the next challenge. The upside is that we keep learning and striving for something better. The downside is that we can never be satisfied, whatever we get.

Our favourite food with enough repetition becomes normal and then dull. Once we get our dream job, it becomes our normal job and eventually perhaps our boring job. We start angling for the next promotion. Winning the lottery makes people happy in the short term, but six months later they have fallen back to their baseline happiness level.[15] The thrill of a new sexual partner does not last. Lasting relationships need to be built on much more than dopamine. In short, dopamine oils the hedonistic treadmill. We work towards what we want, and that becomes the next step towards a higher goal. Clients may work hard for a promotion, a new house, a new relationship or a new level of skill and then start to feel it is not enough. They may think they should be grateful for what they have. But neither achievement nor gratitude will stop them from looking for something more (Figure 8.1). This has a very important implication – the ideal job, partner, house or life does not exist outside you. You cannot find it by looking for it 'out there'. They exist by virtue of the passion and commitment that you bring to them.

Clients come for coaching with goals they think will make them happy. Some of these we call these 'If only …' goals. '*If only* I had … this job, this partner, this holiday, this skill/car/house/, *then* I would be happy'. You can plug anything into the middle of that sentence. Don't mistake us, we are not

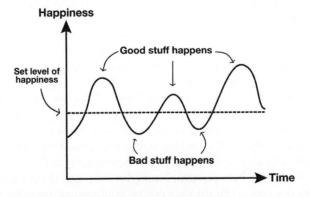

Figure 8.1 Happiness the hedonistic treadmill.

saying these things are bad or will not make a difference in the short term. But they do not work for the long term. 'If … then …' goals make our happiness dependent on something we have no control over. Instead of questioning the 'If … then …' model itself, clients simply plug the next goal between the 'if' and the 'then' and start again.

These goals often come slightly differently packaged: '*If* only my partner/children/boss would stop … nagging/making a mess/shouting at me/picking their nose … *then* I would be happy'. These sorts of goals are even more difficult, making happiness dependent on what others do or stop doing.

The way to get off the hedonistic treadmill is to invest in the journey, not the destination. We are always on a journey. That is where the happiness lies. Success is a bonus. A goal is definite. You may or may not succeed. If you fail, you may be miserable, if you succeed, you will be happy for a while and then want more. Instead, let the goal set the *direction* and pay attention to the *journey* you are on as you try your best to create it. Too many clients are unhappy while they resolutely pursue happiness (Figure 8.2).

We talked about the Mount Everest climber in Chapter 3. Climbers spend months preparing and then weeks on the mountain as they work their way to the top. Then thirty minutes at the top before starting down. Encourage clients to make goals that set a direction. Once it is set, they can put their energy into the journey and enjoy the climb.

In 2015, Andrea walked the Northern Camino de Santiago (Saint James Way) in Spain. She walked for nearly 1,000 km over the course of five weeks. She stayed two days in Santiago de Compostela before heading back home. The destination is the reason to make the journey, and the magic is in the journey. The Camino was a wonderful and worthwhile experience, and it was a marvellous moment to see the spires of the Cathedral of Santiago at the end. The learning was in the journey.

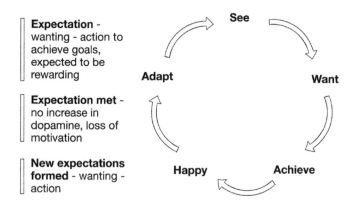

Figure 8.2 The hedonistic treadmill.

As Carlos Castaneda wrote, *All paths are the same: they lead nowhere. ... Does this path have a heart? If it does, the path is good; if it doesn't, it is of no use.*[16]

In our coaching, we always ask clients for the value behind the goal. All goals have a value – something important about that goal that that makes it a priority. The value behind the goal is not always obvious, and you may need several questions to get it. One coaching client talked about how they wanted to progress in their career and move to a higher place in the company. We cycled through several values when we asked questions like 'what is important about that?' 'why do you want that?' and 'when you achieve that, what will it get for you?' He mentioned money, satisfaction, and security. The value where he showed the most involvement and enthusiasm was when he spoke about honouring his parents and working for his children – a *connection* between generations. Not what either of us thought at the beginning. This is a value he could live every moment of his life; he does not need to get the promotion to feel and live this value. Here is the key question we asked: 'Regardless of whether you get the promotion or not, how can you live more of this value of connection in your life right now?' This question energised the client without losing the importance of the goal.

Coaching applications

How can this be used in coaching practice?

First, the brain loves novelty. Something new is exciting and stimulating. That does not make it better, but it does increase dopamine levels and therefore motivation. The most brain friendly coaching is going to be a mixture of exploring new ideas and tackling new subjects and then consolidating them. Good coaching is a balance between challenge and support. Challenge brings novelty, and support gives consolidation to help explore the implications.

We learn fast when we start something new, and then it gets slower by the law of decreasing returns. We are more motivated at the start because the positive prediction error is highest, so dopamine levels are highest. The dopamine signal goes down over time as we get used to the situation. It would be nice to keep the original energy and motivation for longer, but that is not how the brain works. Keeping the same motivation for a long time would block learning anything new, as we would be still happily engaged with the old.

Coaches can use this by working with the client on small, manageable tasks. Each one new and each one a success. All these tasks need to connect to the main goal. Whenever we help clients build action plans, we build in celebrations along the way. Success in each short-term step with a celebration will bring a glow of opioids and an experience of success to build on. The celebration is a reward and can be anything – a meal out, a walk in the park, a party or a weekend break. Some clients use the celebration to do something for someone else – a treat for their children or helping someone at work.

Handling expectations is much easier when you know how dopamine works. Expectations are natural; we need them to set up a prediction error and learn. However, we often blame the world for not meeting our expectations. We feel people should meet our expectations and feel disappointed if they do not. We forget expectations are entirely our own, formed from our experiences and others know nothing of them. They do not know our dopamine levels. For example, you go to a performance from your favourite comedian. You look forward with relish to a fun evening. You listen and gradually, although you want it to be good, it is below standard. You feel let down. Your brain is giving you a lower dopamine signal – a negative prediction error. You feel disappointed. You may project that on the performer; it's their fault. The performer does not have the faintest idea about your expectations or your dopamine levels, and is not responsible for them. They do what they do, to the best of their ability. Certainly, there are many instances where we can and should measure by objective standards. Objective standards are not personal. But, dopamine levels don't respond to objective standards; they respond to your expectations and so the disappointment feels personal.

Disappointment is how we experience a negative prediction error. It is not pleasant; it does not feel good to have dopamine levels go down. Disappointment is less dopamine in the mesolimbic pathway, the 'reward circuit'. But without disappointment, we could not have the happiness and energy that comes from a positive prediction error. We would not learn.

There is also the mesocortical pathway into the prefrontal cortex (PFC). This doesn't have a popular name, so we will call it the 'reframe circuit'. This circuit helps get another perspective on expectation and disappointment – one with value, balance and a time frame. The PFC takes the long view. The PFC helps you consider the consequences and integrates the sense of wanting and disappointment into a bigger picture of life.

Expectations and agreements

Management by expectation is very common in executive coaching. Management by expectation expects people to work but never spells out exactly what they must do nor instructs them how to do it. Expectation takes the place of clear communication and agreement. Standards are not clear, and others may fail to meet the expectations. The managers are disappointed, and the workers are blamed. Management by expectation leads to disappointment, blame and recrimination. Because the request is not clear, the response will probably not be adequate. So, a negative prediction error is very likely. When a worker meets expectations, there will be no positive prediction error, and no extra dopamine. Business as usual. No corresponding praise or good feeling however good the work. Management by expectation is management by dopamine depletion.

Management by agreement is the antidote and will stop dopamine depletion management. This means clear agreements between both parties and bringing the expectations into the open. A worker can be accountable for fulfilling agreements but not expectations. Breaking an agreement breaks trust which is fundamental to business. In an emergency, the worker or manager can always renegotiate the agreement. Now, the expectation is where it belongs, *on keeping the agreement* and not on the task.

Here are the basics of a successful agreement. They work in business and in personal life.

An agreement begins with a request – something needs to be done.

- First, the circumstances are right to make an agreement, and both people are willing and able to do so. For example, an executive can ask their personal assistant to book a flight for them. It is an appropriate request given their respective positions.
- Second, the request is as detailed as necessary to be well completed. It may include when it is to be done and sometimes how it is to be done. The work will not happen all by itself. So, for example, the flight is to a certain city on a certain date, in business class on an Airbus 380. Some things may not matter, like the airline, so do not need to be spelled out.
- Third, closure. The other person can accept, reject or try to negotiate the request. If the request is accepted, then you have an agreement – a promise has been made. If rejected, then this is the prelude to negotiation. Negotiation may be limited at work, but in personal life, it happens all the time.

An agreement is easy if both sides want it. This is usually the case. Agreements do not make anyone right or wrong; they just ensure that something will happen. The obvious principle is keep your promises. A broken promise leads to a legitimate feeling of being let down and leads others to see you as unreliable. There is a legitimate expectation that a promise once given will be kept unless there are exceptional circumstances.

Addiction

Suppose you got a dopamine surge whatever happened? It sounds like fun, but it would be dangerous. You would not learn from experience; you would just want to repeat the same thing, and it would always seem more desirable whatever it was. You would crave the experience because it would always be better than you expected.. This is exactly what happens in addictions. Addiction is the dark side of the dopamine reward circuit. Addictive substances and activities tap into the reward circuits, release dopamine and trigger craving.

Understanding addiction is useful in coaching. The dopamine system is very general. You can get addicted to anything; it does not have to be a drug;

it just needs to give a dopamine surge. Coaches are unlikely to have clients who are drug addicts (however coaching is used increasingly with ex addicts to help them keep their life stable), but behavioural addictions are now better understood and can be part of a client's problem.

Human beings want to change their brain, to go beyond themselves, to access a different state of consciousness. Drugs do this. The second most traded commodity in the world – coffee – contains an addictive psychoactive drug.[17] Caffeine is the psychoactive drug in coffee (and tea and some energy drinks), and it acts directly on your brain. It makes you feel alert and counters feeling tired and sleepy. It is most people's drug of choice when they need to work late. Caffeine is an antagonist for the neurotransmitter adenosine; in other words, it can take the place of adenosine in the synapses. When it does, it blocks the adenosine receptors. Adenosine is made through the day, and the more it binds to the receptors, the sleepier you feel. At the end of the day, lots of adenosine has attached to the receptors with the result that you are ready for bed. Caffeine blocks the receptors, and adenosine can't bind to them, so no tired feelings. But there are consequences (of course). Adenosine keeps being made and accumulates. When the caffeine clears from the body, the tide of adenosine that has been waiting its chance latches onto the receptors. You feel more sleepy and unable to concentrate – a caffeine crash.

Alcohol, another psychoactive, addictive drug, has been around for at least 5,000 years. It reduces the enzymes that break down dopamine, so dopamine stays in the brain for longer. Alcohol also reduces brain activity and leads to a relaxing, 'chill out' feeling.

Nicotine in cigarettes is highly addictive.[18] Roughly one third of adults in the world are estimated to smoke tobacco on a regular basis. Nicotine is not a health problem; the problem is the poisons and carcinogens that are the fellow travellers in cigarettes. Nicotine is an agonist for acetylcholine, the neurotransmitter that is associated with arousal and attention. This means nicotine binds to the acetylcholine receptors at the synapses and strongly activates them. The neurons are fooled into thinking there is acetylcholine and so your alertness goes up. Nicotine is very addictive because the neurons in the VTA that produce dopamine also have receptors for acetylcholine. Nicotine binds to them, and the neurons are stimulated to produce dopamine in large quantities, hence the craving for tobacco.

We find it fascinating that a chapter that started with learning has glided into addiction. The same brain mechanisms are active in both. Learning is trying to make better predictions about the future, based on present experience. It is a beautiful mechanism, so good that we use it to teach artificial intelligence. Learning is pleasant too, when dopamine activates the nucleus accumbens. The downsides are disappointment, dissatisfaction and addiction.

Dissatisfaction is inevitable because we are always looking for something better – we are always trying to learn. We always want to move to a newer, shinier, cutting-edge, hedonistic treadmill. Addiction is when we go faster and faster on the same treadmill believing that it is the best in the world and we are really moving forward.

Learning, pleasure and the PFC

Learning and pleasure are both driven by the more 'primitive' parts of our brains: the basal ganglia and nucleus accumbens. Primitive does not mean stupid; it means necessary for life, so there is much less choice built in. Primitive parts of the brain work automatically. The reward circuit is myopic and impulsive. It pays attention to the moment; it is the ringleader of delay discounting. We also have a PFC which is activated through the mesocortical pathway. The most important parts of the PFC for directing learning are the dorsolateral prefrontal cortex (dlPFC), the OFC and the ACC. The dlPFC is important in planning, reasoning and self-control, fitting learning and rewards into a wider time frame while taking values into account. Your PFC will regulate the reward circuit and inhibit it where necessary.

This is powerful learning for clients. They can understand the dopamine circuits (that are outside their consciousness and control), and how they work. This will lead to more appropriate expectations, more agreements, less disappointments and more acceptance. It can lead to being grateful for past pleasures and better plans for future ones. It can lead to taking a step off the hedonistic treadmill. When we pay attention to the promptings of the dlPFC, those circuits are strengthened by neuroplasticity and become easier to use. If the messages from the dlPFC are ignored, the connections are weakened, and a vicious circle begins. The more you ignore the dlPFC, the weaker the connection and the weaker the voice. Research shows that addictions and eating disorders show first with increased activity in the dlPFC as it sends signals that are increasingly ignored. After that, there is less and less activity. The grey matter linking the reward circuits with the PFC is reduced in addicts. Memory and decision-making are also affected. Learning and its dark side, addiction, are all consolidated through neuroplasticity; the brain changes itself in response to our repeated thoughts and actions.

Behavioural addictions

It is not only drugs that can boost the dopamine system, but behaviours can too. The top eight addictions according to Google in 2016 were drugs, sex, porn, alcohol, sugar, love, gambling and Facebook. We are not sure what 'love' is doing here, but the others are clear. Drugs and alcohol directly affect the dopamine system. The others all seem to be a sort of 'supersize' stimulus, something new (at least in evolutionary terms) that our brain cannot handle.

To understand the idea of 'supersizing', we need to time travel. Imagine a coach had a time machine and was able to coach across time. Their client in prehistoric times was a Cro-Magnon group leader. What would be his valued goals? Probably an endless supply of salt, fat, alcohol and sugar. These were scarce and valuable. He would want them, seize them and consume them as much as possible. They would not be junk food to him. Now, they are not scarce; the local supermarket shelves overflow with sweet, tasty calorie crammed food easy to buy. Our reward circuit is overwhelmed, like a child used to a diet of porridge and dry bread, suddenly let lose in the cheesecake shop. Junk food overpowers the reward circuits that have not changed since Cro-Magnon times.

The same for porn. Sex is one of life's great rewards, but sexually provocative images used to be rare. Now, there is an endless supply at the click of a mouse. Gambling can be addictive; the environment, the stakes and the glamorous surroundings all make it a supersized stimulus, and our reward circuits are entranced. Research shows that chronic gamblers have a smaller pleasure response from the nucleus accumbens.[19] All the normal pleasures of food, sex, games and social contact can overstimulate the reward circuit and increase dopamine if they are supersized. This can lead to craving, a numbing of the reward and pleasure response and wanting that experience more and more just to provide the same level of pleasure: all symptoms of addiction.

Many parts of the Internet are unashamedly built on the model of addiction. Many social media sites are built to consume the users, not vice versa.[20] Unexpected and uncontrolled rewards from social networking sites are one example.[21]

Most digital companies use what is called A/B testing[22] when they want to know what features work best for customers. It can be applied to fonts, colour schemes, page design as well as content. It works like this. A business will create two sites. Identical except for the one difference they want to test. Then, they compare click rates and usage time for each site. The winning site will then be A/B tested for something else. These tests are cheap, easy and no one need ever know. Facebook used to run over 1,000 A/B tests a day. A/B testing is a way to 'supersize' the site for your nucleus accumbens, to make it as attractive as possible. Hundreds of smart people are behind many website pages scheming how to best erode your self-control.

Being addicted means depending on something to feel OK and craving it. At the same time, it causes problems. We have met executives show signs of addiction to increased profits. Others may be hooked on feeling powerful and putting people down. These issues can be complex. The first step is to get the executive to acknowledge the issue. They need insight. They need to notice other people's perspectives, to see the consequences of their behaviour and to understand it. Explaining what is happening from a neuroscientific view can help. They will need a system of behavioural feedback from the coach and from other stakeholders in the company.[23]

Exploring learning, dopamine and addictions has led us to how we try to predict the future and create expectations. These expectations are mental models or beliefs or habits of thinking and will be the subject of the next chapter.

Notes

1   The English comedian Eddie Izzard has a routine where he imagines what would have happened if Pavlov had used cats rather than dogs for his experiment. Although cats are much less predictable than dogs, the experiment would still have worked (perhaps not so well). Cats had to wait until 1935 for Schrodinger to put them on the scientific map (but not in a good way).

2   We don't know if the dogs thought the bell *caused* the food to appear. If they had, then that would have been canine superstition. Superstition is thinking an external event causes something to happen rather than just being associated with it. Superstition is another way to try to control and predict the world. The behaviourist B.F. Skinner ran experiments where he made pigeons superstitious by feeding them at arbitrary intervals. The pigeons developed strange rituals and twitches trying to make the food appear, because it had come when they did those things once before. In an unpredictable environment, they were trying to exert control in the only way they knew – by repeating what they did before, that was successful. We are more intelligent than pigeons and know that if we get a new client on the same day that we wear a new shirt, wearing that shirt again won't get another new client.

3   Latin for 'black substance'. Dopamine gives it the black colour from the pigment neuromelanin. Dopamine is made in one part of the SN called the pars compacta ('Compact part').

4   This is the dorsal or front part of the striatum and is made up of two structures called the caudate and the putamen. Dopamine is important in the basal ganglia to control movement.

5   The ventral striatum and dopamine mesolimbic pathway got an early reputation as the 'pleasure centre' of the brain from the work of Olds and Milner in the 1950s. They implanted electrodes into the brain of rats and then gave them the opportunity to stimulate their brain by pressing a lever. Some rats pushed the lever a few times and then did not bother. Others pressed the lever continuously until they collapsed exhausted. They were not interested in eating, sleeping and having sex. These rats had the electrodes implanted in what we now call the dopamine mesolimbic pathway from the VTA.

See Olds, J., & Milner, P. (1954). Positive reinforcement produced by electrical stimulation of septal area and other regions of rat brain. *Journal of Comparative and Physiological Psychology, 47* (6), 419.

This might be written off as the eccentricity of rats. However, research by Robert Heath in the 1950s, implanting electrodes into the septal region of the brain of psychiatric patients gave similar results. Given the opportunity, they would self-stimulate in preference even to sex and sleep. See Heath, R. G. (1963). Electrical self-stimulation of the brain in man. *American Journal of Psychiatry, 120* (6), 571–577.

These experiments made dopamine a hot research topic for many years.

However, later, it became clear that dopamine was involved in wanting the pleasure but not the pleasure itself. When researchers gave a dopamine antagonist (a chemical that sits in the receptors for the dopamine and blocks the dopamine from working), people would still feel the pleasure from the experience but did not feel driven to have it.

6   This is the back part of the striatum.

7   When dopamine-producing cells in the substantia nigra die, the result is muscle tremors and difficulty in initiating movements, because dopamine controls voluntary movements. This is Parkinson's disease. Parkinson's is treated with the drug L-Dopa which is converted to dopamine in the brain. Dopamine cannot be given directly as it does not pass the blood/brain barrier.

8   Mouse facial expressions are not very scientifically convincing. There is better evidence in another experiment: mice that are genetically engineered not to produce dopamine show no motivation to do anything and will starve to death rather than go to the trouble of getting up to go to the food bowl. Mice without dopamine are the archetypical lotus eaters.

9   The enzyme catechol-O-methyltransferase (COMT) breaks down dopamine once it has been used in the frontal lobes. Some people are born with a gene that reduces the activity of COMT, allowing the dopamine to stay around in the synapses longer.

10   It is now possible through advances in genetics and the Human Genome Project to find out your genetic dopamine profile for under 200 dollars.

11   The prediction error hypothesis was first proposed in 1972 by Robert Rescorla and Allan Wagner. Unsurprisingly, it is known as the Rescorla-Wagner hypothesis. Whether prediction error is the whole story of how dopamine works in learning is still disputed. However, prediction error learning has been found to be remarkable effective in artificial intelligence reinforcement learning.

AIs run through many possibilities (e.g. chess moves) and reinforce the networks that lead to good positions (their programmed reward). After time, the strongest networks are the ones that have the most success. The best moves are worked out purely pragmatically – they are what lead to success – by trial and error. Humans learn more quickly, but machines are more thorough. So far, they have the upper hand in winning rule-based games (Chess, Go) against the top human players.

12   Schultz, W., Dayan, P., & Montague, P. R. (1997). A neural substrate of prediction and reward. *Science, 275* (5306), 1593–1599.

13   Schultz, W. (1998). Predictive reward signal of dopamine neurons. *Journal of Neurophysiology, 80* (1), 1–27.

14   See the book, 'Punished by Rewards' by Alfie Cohn (Houghton Mifflin, 1999) for a good treatment of how business gets rewards wrong. The dopamine research was not known then, but the links are easy to see.

15   There is plenty of research on lottery winners. For example, see Gardner, J., & Oswald, A. J. (2007). Money and mental wellbeing: A longitudinal study of medium-sized lottery wins. *Journal of Health Economics, 26* (1), 49–60.

There is also literature on the influence of income levels on happiness. As you might expect, raising your base income makes you happier in the short term but not in the long term, and there is little correlation between reported levels of happiness and levels of income. Above the level of $60,000, a year reported happiness levels flatline. Money can't buy you happiness, but lack of it can buy you misery.

See Easterlin, R. A. (1995). Will raising the incomes of all increase the happiness of all? *Journal of Economic Behaviour & Organization, 27* (1), 35–47.

16   *The Teachings of Don Juan, a Yaqui way of knowledge.* University of California Press, 1968.

17   Coffee is second only to oil in volume of trade internationally. Coffee has an interesting history. When it first came to England in the 1500s, it was very popular

especially among men, so much so, that in 1674, a group of women circulated a petition called 'The Women's Petition against Coffee'. It stated that 'Coffee leads men to trifle away their time, scald their chops and spend their money, all for a little base, black, thick, nasty, bitter, stinking, nauseous puddle water'. It's been a long journey from there to Starbucks.

18 The success rate of quitting cigarettes is around ten percent, about the same as for heroin. Looking at success rates of quitting, nicotine is as addictive as heroin.

19 See Goudriaan, A. E., Oosterlaan, J., de Beurs, E., & Van den Brink, W. (2004). Pathological gambling: A comprehensive review of biobehavioral findings. *Neuroscience & Biobehavioral Reviews, 28* (2), 123–141.

    Also Reuter, J., Raedler, T., Rose, M., Hand, I., Gläscher, J., & Büchel, C. (2005). Pathological gambling is linked to reduced activation of the mesolimbic reward system. *Nature Neuroscience, 8* (2), 147–148.

20 Sean Parker, a former executive and early shareholder of Facebook, has said that Facebook exploits human psychology as the social media platform is designed to be addictive. He talks about the site giving a little dopamine hit to keep you interested.

    See the full article here: https://www.axios.com/sean-parker-unloads-on-face book-god-only-knows-what-its-doing-to-our-childrens-brains-1513306792-f855e7b4-4e99-4d60-8d51-2775559c2671.html (Accessed 3rd May 2018).

21 This is based on a psychological model called 'variable reward schedule' first described by B.F. Skinner in the 1950s. He showed mice were more responsive to random rewards. They would press a lever and sometimes get a tasty treat. And sometimes nothing. These mice would press the lever repeatedly. Mice who received the same reward every time did not. The repetition is one way to try to control an unpredictable environment. Unexpected rewards give increased dopamine, but these are *randomly scheduled* unexpected rewards, so they cannot learn from them. They could not plan any strategy to get them except keep pressing. The next one could be the tasty treat (or not). Same in gambling. The next play could be the big win (but probably not). The dopamine possibility overrides the dlPFC.

22 Reputedly first used by Google in 2000.

23 There are many good coaching models and interventions for this. A very good place to start is the book by Marshall Goldsmith, 'What got you here, won't get you there' (Hyperion 2007) which shows some of these behaviours and how to deal with them, without the neuroscience parallel explanation.

Bibliography

Castaneda, C. (1968). *The teachings of Don Juan, a Yaqui way of knowledge*. Berkeley, CA: University of California Press 1968.

Cohn, A. (1999). *Punished by rewards*. Boston, MA: Houghton Mifflin.

Easterlin, R. A. (1995). Will raising the incomes of all increase the happiness of all? *Journal of Economic Behaviour & Organization, 27*(1), 35–47.

Gardner, J., & Oswald, A. J. (2007). Money and mental wellbeing: A longitudinal study of medium-sized lottery wins. *Journal of Health Economics, 26*(1), 49–60.

Goldsmith, M. (2007). *What got you here, won't get you there*. London, England: Hyperion.

Goudriaan, A. E., Oosterlaan, J., de Beurs, E., & Van den Brink, W. (2004). Pathological gambling: A comprehensive review of biobehavioral findings. *Neuroscience & Biobehavioral Reviews, 28*(2), 123–141.

Heath, R. G. (1963). Electrical self-stimulation of the brain in man. *American Journal of Psychiatry, 120*(6), 571–577.

Olds, J., & Milner, P. (1954). Positive reinforcement produced by electrical stimulation of septal area and other regions of rat brain. *Journal of Comparative and Physiological Psychology, 47*(6), 419.

Reuter, J., Raedler, T., Rose, M., Hand, I., Gläscher, J., & Büchel, C. (2005). Pathological gambling is linked to reduced activation of the mesolimbic reward system. *Nature Neuroscience, 8*(2), 147–148.

Schultz, W. (1998). Predictive reward signal of dopamine neurons. *Journal of Neurophysiology, 80*(1), 1–27. Retrieved from https://www.axios.com/sean-parker-unloads-on-facebook-god-only-knows-what-its-doing-to-our-childrens-brains-1513306792-f855e7b4-4e99-4d60-8d51-2775559c2671.html

Schultz, W., Dayan, P., & Montague, P. R. (1997). A neural substrate of prediction and reward. *Science, 275*(5306), 1593–1599.

Chapter 9

Mental models

We began this book with three questions:

Where are you now?
Where do you want to go?
What stops you?

The first two questions are about goals and values. Dopamine, the reward circuit, expectations, emotions and the limbic system have given us some answers.

Now the third question – what stops you from achieving what you want?

The main difficulty is usually not the goal, but the way of thinking about the goal.

How we think about the goal is based on our mental models – the ideas that govern how we think about ourselves, others and how the world works.

A mental model is an idea about how things work; it predicts what will happen and creates expectations about the situation, ourselves or other people. We act on our mental models. They may be based on experience or may be picked up from others, (especially when we are young and have little experience about how the world works).

Mental models are constructs that help us to react to events. They are the cognitive crystallisation of what you learn from the dopamine learning system. They are probably constructed and organised by a system named as 'The interpreter'[1] in neuroscience. We will look at this in more detail in a later chapter. The interpreter is the name given to the system that pulls the pieces together into a coherent story. This takes place in the left hemisphere of the prefrontal cortex (PFC). It takes in all the chaotic information and makes sense of it by linking causes and effect and then constructing our mental models. We then behave according to these mental models and are freed from simple stimulus – response behaviour.

Mental models are habits of thinking, learned, repeated and acted on without reflection. They are sometimes known as 'beliefs', but 'belief' has a religious connotation, and coaching does not go there. The word 'belief' also implies a fact about the world and not an idea *we have* about the world. Coaching does not deal with whether beliefs are true, only their effect on the client. We do not deal with mental models about the laws of physics (e.g. we all 'believe' in gravity, in the sense we act as if it is true[2]). In coaching, we deal with mental models that affect the client's happiness and achievements, are not provable either way and have not been properly tested.

There are two types of mental models: those that empower us and those that are limiting.

Those that empower us are inspiring and open up possibilities. They give space for thought. For example, 'The universe is a friendly place' or 'Whatever happens, I can learn from it'. Limiting mental models stop us from achieving, from creating and from being happy. For example, 'I can't win without other people losing' or 'Success only comes with great effort'. Confirmation bias does a lot to keep existing mental models in place. Mental models can be hard to identify; we usually just act them out. We will only challenge limiting ones when we become aware of them and they stop us being happy or achieving something we want. The work of a coach is mainly to help the client identify and challenge limiting mental models.

How we acquire mental models

We like to think we choose our mental models, but we pick them up as we live. Limiting mental models come mostly through misunderstandings based on partial information. Without full information, it is like trying to work out the rules of tennis by watching only one side of the court. You do not see the whole situation, and you draw the wrong conclusions and then think tennis is a weird game.

One common misunderstanding is mistaking correlation for causation. One client recounted how his parents always seemed to be fighting when he was growing up. He thought he was somehow responsible, but the parental fights were over something else entirely. Children do not know how the world works, and it is easy for them to draw the wrong conclusion. One funny example was when the five-year-old daughter of a friend asked her why everyone had to break a bone when they were a child. Our friend said, 'They don't!' and asked why she thought they did. It turned out that every adult the girl knew had suffered a childhood accident and broke a bone. It could be arm, leg, wrist, toe or finger, but everyone had done it. She concluded it was an inevitable *rite de passage* to adulthood. Our friend quickly explained the true situation, or else the girl would surely have found a way to break a bone in order to achieve adulthood. Broken bones in childhood are common – but not necessary.

Another way to acquire mental models is by imitation. Children pick up physical and mental mannerisms from their parents and significant adults in their life – about how people should treat each other, when to lie and how to act socially. Children extract the principles that fuel their parents' behaviour from watching adults behave, just as they extract the grammatical rules of their native language from listening to adults speak. If our actions are a language, then our beliefs are the grammar – the invisible structure that determines why we do what we do. Children pick up these patterns easily.

A third way is by repetition. Once is an occasion, twice is a coincidence, but three times is a pattern. Our brain looks for patterns all the time. Lending money to three people who do not pay it back could create a mental model that people are untrustworthy. It could create a mental model that I am a poor judge of character. Neither of them are good conclusions based on so few instances. Notice system 1 at work here: the principle of availability. Source amnesia magnifies this pattern. Source amnesia means we tend to remember a fact but forget where it came from. Different sources blend into one, even if the circumstances were very different. They all get generalised into one pattern, which could be a limiting mental model.

One significant event can also build a mental model. An example might be lending money to a friend. They abscond (proving they were no friend really). Because it involved a trusted friend, it counts more than several instances with strangers. Again, a mental model might be built – that people are untrustworthy or that I am a poor judge of character. Neither of them are fair based on one occasion. Another example would be investing a lot of money in a business that fails. The size of the investment makes that example significant. Whenever the consequences are painful, the amygdala will be activated and associate a fear response to lending money in future. This will get formalised by the PFC into a mental model that people are not trustworthy.

Finally, the idea may not be based on experience at all. It could be picked up through peer pressure like picking up chewing gum on the soles of our shoes.

Our expectant brain – the spell checker

We do not just react to the world, we interact with it. Our mental models direct our attention and our actions.

How do we make sense of the world?
How do we know what to do?
We use mental models.

The mental models generate expectations.
    The brain modifies these expectations with information from the outside world through the senses.
    This is the opposite to how it appears to us. We naively think we take in the information and make sense of it, but we do not. Your brain *starts* with expectations built from previous experience, uses them to make sense of

incoming sense data and serves up the result. The brain operates like a very sophisticated spell checker with predictive spelling – it makes its best guess about what is happening based on the context and information it has. Smart spell checkers take note of your use of words, how you express yourself, including the abbreviations.[3] It learns from what you do and predicts what is likely to come next. This is exactly what your brain does. without this initial prediction, the process would be much slower. We have already seen this system in operation with the dopamine prediction error. We start with what we know already. Correcting expectations with data is the easiest way to learn, and the brain is always looking for shortcuts. Most of the time, there will be little modification.

Predict – then modify

The brain operates on the principle of predict first – then modify (if needed). The visual system gives the clearest examples. When we look, the occipital cortex sends it predictions to the thalamus. The thalamus is the relay station, sending signals where they need to go. The thalamus compares what comes from the eyes and what is expected by the visual cortex and sends the difference back to the cortex to process. This is how we learn about the world – by noticing the difference between what we expect and what we sense out there.[4] Sometimes, we can almost catch this process on the fly. For example, Joseph went into the bathroom and for a split second, 'saw' a cat sleeping on the pile of towels. It is the cat's favourite spot; the towels had a vague 'cat shape'. He expected to see the cat there. The impression was immediately corrected by the feedback from his eyes – no cat, just towels.

Optical illusions are great examples where the brain's expectation clashes with the outside world. The result is that we see what the brain expects, not what is there (see Figure 9.1).

Figure 9.1 Do you believe your eyes?

Which is the darker, square A or square B?
Obviously, square A is darker. Seeing is believing.
Only it isn't. Both squares are the same colour (see the diagram on the right)

Our visual cortex has some hardwired rules about interpreting light and shadow and direction. We 'see' what these rules predict, not what is there. In this case, we cannot override the built-in rules in our visual cortex. We cannot see the squares the same colour, even when we know they are.[5]

Not only does the visual cortex generate expectations, but it smooths out our perception to fit the expectations. We can swing our eyes across the room and experience one continuous smooth movement, not a crazy jerking sensation where everything swings around. We blink frequently but never experience the world going black several times a minute. Our eyes have a blind spot in the middle where the optic nerve goes into the retina, but we do not see a black hole 'out there'. Your experience of reading is a smooth flow of sensible words, even through your eyes is jumping from pillow to post in short, jerky movement known as saccades. (And we read what we expect to read, so you probably read the last sentence as making sense, when it does not.)

Our predictions influence all our senses. Have you ever wondered how you can move your arm easily and naturally, yet when someone else moves it, you become aware of it in a different way? It is because the brain has not predicted the movement so it feels strange. Have you wondered why you cannot tickle yourself? It is because our brain can predict what we will feel because it is sending commands to the fingers to do the tickling. Tickling must be unpredictable otherwise it does not work. When you are tickled, the skin receptors send a message to the somatosensory cortex which decodes touch sensations. If you tickle yourself, the signal is dampened.[6] We wonder if this applies to self-coaching. When you coach yourself, you know what questions are coming. They are not as stimulating as the unpredictable questions asked by a coach.[7] Our imagination can be very creative, but we need a reality 'out there' for feedback to learn.[8] No feedback, no learning. Self-coaching, like mental rehearsal, only goes so far. Having an external coach is more fun and more effective.

We can easily make mistakes by relying on one source of information, so the brain uses all the senses to construct its predictions. It takes in more information than it needs. We rely primarily on the visual sense, but the brain pays attention to the other senses too. For example, we pay attention to lip reading when listening.[9] When the auditory does not match the visual, it sounds (or looks) odd. Watching a singer lip synch badly makes the song sound wrong. The brain does an incredible job, taking in huge amounts of information through the senses, comparing it with its built-in rules and its learned expectations and generating meaning and actions from the mess. It does this all the time seamlessly, making the world look like it is sensible and predictable. Producing a sensible and predictable world is the brain's greatest miracle.

Implications for coaches

We are not objective observers. We start with expectations and predictions generated by our mental models. The famous saying sums it up, 'It ain't what you don't know that gets you into trouble. It's what you know for sure that just ain't so'.

Our mental models are held by the left PFC gathering and integrating information from many parts of the brain. Emotions from the amygdala, memories from the hippocampus and values from the reward system. To learn, we need to update the mental models with feedback from the outside, but often this does not happen. Feedback about our physical senses is impossible to ignore. If you thought gravity did not apply to you, you would get immediate feedback that would bring you down to earth. Mental models are different, and there are many ways to ignore, distort or reinterpret feedback.

First, we are attached to our mental models. They are ours. They give us certainty in a confusing world. We hang on to them to the last minute.

Second, we use confirmation bias, cherry picking the evidence and ignoring feedback that goes against the mental model.

Third, limiting mental models will limit our actions, and this limits the possible feedback. Mental models become self-fulfilling prophecies because we don't put ourselves in a situation where they can be seriously challenged. For example, suppose a client thinks his team is incompetent. Therefore, obviously (to him), he never delegates and never asks for ideas. Therefore, he never puts himself in a position to get feedback that might challenge that mental model. This is how limiting mental models sustain themselves – by limiting the experience, we allow ourselves. Here is a perfect illustration – how to keep an elephant from escaping using only a thin piece of rope. When the elephants are young, their handlers tie their leg to a stake in the ground, so they cannot wander away. The baby elephant is not strong enough to uproot the stake. They do not try to test their strength again, even when they are fully grown and strong enough to uproot the stake easily, because they 'know' they can't. Their mental model tells them what they can and cannot do, so they do not try.

The best coaching intervention for limiting mental models is to engage the client's system 2 thinking and agree an action for the client that will get good feedback.

Here is an example. Joseph coached a manager who complained of stress and overwork. It was clear that he was doing more work than he needed to or was asked to. We were talking about multitasking and efficient working and he said something quite telling, 'I could ask my assistant to do more, but if you want something done well, you have to do it yourself'. This is a limiting mental model. He went on to say, 'It takes me more time to correct something than it does to do it in the first place'. (Which is only relevant if the mental model is true.) He knew how to delegate, but he hardly ever did. He had a series of incompetent assistants in the past, which had reinforced his mental model. As long as he does not test his mental model in the present moment, he will not learn that *this* assistant, *this* work and *this* time might be different from *that* assistant, *that* work and *that* time in the past. We framed it as a learning opportunity. He was going to discover if this assistant was any good. He agreed to delegate a few small tasks. When those went well, he did more and within a month, his workload was down, and he was much happier and less stressed. He still kept the really important stuff for himself.

This mental model, '*If you want something done well, you must do it yourself*', has three important qualities that are shared by nearly all limiting mental models.

First, it is expressed as if it were about the world, about other people and their capabilities. It isn't. It's about the client. Every idea is expressed by someone. To be pedantic, the full statement would be, '*I think that* if you want something done well, you have to do it yourself'. Now the idea is owned – by the client. It is not about the nature of the world. The client agreed with this rephrasing with the proviso that it was true in his experience. So far so good.

Second, it is expressed as a timeless, general rule. Here is a full unravelling of the thought: 'In the past, I have delegated to certain people in a certain way, in certain circumstances, and the results were not good. Based on that, I am wary of delegating now for fear that this experience will be repeated'. Logically, he could not fault this, although emotionally he started to feel anxious. Joseph assured him that he was not trying to get him to delegate, only to consider testing the idea.

Third, the mental model has two emotional connections. One is away from – the amygdala had stored some unpleasant memories of delegation. The memory gets linked to the present and the thought of delegating activates the memories. Our brain is very good at making associations. Damasio's somatic marker hypothesis would predict that his brain is taking the emotional aspects of his experiences of delegating, together with other ideas and input, and processing them in the orbitofrontal cortex (OFC). The verdict comes out in favour of avoiding the risk now (status quo bias). Instead, he decided to work harder, faster and longer to try to catch up. This short-term solution was not sustainable. The coach must deal with the emotional aspect. One way is to make the client aware of the risks of *not* changing by asking questions like:

What would happen if you did not do this?
How long are you prepared to tolerate this situation?

These will not change the mental model but will make the status quo less comfortable.

The second emotional connection is positive and towards. Good work is important, and Joseph's client took pride in his results. For him, delegation resulted in second-rate work. He cared about the quality of his work. Mental models may be limiting, but there is always a positive value behind them.

To change, the client must see that the mental model is limiting them and be willing to get feedback. They need to step out of the model. The coach does not try to disprove mental models; they do not have any stake in them one way or another. They help the client to take an action to get feedback on the model. With a well-designed action step, they will get balancing feedback and will naturally update the mental model. The update will still express the positive value (in this case, the value of good work).

The neuroscience of 'shoulds'

Mental models are often expressed in the language of 'Should' or 'Shouldn't'. The English language has many words like this: must and mustn't and 'have to'. All imply a rule. Moral and ethical rules are fine. However, usually 'should' implies a self-imposed limiting rule. For example, a client might say, 'I should get a better work-life balance and get home earlier'. This is not the same as saying, 'I want to get home earlier'. Wanting is driven by dopamine; it is an authentic feeling. 'Shoulds' are not backed by dopamine. They are imaginary ideas we impose on ourselves. 'Should' is usually shorthand for, 'I feel a pressure to do this, but I am not doing it'.

We meet this pattern many times in our coaching practice. Executives think they should exercise more, treat their team better and get a better work-life balance. As long as they think they 'should', they are not actually doing it. They have an internal conflict. They want to, but do not. In simple terms, the PFC, and especially the dorsal part that generates rules, puts the idea forward, but the reward circuits are not on board. There is no action from the basal ganglia.

A 'should' goal is not an authentic goal. The values and emotions are not strong enough, and the reward circuit is not engaged. It will not happen unless the client converts it into an authentic goal – something they want. Then, the reward system participates, and they will be spurred to action. Until this happens, the client has the worst of both worlds – feeling they should do something, not doing it and feeling bad about it. If a client says they 'should' get a better work-life balance, it's not a goal. Nothing is happening; it is a weak expression of hope. A coach should never align themselves with a 'should' goal.

Instead, ask some of the following questions:

Why do you want to work on this now?
(Anything significant happened that makes the client want to tackle this issue? If there is nothing new, then there is no reason to change.)

Do you really want this?

(The PFC will say 'yes', but the other parts of the brain will send their own non-verbal message and the answer will not be congruent.)

What stops you – honestly?

(This gives permission for the other parts of the brain to get control of Wernicke's and Broca's area and express themselves verbally.)

What would have to be true for you to really want this?

Then a real discussion can begin. There will be values, emotions and rewards on both sides and only by discussing them will the client understand the issue.

Sometimes, the client agrees a small action designed to try out the change and see how it goes. No commitment to follow up. Dealing with work-life balance is often like this.

The client will commit to the goal only when they can honestly say, with the important parts of their brain on board, that they want the goal. Otherwise, it is best to forget it for the moment.

Doubt and certainty

Mental models are impossible to prove or disprove.

How certain is the client about their idea?

We tend to treat mental models in a linear way: true or false, yes or no. As a result, we do not bother to test, or we are afraid to test (amygdala hijack). A good coach can chip away at the client's belief but even so, strongly held ideas (the ones the client gives the greatest probability), need feedback to shake them.

Find out, on a scale of one to ten how strongly the client believes the idea. Ten represents certainty, 100 percent probability that they are right. Most mental models will score between an eight and a six.[10] The more certain the mental model, the more feedback is required to change it. We ask the question every session when we are working with a client on limiting mental models and chart how their certainty drops.

Here is a coaching process for testing limiting mental models – but make sure the client owns it first – as something they think rather than something that exists as true 'out there' in the world.

•   *Believability*

Ask for the events that led the client to believe the idea. If there are, then the idea is reasonable based on that experience. If there are not, you can ask what leads the client to think it is true. How far can they trust the source of the idea? They may have source amnesia.

- *Influencing factors*

  What were the influencing factors that led to the experience?

  What factors were there at the time that contributed to the result?

  Which one of those influencing factors has changed or can be changed to get a different and better result now?
- *Positive implications*

  Is there an upside of keeping the idea?

  There always is, at the very least it gives some security.

  The client needs to know this.
- *Value*

  What is important about this?

  What value does it represent?

  Why did they adopt this idea rather than let the experience go as a transient event?
- *Preferred idea*

  What mental model would they prefer?

  (This cannot be a direct opposite of the existing one.)

  It needs to have the first-person pronoun 'I' in it, and it needs to honour the value.

  So, for example, if the limiting idea is *'I cannot trust people to do a good job if I delegate',* then the preferred idea might be, *'I am willing to delegate work to find out how trustworthy people are to create good enough work and I can control the consequences'.*
- *Action*

  What small action step can you do that is safe and tests this factor, so you can get better feedback on the idea?

  These questions will help the client create an action to get feedback. In the example of delegating, a client could vary the way they delegated. They might delegate a small piece of work to two different people and give themselves time to correct it if needed. If that does not work, try something else. Keep the goal and value and be as flexible as necessary with the means.

  Your mental models are not you. The Internet entrepreneur Marc Andreessen has a nice saying, 'Have strong beliefs, loosely held'. In other words, hold your ideas strongly and fight for them. But keep testing them so you have *the best ones you can at any time.* Always look for the best ideas and be prepared to abandon them when a better one comes along.

Notes

1 Gazzaniga, M. (2012). *Who's in charge? Free will and the science of the brain.* Hachette, UK.
2 The gravity example is one extreme – believed by nearly everyone and supported by fact and experience. All our experience to date leads us to predict that if we

fall off a chair with no extra technology or supports, we will hit the floor rather than the ceiling.

3   Even very good spell checkers can make hilarious mistakes and we all know examples. We like the one where a friend texted his wife that she was vehicular. (He said he meant beautiful, but who knows?)

4   Our brains work on difference. A normal, healthy person in a sensory deprivation tank with all sound, sight and temperature fixed will begin to hallucinate within fifteen minutes. The hallucination is the brain losing patience – if there is no difference out there, it starts to make some.

5   There are many fascinating optical illusions and tricks on www.michaelbach.de/ot/index.html (Accessed 5th May 2018).

6   Blakemore, S. J., Wolpert, D. M., & Frith, C. D. (1998). Central cancellation of self-produced tickle sensation. *Nature Neuroscience, 1* (7), 635–640.

7   But they must be good questions. Self-coaching is better than unskilled questioning.

8   We can get an idea and then test it, by acting on it and getting feedback. But you cannot learn anything from the idea itself.

9   This accounts for the so-called McGurk effect. The sound we hear depends on how we see the speaker's lips moving. An 'Ah' sound will sound like 'baa' if we see the speaker's lips making a shape for saying a 'b' sound. It will sound like 'faa' if we see the lips framing an 'f' sound. This is an auditory illusion, and we cannot override it. (Except by closing our eyes.)

    See https://www.youtube.com/watch?v=jtsfidRq2tw for the full effect.

10 We have never had a client give a score of ten. If they did, we would ask them to give a score to their belief in gravity and ask if it was on the same level of certainty.

Bibliography

Blakemore, S. J., Wolpert, D. M., & Frith, C. D. (1998). Central cancellation of self-produced tickle sensation. *Nature Neuroscience, 1*(7), 635–640.

Gazzaniga, M. (2012). *Who's in charge? Free will and the science of the brain*. Hachette UK.

www.michaelbach.de/ot/index.html

https://www.youtube.com/watch?v=jtsfidRq2tw

Chapter 10

Our social brain

No man is an island,
Entire of itself.
Each is a piece of the continent,
A part of the main.
If a clod be washed away by the sea,
Europe is the less.
As well as if a promontory were.
As well as if a manor of thine own
Or of thine friend's were.
Each man's death diminishes me,
For I am involved in mankind.
Therefore, send not to know
For whom the bell tolls,
It tolls for thee.

John Donne 1624

Our social brain

We have been writing about the brain as if it were an island, entire of itself, but the reality is much closer to the poetic lines of John Donne. We all have an individual and unique brain; yet its individuality and uniqueness are made through others. We are social beings, unable to live fully without others and our brain reflects that. Our brain needs care, love and attention from others to develop at all. These are essential brain nutrients. Our brain is formed through our interaction with others and connects us to others. This chapter will explore some of those ways.

Our brain is rather like a river. The river looks separate, and it can be studied as a separate system, but the more you study, the more you realise that it is a flow of water connecting to other flows, constantly changing. It stagnates and dries up without a supply of water. It looks separate only because of our limited perspective.

The social connection pervades many business themes. Leadership was studied for many years as a group of individual qualities: charisma, vision and communication skills, but leadership is a social phenomenon 'Leaders' cannot exist without 'followers'. They must be good at connecting with others on an individual level. But leaders are also part of a group and represent their group against other groups. Leadership is a neurological, a psychological, a cultural and a sociological experience. The social dimension is an integral part of us. Therapists, mentors, trainers and coaches all need to understand how we connect with each other.

Let's start with happiness. Our happiness depends on others. Being with friends and connecting with others gives pleasure, and pleasure is evolution's way of telling us we are doing something right. Having many good social relationships correlates well with a higher level of happiness. Being lonely makes us unhappy. There is a difference between being alone and being lonely. Being alone is not negative. It means you are not with anyone else at that moment. Most people like to be alone if it is on their own terms and they have a network of good relationships they can call on. Being lonely is being alone too often without wanting to. Being lonely is feeling you do not have a good supporting network of people. Being lonely is painful and you can be lonely in a crowd. Loneliness seems to make us more alert to threats, activates the amygdala and increases levels of stress hormones.[1] Recent studies[2] have shown perceived isolation is associated with a shorter life and a greater risk of heart disease. Lonely people are also more prone to cognitive decline. A very large social study in 1979 reported that people with few social contacts were between two and three times more likely to die of any cause than others with a normal social life.

Social isolation is painful. In one cunning experiment, volunteers were invited to take part in research and then ignored. (To be ignored was the research they were invited to take part in, but they did not know that.) These people reported very high levels of anger and sadness.[3] This is not surprising as ostracism from your group meant death for most of human evolutionary history.

Friendship is very important. We want and seek friends, so it is important we show we are valuable for others to attract friends. We do this through good appearance, good health, looking powerful and helping others. We do good, and we want others to see we are doing good. We want to fit in socially. (Remember Cialdini's social pressures?) We frequently compare ourselves to others, regarding our social worth and reputation. We want to be part of a group as a valued and important member. However much we encourage clients to measure their own progress by comparing themselves now with themselves in the past, they still compare themselves to others. It comes naturally. It is the basis of social media.

Levels of the neurotransmitter serotonin are linked with social status. High serotonin level seems to go with high self-esteem and social rank, which may be partly how serotonin modulates mood. It is impossible to claim a cause effect link either way. We don't know if high serotonin will take you to the top of the social ladder, or that climbing the social ladder will lead to higher serotonin levels. However, it is another example of how social factors influence individual neurochemistry. We also know serotonin levels link with increased self-confidence and better health. Low serotonin levels are linked with decreased confidence, higher response to stress, depression and higher probability of ill health.

How do we connect with others?

The brain has developed a very clever way.

Mirror neurons

Mirror neurons are one of the most important recent discoveries in neuroscience. Mirror neurons are neurons that fire when we act, *and* when we see the same action performed by others. They 'mirror' the action. (They are called 'mirror neurons', but single neurons do not control actions, they are part of a circuit.)

Mirror neurons are your brain's way of connecting with others by imitation. We learn from and depend on others from the moment of birth. Imitation is the way we learn. Not knowing, we copy someone else who seems to know. Newborn babies can imitate facial expression within minutes of birth, although they cannot control the rest of their bodies.

It may be that mirror neurons were discovered by accident. In the late 1990s, a group of scientists led by Giacomo Rizzolatti from the University of Parma in Italy were studying the motor command neuron circuits in monkeys in the premotor cortex – the part of the cortex that deals with planning and executing actions. According to the story, one of the scientists reached for something in the laboratory, and there was immediately a burst of electrical activity from the brain of a monkey sitting passively. (The monkey had electrodes implanted in its brain.) This was odd. The monkey had not moved. The researchers followed this up and discovered the mirror neurons – the first time these had been directly observed.[4] Neurons in the monkey's motor cortex controlling movement had fired in response to observing the researcher's movement.

This led to a huge interest in mirror neurons, especially to establish their presence in humans. Sure enough, later research by Fadiga using transcranial magnetic stimulation showed that mirror neurons were also present in the human brain.[5] More experiments made direct recordings from mirror neurons in humans.[6] Mirror neurons have been intensely studied since then and are helping us understand many neuroscientific puzzles. Some mirror neurons fire for the same action whether it is performed or observed. Others fire for actions that achieve a similar goal. It is remarkable that cells in the brain seem to be able to respond to intentions. They will fire when someone reaches for a cup of coffee, but not when they make an identical movement with no goal. Mirror neurons mirror goals as well as actions. For us, it is intentions that matter, not actions. Movement can have many possible intentions, and it matters which one it is. Is it a greeting? Is it a threat or is it random? We do not know how mirror neurons distinguish between intentions, but these give a partial answer to how we mind-read other people. Actions are visible, but goals and intentions are invisible. In effect, the mirror neuron system allows us to adopt another person's point of view – it is the neuroscientific parallel of being able to 'walk in another person's shoes'.

Another person's shoes

How do we metaphorically walk in another person's shoes? It is a walk of empathy – a skill we take for granted. The dominant explanation for a long time was that we observe others' behaviour and theorise about what mental state could give rise to it, rather like scientists observing nature and trying to explain it by making hypotheses. This is long winded, complicated and much too cognitive. It puts too much faith in the prefrontal cortex (PFC) and makes the brain into a little scientist, whereas it is more like a creative opportunist.

It seems we automatically simulate, by means of mirror neurons, what other people do and intend, to understand what they are feeling and thinking. Mirror neurons generate a kind of virtual reality recreation. They put us in touch with others' actions and intentions and give us the possibility of 'mind-reading others'. They provide a sort of embodied simulation.

How does the brain know who is moving – you or another person? The answer seems to be in an area called the parietal operculum in the right hemisphere. This area is involved in representing our body image, so much so that damage to that area leads to strange mistakes about the body, where it is and how it works.[7] This area is not part of the mirror neuron network and is activated only when *we do the action*, not when we observe it. The activity marks that we are the actor, not another. Furthermore, the mirror neurons discharge much more strongly for actions of self than actions of other. So, even with mirror neuron simulation of activity, our brain keeps track of who is really acting.

Another important area is the right supramarginal gyrus (RSG), which controls your perception of yourself as opposed to others.[8] It is in the somatosensory cortex and is part of the mirror neuron system. Disruption to this area disrupts the ability to distinguish our judgements from those of others. When this area is not working well, people project their ideas onto others.

It is likely we have 'super mirror neurons' that modulate other mirror neurons, otherwise we would be too influenced by the actions of others.[9] Some mirror neurons have been discovered[10] (in the orbitofrontal cortex [OFC] and the anterior cingulate cortex [ACC]) that fire when the person does an action but shut down completely when they only observe the action. It seems these cells inhibit other cells, telling motor neurons that the observed action should not be imitated.

Mirror neurons may also respond to language, helping us to understand it by internally simulating what we read. We have many linguistic metaphors using the body. We talk of 'grasping a subject', 'giving a hand', 'a kick in the pants', 'The kiss of death', 'stretching the truth' and so on. It may be that mirror neurons fire for these actions to give us an embodied understanding.[11] If this is so, then coaches should make use of embodied language and concrete metaphors, as these will be more easily understood than abstract concepts. *Mirror neurons do not fire for abstract concepts.*

Empathy

Empathy is our emotional connection with others. It is not an all or nothing trait, possessed by some and not by others. Some people are more empathic by nature, some less so. Genetics no doubt plays a part. Different parts of the brain need to work together for empathy, and it varies from person to person.[12]

Empathy is a combination of three abilities:

- the ability to understand the feelings of others.
- the ability to share the feelings of another.
- the ability to respond with an appropriate emotion or action to the feelings of another.

These three parts – understanding, sharing and responding – do not always go together.

Understanding the feelings of others is *cognitive empathy*. Most people have cognitive empathy; they can understand intellectually what another person is feeling. Cognitive empathy is our ability to mind-read. We are as good as we need to be, not so good that we might consider other people's interests greater than our own. A study by William Ickes[13] concluded we are about twenty percent accurate with total strangers, thirty percent with close friends and about thirty-five percent between spouses. These are not very impressive figures. Yet any mind-reading is a miracle, as we have no access to the mind of another.

We can only understand what another person is thinking if we assume that others have minds like our own. Then, we attribute desires, goals and thoughts to them and predict their actions. This is known as 'Theory of Mind' and develops in children between the ages of three and five. The right temporoparietal junction (RTPJ)[14] seems to be a key part of our ability to understand others.[15] This must involve somehow putting our self in their place, as the RTPJ is also involved in 'out of the body' experiences. Another area of the brain involved in theory of mind is the posterior superior temporal sulcus (PSTS).[16] This is activated when you follow the direction of someone else's gaze.[17] We are sensitive to where people look, not just where they point. We look into another person's eyes when we want to know what they are interested in and what they are feeling. We need and expect a certain amount of eye contact. Working out a person's intention and their internal state must involve some planning, so it is no surprise that the PFC is also involved, in particular the dorsal medial PFC.[18] This part of the brain is also active when we think about our own actions, which makes sense if the mirror neuron theory is right; we understand others by mentally simulating them as if they were us (Figure 10.1).

Cognitive empathy is the first step – you understand what another is feeling, but you don't feel it; there is no emotional connection. Psychopaths have cognitive empathy only. To make a connection with others, to be 'touched' by them, we need the ability to share feelings.

The second type of empathy is *emotional empathy*. This means feeling with the other person, not just understanding it. Emotional empathy involves many more systems in the brain than cognitive empathy.[19] The amygdala, as the key part of the emotional system, is involved. Damage to the amygdala makes it difficult to make eye contact and therefore to recognise emotion in others.

The inferior frontal gyrus (a fold in the lower part of the PFC) is a region involved in emotional empathy. It is activated when we see pictures of basic emotions and is probably necessary to recognise these.[20] The ACC is active when you experience pain yourself and when you observe others in pain.[21] This makes it part of our emotional system as well. The activity of the ACC increases when we recall emotional experiences or see an emotional film. This happens because you imagine yourself as that other person, and the mirror neuron circuits simulate in you what the other person is feeling. If you have ever seen anyone shut their fingers in a door and cringed, your mirror neurons are active. (Even if you imagine this, it is hard not to cringe.)

Our goals influence our degree of emotional empathy. In one experiment,[22] researchers observed the brain activity of professional acupuncturists.

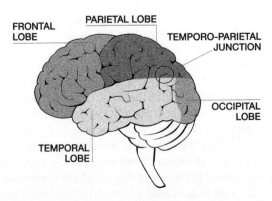

Figure 10.1 Theory of mind: temporoparietal junction.

These practitioners need to detach themselves from the idea of administering pain to focus on the health aspect. The study found that regions associated with pain (the insula and ACC) were not significantly activated when professionals did acupuncture, instead executive planning regions were activated (dlPFC). When non-professionals did acupuncture, their pain regions were activated (and probably the pain regions of their volunteer patients as well). The same mechanism must also act in the medical profession although we do not know of any research in that area. Doctors need to be able to control emotional empathy and by implication their mirror neuron system, otherwise their work would be unbearable. If this is true, then it must be possible to increase emotional empathy as well.

Mirror neurons help us understand others' emotions through inner imitation.[23] For this to work, the system must communicate with the emotional parts of the brain (the limbic system) for us to connect emotionally with others and feel their emotion. The link seems to be the insula. The insula (Latin for 'Island') is anything but an island; it is one of the most connected parts of the brain. It is closely involved in self-awareness, including awareness of our body and connects to the mirror neuron system and the limbic system. Research was done with volunteers who watched faces that showed some basic emotions: disgust, fear, sadness, anger and happiness. One group imitated the expressions, and the other group only watched. Functional magnetic resonance imaging (fMRI) showed activation in the mirror neuron network, the anterior insula and the limbic system for both groups. Further studies showed that the ACC and the insula were active when watching someone's hand caught in a door.[24] Damage to the ACC and the insula interferes with our ability to recognise emotions in others. Finally, the OFC, the region responsible for integrating emotions and cognition in decision-making (somatic marker hypothesis), is also active. Damage to the OFC always results in a lack of social awareness – not knowing or caring about social rules.

The last stage is *Compassionate empathy*.

At this level, you not only understand the suffering cognitively and emotionally but also want to do something about it. Compassionate empathy links thinking and feeling with the will to help. Compassionate empathy depends on a balance of cognitive empathy and emotional empathy and brings a will to help, but the help must be appropriate and accepted by the other.

Barriers to empathy

What gets in the way of empathy?

Threat. This hijacks the amygdala and shuts down empathic parts of the brain. Threats to authority, power, values and self-image can stop empathy. We do not empathise with someone threatening us. Other strong emotions will interfere with empathy, especially anger, disgust and contempt. And it is hard to be empathic if you are tired, hungry or drunk.

Cultural factors may stop empathy. Cultural rules may allow classes of people to be unfairly treated. Others may see them as different or even threatening. Identification with one group will stop empathy towards people in an opposing group. The 'in group' can be family, extended family, work, department, industry sector, football team, race or religion. As people identify with many different, overlapping groups, this can lead to a lot of confusion. This is the dark side of social connection – connecting with some people at the expense of others.

Implications for coaches

Coaches need to follow the client's thought process and connect with them emotionally. They need a balance cognitive and emotional empathy. Too much cognitive empathy can seem aloof. Too much emotional empathy can be suffocating. Cognitive empathy gets us close to the client's thought process, but the client is the expert and the coach cannot jump to conclusions. We may have a good idea of how the client is thinking, but why mind-read when you can ask a direct question?

Coaches may feel the client's emotion quite strongly. They pay close attention to their client, especially their facial expressions. The mirror neuron hypothesis predicts that the coach will mirror those expressions with tiny and unconscious muscle movements of their own. The face and the limbic system are connected – emotions trigger facial expressions and facial expressions trigger emotions. Therefore, a coach may feel the client's emotion. The coach must be clear about their own feelings or they will get confused. For example, a client may be describing their boss, and suddenly the coach feels angry for no reason. This could be because the client is angry at the boss and the coach is picking up this anger. In this case, the coach might ask a question based on their intuition like 'I have an idea you may be angry with your boss … what do you think?' This leaves it open for the client to speak about their anger, if they want.

Finally, the ethical issue. There is an ethical dilemma for the coach if a client has an issue that the coach is currently struggling with. It is much harder for the coach to remain an impartial partner, because the client's issue trigger and amplifies the feelings and doubts the coach already has. It is wise for coaches not to coach a client in this situation.

Face to face is best for empathy. It is a real connection. Mirror neurons work when you are facing a video of the other but less strongly. We are physical and regardless of the rise of virtual reality, we have millions of years of practice and adaptation to a physical reality. That is where we grew up. Research backs this up. Volunteers playing a game face to face cooperated far more than when they played the same game by computer messaging.[25] All the research suggests that coaching face to face is going to be the most effective in producing cooperation, trust and commitment. There are practical difficulties, but they are worth overcoming. We always ask for a small number of face-to-face sessions with our clients, and the majority can still be done by videoconferencing.

All coaches empathise and need to keep their emotional balance. Over empathising can leave the coach at the mercy of the client's emotions. Too much emotional empathy risks burnout. All coaches need a ritual after each session to clean and reset their mirror neurons and shake off any residual feelings. No one wants the emotional imprint of the last client carried into the next session. A short relaxation, mindfulness or meditation after each client session will help to reset our mirror neurons. Compassionate empathy is the best way to avoid the dangers of being absorbed by emotional empathy.

Spiritual traditions, especially Buddhism,[26] are the best sources of understanding and practising compassionate empathy. There are some good summaries on the Web.[27] Compassionate empathy can be learned with mindfulness meditation and loving kindness meditation; practice builds the circuits by neuroplasticity.

When you have empathy, you feel close to the other person, like walking along beside them – not forcing the pace and not lagging. You understand what they are feeling, it seems reasonable. You may feel what they are feeling quite strongly. Empathy adds to the coach's presence. A lot has been written on presence, and the neuroscience of presence is still to be discovered. Not easy to research as presence is rated by the other person – do they feel you are present. Presence is something a coach *does*: they pay attention, they are fully present and their mental chatter is quiet. They backtrack regularly to ensure they have understood, rarely interrupt and do not jump to conclusions. They talk for less than twenty percent of the session, and the other eighty is for the client. It may link with some neuroscientific markers. Our best guess at this time would be activation of the parts of the brain involved in empathy and focused attention and a reduction in the coach's default network.

The coaching conversation is based on accepting the client's reality – their circumstances, emotions and thoughts. This does not mean all is well and nothing will be changed. Often the client does not accept their present state, so it is imperative that the coach does. Understanding only comes from acceptance. Neither coach nor client will understand the situation without accepting it. Without understanding it, they will not be able to change it. Outlaw the word 'should' from the coaching conversation; it always shows rejection of the present state.

From the outside, you can see two people who are connected, because they seem to be in sync, like dancers – not imitating, but reflecting each other. This happens naturally. Matching with body and voice is a consequence of connection, not a means to it. (Once you try to imitate and match voice and body, it looks phony, like bad lip synching.) Your mirror neurons will do it for you effortlessly if you let them. Empathy gives connection. Connection gives trust.

Trust

Trust is one of the strongest social bonds. The word that comes from a root meaning 'support'. Lean against the nearest wall – if you trust it, give it your whole weight and if it is trustworthy, it will not let you down. You would not lean on a lace curtain – it wouldn't support you and you would take a tumble. It is not trustworthy. People are not all or nothing trustworthy – brick wall or lace curtains – that would be the fundamental attribution error. People are trustworthy depending on context. Trustworthy in some situations but not others. Trust and verify is a good rule, especially in business.

Deciding about trust needs cold cognition – the dlPFC. You weigh up the person and the situation. What do you know if the person? What is the issue? Money, business dealings and romance are very different, and being trustworthy in one area does not necessarily carry over to another area. Trust is also an emotional issue. There has been a lot of research into oxytocin which has been promoted as the 'trust hormone' after research showed higher levels made people more generous and willing to lend money to strangers.[28] Oxytocin is a hormone, made by the hypothalamus and released by the pituitary. It is released during sex and breastfeeding and plays a strong role in establishing maternal bonding of mother to baby. It can also act as a neurotransmitter.

Oxytocin seems to have a calming influence on the hypothalamus–pituitary–adrenal (HPA) circuit – the circuit that releases the stress hormone cortisol. The HPA circuit jumps into play when we feel threatened by anything from physical danger to work deadlines or a bad position on social media. Oxytocin reduces the level of cortisol and lowers blood pressure. It may promote trust by reducing fear and anxiety, perhaps by interacting with the amygdala, which has oxytocin receptors.

The shadow side of group cooperation is the rejection of others who are seen as outside 'our' group. Research suggests that oxytocin promotes trust and co-operation but only within an 'in group'. (For example, oxytocin increases the likelihood of a person lying if that serves the group they are part of.) It may be that oxytocin contributes to ethnocentrism and group favouritism, and it may limit wider cooperation. Humans develop through stages. Strong group identification is part of the first stages of human development; it would not be surprising if oxytocin reinforced this at the expense of other groups.[29]

Oxytocin plays a part in empathy. It might act as a signal to seek out social support. People living with unsupportive partners have been found to have higher levels of oxytocin – which normalise when they get more support.[30] Oxytocin may also work by reducing tolerance to our 'feel good' chemicals in the brain – the opioids – making the pleasurable feelings last longer.

The power of 'we'

'We' is the pronoun for connection. This little word is very powerful. Without it, you are alone. Without it, there is no leadership – leaders need followers.

Most leaders underuse the word 'we' and think leadership is all about themselves. Instead, they use too many first-person singular: 'I', and too many second person singular: 'you'. I and you are separate. 'We' means together. Listening to how an executive leader talks about their team can be revealing. (Even more revealing for the coach to shadow the leader and do this in real time.) 'We' is only powerful for leaders if used in the person sense – you and I together. There are at least three other ways people can use the pronoun 'we' which have nothing to do with cooperation.[31]

The first-person pronoun is the most commonly used word in the English language.[32]

People assume that women use first-person plural words ('we', 'us', 'our') more than men, but research shows that there is no difference between the genders in this matter. (Women do use more social words than men, like 'they', 'friend, 'parent'.)

Leaders who talk of cooperation and co-creation and more important demonstrate those values in their behaviour will be more successful and more persuasive than those who try to be ooze charisma and attract followers. Individualistic, charismatic models of leadership are long gone. Leadership is not about just one person. It is about a group of people, one of who is an inspiring representative of the group, who creates something for everyone out of shared values and vision.

Finally, can a coach talk about 'we' rather than about 'you and I' in a session?

Plenty of arguments for both sides. A good argument in favour of using 'you and I' is that using 'we' might encourage a kind of comfortable symbiosis, rather than accountability for the client. On the other hand, you want to establish rapport, you want to be with the client and foster connection, so it makes sense to use 'we'.

Both are right. Use 'I' and 'You' when you want to emphasise accountability and the actions the client will take. Their goals, their values and their mental models belong to them, so that needs to be clear. When talking about *content* of the session, use 'I' and 'You'. When talking about the *process*, use 'we'. You and the client co-create the session together, but the client takes away the results.

Fairness

We have a built-in sense of fairness. When an offer is not fair, many will reject it even though this means they also lose. Researchers use the ominously named 'Ultimatum Game' to explore the sense of fairness.[33] In this game, one player must split an amount of money (e.g. 100 pounds) with another player. They can split it any way they like, but if the second player rejects the offer, neither gets any money. From a purely rational point of view, the second player should accept whatever they are offered (free money!). But that is not what happens. The second player will often reject unfair offers (e.g. ten or twenty pounds). When they do, they show activation of the dlPFC and the insula. The dlPFC is normally involved in rational calculations. The insula is involved with emotions such as disgust or anger. The more insula activity, the more likely the second player will reject the offer. Rejecting an unfair offer might have to do with anger at being taken advantage of, as this can lower one's social standing. Rejection also punishes the first player for being unfair.

Another experiment extended the idea.[34] Here, the pot was ten dollars. A player could choose between two options. Option 1 was five dollars for themselves and five dollars for the other player. The second option was six dollars for themselves and one dollar for the other player. In the first study, about two thirds of the players went with the fair choice – option 1. The next round was a clever variation. The first player could still choose to keep five dollars or six dollars but did not know what the second player would get. The second player might get one dollar or five dollars, and it no longer depended on the first player's choice. Here's the catch. The first player was given the option of seeing what the other player would get *before* making their choice. About half the participants chose not to discover the payoff for the second player and most chose to keep six dollars. They could honestly claim they did not know the consequence of their choice, so their conscience was clear. It looks like fairness is important, but a clear conscience may be more important. Part of us wants to be fair. Another part of us wants more reward. What makes the difference – on average of course – are the external circumstances. You get to keep the extra dollar because you can claim you do not know for sure it was unfair because you do not know what the other player got. 'When ignorance is bliss, 'tis folly to be wise'. This conclusion agrees with all the research that shows people will generally not deceive or act unfairly if everything is in the open. If they can get away with it however (other people do not know what they have done), then they are substantially more likely to cheat.

Other research into cooperation in the prisoner's dilemma game[35] suggested strongly that social acts that help others are intrinsically rewarding, activating the nucleus accumbens and the OFC. The same brain areas that are active when we have a tangible reward like food. Seeing other people rewarded makes us feel good.[36]

Our brain is part of a network, and connecting with others is essential to our health and survival. Social neuroscience is just beginning, and there are sure to be more important findings.

Notes

1 Only in general – an introvert made to participate with others would be stressed.
2 Bhatti, A. B., & ul Haq, A. (2017). The pathophysiology of perceived social isolation: Effects on health and mortality. *Cureus, 9* (1), e994. Retrieved from http://doi.org/10.7759/cureus.994
3 Williams, K. D. (2007). Ostracism. *Annual Review of Psychology, 58.*

4 Kohler, E., Keysers, C., Umilta, M. A., Fogassi, L., Gallese, V., & Rizzolatti, G. (2002). Hearing sounds, understanding actions: Action representation in mirror neurons. *Science, 297* (5582), 846–848.

5 Fadiga, L., Fogassi, L., Pavesi, G., & Rizzolatti, G. (1995). Motor facilitation during action observation: A magnetic stimulation study. *Journal of Neurophysiology, 73* (6), 2608–2611.

6 Iacoboni, M., & Dapretto, M. (2006). The mirror neuron system and the consequences of its dysfunction. *Nature Reviews Neuroscience, 7* (12), 942.

7 For example, anosognosia. This is a strange syndrome where a patient will deny the fact that they have part of their body paralysed (by a stroke for example). The most famous example was Woodrow Wilson, President of the United States from 1913 to 1921. He had a stroke that paralysed the left side of his body, but he insisted that he was fine. Many patients with anosognosia also deny that other disabled patients are also paralysed. This may be because their own mirror neurons are damaged, so they cannot make accurate judgements about other peoples' movements either.

8 This part of the brain is strongly activated when we imagine anticipated actions. When it is damaged, the result is known as apraxia, where the patient cannot carry out skilled actions, they have difficulty translating a thought into an action.

9 We are already very influenced by what others do and say, not always in a good way. The studies on the effect of violence in the media overwhelmingly suggest it encourages imitation.
    See: Paik, H., & Comstock, G. (1994). The effects of television violence on antisocial behavior: A meta-analysis1. *Communication Research, 21* (4), 516–546.

10 Mukamel, R., Ekstrom, A. D., Kaplan, J., Iacoboni, M., & Fried, I. (2010). Single-neuron responses in humans during execution and observation of actions. *Current Biology, 20* (8), 750–756.

11 There are many papers studying this, and it makes a fascinating case for how we understand metaphor. It may also explain why priming works – our brains are running simulations of what is happening in the environment which we are not aware of, but which influence our thinking and therefore our actions.
    See: Gallese, V., & Lakoff, G. (2005). The brain's concepts: The role of the sensory-motor system in conceptual knowledge. *Cognitive Neuropsychology, 22* (3–4), 455–479. and, Aziz-Zadeh, L., Wilson, S. M., Rizzolatti, G., & Iacoboni, M. (2006). Congruent embodied representations for visually presented actions and linguistic phrases describing actions. *Current Biology, 16* (18), 1818–1823.

12 One of the best books on empathy for coaches, as well as being a very interesting read, is 'The Science of Evil' by Simon Baron-Cohen, who is one of the foremost researchers into empathy in neuroscience. The book gives many examples and shows how empathy varies and a way to measure and understand your own degree of empathy.

13 Ickes, W. (1993). Empathic accuracy. *Journal of Personality, 61* (4), 587–610.

14 This is the place on the right where the temporal lobe meets the parietal lobe.

15 Saxe, R., & Kanwisher, N. (2003). People thinking about thinking people: The role of the temporo-parietal junction in 'theory of mind'. *Neuroimage, 19* (4), 1835–1842.

16 A sulcus is a shallow groove in the surface of the brain. So, the PSTS is the groove that is further back at the top of the temporal lobe.

17 Campbell, R., Heywood, C. A., Cowey, A., Regard, M., & Landis, T. (1990). Sensitivity to eye gaze in prosopagnosic patients and monkeys with superior temporal sulcus ablation. *Neuropsychologia, 28* (11), 1123–1142.

18   Mitchell, J. P., Macrae, C. N., & Banaji, M. R. (2004). Encoding-specific effects of social cognition on the neural correlates of subsequent memory. *Journal of Neuroscience, 24* (21), 4912–4917.

19   Studies of people with psychopathic traits have also shed light on emotional empathy. Psychopaths generally have excellent cognitive empathy, but little or no emotional empathy. The sight of another in pain does not affect them. Psychopathy is a complex subject, but studies suggest people who score highly on the Hare checklist of psychopathy have less activity in the ventromedial PFC (hot cognition pathway) and the OFC. They also have more activity in the amygdala and the reward circuit when seeing other people suffer. This may mean they enjoy the suffering of others – the reverse of compassionate empathy. Empathy does not correspond with any particular brain region, but research suggests that people who lack empathy are sensitive to the thought of pain in themselves but lack the ability to put themselves in another person's shoes to feel their pain.

See Buckholtz, J. W., Treadway, M. T., Cowan, R. L., Woodward, N. D., Benning, S. D., Li, R., … Smith, C. E. (2010). Mesolimbic dopamine reward system hypersensitivity in individuals with psychopathic traits. *Nature Neuroscience, 13* (4), 419. also: Paulhus, D. L., & Williams, K. M. (2002). The dark triad of personality: Narcissism, Machiavellianism, and psychopathy. *Journal of Research in Personality, 36* (6), 556–563.

20   Shamay-Tsoory, S. G., Aharon-Peretz, J., & Perry, D. (2009). Two systems for empathy: A double dissociation between emotional and cognitive empathy in inferior frontal gyrus versus ventromedial prefrontal lesions. *Brain, 132* (3), 617–627.

21   Hutchison, W. D., Davis, K. D., Lozano, A. M., Tasker, R. R., & Dostrovsky, J. O. (1999). Pain-related neurons in the human cingulate cortex. *Nature Neuroscience, 2* (5), 403.

22   Cheng, Y., Lin, C. P., Liu, H. L., Hsu, Y. Y., Lim, K. E., Hung, D., & Decety, J. (2007). Expertise modulates the perception of pain in others. *Current Biology, 17* (19), 1708–1713.

23   Carr, L., Iacoboni, M., Dubeau, M. C., Mazziotta, J. C., & Lenzi, G. L. (2003). Neural mechanisms of empathy in humans: a relay from neural systems for imitation to limbic areas. *Proceedings of the National Academy of Sciences, 100* (9), 5497–5502.

24   Jackson, P. L., Meltzoff, A. N., & Decety, J. (2005). How do we perceive the pain of others? A window into the neural processes involved in empathy. *Neuroimage, 24* (3), 771–779.

25   Sally, D. (1995). Conversation and cooperation in social dilemmas: A meta-analysis of experiments from 1958 to 1992. *Rationality and Society, 7* (1), 58–92.

26   A good place to start is: https://www.dalailama.com/messages/compassion-and-human-values/compassion (Accessed 12th June 2018).

27   https://www.psychologytoday.com/intl/blog/irrelationship/201408/new-understanding-compassionate-empathy (Accessed 12th June 2018).

28   Zak, P. J., Stanton, A. A., & Ahmadi, S. (2007). Oxytocin increases generosity in humans. *PLos One, 2* (11), e1128. Lending money to strangers because you are primed with a chemical, has a mixed message. Hopefully the experiment was well controlled.

29   De Dreu, C. K., Greer, L. L., Handgraaf, M. J., Shalvi, S., Van Kleef, G. A., Baas, M., … Feith, S. W. (2010). The neuropeptide oxytocin regulates parochial altruism in intergroup conflict among humans. *Science, 328* (5984), 1408–1411.

30   Taylor, S. E., Gonzaga, G. C., Klein, L. C., Hu, P., Greendale, G. A., & Seeman, T. E. (2006). Relation of oxytocin to psychological stress responses and

hypothalamic-pituitary-adrenocortical axis activity in older women. *Psychosomatic Medicine, 68* (2), 238–245.

31 One use means 'you' and 'I' in a shared group. Another means 'you' as in, 'We are not very good at this are we?' There is also the politicians 'we', meaning people in general (who agree with them) as in, 'We need a better government …'. Then, there is the 'royal we', at least for the UK Royal Family.

32 Accounting for about 3.6 percent of all words sampled. The next three are 'the', 'and' and 'to' weighing at 3.48 percent, 2.92 percent and 2.91 percent, respectively.

33 Sanfey, A. G., Rilling, J. K., Aronson, J. A., Nystrom, L. E., & Cohen, J. D. (2003). The neural basis of economic decision-making in the ultimatum game. *Science, 300* (5626), 1755–1758.

34 Dana, J., Weber, R. A., & Kuang, J. X. (2007). Exploiting moral wiggle room: Experiments demonstrating an illusory preference for fairness. *Economic Theory, 33* (1), 67–80.

35 Padoa-Schioppa, C., & Assad, J. A. (2006). Neurons in the orbitofrontal cortex encode economic value. *Nature, 441* (7090), 223.

36 And perhaps explains the popularity of game shows.

Bibliography

Aziz-Zadeh, L., Wilson, S. M., Rizzolatti, G., & Iacoboni, M. (2006). Congruent embodied representations for visually presented actions and linguistic phrases describing actions. *Current Biology, 16*(18), 1818–1823.

Baron-Cohen, S. (2011). *The science of evil.* New York, NY: Basic Books.

Bhatti, A. B., & ul Haq, A. (2017). The pathophysiology of perceived social isolation: Effects on health and mortality. *Cureus, 9*(1), e994. doi:10.7759/cureus.994

Buckholtz, J. W., Treadway, M. T., Cowan, R. L., Woodward, N. D., Benning, S. D., Li, R., … Smith, C. E. (2010). Mesolimbic dopamine reward system hypersensitivity in individuals with psychopathic traits. *Nature Neuroscience, 13*(4), 419.

Campbell, R., Heywood, C. A., Cowey, A., Regard, M., & Landis, T. (1990). Sensitivity to eye gaze in prosopagnosic patients and monkeys with superior temporal sulcus ablation. *Neuropsychologia, 28*(11), 1123–1142.

Carr, L., Iacoboni, M., Dubeau, M. C., Mazziotta, J. C., & Lenzi, G. L. (2003). Neural mechanisms of empathy in humans: A relay from neural systems for imitation to limbic areas. *Proceedings of the National Academy of Sciences, 100*(9), 5497–5502.

Cheng, Y., Lin, C. P., Liu, H. L., Hsu, Y. Y., Lim, K. E., Hung, D., & Decety, J. (2007). Expertise modulates the perception of pain in others. *Current Biology, 17*(19), 1708–1713.

Dana, J., Weber, R. A., & Kuang, J. X. (2007). Exploiting moral wiggle room: Experiments demonstrating an illusory preference for fairness. *Economic Theory, 33*(1), 67–80.

De Dreu, C. K., Greer, L. L., Handgraaf, M. J., Shalvi, S., Van Kleef, G. A., Baas, M., … Feith, S. W. (2010). The neuropeptide oxytocin regulates parochial altruism in intergroup conflict among humans. *Science, 328*(5984), 1408–1411.

Fadiga, L., Fogassi, L., Pavesi, G., & Rizzolatti, G. (1995). Motor facilitation during action observation: A magnetic stimulation study. *Journal of Neurophysiology, 73*(6), 2608–2611.

Gallese, V., & Lakoff, G. (2005). The brain's concepts: The role of the sensory-motor system in conceptual knowledge. *Cognitive Neuropsychology, 22*(3–4), 455–479.

Hutchison, W. D., Davis, K. D., Lozano, A. M., Tasker, R. R., & Dostrovsky, J. O. (1999). Pain-related neurons in the human cingulate cortex. *Nature Neuroscience, 2*(5), 403.

Iacoboni, M., & Dapretto, M. (2006). The mirror neuron system and the consequences of its dysfunction. *Nature Reviews Neuroscience, 7*(12), 942.

Ickes, W. (1993). Empathic accuracy. *Journal of Personality, 61*(4), 587–610.

Jackson, P. L., Meltzoff, A. N., & Decety, J. (2005). How do we perceive the pain of others? A window into the neural processes involved in empathy. *Neuroimage, 24*(3), 771–779.

Kohler, E., Keysers, C., Umilta, M. A., Fogassi, L., Gallese, V., & Rizzolatti, G. (2002). Hearing sounds, understanding actions: Action representation in mirror neurons. *Science, 297*(5582), 846–848.

Mitchell, J. P., Macrae, C. N., & Banaji, M. R. (2004). Encoding-specific effects of social cognition on the neural correlates of subsequent memory. *Journal of Neuroscience, 24*(21), 4912–4917.

Mukamel, R., Ekstrom, A. D., Kaplan, J., Iacoboni, M., & Fried, I. (2010). Single-neuron responses in humans during execution and observation of actions. *Current Biology, 20*(8), 750–756.

Padoa-Schioppa, C., & Assad, J. A. (2006). Neurons in the orbitofrontal cortex encode economic value. *Nature, 441*(7090), 223.

Paik, H., & Comstock, G. (1994). The effects of television violence on antisocial behavior: A meta-analysisl. *Communication Research, 21*(4), 516–546.

Paulhus, D. L., & Williams, K. M. (2002). The dark triad of personality: Narcissism, Machiavellianism, and psychopathy. *Journal of Research in Personality, 36*(6), 556–563.

Sally, D. (1995). Conversation and cooperation in social dilemmas: A meta-analysis of experiments from 1958 to 1992. *Rationality and Society, 7*(1), 58–92.

Sanfey, A. G., Rilling, J. K., Aronson, J. A., Nystrom, L. E., & Cohen, J. D. (2003). The neural basis of economic decision-making in the ultimatum game. *Science, 300*(5626), 1755–1758.

Saxe, R., & Kanwisher, N. (2003). People thinking about thinking people: The role of the temporo-parietal junction in 'theory of mind'. *Neuroimage, 19*(4), 1835–1842.

Shamay-Tsoory, S. G., Aharon-Peretz, J., & Perry, D. (2009). Two systems for empathy: A double dissociation between emotional and cognitive empathy in inferior frontal gyrus versus ventromedial prefrontal lesions. *Brain, 132*(3), 617–627.

Taylor, S. E., Gonzaga, G. C., Klein, L. C., Hu, P., Greendale, G. A., & Seeman, T. E. (2006). Relation of oxytocin to psychological stress responses and hypothalamic-pituitary-adrenocortical axis activity in older women. *Psychosomatic Medicine, 68*(2), 238–245.

Williams, K. D. (2007). Ostracism. *Annual Review of Psychology, 58*.

Zak, P. J., Stanton, A. A., & Ahmadi, S. (2007). Oxytocin increases generosity in humans. *PLos One, 2*(11), e1128.

https://www.dalailama.com/messages/compassion-and-human-values/compassion

https://www.psychologytoday.com/intl/blog/irrelationship/201408/new-understanding-compassionate-empathy

Chapter 11

Identity – who are we?

Our brain – the magician

Now the final miracle. Somehow our consciousness, our personality and our sense of 'me' emerge from the brain. If our brain in damaged, our personality and sense of self changes. One strange example is the 'gourmand syndrome'. Injury to a specific part of the right frontal lobe gives an overwhelming preoccupation with fine dining. One Swiss political journalist who suffered a stroke which damaged that area of his brain became a food columnist.[1]

So, there is no 'ghost in the machine', no separate consciousness sitting on top of it all. A consciousness running the show from the top would need a ghost in their machine to run them and so on ad infinitum.[2] We have talked about 'top-down' and 'bottom-up' processing, but this is a simplification. There is no processing that is completely top down, because there is no part of the brain that does not have feedback from other parts of the brain. No part of the brain is independent, running the show. All processing is mixed, ranging from extremes of bottom up (reacting to pain) to top down (sitting comfortably, reviewing the plan of your day).

The brain is a brilliant magician; it creates the show and then makes itself invisible and fixes 'your' attention on the show. It is a wonderful entertainment; every part of the brain contributes, and the show emerges from the interaction, but there is no script and no director. The brain is the cast, the crew, the director, the show and the audience all at once. The cast and crew work together to produce the play, but they also have their own agendas. They argue on stage about the plot – which is incorporated into the drama.

We are not saying consciousness is only material and has no other dimensions. Nothing in this book rules out a spiritual ground of being on which everything depends – something so close and intimate that it seems unreachable. All we are saying is that as far as we know, a material brain is necessary to manifest consciousness in this world.

Here is another metaphor – the brain is like a tablet computer running lots of different apps – small, specialised programmes. The tablet relies on you, the user to overview, select and run the app you want, but some of the apps may have a 'mind of their own'. When you are lost, you want to run Google maps, but you might get interference from the YouTube app wanting to play you videos of survival skills. Let's look at the apps in more detail – their conflicts and their cooperation.

The team in the closed room part 2

Remember in Chapter 1, you had job of coaching the mysterious management team. Peter, Mary, Jan and the others were personifications of what happens in the brain.

What happens behind the closed door?
How far do they work as a team?
Like every team, they do not always see eye to eye.

The most obvious case is the division into two hemispheres. Popular science has cast the left hemisphere as the intellectual and the right as the quirky artist. In fact, both hemispheres can do everything, although each is specialised in some areas. The left hemisphere looks for patterns, causes and effects. The right hemisphere is more direct, looking at the big picture. There is a lot of redundancy.[3] The two hemispheres are connected by a thick band of white matter fibres known as the corpus callosum, so each hemisphere can access the information from the other. When the corpus callosum is cut, each hemisphere is on its own and cannot share its knowledge with the other. Emotional states seem to transfer subcortically, so cutting the corpus callosum does not stop emotions transferring between the hemispheres. (The perceptions that triggered the emotions are still isolated however.) Split-brain surgery (severing the corpus callosum) has been performed since the 1940s usually to help severe epilepsy, and afterwards patients feel the same. Studies of split-brain patients show each hemisphere has 'a mind of its own'. The left can speak,[4] and the right is mute, it can only use the left hand to point or indicate what it wants. Split-brain patients cannot name or describe things without left hemisphere awareness, but that does not mean they are not aware of them.[5]

Joseph LeDoux and Michael Gazzaniga conducted one of the most well-known experiments with a split-brain patient in 1978.[6] They showed a picture of a chicken claw to the left hemisphere's visual field, and a picture of a snowy landscape to the right hemisphere's visual field. The patient was asked what he had just seen. He (his left hemisphere) replied 'chicken'. Then, he was shown two cards, one with a picture of a chicken and one with a picture of snow shovel and asked to *point* to the one he had seen. His left hand (under the control of the right hemisphere) pointed to the snow shovel. His right hand (under the control of the left hemisphere) pointed to the chicken.

But ... they can't both be right. When he was asked why he was pointing to the snow shovel, he said it was to clean out the chicken shed. The left hemisphere had created a story to make sense of the contradiction. Different parts of our brain are aware of different things, but not all have access to language. The part that has access to language is at an advantage. It can spin a plausible story.

The interpreter

Gazzaniga called the part of the brain that made up the story to make sense of the situation, 'The interpreter'. The interpreter smooths out the conflicts and presents a coherent story to you and others. The interpreter uses the information it gets to make up a narrative that keeps our reality consistent. It is like a press secretary, spinning the best story. The interpreter seems to be an important part of the ego – the part of us that wants to appear in the best light, be well thought of by others and be right whenever possible (and if we are wrong, concoct a good reason to explain it).

The interpreter can't be pinned down to one place in the brain, but it is likely to be a left hemisphere function, as it depends on making cause-effect deductions and finding patterns.[7] Patterns give information. Patterns mean things are not random. The interpreter is one of the main actors in making our experience consistent and meaningful. Anything that does not fit is rationalised by the interpreter. ('I am a very good leader. These people are not following me because they have been corrupted by messages from my competitor'.)

We overestimate our insight into our reasons. We rationalise conflict and we rationalise the effects of priming. One nice example is the research carried out by Nisbett and Wilson.[8] People were shown four *identical* night gowns laid out from left to right and asked which one they preferred. There were 378 shoppers, and their choice was overwhelming – the one on the extreme right. People gave a wide variety of reasons for their choices (e.g. colour or texture). Location was not one of the explanations, because choosing by position does not make sense. Perhaps, people have a bias for articles on the right. Perhaps, they looked from left to right looking for the best, and as all were the same, chose the one on the right as that was the last place they looked. We do not know. We do know that we do not understand our reasons very well, but are very good at making up explanations that make sense.

Making sense of conflict

There are many fascinating examples that show the different parts of the brain going their separate ways, and the interpreter is always there to explain. Anosognosia came up in a previous chapter – when a person will deny they are disabled when it is obvious to everyone else. A stroke damages the brain and can cause paralysis in one side of the body. A significant number of people deny they are paralysed and insist they can move normally. It is not clear why this happens; it may be damage to part of the right hemisphere. The right hemisphere deals more with holistic patterns and the big picture. There may be a part that balances and keeps the left hemisphere interpreter in check. An unchecked interpreter would be a grandiose tyrant, making up ridiculous stories to explain their difficulties. So, if this balancing part is damaged, the left hemisphere interpreter has free rein to make up whatever story it likes, however ridiculous. We all like to smooth reality in our favour in normal life, but anosognosia takes it to extremes. The interpreter must somehow explain the paralysis. The person may deny it (I am not paralysed), rationalise it (I am too tired to move my leg) or simply make excuses (I will move it later when I feel like it). They are not lying. They are expressing part of their experience as if it was all of it.

Neglect is another example. This is when injury or stroke in one hemisphere damages the ability to pay attention to one side of the body. For example, a patient with right hemisphere damage may completely ignore the left-hand side of their body and not 'see' anything in their left visual field. Such patients may only wash the right-hand side of their face and their right hand. They may eat only what is on the right-hand side of their plate and only pay attention to the right side of a clock face. They do not suppress or deny it; they just do not see it.

Blindsight is further example. A person may not be able to see objects but can correctly point out where they are and how they are moving a much higher rate than chance. This is because visual information travels down two pathways in the brain. One part of the brain is aware of the object's location and can point to it, but the person is not aware of seeing it because information from the other pathway is blocked. We don't know what we don't know – even when part of the brain is aware of it.

Finally, the 'alien hand' syndrome, made famous by the Stanley Kubrick film, 'Doctor Strangelove'.[9] Alien hand syndrome is when a patient's hand seems to have a 'mind of its own'. It will grab objects, people and food, while the patient protests they do not want them. The other hand will grab the misbehaving hand and the hands will battle for control. The patient cannot control their hand and does not feel responsible for what it does. Alien hand syndrome is caused by damage to the anterior cingulate cortex.

Alien hand syndrome is the extreme, embodied version of internal conflict which we all experience, 'being in two minds', when one part of us pulls one way and another pulls the opposite way. We resolve this one way or the other or with some compromise. We have modules and routines in our brain that we do not control, but they are kept behind the curtain and normally everything works well. All the hard work is hidden from us. Our conscious mind, our sense of 'I', floats in happy ignorance over this teeming activity.

Unconscious bias

We have many modules in our brain all doing different things, and the results can be confusing. There is a test called the implicit association test (IAT[10]). Devised in 1995, it has been used to measure attitudes to many controversial subjects, such as race and gender. In a typical test, participants see a category of people (e.g. lawyers) but at the same time evaluating a stream of words as good or bad (e.g. excellent, terrible, fantastic). When the group category interferes with the judgement, there is a longer reaction time and shows there is an 'implicit association' between the group and a judgement. In theory, this can measure a person's implicit judgement about anything, and it may conflict with what the person says they believe. For example, you might strenuously protest that you hold lawyers in high repute, but the test might show you associate lawyers with negative words. Most people show biases when taking the IAT, but this does not mean they are prejudiced or they act in a prejudiced way. It does not predict behaviour. Also, your score can be different if you take the test a second time. What is happening is that parts of your brain are noticing patterns and taking in information while you do the test, and this interferes with the speed of your reactions. This test has been advanced as evidence of prejudice, but that is not right. Attention, emotion and associations can all interfere with reaction times, and one or more modules can make a 'minority report' on the question. So, it is no surprise that you can say one thing and your reaction time tells a slightly different story. The test does not tell you what you 'truly' think and certainly not how you would act. It makes the internal argument visible. There is more going on than we are aware of.

Applications for coaches

The coach helps the client to create a richer story, one with new insights, new perspectives and new distinctions. It is like giving the client a better language to construct a good story. This story is not more correct than the last one; it just has a larger vocabulary and a better plot. It is more liberating, a happier story to live; it brings more of the client into awareness. When the client gets a better story, they will follow it.

The client's interpreter tells a story, and it will be coherent and put the client in a good light. This does not mean they are lying, but everyone is selective about what they say. The interpreter gives out the best and most defensible message about a person, and the coach works with this. It is not wrong, and there is a 'real true' story hiding behind it.

The story depends on other people as well. Imagine a client who has a trusted friend. They have known them from childhood, they trust them completely. Imagine this friend betrays them. Several things happen as a result. First, the friend changes from someone they knew into a scary stranger.

That is bad. But worse still, the client will question themselves. Their story about themselves disintegrates. Did they ever really know the friend? Are they a gullible fool? They question themselves. What is wrong with them – that they can be so wrong? They become a stranger to themselves. This is what makes betrayal so devastating. The story has to be rewritten.

The interpreter is not good at living with ambiguity and multiple perspectives. There is a big temptation to jump in, resolve ambiguity and give an explanation like the detective in the last act of a murder mystery. So, the coach must be careful. It is usually better to wait, to test and to ask more questions. This is one reason why questions beginning with 'why' do not work well in coaching. They encourage justification, and the interpreter jumps in with a feasible explanation.

The interpreter is a linear thinker. It tends to attribute big effects to big causes, will mistake correlation for cause and will not connect events if there is a long time lag between them. It will also explain things in terms of the person's internal mental world (fundamental attribution error). So, for example, shouting at a work colleague will be explained by a lot of stress, deadlines for the work or the colleague being clueless. We look for plausible justifications for what we do. We are blind mostly to the environment and to the effects of priming. The shouting might be down to a bad night's sleep or too much coffee. We have little insight into the reasons why we do things but are good at making up a good reason afterwards.

Knowing how the brain works also gives us a new view on intuition. Intuition has been called many things. It may be a part of the brain that has information but no access to language. So, it gives you a 'minority report' as a feeling about the situation. An intuition may not be backed by language and logic, but it may have good information. We are not saying follow every intuition. It is another point of view from the team. The same goes for the client's intuition. It may be weird or useless, but sometimes it can be valuable.

Our view of the brain saves the coach from asking silly questions like 'What do you *really* think about this?' or 'What is the real answer to this?' All thoughts and all perspectives are real. They may be different; it is the job of the coach and client together to create an integrated story that takes them all into account in some way.

Every result in real life, positive or negative, is a mixture of chance, effort and other people. However, everyone overestimates their own talents, even when the evidence is against them.[11] When people get a good result, they are more likely to attribute it to their efforts. They are more likely to attribute a bad result to chance or other peoples' interference. Worth remembering when listening to clients' stories.

There is plenty of research on this theme. In one experiment, subjects were asked to take a supposed intelligence test. You might be suspicious as to whether this really was what it said it was ... your suspicions would be justified. Subjects were given random false scores and then asked why they think they got that score. If their score was good, subjects put it down to their efforts, if bad, there were various excuses.[12] This happened even when subjects were hooked up to a machine they thought was a lie detector (it was not). They would still attribute their (false) high score to their intelligence and their (false) low score to bad luck or other factors.[13] There are cross-cultural differences,[14] and some people do consistently take the opposite view (a good result was chance and taking responsibility for a bad result). There is good evidence that optimistic attribution is better for your health than pessimistic attribution.[15]

By now, you will not be surprised that clients express mutually inconsistent ideas. Incongruence is normal. The coach collects all the different views and helps the client integrate them into a better story.

Self-control

Now, the philosophical question buried in the discussion so far. If we are free agents and have self-control, then what self is controlling who? There are many times when we are in conflict with 'ourselves', some members of the team want one thing, while other members what something else. The reward circuit pulls one way, and the PFC another.

We all have things we would love to do but know we would regret the next morning (food, sex, alcohol, shopping and parties figure prominently here). Then, there are those things we need to do but are not attractive, so we put them off. (Tax returns, homework, visiting in-laws come to mind here.)

In practice, self-control means resolving the 'team brain' discussion in the best way – usually forgoing the quick reward for longer benefit. When we are conflicted and there are two or more possible paths, then self-control may be needed to choose the path less immediately attractive, but better in the long run. The PFC argues for the long-term benefit and doing the right thing but it does not always get its own way.

As Saint Augustine summed it up 1600 years ago, 'Lord give me chastity, but don't give it yet'. Homer Simpson, drinking a mixture of vodka and mayonnaise, expressed it more graphically, 'That's a problem for future Homer. Man, I don't envy that guy'.[16]

Ego fatigue

This 'self-control' struggle results in what is called 'ego fatigue'. Will power seems to be like a muscle; the more you use it, the more tiring it is and the more you need a breathing space. Ego fatigue is like decision fatigue. What happens in the brain is not clear.[17] Some researchers say resisting temptation is effortful because the brain uses more glucose. But this does not make sense. The brain uses less than half a calorie per minute and exercise does not erode self-control, quite the opposite. Nor does a bar of chocolate help self-control, so it is not about glucose.

Different parts of the brain are probably arguing about what to do and calculating cost against reward. Context is also important. It is hard to turn down a drink with a group of friends in a good bar. Much easier when you are alone. Time of day, emotional state, other people all affect the decision. Priming also plays a part. In a balanced argument, context is often the deciding factor. ('Don't go grocery shopping when you are hungry'.)

The psychologist Roy Baumeister conducted some classic research on self-control and ego fatigue.[18] In one experiment, a group of subjects sat at a table laden loaded with freshly made chocolate chip cookies. The researchers then asked them to eat … radishes … instead of the tempting cookies on display. Another luckier group of subjects were allowed to eat the cookies. Each subject was left 'on their honour' to eat whatever they had been asked to eat, while the researcher left the room for five minutes. Of course, another researcher was watching and meticulously recorded what they ate. After that, they gave all the subjects puzzles to solve. The subjects did not know these puzzles were impossible to answer.

The subjects who had to exercise 'self-control' (by eating the radishes) gave up on the puzzles sooner and reported feeling more tired after the experiment. No one cheated and scoffed the cookies.[19]

Baumeister followed this with another experiment. He asked some students to make a speech supporting higher tuition fees. Others made a speech opposing higher tuition fees. Then, they all got to do the impossible puzzles. The students who argued for higher tuition fees gave up sooner. Assuming students do not support higher tuition fees, it looks like speaking out publicly against your values or beliefs also induces ego fatigue.

In a third experiment, students were invited to watch a sad movie. Some were told to react as they normally would, and others were told to suppress their emotions. Those that suppressed their emotions solved fewer puzzles than those who did not. So, emotional suppression gives ego fatigue, reframing emotions does not.

These are interesting experiments. In every experiment, the subjects were obeying outside instructions. Would the result be the same if the 'self-control' was freely chosen?

Implications for coaches

Everyone struggles with issues of 'self-control' and inner conflict. Clients struggle with health issues, diets and exercise. They struggle with issues of temper, treating colleagues badly and petty jealousies.

Trying harder does not work, because both sides are 'you'. You are fighting with yourself, and there can be only one winner. One helpful thing the coach can do is reframe the problem. Rather than thinking of one ultimate self-battling subordinates, think of it like a team, where every voice needs to be heard, and the action comes from the discussion.

The coach can also help the client to leverage the context. We pay attention to the comfort of our office, the furniture, lighting, heating and so on, because we know they matter and affect our state. The client can avoid cues, environments and people associated with their problem. They can use a variation of the Ulysses contract to avoid difficult situations. The problem is managing the diverse pulls on their attention.

Ego fatigue is like decision fatigue. Do not let the client struggle with too many issues at once. One at a time. Finally, help the client to reframe challenges. They are not resisting temptation; they are testing their strength with a challenge or trying a new alternative. Finally, small rewards help to slow ego fatigue. Kind words and congratulations count as rewards.

The Marshmallow effect

We can't leave self-control without mentioning the Marshmallow effect. The original research was carried out in the 1960s by Walter Mischel and numerous papers[20] and a book have followed.[21] In 1960, Walter Mischel was working with four-year-olds in Stanford University Nursery School. Each child sat in a room with a tasty marshmallow treat on the table in front of them. They were told Mischel would go out of the room for about fifteen minutes. In this time, they could eat the marshmallow if they wished, but if they waited until Mischel returned, they would get a second marshmallow.

About one third of the children ate the marshmallow immediately. Another third waited, but still ate it before Mischel returned. A third were able to wait until he returned and were rewarded with a second marshmallow, as promised. Mischel had two daughters at the school, and as he followed the children's progress, he noticed some patterns. Does how long a child waited for a treat at the age of four predict anything about their future life?

Yes it does. Over the years, the Marshmallow test has proved a remarkable predictor of future success of these children. The longer a child waited, the higher their SAT scores (a Standardised Test of Academic Achievement used for admission to University). The longer they waited, the more likely they would have a lower body mass index. As the research progressed and was duplicated by other researchers, it appeared that the children who waited the longest were likely to be successful in life – defining success by health, wealth and happiness.

Mischel summarised the study as follows, 'children who were able to wait longer at age four or five became adolescents whose parents rated them more academic and socially competent, verbally fluent, rational, attentive, planful and able to deal well with frustration and stress'.[22] Mischel called this ability self-regulation. This is a remarkable result, showing a far-reaching effect. It may be a more important psychological construct than many in common use.[23] It also merits much more research and exploration of its effects in teams, leadership and coaching.

These children were able to tolerate delay even at a young age. The left PFC seems to be the region most activated by delayed rewards.[24] The PFC has two very important tasks, one is to inhibit actions for a good reason, and the other is to place the person in time, looking forward and backwards. We know that the brain takes many years to mature, and the PFC is one of the last parts to mature, hence the legendary impulsiveness of adolescents. It is not surprising that most four-year-olds took the marshmallow. The surprise is so many held out successfully.

Children are in the moment, tomorrow is a long way away. A fifteen-minute wait would seem endless. The children employed several strategies to try to wait. Some covered their eyes, so as not to see the tempting sweet. Some tried to hide the sweet itself. Some tried to think about the shape rather than the taste and distract themselves. We know that reframing is effective for managing emotions, but a four-year-old will not have the cognitive maturity to do this. Gender was a factor too, girls were able to wait longer than boys on average, a finding that continued throughout their years of education.

A couple of things were taken for granted in the experiment. First, they assumed the children wanted the reward. One marshmallow was tempting, but two was even better. The extra reward for waiting must be valued. The extra reward for waiting can be more of the same the same (e.g. saving money for a bigger party later rather than maxing the credit card now). It can also be something different but also valuable (e.g. saving the money for a family holiday later).

Second, the children trusted the researcher – they believed they would get the second marshmallow if they waited – and that is critical. A study in 2012 changed the experiment slightly.[25] The experimenter made a promise to two groups before the test. He broke the promise with one group but kept it with the second group. The second group waited up to four times longer for the second marshmallow. There is more going on here than self-control. The children were weighing up the likelihood of the experimenter delivering on his promise of the second marshmallow. Even at the age of four, trust matters. What is the point in denying yourself now if you may not get the future reward? It may be that children who had been raised in a trustworthy environment, where promises were kept, were more likely to delay gratification. Trust may be the key issue, in self-regulation.[26] A trustworthy childhood environment probably also impacts health, wealth and happiness in later life.

Free will or free won't?

How far we are free agents in control of our actions?
Does the loudest voice in the brain win the day?
Who decides anyway?

Benjamin Libet conducted a series of experiments in the 1980s to explore these questions. In one experiment,[27] subjects were attached to an electro-encephalogram (EEG) machine and told to move a finger whenever they wanted. They noted the exact time when they were conscious of the decision to move a finger. The EEG machine recorded what was happening in their brain at the time. The results were clear – and controversial. The readiness potential signal showed in the brain about 200 milliseconds *before* they re-ported the conscious decision to move the finger and half a second before they moved the finger. The sequence was – brain activity – one fifth of a second later came the conscious decision and three fifths of a second after that the movement itself. It does not go how we think it does – conscious decision, followed by brain activity, followed by movement. With more so-phisticated scanning technology (fMRI), other researchers could predict whether the subject would use the left or right hand to press a buzzer up to ten seconds before they reported making the choice. It seems the conscious 'you' does not know what 'you' are going to do until after the brain decides and lets 'you' know. This area is still subject to a lot of discussion among neuroscientist, philosophers and legal experts from the point of view of in-tention and criminal responsibility.

What can this mean? It is not surprising given the modular nature of the brain, with all the parts that need to coordinate. The brain hides so many things from us in the closed room, why not this? It is not a problem that our conscious mind is one of the last to know about the action; it cannot all happen at the same time. When our conscious mind becomes aware of the action, it has a short time to override the intention. The ultimate power is the conscious mind can stop the action – the conscious mind has the power of *veto*. Our conscious power comes from deciding what not to do. The brain team can make a proposal, which may carry the day. But the PFC has the power of veto, not the power to compel the team to decide the way they want it to. To stop an act is as powerful as committing one. Our experience of free will is more like 'free won't'. We can consciously choose to allow or stop an action, even if the preparation for it remains forever inaccessible to consciousness. Most of the Ten Commandments are phrased as 'Thou shalt not ...' and five of the basic moral principles of Buddhism are restraints on actions rather than principles of action. 'Do no harm' is also the basic rule of the oldest healing profession – Medicine.

Notes

1 Regard, M., & Landis, T. (1997). 'Gourmand syndrome' Eating passion associ-ated with right anterior lesions. *Neurology, 48* (5), 1185–1190.
2 The 2015 film, 'Inside Out', had the great idea of showing emotions as characters in an eleven-year-old girl's head. These emotions then ran her brain and her ac-tions. It was a nice film, but when the personified emotions reacted emotionally, did they have emotional characters inside their heads?

3   There are rare, but well-documented cases of babies being born with one hemisphere only. They grow, thrive and live normal lives nevertheless. The remarkable neuroplasticity of the brain allows parts to take over and run different functions.

4   Ninety-six percent of people regardless of handedness have language function in the left hemisphere.

5   Different parts of the brain communicate in different ways. For example, galvanic skin response (GSR) measures the electrical resistance of your skin. When you see something arousing, like a gorgeous pin up or a disgusting injury (arousal can be good or bad), you sweat very slightly, and the GSR machine shows a difference. Remember the Iowa card experiment? The subjects were not consciously aware of the bad decks, but GSR picked up a stress reaction. This is one way the non-verbal parts of the brain can communicate. The polygraph works on this principle (popularly known as a 'lie detector'; but it does not detect lies, it detects stress that may result from lying).

6   Risse, G. L., LeDoux, J., Springer, S. P., Wilson, D. H., & Gazzaniga, M. S. (1978). The anterior commissure in man: Functional variation in a multisensory system. *Neuropsychologia, 16* (1), 23–31.
    See a review of the studies and implications in:
    Gazzaniga, M. S. (2005). Forty-five years of split-brain research and still going strong. *Nature Reviews Neuroscience, 6* (8), 653.

7   Nisbett, R. E., & Wilson, T. D. (1977). Telling more than we can know: Verbal reports on mental processes. *Psychological Review, 84* (3), 231.

8   Also, it is a plot device in *Evil Dead 2* when the central character's right hand tries to kill him.

9   Greenwald, A. G., & Banaji, M. R. (1995). Implicit social cognition: Attitudes, self-esteem, and stereotypes. *Psychological Review, 102* (1), 4.
    This test has been used for many different associations.
    You can try it for yourself at:
    https://implicit.harvard.edu/implicit/ (Accessed 29th May 2018).

10 Known as the 'Lake Wobegon Effect'. In one study, two groups of fifty drivers were asked to rate their skills. Both groups gave themselves very good ratings as you might have expected, and the average of the two groups was almost the same. What was striking was that one group was made up of people who had been in traffic accidents and been hospitalised as a result. Most of them were judged to be at fault by the police.
    See Preston, C. E., & Harris, S. (1965). Psychology of drivers in traffic accidents. *Journal of Applied Psychology, 49* (4), 284.

11 Blaine, B., & Crocker, J. (1993). Self-esteem and self-serving biases in reactions to positive and negative events: An integrative review. In *Self-esteem* (pp. 55–85). Boston, MA: Springer.

12 Riess, M., Rosenfeld, P., Melburg, V., & Tedeschi, J. T. (1981). Self-serving attributions: Biased private perceptions and distorted public descriptions. *Journal of Personality and Social Psychology, 41* (2), 224.

13 Mezulis, A. H., Abramson, L. Y., Hyde, J. S., & Hankin, B. L. (2004). Is there a universal positivity bias in attributions? A meta-analytic review of individual, developmental, and cultural differences in the self-serving attributional bias. *Psychological Bulletin, 130* (5), 711.

14 Seligman, M. E. (2004). *Authentic happiness: Using the new positive psychology to realize your potential for lasting fulfillment.* New York: Simon and Schuster.

15 The Simpsons (Season 22, Episode 3).

16 For a review of the topic, see: Gibson, E. L. (2007). Carbohydrates and mental function: Feeding or impeding the brain? *Nutrition Bulletin, 32* (s1), 71–83.

17   Baumeister, R. F., Bratslavsky, E., Muraven, M., & Tice, D. M. (1998). Ego depletion: Is the active self a limited resource? *Journal of Personality and Social Psychology, 74* (5), 1252.
18   They were tired and unhappy. They were hungry, put in a room, smelling of chocolate, told to eat radishes and then given an impossible problem. And they were misled the whole time about the true nature of the experiment.
19   Mischel, W., Shoda, Y., & Rodriguez, M. L. (1989). Delay of gratification in children. *Science, 244* (4907), 933–938.
20   Mischel, W. (2014). *The marshmallow test: Understanding self-control and how to master it.* New York: Random House.
21   Shoda, Y., Mischel, W., & Peake, P. K. (1990). Predicting adolescent cognitive and self-regulatory competencies from preschool delay of gratification: Identifying diagnostic conditions. *Developmental Psychology, 26* (6), 978.
22   The 'big five' psychological dimensions are Extraversion (your level of sociability), Agreeableness (your level of friendliness), Conscientiousness (your level of work motivation), Emotional Stability (your level of calm) and Intellect (your level of curiosity). These are combined to give a personality style. Perhaps there should be a sixth: the marshmallow dimension.
23   Figner, B., Knoch, D., Johnson, E. J., Krosch, A. R., Lisanby, S. H., Fehr, E., & Weber, E. U. (2010). Lateral prefrontal cortex and self-control in intertemporal choice. *Nature Neuroscience, 13* (5), 538–539.
24   Kidd, C., Palmeri, H., & Aslin, R. N. (2013). Rational snacking: Young children's decision-making on the marshmallow task is moderated by beliefs about environmental reliability. *Cognition, 126* (1), 109–114.
25   Mischel did establish trust with all the children in the original experiments, but subsequent experiments did not always do this.
26   Libet, B., Gleason, C. A., Wright, E. W., & Pearl, D. K. (1983). Time of conscious intention to act in relation to onset of cerebral activity (readiness-potential) the unconscious initiation of a freely voluntary act. *Brain, 106* (3), 623–642.

Bibliography

Baumeister, R. F., Bratslavsky, E., Muraven, M., & Tice, D. M. (1998). Ego depletion: Is the active self a limited resource? *Journal of Personality and Social Psychology, 74*(5), 1252.

Blaine, B., & Crocker, J. (1993). Self-esteem and self-serving biases in reactions to positive and negative events: An integrative review. In R. F. Baumeister (Ed.), *Self-esteem* (pp. 55–85). New York: Plenum Press.

Figner, B., Knoch, D., Johnson, E. J., Krosch, A. R., Lisanby, S. H., Fehr, E., & Weber, E. U. (2010). Lateral prefrontal cortex and self-control in intertemporal choice. *Nature Neuroscience, 13*(5), 538–539.

Gazzaniga, M. S. (2005). Forty-five years of split-brain research and still going strong. *Nature Reviews Neuroscience, 6*(8), 653.

Gibson, E. L. (2007). Carbohydrates and mental function: Feeding or impeding the brain? *Nutrition Bulletin, 32*(s1), 71–83.

Greenwald, A. G., & Banaji, M. R. (1995). Implicit social cognition: Attitudes, self-esteem, and stereotypes. *Psychological Review, 102*(1), 4. Retrieved from https://implicit.harvard.edu/implicit/

Kidd, C., Palmeri, H., & Aslin, R. N. (2013). Rational snacking: Young children's decision-making on the marshmallow task is moderated by beliefs about environmental reliability. *Cognition, 126*(1), 109–114.

Libet, B., Gleason, C. A., Wright, E. W., & Pearl, D. K. (1983). Time of conscious intention to act in relation to onset of cerebral activity (readiness-potential) the unconscious initiation of a freely voluntary act. *Brain, 106*(3), 623–642.

Mezulis, A. H., Abramson, L. Y., Hyde, J. S., & Hankin, B. L. (2004). Is there a universal positivity bias in attributions? A meta-analytic review of individual, developmental, and cultural differences in the self-serving attributional bias. *Psychological Bulletin, 130*(5), 711.

Mischel, W. (2014). *The marshmallow test: Understanding self-control and how to master it.* New York, NY: Random House.

Mischel, W., Shoda, Y., & Rodriguez, M. L. (1989). Delay of gratification in children. *Science, 244*(4907), 933–938.

Nisbett, R. E., & Wilson, T. D. (1977). Telling more than we can know: Verbal reports on mental processes. *Psychological Review, 84*(3), 231.

Preston, C. E., & Harris, S. (1965). Psychology of drivers in traffic accidents. *Journal of Applied Psychology, 49*(4), 284.

Regard, M., & Landis, T. (1997). 'Gourmand syndrome' Eating passion associated with right anterior lesions. *Neurology, 48*(5), 1185–1190.

Riess, M., Rosenfeld, P., Melburg, V., & Tedeschi, J. T. (1981). Self-serving attributions: Biased private perceptions and distorted public descriptions. *Journal of Personality and Social Psychology, 41*(2), 224.

Risse, G. L., LeDoux, J., Springer, S. P., Wilson, D. H., & Gazzaniga, M. S. (1978). The anterior commissure in man: Functional variation in a multisensory system. *Neuropsychologia, 16*(1), 23–31.

Seligman, M. E. (2004). *Authentic happiness: Using the new positive psychology to realize your potential for lasting fulfillment.* New York: Simon and Schuster.

Shoda, Y., Mischel, W., & Peake, P. K. (1990). Predicting adolescent cognitive and self-regulatory competencies from preschool delay of gratification: Identifying diagnostic conditions. *Developmental Psychology, 26*(6), 978.

Chapter 12

What now?

Writing this book has been an absorbing journey for us and we hope an absorbing read for you. All that remains is to pick out the most important action steps that have emerged, so you can be a 'facilitator of the client's self-directed neuroplasticity'.

Here are the themes that have stood out for us.

Embodiment

The brain is part of our body and cannot survive without it. (At least not at the time of writing in 2018.) Coaches focus on the mind and talk to the client, relying mostly on what they say back. Knowing the brain as we do, we need to expand our perspective and think of ourselves as coaching the whole person rather than restricting our attention to the part above the neck that has access to Broca's area. Some members of the 'brain team' are not able to get control of the language faculties, but they have influence nonetheless.

Sleep

Sleep is essential to high performance. We have read many books on high performance, but none seem to mention sleep. Many executives think they can push themselves to higher levels while neglecting the basic brain essentials. Sleep has come up quite a few times during the book. It is without doubt the single most effective action you can take to refresh your brain and body each day. We know that consistently getting less than six hours sleep affects the immune system and is correlated with many illnesses in the long term.

Sleep consolidates muscle memory and enables neuroplasticity. Sleep updates the memories of the previous day and increases memory retention by up to forty percent. Deep sleep seems to take the short-term memories from the hippocampus and store them in the cerebral cortex. The REM sleep takes consolidated memories and integrates them, through your unique autobiographical magic theatre of dreams. This creates networks of associations in the brain, critical not just for memory but also for creativity. What is more, you cannot catch up. Unless the memories are consolidated the same night, they are weaker and will not be strengthened even with a good night's sleep the following night.[1]

Research with adults who experienced six hours or less sleep a night for ten days showed this impaired their performance on cognitive tasks to the same extent as going without sleep for twenty-four hours. (We have all done that and it does not feel good.)

We know from daily experience that we are more likely to overreact when we are short of sleep. Brain scans for subjects shown emotional images showed that the amygdala signals are amplified by about sixty percent when sleep deprived, with clear consequences for emotional regulation.[2] Sleep is a very big deal for the brain, and it would be good if its importance permeated coaching as well. We always ask a client to pay attention to their sleep patterns, and especially when they are involved in high performance, leadership and creativity.

Physical exercise

Physical exercise is another important aspect of high performance, hiding in plain sight. Many people do not find time for it, because they are busy chasing high performance. The body benefits from exercise and so does the brain. The body supports the brain, and the healthier the body, the better it can support the brain.[3] Again, we ask executives to make physical exercise part of any high-performance plan.

Mindfulness

Mindfulness completes this triumvirate of embodied practices.

Mindfulness and meditation practices have cropped up many times in these pages. The benefits of mindfulness practice are very well researched. Mindfulness practises attention. Our choice every moment of our lives is where to put our attention. This determines our learning, our emotional state and our results.

There are two types of attention. The first is wide-open attention; you are alert and aware and let the world come to you. You are in the moment, non-judgemental and notice all stimuli without being drawn in to any of them. You can do this right now. Simply sit back and notice whatever comes into your mind. Simply observe it and treat everything equally. Do not label it as good or bad and do not be drawn into it. This is mindfulness – becoming a witness to your experience. You will be calmer, more objective and less stressed by what happens. You notice trains of thought and emotion going past, but you do not jump on them automatically. Mindfulness practice cultivates open attention. Mindfulness practice strengthens the link between the medial prefrontal cortex (PFC) and the amygdala, so we are less emotionally reactive and disturbed by what happens.[4] It helps people to become more self-aware by amplifying the signals from the body. At the same time, paradoxically it reduces uncomfortable self-consciousness.

Attention is affected by the phenomenon called 'attentional blink'. When we are looking for something and the information is rapidly changing (e.g. listening to a client for important information, body language, facial expression), we miss information if it occurs very close to another important piece. When we register information, there is a small period – a 'blink' where we miss what comes next (it lasts from two fifths to half a second). Meditation training has been shown to reduce this attentional blink by about thirty-three percent. Mindfulness can help us to become more observant coaches.

The second type of attention is focused attention – you choose what to focus on. We have called it 'top-down attention', as it is controlled by our goals and values. Our focused attention jumps from one thing to another, it is not easy to keep focus on one thing. Focus is essential to be able to study, remember and understand. A multimillion dollar pharmaceutical industry is focused on helping people focus better. Mindfulness practice helps focus. It increases phase locking[5] – the degree to which the brain waves become synchronised to an external stimulus – which is a sign of focus. The more scattered our attention, the less phase locking. The more phase locking, the more capacity for selective attention – the more the ability to focus.

Mindfulness practice also helps as a relaxation and refreshment between clients. It gives pause to let the mirror neuron activity die down, so you do not take the emotions and problems of the last client into the next session.

Mindfulness practice affects the default network.[6] The default network is made up of parts of the brain that are active when we are doing 'nothing', chilling and daydreaming. There is no focused attention. It includes the medial prefrontal cortex (mPFC), parts of the parietal cortex and the posterior cingulate cortex (PCC). The default network also connects to the memory system (hippocampus). There are no motor parts of the brain involved, so no action. When we are thinking of 'nothing', we are really thinking about ourselves. Past triumphs and failures, future ambitions, real and imagined slights, daydreams and nightmares; it is all about us. When the default network holds sway, we are the hero of the story. Goal-directed action takes you off the default network, and so does thinking of others. There must be some connection to the interpreter, but it is hard to demonstrate as both the default network and the interpreter functions are dispersed across the brain.

Research on experienced meditators using functional magnetic resonance imaging (fMRI)[7] found their default network was much less active. Empathy is connection with others and the default network all about self. It seems very likely from research that mindfulness meditation builds compassionate empathy, by quieting the default network.

Other studies with experienced meditators show that the activity in their default network is more in sync with networks associated with attention and executive control in the PFC. It looks like a greater ability to maintain attention and less time in mind wandering.

Finally, we know that mindfulness meditation helps in emotional self-regulation, strengthening the feedback loop between the PFC and the amygdala, leading to faster calming from emotional upset.

Enough quality sleep, regular physical exercise and regular mindfulness practice are the best practices for you and your brain. We believe that coaching must pay much more attention to these areas, regardless of the client's goal.

Inhibition

The brain team has many members, but no overall CEO. The team do not obey any one member; there is always a debate, and the different members (e.g. the amygdala, the default network, the reward system) all have different functions and agendas. They all discuss the issue, and the answer emerges for 'you' to carry out. The PFC is the nearest there is to a CEO because it has the power of *veto*. It may struggle to impose it, but the 'free won't' power is crucial. Sometimes, the PFC may be drunk, overwhelmed by the situation, half asleep or otherwise engaged and does not exercise the veto. Afterwards you may wish it had.

The PFC is the master of inhibition. Without it, the reward centre would run riot, the amygdala would be hijacked regularly, and the interpreter would spin ever more fantastic and self-serving tales. Many of the connections between the PFC and the reward centre are inhibitory. Focused thinking is not something that comes naturally; it comes when various impulses, distractions and irrelevant thoughts are stopped. The ability to inhibit impulses, distractions and irrelevant thoughts is crucial to focused thinking.

The PFC also stops habitual responses and allows creativity. It gives the space for new thinking to emerge. We need the PFC to stop that obvious, yet wrong answer that comes quickly from system 1, to make way for the reflective, more considered answer from system 2. Damage to the PFC leaves people reacting to the surroundings, neither goal driven nor creative. The PFC inhibits distractions to working memory, so you can get on with the work you want to do. The brain is a playground of infinite possibilities, and this playground would be chaos without the PFC to impose some order by selecting what is important, what to pay attention to and then keeping the focus by stopping distractions.

The PFC decides whether you go ahead and act. It is the arbiter of 'free won't'. When the PFC is working well, it will make its voice heard above the bickering team. It has one other power possessed by no other committee member – the power of perspective, particularly the power to choose different time horizons.

Time travel

The brain team members mostly have a short time horizon – the immediate risks, threats and rewards. The PFC can take a wider perspective which grows as we mature. You cannot reason a baby out of its hunger by saying they will get double ration of milk later. As we grow, so the PFC matures, and we gain gradually the ability to delay gratification, to veto the rest of the team. No one is sure when the PFC matures completely. Researchers say at about the age of twenty-five for men and a few years earlier in women, but some circuits may not be complete until years later. Wisdom is a journey, not a destination.

The PFC can imagine different futures. We can try out different future scenarios and test them. This power seems uniquely human. We do not need to act to know how it will turn out. The PFC ranges over the past, the present and constructs possible futures. This gives us tremendous power over our lives. It may be the one important defining characteristic of the human brain. Writing this book has made us incorporate a couple of questions into our coaching practice and ask them when the client is considering acting.

For example, the client is thinking of turning down a job offer.

We ask, 'Imagine it is one week's time. You have turned down the job offer. How do you feel?'

The second question is: 'Imagine it is one week's time. You have turned down the job offer. What do you think about that decision and how has it turned out?'

Make sure the client is associated into the future time. They need to imagine themselves into the future and then speak in the present tense. 'I feel this ... I think this ...'. You can vary the time frames depending on the decision or action. For some actions, it might be a day, for others a week and for others a month or even a year.

If the client is not happy, or has misgivings in the imaginary future, we ask another question:

'What would have to be true for you, (in this future time), to feel good about the action?'

This question goes for something the client needs to do in the present now, for them to feel good about the decision in the future 'now'.

Planning over time needs the idea of a continuous self. We feel more or less the same person as yesterday and will not change much tomorrow. What does it mean to have a continuous self? To accept and have compassion for our previous selves. Compassionate empathy is not only bestowed on other people. Looking to the past, we see actions that we label as mistakes now, but the self at the time was doing it for good reasons at the time. Everyone is doing the best they can, including yourself in the past. We are not one unchanging monolithic self, but an ever-changing team process. We have a sense of self, of a person, of a significant unique continuity, not with sharp edges but with rather fuzzy edges, moving through time. We recognise who we see in the mirror. Embrace our past selves, so that our future self can embrace us as we are now.

Neuroplasticity

We began this book with neuroplasticity because it underpins everything else. Without it, we would not learn, adapt or mature. It makes new thoughts and new habits and destroys old ones. It means making habits of thinking and action that work for us, so we do not have to review them all the time. We can change our brain. We create our brain through our thoughts and actions, and our changed brain can see wider horizons. And ... like all great gifts, it comes with a significant downside. Whatever we repeat becomes stronger. The brain makes no judgement about what is good or bad. Limiting habits of thinking are as easily formed as empowering ones. Repetition and attention build new brain networks. Repetition without attention will still build the network, but it will do it more slowly. It is significantly harder to change a network of connections making a habit than it is to build one. Habits should be treated with great respect. They are our greatest allies when we are happy with our life, and our greatest enemies when we want to change.

Context

Many times, during this book, we have seen the power of context – where you act, when you act, who you are with and what else is going on. The PFC lets takes in the context and adjusts your actions accordingly. Sometimes you do not want to be influenced by context. You do not want to be primed, anchored and influenced out of your awareness. System 1 has trouble with context. Either it takes it too seriously, as in priming, or it ignores it, as in the fundamental attribution error. System 2 gives context its proper place. System 2 uses decontextualised thinking – abstract thinking. It can reflect on ideas and separate principles of action from the context. The more we wake up the power of context, the more we can help ourselves and our clients.

Context can help us. We need to use the power of the environment. For example, I am sitting at my desk in my office typing this chapter. The afternoon sun is shining through the windows and the birds are singing. It is quiet, and I am undisturbed. The cat is sleeping on my desk and will probably make a bid for my attention in a minute by strolling languidly across the papers and sitting on my computer to compel me to pay attention to her and not to the writing, but that is a problem for later. The keyboard on the computer is working well. All these things help me to write. If I had an uncomfortable chair, a cramped desk and a computer that kept crashing, I might be the greatest writer on earth, but it is going to be difficult to concentrate. With the right context, I do not have to be the greatest writer on earth, (thank God). And yet so often, we expect people to adjust themselves to the situation, instead of getting the situation to adjust to them. Clients may think the environment is fixed, and they must change. Help clients to make it as easy as possible for themselves. This also means associating on a regular basis with people who are helpful and kind, and support them.

The environment is full of triggers and cues – the chime of the cell phone, the smell of coffee, the office layout – they tug at the coat tails of your mind for attention. They are hard to resist. The more you can control your environment, the more you can control your attention. The Ulysses contract is the extreme example – you take steps to control the future environment knowing the danger that will be there. Help your future self. Be a good friend to your future self. Don't be Homer Simpson and let your future self take care of the mess. Your future self is still – you.

The power of expectation

We learn by predicting the future, acting on the prediction and then adjusting our mental models through the feedback we get. We cannot operate without expectations, but we can own them as ours and not expect the world to live up to them. When expectations are confounded, that is the chance to learn. Instead, many people take it as a chance to be disappointed. Disappointment is that mixture of sadness and anger when your expectations are not met.

What is the opposite of disappointment?

Gratitude.

Gratitude is a feeling of appreciation mixed with pleasure for what you have now. It is complete. Gratitude gives value to what happened. It doesn't mean it's perfect and couldn't be better. It doesn't mean giving up striving for more. Gratitude is not an emotion in the sense of happiness or sadness, it is more an act of will. There have been several studies of gratitude; it is associated with more feelings of well-being[8] and better social relationships[9] and ability to deal with impatience and delay discounting for money.[10]

Gratitude activates many areas of the brain including the reward centre, the anterior cingulate cortex and the parts of the PFC and OFC associated with moral understanding and self-reference (ventromedial PFC and the insula).[11] It seems to be one of the most important moral emotions. Gratitude and happiness are both feelings with health and well-being benefits. We recommend all our clients keep a gratitude journal, and this practice is very helpful especially for clients who are very demanding of themselves and others. (They are likely to have high expectations and be disappointed more often.)

The future

What will neuroscience bring to the study and practice of coaching? It is difficult to predict, because coaching is not one practice; there are many different models of coaching, although all the main streams share the same basic philosophy and practice.[12]

We think neuroscience will keep adding to our understanding of coaching. The subjects explored in this book will be incorporated into coaching in the next few years. Thinking, memory, emotion, learning – these are all fundamental to coaching.

One future scenario is where very little changes. Neuroscience is used to bolster existing practice. This will probably happen over the short term. In the long term, we see several connected trends.

First, there will be more attention for the body. Whatever the goals – health, happiness, better relationships, leadership skills – they depend on the mind and body. We will understand more about how our mind arises from our brain and how our brain is embodied. Taking care of the body will become more important. It is ridiculous to expect a leader to function well on too little sleep, not enough exercise, inadequate relaxation, poorly designed environment and little knowledge of how their brain works.

Already in international companies, there are gyms, mindfulness sessions and a focus on healthier eating. All are trends in supporting the mind through the brain through the body. Sleep will probably be the next focus for high performance. We can soar to the stars, literally and artistically, but we cannot leave our bodies behind.

Sleep, exercise and mindfulness all help focus and motivation. What other possibilities are there? Smart drugs or nootropics to give them their proper name are a growing trend. An article[13] in June 2018 reports that one in twelve adults admit to taking 'smart drugs'.[14] The true number is likely to be higher. Most people use them at work to cope with workload pressures according to the report. It is likely that many people are missing good quality sleep, exercise and relaxation practice and are turning to smart drugs to make up for this. This is a moral, ethical and legal question and more complicated than the question of performance enhancing drugs in sport. It will need serious consideration in the next five years.

In a sense we are all on drugs – dopamine, serotonin, oxytocin and acetylcholine are all chemical compounds that can be supplemented directly or indirectly. We need these to function. These natural chemicals are not addictive or dangerous to health in their natural state. We need them to run the physical processes of the brain which result in the experience of focus, mood and memory. Everybody starts with different levels. For example, the feeling of motivation needs dopamine (as well as many other things). To get enough dopamine, you need to take enough of the precursors of dopamine as dopamine cannot be supplemented directly; it does not pass the blood–brain barrier. Phenylalanine is a compound in many foods: eggs, meat and milk (and diet soda) that is converted in our brains to the amino acid tyrosine and then through other stages to dopamine. Dopamine is itself used in the making of noradrenaline and adrenaline, two further important neurotransmitters. Dopamine depends on diet for its constituents. Genetics also plays a part in how well and effectively dopamine can be used.

Nootropics, or cognitive enhancers, are supplements that can be taken to help to boost the natural neurotransmitters and enhance brain function. The result can be improved memory, focus and concentration. Nootropics are the cognitive equivalents of vitamin and mineral supplements. Many people are using these. Some occur naturally in the body. Examples are alpha glyceryl phosphoryl choline (GPC), Ginkgo biloba and omega 3 and 6. The evidence for what smart drugs and nootropics do to the brain is not clear, but many people report better concentration and memory. Coaches help well-functioning people function better. Nootropics do the same on the physical level. Do they work and if so are they worth using? The coach of the future will have to engage in this debate.[15]

We do not think brain scans will be used in coaching in the foreseeable future. Scans are very limited in what they can tell us about the brain for coaching purposes; they can tell us what is working and what is not, but now, it is hard to see how this could be applied in coaching.

We opened this book by talking about our brain scans in New York.

What of those?

They brought us a new understanding of ourselves. They opened a door on our experience that has been fascinating and rewarding. It has deepened and expanded our coaching practice and started us down a path that has helped us personally and professionally. Brain-based coaching does not try to upend existing knowledge. Everything in this book is intended to strengthen, augment and expand what coaches already do. When it backs up existing practice, it gives coaching added credibility. When it points in other directions, it gives us an opportunity to learn, revaluate and change.

Clients have very little idea of how the brain works and knowledge gives power. The more we know about ourselves, the further we can go. Looking at the intricate and incredible workings of our brain, we feel humble. We all have depth – more than we can fathom, perhaps than we can ever fathom. We can generate questions about ourselves that are impossible to answer. The mind is not a place; it is a process maintained by neurons and neurotransmitters. The brain lives on proteins and glucose, but it also lives on experience. Experience is the food of the brain. The brain converts experience into learning and then into more (and hopefully better) experience. It produces what we call reality as a final draft from all the inputs. Somehow, our consciousness floats above the turbulent team and expresses them as best it can through attention and action. We can choose where to put our attention and whether to act or not. The result will change ourselves and the world.

We began this book with a quotation from the American Psychologists William James, so it is fitting we close with another. In 1890, he wrote,

> The great thing then in education is to make our nervous system our ally instead of our enemy, for this we must make automatic and habitual, as

early as possible, has many useful actions as we can, and guard against the growing into ways that are likely to be disadvantageous to us, as we should guard against the plague.

When coaches help clients to understand their evolving team of selves, with acceptance of the past and excitement about the future, then they serve their clients well.

   This book has changed you, because you remember it. Your brain is not quite the same as it was when you started. We hope your team has enjoyed it and will convert it to great happiness and learning.

Notes

1 Stickgold, R. (2005). Sleep-dependent memory consolidation. *Nature, 437* (7063), 1272.
2 Yoo, S. S., Gujar, N., Hu, P., Jolesz, F. A., & Walker, M. P. (2007). The human emotional brain without sleep—A prefrontal amygdala disconnect. *Current Biology, 17* (20), R877–R878.
3 That exercise is good for health is a cliché, although like many cliché, more honoured in the telling than in the doing. There is a good summing up of the cognitive benefits in: https://www.psychologytoday.com/intl/blog/the-athletes-way/201404/ physical-activity-improves-cognitive-function (Accessed 1 June 2018).
    There are many claims for the cognitive benefits of purely cognitive exercises. There are many apps, websites and plans offering these. The jury is still out on whether these offer a clear benefit, and how big it might be. On the other hand, the cognitive benefit of physical exercise is very well established.
4 Desbordes, G., Negi, L. T., Pace, T. W. W., Wallace, B. A., Raison, C. L., Schwartz, E. L. (2012). Effects of mindful-attention and compassion meditation training on amygdala response to emotional stimuli in an ordinary, non-meditative state. *Frontiers in Human Neuroscience, 6*, 292. doi:10.3389/fnhum.2012.00292.
5 Paulson, S., Davidson, R., Jha, A., & Kabat-Zinn, J. (2013). Becoming conscious: The science of mindfulness. *Annals of the New York Academy of Sciences, 1303* (1), 87–104.
6 Brewer, J. A., Worhunsky, P. D., Gray, J. R., Tang, Y. Y., Weber, J., & Kober, H. (2011). Meditation experience is associated with differences in default mode network activity and connectivity. *Proceedings of the National Academy of Sciences, 108* (50), 20254–20259.
7 Brewer, J. A., Worhunsky, P. D., Gray, J. R., Tang, Y. Y., Weber, J., & Kober, H. (2011). Meditation experience is associated with differences in default mode network activity and connectivity. *Proceedings of the National Academy of Sciences, 108* (50), 20254–20259.
8 Froh, J. J., Sefick, W. J., & Emmons, R. A. (2008). Counting blessings in early adolescents: An experimental study of gratitude and subjective well-being. *Journal of School Psychology, 46* (2), 213–233.
9 Algoe, S. B., Haidt, J., & Gable, S. L. (2008). Beyond reciprocity: Gratitude and relationships in everyday life. *Emotion, 8* (3), 425.
10 DeSteno, D., Li, Y., Dickens, L., & Lerner, J. S. (2014). Gratitude: A tool for reducing economic impatience. *Psychological Science, 25* (6), 1262–1267.
11 Fox, G. R., Jonas, K., Hanna, D., & Antonio, D. (2015). Neural correlates of gratitude. *Frontiers in Psychology, 6*, 1491.
    https://www.frontiersin.org/article/10.3389/fpsyg.2015.01491

12 O'Connor, J., & Lages, A., (2007). *How coaching works*. London, England: AC Black.
13 https://www.telegraph.co.uk/news/2018/06/15/smart-drug-epidemic-one-12-adults-admit-taking-trying-work/ (accessed 19the June 2018).
14 The most popular being Adderall and Modafinil, both cognitive enhancers that increase focus, although Adderall, because it interferes with the dopamine system and carries a substantial risk of addiction. They are not illegal.
15 See the book, Bad Moves, by Barbara Sahakian and Jamie Labuzetta (Oxford University Press 2013) for an ethical discussion on the future of smart drugs and nootropics.

Bibliography

Algoe, S. B., Haidt, J., & Gable, S. L. (2008). Beyond reciprocity: Gratitude and relationships in everyday life. *Emotion, 8*(3), 425.

Brewer, J. A., Worhunsky, P. D., Gray, J. R., Tang, Y. Y., Weber, J., & Kober, H. (2011). Meditation experience is associated with differences in default mode network activity and connectivity. *Proceedings of the National Academy of Sciences, 108*(50), 20254–20259.

Desbordes, G., Negi, L. T., Pace, T. W. W., Wallace, B. A., Raison, C. L., & Schwartz, E. L. (2012). Effects of mindful-attention and compassion meditation training on amygdala response to emotional stimuli in an ordinary, non-meditative state. *Frontiers in Human Neuroscience, 6*, 292. doi:10.3389/fnhum.2012.00292.

DeSteno, D., Li, Y., Dickens, L., & Lerner, J. S. (2014). Gratitude: A tool for reducing economic impatience. *Psychological Science, 25*(6), 1262–1267.

Fox, G. R., Jonas, K., Hanna, D., & Antonio, D. (2015). Neural correlates of gratitude. *Frontiers in Psychology, 6*, 1491.

Froh, J. J., Sefick, W. J., & Emmons, R. A. (2008). Counting blessings in early adolescents: An experimental study of gratitude and subjective well-being. *Journal of School Psychology, 46*(2), 213–233.

O'Connor, J., & Lages, A. (2007). *How coaching works*. London, England: AC Black.

Paulson, S., Davidson, R., Jha, A., & Kabat-Zinn, J. (2013). Becoming conscious: The science of mindfulness. *Annals of the New York Academy of Sciences, 1303*(1), 87–104.

Sahakian, B., & Labuzetta, J. (2013). *Bad Moves*. Oxford, England: Oxford University Press.

Stickgold, R. (2005). Sleep-dependent memory consolidation. *Nature, 437*(7063), 1272.

Yoo, S. S., Gujar, N., Hu, P., Jolesz, F. A., & Walker, M. P. (2007). The human emotional brain without sleep – A prefrontal amygdala disconnect. *Current Biology, 17*(20), R877–R878.

https://www.psychologytoday.com/intl/blog/the-athletes-way/201404/physical-activity-improves-cognitive-function

https://www.frontiersin.org/article/10.3389/fpsyg.2015.01491

https://www.telegraph.co.uk/news/2018/06/15/smart-drug-epidemic-one-12-adults-admit-taking-trying-work/

Bibliography

Recommended reading (2018)

Here is a personal list of books we found useful and interesting.

There are sure to be some we missed. Neuroscience is a fast-growing field; we have given the most recent books, and no doubt, there will be many more.

On neuroscience

Austin J. H. (1998). *Zen and the brain: Toward an understanding of meditation and consciousness.* MIT Press.

Baron-Cohen, S. (2011). *The science of evil.* Basic Books.

Damasio, Antonio, (2000). *The feeling of what happens.* Vintage books.

Davidson, R. J., & Begley, S. (2012). *The emotional life of your brain: How its unique patterns affect the way you think, feel, and live--and how you can change them.* Penguin.

Doidge, N. (2007). *The brain that changes itself: Stories of personal triumph from the frontiers of brain science.* Penguin.

Eagleman, D. (2011). *Incognito: The secret lives of the brain.* New York: Pantheon.

Eagleman, D. (2015). *The brain: The story of you.* Vintage.

Fallon, J. (2013). *The psychopath inside: A neuroscientist's personal journey into the dark side of the brain.* Penguin.

Frith, C. (2013). *Making up the mind: How the brain creates our mental world.* John Wiley & Sons.

Gazzaniga, M. S. (Ed.). (2014). *Handbook of cognitive neuroscience.* Springer.

Iacoboni, M., (2008). *Mirroring people.* Farrar, Straus & Giroux.

Johnson, S. (2004). *Mind wide open: Your brain and the neuroscience of everyday life.* Simon and Schuster.

Kurzban, R. (2012). *Why everyone (else) is a hypocrite: Evolution and the modular mind.* Princeton University Press.

LeDoux, J. (1998). *The emotional brain: The mysterious underpinnings of emotional life.* Simon and Schuster.

Levitin, D. J. (2006). *This is your brain on music: The science of a human obsession.* Penguin.

Lewis, M. (2015). *The biology of desire: Why addiction is not a disease.* Hachette UK.

Macknik, S., Martinez-Conde, S., & Blakeslee, S. (2010). *Sleights of mind: What the neuroscience of magic reveals about our everyday deceptions.* Henry Holt and Company.

Mischel, W. (2014). *The Marshmallow test: Understanding self-control and how to master it.* Random House.

Quartz, S. R., & Sejnowski, T. J. (2003). *Liars, lovers, and heroes: What the new brain science reveals about how we become who we are.* Harper Collins.

Ramachandran, V. S., Blakeslee, S., & Shah, N. (1998). *Phantoms in the brain: Probing the mysteries of the human mind* (pp. 224–225). New York: William Morrow.

Sahakian, B., & LaBuzetta, J. N. (2013). *Bad Moves: How decision making goes wrong, and the ethics of smart drugs.* OUP Oxford.

Schwartz, J. M., & Begley, S. (2009). *The mind and the brain.* Springer Science & Business Media.

Walker, M. (2017). *Why we sleep.* Allen Lane.

Coaching

O'Connor, J., & Lages, A. (2009). *How coaching works: The essential guide to the history and practice of effective coaching.* A&C Black.

Stober, D. R., & Grant, A. M. (Eds.). (2010). *Evidence based coaching handbook: Putting best practices to work for your clients.* John Wiley & Sons.

Further reading in neuroscience and coaching

Azmatullah, S. (2013). *The coach's mind manual: Enhancing coaching practice with neuroscience, psychology and mindfulness.* Routledge.

Bossons, P., Riddell, P., & Sartain, D. (2015). *The neuroscience of leadership coaching: Why the tools and techniques of Leadership Coaching Work.* Bloomsbury Publishing.

Brann, A. (2017). *Neuroscience for coaches: How to use the latest insights for the benefit of your clients.* Kogan Page PublishersDehaene, S. (2014). *Consciousness and the brain: Deciphering how the brain codes our thoughts.* Penguin.

Damasio, A. R. (2000). The feeling of what happens: Body and emotion in the making of consciousness. Vintage Books.

Glaser, J., (2014). *Conversational Intelligence.* Bibliomotion.

Greenfield, S. (2017). *A day in the life of the brain.* Penguin.

Higbee, K. L. (2001). *Your memory: How it works and how to improve it.* Da Capo Press.

Kandel, E. R. (2007). *In search of memory: The emergence of a new science of mind.* WW Norton & Company.

Lehrer, J. (2008). *Proust was a neuroscientist.* Houghton Mifflin Harcourt.

Pillay, S. S. (2011). *Your brain and business.* Pearson Education India.

Rock, D., & Page, L. J. (2009). *Coaching with the brain in mind: Foundations for practice.* John Wiley & Sons.

Sacks, O. (2009). *The man who mistook his wife for a hat.* Picador.

Swart, T., Chisholm, K., & Brown, P. (2015). *Neuroscience for leadership: Harnessing the brain gain advantage.* Springer.

Website

There are many websites dealing with Neuroscience. One we found particularly helpful was www.neuroscientificallychallenged.com

Key to the Team in the closed room

CEO:

Peter Bach – Prefrontal Cortex

Translators:

Vera Score – Wernicke's area

John Broker – Broca's area

CFO:

Victor Strickland – Ventral tegmental area

Risk assessment:

Della – Amygdala

Head of security:

Andrew Solo – Anterior cingulate cortex

Organizer:

Jan Sanctum – Thalamus

Mary Island – Insula

Global HR manager:

Richard Border – Supramarginal gyrus

Data Processing:

Mary Steed – Hippocampus

Glossary

Acetylcholine   A neurotransmitter essential for movement, also involved in attention and memory.

Agonist   A substance that binds to a receptor on a neuron and activates it, replacing the usual neurotransmitter.

Amnesia   Memory difficulties or loss, often the result of brain damage.

- Anterograde amnesia   Inability to form new memories.
- Retrograde amnesia   Loss of memory for past events.

Amygdala   Specialised part of the brain in the medial temporal lobe associated with emotional processing and memory, especially fear.

Antagonist   A substance that binds to a receptor and blocks it, so the usual neurotransmitter cannot bind to it.

Anterior cingulate cortex (ACC)   Front portion of the cingulate cortex below the frontal lobes. Associated with error detection, attention control and the sensation of pain.

Aphasia   Language difficulty due to brain damage.

Attention   The process by which we become conscious of a stimulus. There are many types of attention, and many brain areas are involved. The main types are bare attention and selective attention. Our attention is directed either top-down (goal oriented) or bottom-up (reactive to a stimulus such as pain).

Attentional blink   A gap in attention for a second visual stimulus that comes too quickly after a first stimulus.

Autonomic nervous system   Part of the peripheral nervous system that regulates many processes like digestion and temperature and heart rate. It consists of the sympathetic (excitatory) and parasympathetic (calming) systems.

Axon   An extension of the cell body of a neuron sending information through the action potential to other cells.

Basal ganglia   A group of structures deep in the brain including the caudate nucleus, the putamen, the globus pallidus and the substantia nigra. They play a defining role in the control of movement.

Blindsight A condition where an effectively blind person can still point out objects, although not able to consciously see them. This is because visual information travels on two pathways to the brain. A person may not be able to see an object but still know its location and orientation.

Bottom-up processing Processing in response to a stimulus that compels our attention (e.g. pain).

Brainstem The base part of the brain. It sends and receives information from the spinal cord and controls many automatic functions like breathing and heart rate.

Broca's area The region usually in the left frontal lobe that controls the production of speech.

CAT scan Computerised axial tomography – a way of using X-rays to give three-dimensional images of the brain.

Caudate Part of the basal ganglia, making the striatum.

Central nervous system (CNS) Brain and spinal cord.

Cerebellum A large area of the brain that controls movement, coordination balance and has a role in memory and cognition.

Cerebral cortex The outer layer of the cerebral hemispheres, responsible for abstract thinking and planning.

Cerebral hemispheres The two halves of the brain – mirror images, but with some specialisation, the left for aspects of speech and language and the right for spatial ability and music.

Cingulate cortex The inside area of the cerebral cortex that surrounds the corpus callosum.

Cognition The process whereby we become aware of events and thoughts and using the knowledge for problem-solving.

Cognitive neuroscience The biology of the mind – providing explanations for perceptions and thinking.

Conditioning Learning mechanism where a stimulus is paired to a response.

Consolidation The process of memory that transfers the memory from short-term to long-term memory.

Corpus callosum The structure that connects left and right hemispheres and allows signals to pass between them.

Cortisol Stress hormone produced by the adrenal glands through the hypothalamus–pituitary–adrenal (HPA) axis.

Deep brain stimulation (DBS) Stimulation of the brain directly through electrodes planted in the brain.

Default network A group of structures including the medial prefrontal cortex, cingulate cortex and part of the parietal lobe that are thought to be active when one is awake but not attending to anything in particular. It is most active when we are daydreaming.

Dendrites Extensions of the neuron that receive information from other neurons.

Dopamine   An important neurotransmitter involved in movement, motivation, attention and wanting.

Electroencephalography (EEG)   A measurement of electrical activity in the brain, by placing electrodes on the scalp.

Emotion   A feeling or response to events or our interpretation of events. They are deep evolutionary important responses, change our physiology and orient us to important events. The basic emotions are happiness, anger, sadness, fear and disgust.

Empathy   The ability to identify what someone else is thinking and/or feeling and making an appropriate response.

- Cognitive empathy is the ability to identify what someone else is thinking.
- Emotional empathy is the ability to identify what someone else is feeling.
- Compassionate empathy is the ability to make an appropriate response to what someone else is thinking and feeling.

Epinephrine   A hormone and a neurotransmitter involved in the fight or flight fear response. It increases the heart rate and the amount of glucose in the blood. Also called acetylcholine.

Episodic memory   Memories of actual personal experiences in the past.

Event-related potential (ERP)   A specific, electrical brain response to a sensory, cognitive or motor stimulus and can be measured directly by EEG.

Feeling   A physical awareness of sensation.

Frontal lobe   The part of the cerebral hemispheres at the front. It contains the primary motor cortex and is the centre for executive planning, learning and cognition.

Functional magnetic resonance imaging (fMRI)   A way of measuring which parts of the brain are active when a person engages in a task by detecting changes in cerebral blood flow.

Fusiform gyrus   A fold in the temporal lobe specialised for recognising faces.

Gamma-aminobutyric acid (GABA)   An important inhibitory neurotransmitter.

Ganglion   A group of neurons.

Glial cell   Supporting cells in the brain. All cells in the brain that are not neurons. There are many varieties with many functions. There are as many glial cells in the brain as there are neurons (about ninety billion).

Goals   Those things we do not have and want to achieve or create.

Gyrus   A ridge in the cerebral cortex because of the way it is folded.

Habit   An automatic thought or action that is not under conscious control. Habits are expressed in the brain by systems of neurons that have strong connections between them because of repetition. Neuroplasticity makes habits possible, keeps them current and allows them to change.

Hebb's law 'Cells that fire together, wire together'.

Hippocampus A small structure located in each temporal lobe, important in coding and consolidating memories.

HPA axis The interaction between the hypothalamus, the pituitary and the adrenal glands, important in the stress response.

Hypothalamus A brain structure, often included in the limbic system that controls the pituitary gland and so regulates parts of the autonomic nervous system.

Insula An important area deep in the brain that appears to modulate our sense of awareness. It has strong connections to other areas, including the amygdala and the anterior cingulate cortex.

Learning Gaining more knowledge and skill in the world by updating predictions and expectations through feedback.

Limbic system Name for the structures forming the emotional network in the brain, with the amygdala as the principal part.

Long-term memory Memories that are stored and distributed across many parts of the brain that can be retrieved given an appropriate stimulus.

Long-term potentiation The strengthening of synapses due to repetition. The basis of Hebb's Law, neuroplasticity and habit formation.

Magnetic Resonance Imaging (MRI) A method that uses magnetic resonance technology to give high-resolution images of the brain.

Medulla The part where the spinal cord connects to the brainstem.

Memory The ability to code, consolidate and recall past information. Dependent on the hippocampus and associated parts of the temporal lobe.

Mental models Beliefs, assumptions or expectations about the world that we act on as if they are true.

Mesocortical pathway One of the two dopamine pathways in the brain; it runs from the VTA to the cerebral cortex. It modulates the experience of wanting with executive planning.

Mesolimbic pathway The dopamine pathway that runs from the VTA to the NA and amygdala. It influences the feeling of pleasure and reward.

Midbrain The upper part of the brainstem.

Mirror neuron network Neurons that fire not only when the person themselves performs an action but also when they observe someone else doing that action. Mirror neurons appear to be the basis of empathy and our ability to understand the intentions of others, by making a simulation of the action.

Motor cortex The area of the cortex that controls movement.

Motor neuron A neuron that carries information from brain to muscle.

Mu waves Brain waves that are suppressed during acting and observing an action, thought to be part of the default network.

Myelin   The fatty sheath round an axon. It insulates the axon and allows the signal to pass quickly.

Neocortex   The outermost layer of the cerebral cortex and the most recently evolved. It is associated with functions of higher intelligence.

Neuron   Nerve cell, consisting of a nucleus, an axon and dendrites. The brain consists of about ninety billion neurons.

Neuroplasticity   The ability of the brain to change itself.

Neurotransmitter   A chemical released at the synapse of a neuron to allow the signal to continue to the next neuron.

Nucleus accumbens   Part of the basal ganglia involved in the experience of wanting, gaining rewards and subsequent pleasure.

Occipital lobe   One of the four lobes of each cerebral hemisphere, specialising in vision. It is situated at the back of the brain.

Opioids   Chemical released in the brain giving the experience of pleasure. They are linked to dopamine and the reward system.

Orbitofrontal cortex (OFC)   Part of the PFC directly above the eye orbits. It is involved in decision-making, emotional processing and learning.

Oxytocin   Hormone produced by the hypothalamus, also a neurotransmitter. It plays a part in maternal bonding, childbirth and lactation. It may also be important in social bonding and the experience of trust.

Parietal lobe   One of the four divisions of each cerebral hemisphere, situated behind the frontal lobe. It contains the primary somatosensory cortex. It is involved in orienting attention and spatial orientation.

Peripheral nervous system   The part of the nervous system outside the brain and spinal cord.

Pituitary   Endocrine gland at the bottom of the hypothalamus that secretes many hormones.

Pons   Part of the base of the brain near the spinal cord. It regulates breathing and heart rhythm.

Positron emission tomography (PET)   Injecting radioactive particles and then using them to image the brain activity in real time by following the particles in the blood flow.

Prediction error   The difference between what was predicted and what was experienced. Essential for learning, it appears to be measured by differences in dopamine levels in the brain.

Prefrontal cortex (PFC)   The frontal area of the frontal lobes. Responsible for executive planning.

Premotor cortex   Motor area in front of the primary motor cortex, involved in planning movements.

Primary motor cortex   Part of the brain controlling voluntary movement, situated at the back of the frontal lobe.

Priming   The effect of context on our thinking. Objects and ideas in the environment influence the way we think about unconnected subjects without our knowledge.

Procedural memory Memory for skills.

Putamen Part of the striatum that forms the basal ganglia.

Qualia Subjective sensations.

Refractory period The time after feeling an emotion where we interpret events in the light of that emotion.

Reversal learning The ability to inhibit previously learned actions when they are no longer rewarding.

Reward system Several brain structures, including the nucleus accumbens and the ventral tegmental area that help learning. The reward system is involved in the experience of wanting and pleasure in achievement.

Semantic memory Memory for the meaning of an event or concept. The brain's dictionary of general knowledge.

Serotonin A neurotransmitter linked to regulating mood, social behaviour, sleep and sexual desire.

Short-term memory Memory for events before being consolidated into long-term memory, ranging from several seconds to several hours. It is divided into sensory memory and working memory.

Somatic marker hypothesis The idea put forward by Antonio Damasio that we decide by balancing emotions and feelings associated with ideas and experiences that are stored in the body. The orbital frontal cortex is the main brain area involved in integrating the feelings to decide.

Somatosensory cortex Area of the brain processing sensations of touch.. Situated in the parietal lobe.

Stimulus Something we can detect by our senses, leading to a response.

Striatum A structure incorporating the caudate, nucleus accumbens and putamen. It is part of the basal ganglia and the reward circuit.

Structures Reminders in coaching for the client to take a course of action or a new perspective.

Subcortical Under the cerebral cortex.

Substantia nigra Part of the brain that makes dopamine and supplies dopamine to the basal ganglia. Also part of the reward circuit.

Sulcus A groove in the folding of the cerebral cortex.

Supramarginal gyrus A fold in the parietal lobe associated with self-perception and empathy.

Sylvian fissure The large groove that separates the temporal lobe from the frontal and parietal lobes.

Sympathetic nervous system Branch of the peripheral nervous system that is concerned with arousal.

Synapse A gap between two neurons, where the signal crosses usually by means of a neurotransmitter.

Top-down processing Proactive processing driven by goals and values.

Temporal lobe One of the four lobes of each cerebral hemisphere. The temporal lobe is involved in hearing, language, memory and emotion.

Thalamus   A small structure in the middle of the brain that serves as a relay station, sending information to different parts of the brain as required.

Theory of mind   The idea that we can imagine the thoughts and intentions of others as separate to us.

Values   Those concepts that are emotionally important to us and guide our actions.

Ventral tegmental area   A subcortical area, with many dopamine neurons. Part of the mesolimbic dopamine pathway and the reward system.

Wernicke's area   The brain region, usually in the left temporal lobe, that is responsible for understanding language and producing meaningful language.

Working memory   The part of short-term memory that stores information we are currently working on and needs to be available.

Further resources

We hope you have enjoyed this book.

We believe Neuroscience will form a larger part of coaching in the future.

We conduct many trainings all over the world on Leadership, Coaching and Neuroscience and also run many distance learning courses on these subjects.

Our distance learning course, 'Coaching the Brain' was built to put this book into practice and can be taken individually, or in groups.

For details of 'Coaching the Brain' and our other neuroscience courses, go to:

www.neurosciencecoaching.net

For coaching and leadership courses, go to:

www.lambent.com and, www.internationalcoachingcommunity.com

We can be contacted directly through any of the above websites.

Index

TANNER

CALHOUN MEN BOOK 6

KATHI S. BARTON

This is a work of fiction. Names, characters, places, and incidents are products of the author's imagination or are used fictitiously and are not to be construed as real. Any resemblance to actual events, locations, organizations, or persons, living or dead, is entirely coincidental.

World Castle Publishing, LLC
Pensacola, Florida
Copyright © Kathi S. Barton 2018
Paperback ISBN: 9781629899244
eBook ISBN: 9781629899251
First Edition World Castle Publishing, LLC, April 30, 2018
http://www.worldcastlepublishing.com
Licensing Notes
Cover: Karen Fuller
Editor: Maxine Bringenberg

Table of Contents

Chapter 1

Tyrrell watched the little plane land. He'd been in Ohio for a whole day now, and he'd decided that it was a cute place. The town that he was staying in, a quaint little burg, had all the amenities that one might need—a grocery store, library, schools, as well as a doctor or two. The only thing that he could find fault with, and that wasn't such a big deal, was that it lacked places to eat. Not that the few that were there didn't cater to your every whim, but all he could get delivered to him was subs and pizza. Laughing, he wondered what his sister would think after living in a part of Ireland that was mostly farmland and sheep. She'd think she was living in a metropolitan area around here.

He was at the end of the gate when she came into the building. Tyrrell felt his eyes fill with tears at the sight of her. She'd changed so much that he was surprised. It had been just over ten years since he'd laid eyes on her, but he had talked to her often.

Giyanna had her red hair pulled back in a long braid that had pulled loose in several places, but she had the face of a porcelain goddess, freckles and all. He had missed her so much, and it occurred to him then that it had been far too long since they'd even spoken.

They hugged for a full five minutes, both saying how much they'd missed each other, their words tumbling over one another like they used to as children. He had missed her so very much. And she him, she told him.

"The flight was long and I'm exhausted. Hungry too. The food on the plane was good, but far too little to sustain someone for hours, I think." He helped her with her luggage, just one bag and a carry on. "I didn't know how long I'd be here, so I took two months off. It was difficult to find someone to watch my house, so you owe me half of that as well, Tyrrell." She told him that she was joking, that she had it covered.

"No, no, I told you that I'd go half. Just tell me what you want. Anything you need, I'll do it. I'm just so very glad to see you. But two months and you have one bag? Are you planning to spend some time while here to shop?" She glared at him. "Ah, so you're a better packer than I. I don't doubt that either. I just haphazardly throw things toward the suitcase, and if it lands in it, it goes with me. God, it's so good to see you after all this time. We should have done this years ago, Giyanna."

"Yes, we should have, but I'm telling you right now, I won't be drawn into Rogan's mess other than to try and get him a reduced sentence. What is it he's been taken in for?" Tyrrell handed her a thick file as he carried her bag out to the car. "Restraining order violation? That's it? Damn it. I thought for sure I could just let him float his arse to prison.

6

How is Bridgett? Have you spoken to her yet?"

"No, I've not, and your Irish is showing. But yes, there is more. Breaking and entering. Parole violation. Also, he has a list of other charges about a mile long that he's been avoiding. And by avoiding, I mean that he's been not seeing his parole officer when he was supposed to. Intoxication. Robbery. Selling stolen goods. They decided that since they know where he is right now they'll hit him up for them all at once. So you might get your wish after all with him. But he's been beating Bridget, and that has gotten him into the worst of it." She was still reading over the file when she asked him where he was now. "Jail. Apparently, he was asked to leave the house that Bridgett was living in with him and he didn't cooperate. He beat one of the men nearly to death, and the other man has a broken arm. They're also charging him with the destruction of a government building. He tore up the house pretty good. His defense on that was that when Bridgett returned, she'd fix it up. And she is going to return, as he's told everyone that will listen."

"He's a moron and a bully. It saddens me on so many levels that she had to do this. Running away is seldom the answer, but in her case and ours it was the only way to survive him. And she had to take his children so far away to hide from him." Tyrrell told her that he'd sent her some money. "I did as well. At least she'll be able to feed them until she can get a job. I'm to understand that her brother is there with her, and he's already lined up a job for himself. These people that are helping her…do you know anything about them?"

"I've been doing some research, and they're about the best thing this town has ever seen. They're wolves that are

7

wealthy beyond anything I've ever heard of." She nodded as they drove to the local bed and breakfast. "One of them is an attorney that has been asked to take on the case, but he declined. Something to so with him being in private practice. I don't know. But it's probably just as well. He's really the best they have around here. And as much as I'd hate to say it, I do not want Rogan free to run around any more than Bridgett does."

"I'm better as an attorney, I bet." She laughed with him. "But I have to tell you, Tyrrell, I don't want to do this. You have to know that." He said that he'd do it if she would be the second chair. "I don't even want to do that. I really dislike him. Rogan has been nothing but a bully since we were children. I'd just as soon he went to prison and never got out."

"When he called me, all I could think about was finding the state's prosecutor, whoever that might be, and giving him even more shit to pile onto whatever they have on him. And as you can tell, there is a great deal of it." She closed the file and leaned back. "Honey, you're tired. Why don't you take a long nap when we get there? That way when you wake, you'll be fresh enough to go see him with me."

"I think I'll sleep for a week." He just grinned at her when she looked at him. "I want to spend time with you, and before I have to go back, I want us to go out and see the kids. Hopefully they'll be all right out there. I have to admit, though, I'm so glad that she was able to do this. Even if she had to take them all the way across the country to do so."

"Bridgett is terrified that she'll lose the kids if he's able to get out. I don't foresee him getting even visitation rights, but I don't practice in this state, so things could be different.

With him having a criminal record it might go in her favor. But they're not hers, remember." She said that she did. "The fact that they're his might not go so well for her since she's unemployed and took them out of the state. However, she has called the police on him several times, and I'm to understand there is a restraining order that he broke too. I'm thinking she'll be all right, but I don't want to promise her anything."

"She took them for safety reasons, and that alone will keep her from getting into trouble. That's what I would do if I were on her side. Where, I might add, I wish I was." He said that he did as well. "Oh well, so we're here. When do we go and see the dumbass?"

"When you're rested. I think right now you're not in the mood to talk to him, am I right?" Giyanna yawned and nodded. "You get some rest. I'll go tell Rogan that we're both here and see what he has to say for himself. I've been sort of avoiding him since I got here. For good reason, I think, but I still have no desire to even be in the same room with him."

Their brother had been cruel to them when they were children. It was the reason that they'd left home so young and never returned. Not even to talk to their parents, who Tyrrell had lost contact with years ago. He wondered if Giyanna had spoken to them, but she was exhausted, and he didn't want to upset her more.

"All right then, seeing him has to come first, I guess. But wait for me. I'll go with you, and that way we can try and hold onto our tempers as a tag team." She was nearly asleep when he laughed. "I'm really exhausted. I would have slept on the plane, but there was this kid behind me that I swear to you had daggers at the end of his shoes, and he was using

9

them to hit me in the back. The entire trip."

Tyrrell glanced at her every so often to see that she was sleeping again. He didn't envy her the trip back, nor seeing Rogan. As he'd said, he had no desire to see him either. And when he thought of that, it sometimes hurt his heart. They had never been close as a family, except for Giyanna and himself. But they were twins, so that helped a little, he supposed.

She woke once the car stopped. He helped her into her room and then went back for her luggage. Giyanna was asleep on the bed when he got back. Taking off her shoes, he covered her up with the blanket at the end of the bed and left her. He'd talk to her when she was up and around. To deal with Rogan, they'd need all the strength they could get. He decided to go and see his brother, just to test the waters.

The jail where he was being held was a nice one. It sort of reminded him of the jail on a black and white show that he'd watched in reruns as a kid. There was even a rocking chair down the long hall where the cells were. Rogan was in the last cell. It looked like he'd never broken his habit of being a slob since they'd left home.

"Hello, Rogan. I've come to help you out as you asked." Rogan just glared at him. "I could just go back home and tell Giyanna that you don't need either of us."

"She came? Well la-de-da. The bitch wouldn't even take my calls when I tried to call her and ask her to come here. She still a bitch like she always was?" Tyrrell told him she was never a bitch to him. "Yeah, because she has you all pussy whipped. Either of you bring me any money? I want you to bail me out. That's the least you can do for making me sit around here and wait on one of you to come around."

"There is no bailing you out of this, Rogan. I'm sure you were told that. The judge didn't set you one because he thought you'd be a flight risk. Not to mention there are too many things in your jacket for them to think that you'd not just hide out until they forgot about you." He said that they've told him a lot of shit. "Perhaps it would do you better to listen next time. Giyanna and I are going to try to get you a reduced sentence, and after that—"

"Reduced? That's bullshit. I want out of here for good. I don't belong in here anyway. You tell her to get me out of here, and all them charges they're supposed to have on me dropped. Some of that shit is really old. There should be some kind of expiration date on them. Hell, even my milk has one of those." Tyrrell just stood there. "Did you hear me, moron? I said for you to get me out of here. Right now."

When his brother stood up, Tyrrell backed from the cell. It was then that he realized that his brother was more of a mess than his cell was. And not just because he was in jail, but about three hundred fifty to four hundred pounds of fat was hanging out of the too small jumpsuit they'd given him, and his chins were touching his chest. His dirty hair, usually pulled back in a ponytail when he was younger, now hung down his back in a stringy mess, and he was bald on top.

"When was the last time you had a bath?" Rogan just grunted at him. "You'll need to clean up before we take you to court. And I'm warning you right now, Rogan, you piss either of us off too much and we'll go back home. You're not going to fuck this up by being yourself. You asked for us, and we dropped everything to come here and help you out. The very least you can do is behave."

11

"Don't be a shit, Ty. It's your big brother you're talking to. Bridgett has to pay, and pay big. She took my damned kids." Tyrrell told him they were better off without him. "What a thing to say to me. They're my damned kids, and she had no right to do that to me. And I'm betting she took that fucking card with her too."

"Really? Tell me, Rogan, how old are they? Just one of them. Tell me how old the oldest is." Rogan stared at him with that blank stare he always had when he didn't want to answer. "You don't know, do you? Then tell me. What are their names? I'm betting that you don't even know that, do you? You're a terrible person, and a worse father. And as far as I can see, nothing about you has changed in ten years. Your kids and Bridgett are better off where they are. They deserve more than they ever had in you. Instead of beating her to shit every time you could, you should have been telling her thank you daily for raising your children to be better people than you are or ever will be."

"I'm a good person. She asks me for it when I have to knock her around." Tyrrell asked him how she ever did that. "By not doing what I told her to do. All I wanted was peace and quiet when I came home, and she couldn't even do that. Always harping on this or that. Making me get out and find a job. What do I need a job for? The government, they take from you if you work, and that ain't right. Also, when I have a job, I can't go hang out with my buds. You know how much I like doing that—don't you remember, Tyrrell? We have shit to do, my friends and me. And that brings me to her card again. She spends it on shit that I don't want her to. Going to the grocery store and spending almost every dime of it so I can't go and

12

trade it off for other shit. Shit that I want."

"Yes, I'm sure that you having your shit is much more important than your children you want back having food in their bellies when they need it. What must she have been thinking to take the card and use it for what it was intended for?" Tyrrell just looked around the cell and shook his head. "Is this the kind of mess you left her when you got into her house? If so, it's a small wonder that she didn't leave you long before this."

"Not for lack of trying, I'll tell you. Once a week she'd leave and take the kids. I'd have to beat her hard after that. And one of the kids. That'd be all it took to bring her in line. Of course, all they did was whine when I hit them, but that's what she needed — and it's always her fault too." He laughed like it was a huge joke to hurt one of his own children. "And she was starting to hide the card on me. Or spending it all before I could get me a handle on it. I think she has another mail box or something. If she does, I'll find it. And that card should be mine. I'm the reason that she gets it anyway. That card was as high as it was because of my kids. Damn it, I should have had it when I wanted it."

"You don't want her to spend it on food for the children?" Rogan told him how they got government handouts all the time. "I see. And how much of that do you eat? Of this government food? You look like you eat more than your fair share of it."

"I think you're not being nice to me, Tyrrell. You know I don't like that. Come over here and let me plunk you like I used to do when you was a kid." Rogan laughed at him when he took another step back. "You're a pussy. It's a wonder that you ever made it alive out on the streets when you left me. And don't think I'm not mad about that either. The two of you left me without any kind of help around the house. You should see that place now. It's going to shit. I go there sometimes when I need some breathing room. It's mine, you know."

Tyrrell knew just who owned the house and why. He hated it, but when the bank had called him and not Rogan, he did the only thing he could think of and paid the back taxes. And in return, he was given the deed to the house so long as he kept up on the taxes.

"Whatever. You clean up and Giyanna and I will be back tomorrow. And you'd better be nice to her, Rogan. If she leaves, then I do as well." Rogan told him they'd better do right by him or when he was out, he'd take care of them too. "It's tempting to not do right by you. As far as I'm concerned, everyone is better off with you right where you are."

"That ain't right, Tyrrell. We used to have fun as kids." Tyrrell asked him when that was, and Rogan looked like he was thinking about it. "All right. I used to have fun. But you and Giyanna, you begged me to hurt you. Just like Bridgett did all them times. Then she goes to the police, so they'd tell me to stop. Not going to happen, I told her. She belongs to me. And both of you were always stashing away cash and not letting me have it. That ain't the least bit fair. I'm the oldest, and you should be proud to have me as your brother. And giving me all that you had, that's only fitting because you should want me to have it."

"By letting you have all we had? You think that's the way it should be?" Rogan said that was right. "No, it's not right.

14

Giyanna had to go to another country to get away from you. And I had to change my number over and over to get away from you too. You're not a nice person, and I don't care that you are my brother, I don't like you at all. And it's doubtful that you care, but you should know that as soon as this trial is over, I'm going to wash my hands of you completely, Rogan. I'm no longer going to answer the phone when you call."

Tyrrell left him after that. All Rogan could focus on was how much he'd been wronged. It had been that way their entire lives. He wanted, he took. When he was hurt, everyone was hurt. And he had been a bully, a bastard all his life. Tyrrell went back to the bed and breakfast thinking that it was a mistake to have come to this town for him. He just hoped that they lived, first of all, and didn't live to regret this. Rogan was going to cause them trouble, even from behind bars.

~~~

Tanner looked over the calendar to figure out what was going to happen today. Mostly it was just over the phone meetings that he had to take care of for Noah. Then he had a luncheon with his mother on her projects. Life wasn't as boring as he'd thought it would be taking on a single client.

"You have a call on line one. Its Chris Bentley."

Excited to have his day interrupted by the witch, he picked up the phone. He'd drop everything just to talk to the wonderful woman. "Hello, and how the heck are you? You should see my house. Myra did a fantastic job of it." She laughed with him. "I'm sure that she told you. But anyway, what can I do for you today, my dear?"

"I have a favor to ask of you. There is this fellow that you've been dealing with. Rogan McGowan. I'm to understand that

15

you and your family have taken his wife and children under your wing, so to speak. You've sent them away to keep them safe, right?" He told her what they'd done. "Sending her away is the best thing for her, I think. She'll be safe, and the children will as well. But it's her that this is about. She needs to never return. No matter what happens, do not let them make her return. She's safe, and that's what she needs to be from now on."

"I think that you're right. Being here, that's not terribly safe for anyone, but especially her and those children. I mean, you just said how she's going to be fine out there." Chris said that Bridgett needed closure on this, but she could get that from a distance. "I'm afraid that she has to deal with her husband at some point. But I will try my best to make them see the big picture when it comes to her returning."

"Yes. Otherwise, those poor children will become a ward of the state and never have anyone to love them as she does. She's terrified of men, and with good reason, I think." He could understand that and told her so. "Also, I know that you can't help with the attorneys representing Rogan, but they're in town, and not from around there. They'll need someone to show them around. I was wondering if you could get one of your brothers to help them out."

"Is this a ploy for me to meet my other half?" She asked why he'd think that. "I don't know. I'm the last of the Calhoun men that is unattached. I have my house in order. I've a good job, money in the bank. I'm surprised every time I see someone new in town that she's not falling all over me saying that she's the one."

They both laughed, and he was embarrassed that he'd

voiced that out loud. He really had been worried about that. Not worried, but concerned enough to start avoiding the grocery store, as well as any place that had a crowd of people.

"Yes, you are, but I'm reasonably sure that you can find yourself a mate all on your own. Besides, they're Rogan's sister and brother." He wondered if they were like him, but said nothing. "The woman, I think her name is Giyanna, is from Ireland. Been living there since she was about seventeen. The brother, Tyrrell, he's been living in Texas for the most part, moving around where the job he has takes him. They're both single—yes, I'm aware of that—but I don't think that she'd be suited to you. Not with you being so close to your family."

"Which, I'm saying this because you've always been there for us, she's going to take me back with her because of her being my mate. And I'll be singing 'Wild Irish Rose' and eating haggis with every meal." They both laughed. "Is she? My mate? I've never come right out and asked you before, and you did promise me that you'd never lie to me."

There was a pause there, and he was sure that he had his answer. So, when she finally did speak, he wasn't the least bit surprised when she told him she was.

"I wanted it to be something that you took care of. I did." He said that he understood. "I don't think you do. But that's all right as well. She's been hurt, and badly so, by her brother, Rogan, and hasn't had a moment's peace since leaving home. Giyanna lived with an elderly aunt until she passed away, and in all that time, she never dated. Not once since she moved there, and that's just sad. She's a wonderful woman, and you couldn't do better than if I had picked her for you myself."

"Is she afraid of men as well? I mean, is she going to hurt

me if I touch her in the wrong way? I don't want to make her upset with me right away. I'll save her being pissed off at me till when we're together for a little while." Chris said that she was more than afraid of them. "Because of Rogan. And this guy, they're here to get him off? To let him out with people that he can and will harm? Or are they only going through the motions with him?"

"It's not like that, and it is. Her and her brother are here to make sure that he gets a fair trial, but they'd just as soon he ended up in jail for the rest of his life too." He asked why they were helping him then. "Family, I think. And maybe a little bit of closure. You know more than most what you'd do for your family. And I think that the only reason that they agreed was so that they could have time to see each other. Tyrrell and Giyanna are twins, and used to be very close."

"I understand that. I don't like it, but I understand. And since she's going to be my mate, no matter how much I'm not ready for her, I can't take the case against him. Not now." Chris thanked him. "Don't thank me yet. I still must convince her that I'm her mate. And knowing how well that went over for my brothers, she's not going to go easy on me."

"No, she won't." He wondered what she'd say to him if he decided to leave town and not return until Giyanna was gone. "It wouldn't work, and you know that. When the fates have your life planned out, it matters little when you get together, but you know that you will."

He did, but said nothing else. His mind was going over the things that he still had to finish up. Not just his home, but there were a few things that he wanted to take care of here as well. Tanner had his life planned out too, right down to what he was going to have for dinner tonight and tomorrow. But this, having a mate, he knew as well as Chris did that it would consume him when they came together.

"You have such a shitty outlook in all this. Why is that?" He told her that he didn't know, but he wasn't keen on having a mate. And asked her to stop reading his mind. "I don't have to tell you what she'll bring to you. Or how you're going to feel when she comes into your life, do I?"

"You know me and what I've had going on since I was a kid, so you know what sort of things I'm dealing with." She said that she didn't. "Chris, I might be the youngest, but I think that I'm more set in my ways than even Joe is. I don't care for change. It was the most difficult thing I've ever done, quitting my job and working for Noah. I can't give a woman, any woman, what she will want. I'm not built like that."

"And what is it, Tanner, that you think a woman might want from you other than your undying love?" When he didn't have an answer for her, she didn't continue her train of thought. "If you could please tell Bridgett not to come home. No matter if she wants to face her demons or not, that would be disastrous."

"Are you mad at me?" She said that she wasn't, just disappointed, but not mad. "I don't want you disappointed either. But I know what I am."

"Yes, and so do I. All right then. We're planning a large picnic for the summer. You all will be invited as well. And we hope to be notified when Noelle has her babies. It's soon, correct?" He told her in two weeks. "Good. Let me know, and I'll come out to see her. Thanks again, Tanner."

Then she hung up. He felt all twisted up inside when

19

he couldn't give her what she wanted. A mate would want children, and he just couldn't give that to her. Not like the others could. As he worked through the rest of the morning, he tried hard not to think about what was going on. His mate was here. And she was an attorney. He decided to do a little digging on his own about Rogan McGowan, and see what he could find out to either hurt or help their case. It was funny really—he'd never thought of himself as not being able to take a side on something like this. He knew just what he wanted as soon as he'd been approached with a case. But this one, he knew that it was going to change a lot of lives, his included.

"Sir, there is a Mr. McGowan to see you." He looked at his cook and friend, Mabel, his heart doing a little jump. He asked her where her husband was. "He's gone to the market, and the young man said to tell you that he's Tyrrell, not Rogan."

"Send him in, please." She said that she would, and would bring refreshments as well since he'd worked through lunch again. "I'm sorry. Did you go have some?"

"I did. And I've made you a bowl of beef and vegetable soup. You can have it later. If you don't piss this young man off. He looks like he's had a rough time of it. I'm sure he has too." Tanner asked her why she'd think that. "He's related to that dreadful man, isn't he? Poor man. I'd hate to have him on my coattails. You need to know something about him, just gossip mind, but I can tell you." Tanner thanked her and shut off the monitor on his computer when she went to get Tyrrell.

Tyrrell looked just like he thought he would except for the hair. While Rogan's was silvery white as the clouds and nasty stringy, Tyrrell's was as red as the roses that were blooming in his mother's garden. He had a moment to wonder what

20

his own mate's would look like, and squashed that thought down. Not now, he told himself.

"Hello, Mr. Calhoun. My name, as you know, is Tyrrell — Rogan McGowan is my brother. And I assure you, we're nothing alike." They both laughed as they shook hands. "I'm new to this area and state, but I do have a federal license that takes me pretty much where I need to go. I work for the government. Mostly to do with paperwork, but I wanted to let you know that I won't be representing him without a license."

"He's got a lot on his plate right now. And, I would imagine, you as well if you're taking this on." He said that he knew that. "I'm not going to be involved in this. First, he had an issue with a public defender — I think you know who that is." He said that it was his sort of brother-in-law. "Yes, that's him. Phillip Chester is now safe, as is Bridgett. The second thing, along with a list of other items that they've put on his docket, is that he destroyed a public housing home and made a public nuisance of himself."

"Yes, I called and got Bridgett's address from your sister-in-law before coming here. My sister, Giyanna, came to the States to second chair with me. I'm going to be honest with you, sir, I have no desire to be here any more than Bridgett did." He asked why he was here then. "My sister and I haven't seen each other for a very long time. Just once since we turned seventeen. She went off to Ireland to be with a relative, and I stuck around to get my law degree here. This is a way for us to — sort of, I guess — write off a way to see each other and have a little time together. We don't want him out of jail any more than anyone else might. Rogan is and always will be a bully."

"I've been reading up on him. He's a bit more than that, I'd say. But as for you and your your sister, that's a very long time to not see someone you're related to, I think. My entire family lives near here. It can be both a blessing and a pain in the butt most of the time. But I do love them." He said he knew about pains in the butt. "What can I do for you?"

"I was hoping that you could help Giyanna and I out with the judges. As I have said, neither of us wants to help Rogan out, but we're stuck with him as a brother. But I do have to go through the motions so that he can't say he didn't get a fair trial. That would just piss him off, and he'd take it out on a lot of people." He said he understood. "Also, we don't know the area, and we were kind of hoping you could steer us in the right directions of a nice place to have a meal. It doesn't have to be fancy, but Giyanna will want cloth napkins. It's been a sort of requirement of hers since we were kids when a nice dinner was suggested."

"She sounds like a stickler." He said that she was usually laid back, but he'd not seen her in ages. "I take it she's here?"

"Yes, today as a matter of fact. She's resting now at the local B&B. It was a long flight."

Tanner told him that was good that they were staying so close. "Why don't you come to the house tonight? The two of you can meet my family—they're a little on the large size—and then we can figure out a plan for the two of you to find a nice place. There are several in Columbus, but around here, about all we have is burgers and pizza. The one restaurant that we do have, they're not open on Mondays. But the food is good and filling."

"We don't want to impose. We can just have dinner at

the pizza place." Tanner told him he insisted. "Well, if you're sure no one will mind, then yes, we'd love to have dinner with you. Is there anything I can bring? Not that I know what it would be, but I'm sure I can bring something."

"No, that's all right. Just come casual. We are a big family, as I said, and they're very casual about things. My sister-in-law is due in two weeks, so we're sort of on pins and needles too." He nodded. "I'll send a car for you, and that way you won't get lost. It'll be at my parents' house. They'll be happy to see you."

After he left, Tanner wondered what the hell was wrong with him. He'd just invited his mate to meet his family. A mate that he'd not met yet. Laying his head on the desk, he was still there when his cook cleared her throat. He took the soup and thanked her. He was so fucked right now. Tanner had no idea where to begin. But changing his attitude might be a good place to start, he thought as he ate his soup.

Chapter 2

Giyanna wasn't sure that this was a good idea. Having dinner with strangers was never anything that she would do at home. Hell, she thought, she didn't even enjoy having dinner with people that she did know anymore. She looked at her brother in the mirror, and saw that he was in jeans and a polo shirt.

"Tanner said casual." She told him this was as casual as she had with her. "Don't you ever just let go? I mean, I bet you've not had a good time since we spent that week together before you left home."

"That was a lot of fun, wasn't it? I mean, I think that I put on ten pounds for all the junk food that we ate." She hugged him and asked him if she looked all right. "I want to make a good first impression. Maybe that'll get us in good with the judges here because of how important this family is. And then he can say that he's guilty no matter what we've sort of thrown at him, and we can all go home."

"I doubt very much that anyone will want him to be anything but guilty, don't you? And how do you know that the Calhouns are important?" She told him that she'd looked them up. "I did as well, but I never got that they were important. Just rich and well known."

"I also talked to Bridgett. She told me that they have a fundraiser every year for the kids around here. For backpacks and coats and gloves. And not only that, but for the food pantry as well as a lot of other charities that they run and donate to. One of them is a teacher, and Bridgett's son was in his class. Bridgett said that he has a closet full of food that the kids can take from when they don't have enough to eat." He asked her how many times her kids had eaten from it. "I don't know, but I would say a great deal. Rogan has been taking her food card from her until she got a post office box to have it mailed to. They refill it on the first of the month, but he'd lose the card after emptying it, and she'd have to apply for another one."

"He's a bastard." Giyanna nodded her agreement and looked at herself in the mirror again. "You look lovely, spring like. And you look very good in green with all your red hair. Not that you've changed that much, but you've grown up, and I guess in my excitement to see you, I didn't think of that. In my mind you were still going to be that kid that told me to make something of myself before you got on that plane."

"It's funny, I was thinking the same thing before I saw you. Then I realized that you'd be older and might not be the same as before. I have no idea what I assumed would change, but I didn't care for my thoughts." Tyrrell told her that he loved her. "And I love you too. We've been apart for too long, and I would like to change that."

"Me too. Since you're going back home when this is finished, perhaps I'll go there to see you once in a while." She nodded, and he could see the tears as they filled her eyes. "Don't cry, Giyanna. I still can't stand to see you cry."

"Ty, what are we going to do if we get him off from all these charges? He'll hurt her if he manages to find her. And I don't know about you, but I'm good at what I do. Even though I'll only be second chair with you, we can't fuck this up—we'll look bad if we do. And he'll be free to do whatever it is that he does to people. No one around here likes him." He said he had a plan. "You do? Let's hear it. I'm game for anything about now."

"You don't second chair with me." Giyanna just stared at him. "Let me finish. You'll be there with us, but I think that we should ask Tanner to help us out. He hates him as much as we do, and if we do fuck up, he'll be there to save us."

"You mean for him to take the fall." He shook his head. "He's not going to do this. I'm not even sure that I'd want him to. He's a pillar of this community. If he is as good as Bridgett says he is, then I don't want people to dislike him simply because we don't want to get Rogan out of jail."

"I don't know what else to do, Giyanna. Rogan strongly believes that the state has him on trumped up charges. And he's pissed off. And you know Rogan when he's pissed off. He tends to hurt those around him." She shivered, thinking of the last time she'd seen him. "I won't let him hurt you again. I will do everything within my power to make sure that he doesn't. But we have to do something, or he's going to terrorize this town because they've had the nerve to arrest him."

"He will, and we both know it. Then he'll wonder why everyone is so upset with him when he gets caught again. Did you hear what he did to Phillip? He stabbed him with a pen right there in the frigging jail. He hit Phillip with it so hard he had to have surgery to remove it from the bone. What sort of person does that shit and thinks that it's all right?" Ty told her that they had to do something. "No, we don't. Now I have an idea. Why don't you and I hire this Tanner person to be his attorney, and we're his second chair. That way, when the shit hits the fan with Rogan, and we both know that it will, then perhaps this guy will be able to take him down. You said he was a big man."

"I did, but don't you think that's a little unfair? To Rogan, not Tanner. I think he can handle himself." She laughed with him. "He's a wolf, I think I told you that. And he'll have his beast on his side. That's more than you and I would have if Rogan gets mad. And you know as well as I that it doesn't take much for him to get upset. It doesn't even have to be centered around him. He's always had a short fuse."

"Not to mention, Tanner could know things that we can't about Rogan. They've lived in the same town for ages, and he'd know what sort of person Rogan is. We've not seen him in a decade—not that I think Rogan has changed all that much, not for the better anyway—but we don't know our brother all that well, and he should be represented by a local." She knew that they were stretching the truth of this. And there was a good likelihood that the man wouldn't help them out. She'd not. She would be telling Rogan that he was on his own and that he wasn't worth the effort anyone would put forth for him. They were both worried, she was at least, and wanted

28

the same thing as Tyrrell. But they had no way of getting it.

"I'll talk to Tanner about it at dinner." Giyanna hugged her brother and grabbed her sweater. To her it was still chilly out, but to Tyrrell, it was nice and warm. "You'll back me up on this? Tell him how much we dislike Rogan and want him to stay just where he is?"

"I think if the man has a lick of sense, he'll know that we're not fans of our brother." The limo was pulling up just as they were coming out of the B&B. "Wow, I could get used to this kind of service. I had to max out my cards just to come here."

"I'll pay you back. I promise." Giyanna told him not to worry about it. She had it covered. "Well, I begged you to come, and I did make a promise. I have the money. I don't spend much on things, so I just stash it away."

"I do the same thing because I'm terrified of being without money. But you pay for dinner when we go out. All right?" He nodded as they slipped into the limo. "And lunch too, while we're here." He said it was a deal.

Giyanna had money. When her aunt had died a couple of years ago, she had left her everything in her will, including the house that she still lived in, as well as the farm. And being the way that she'd grown up, Giyanna still saved all that she could, stashing it away in the bank since she'd gotten out of law school and had landed a good job.

The limo came to a smooth stop, and she looked at her brother. She had a feeling that he knew something that she didn't. But he'd not tell her. They were twins, but couldn't read each other's thoughts nor feel what they were feeling. She supposed that was both good and bad. She'd been feeling down a great deal lately. And now this.

"You ready?" She nodded at him. "Good. So am I. I've not had a home cooked meal in so long I don't know if my belly can take it tonight. Fast food is not the way a grown man should eat."

They were both laughing when he got out of the limo. When a hand came in to help her out, she didn't even bother looking but grabbed it and got out of the car. As soon as they touched, she felt the tingle of something strange go up her arm. Then she was staring into the eyes of the most incredibly good-looking man that she'd ever seen.

"Hi." Giyanna nodded, not sure how to make her tongue work at the moment. "I'm Tanner Calhoun. You must be Giyanna McGowan. Welcome to our family."

"Welcome to your family?" He nodded and pulled her along to the porch, where it seemed they'd taken a photo of the eldest man and had made younger copies of him for some kind of trick. They were all handsome, with dark hair and nice smiles. The women looked as if they had only just stepped off the runway to greet her and were planning to go back to work. Except for one. She was still gorgeous, but large with child. Christ, the size of the men was intimidating.

Backing from them when they seemed to move as one to come greet them, she tried to smile through her panic. They weren't just big men, but they were scary big. They all had to top over six foot tall. The man with her cleared his throat.

"They mean well." Giyanna told him they were scaring her. "Yes, I've told them to back off. They'll go in the house now and give you a moment to regroup. You need that, right?"

"Yes. I think...I shouldn't think that they'd hurt me,

would they?" He promised her that they wouldn't live long, no matter what the witch had told them, if they tried. "You're very odd."

"You have no idea." That wasn't want she expected, but he pulled her along again to the house. The elder couples still there didn't say anything until Tanner introduced her to them. "This is my mom and dad, Christine and TJ Calhoun. The other couple are my grandparents, James and Jasmine Calhoun. The others were my brothers and their wives, and they'll try not to frighten you again."

By the time she entered the house, after being welcomed to their home, she was starting to get her feet under her. She'd made a fool of herself, and that didn't sit well with her. As the others were being introduced to her and her brother, each of them said the same thing, welcoming her not only to their home but to the family. When they were seated in the living room, she asked why.

"We're not ones to hold back on something when pulling off the Band-Aid is much quicker, and usually less painful. You know what we are, don't you?" She nodded to the man; she thought his name was Trent. "Well, we're saying that—"

He was cut off by Tanner. "We're saying that we are making you a part of the family because of your relationship with Bridgett and the kids."

She didn't believe him any more than she felt safe when one of the men came toward her and offered her a drink. "No thanks, I don't drink." They were all pleased by that, and she had a moment of panic. "Are you all all right? I mean, you're not usually this strange, are you? I don't mean to be rude here, but if something has happened, I don't like being fobbed off."

31

"I told you that was gonna make her upset with us." James laughed as he came toward her, slowly this time. "I'm Grandpa. I'm also a great grandpa. Nothing to do with the way we're acting really, but I'm as tickled about that as I am you being here." She nodded at him. "We're welcoming you to the family because you are a part of it. Like all the other women are here."

She asked him what he meant, and he laughed then did the strangest thing—he danced a little. She looked at Tanner, the man who had made her tingle a little.

"You're my mate." Giyanna didn't know what to say to that so she didn't speak. This was just too surreal. "They're trying very hard to slide you into this madness of a family slowly. The only sane ones here are my grandparents and parents. The rest are looney. You might want to run now."

"I know what a mate is, but how can you be sure about this? I mean, you're certainly acting as if— Ah, the welcome to the family line. I don't want to be a part of your family. Again, I'm not being rude here, but I'm not the joining of a family type. I don't even know any of you. I'm here to try very hard not to let Rogan out of jail without losing my license while I'm at it." She stood up. "If this is some kind of ploy to get me to do something I don't want, I want you to know that I might be little, but I'm smart enough to beat you at this game. I don't like my job as an attorney, but it was the most well-paying job that I could think of and not be a surgeon. I don't care for other people's blood. And...and I have no idea why I just said that to you all."

"What game would you think this would be?" She looked at Tanner again. "This isn't a game. This is life, and I'm not blaming you for this, but I don't need you anymore than you seem to not need me."

"Tanner." His mother looked at him sternly, then at her with a gentle smile. "He's the last one to find his mate, and he's a little on edge."

"I'm not going to do this." She stood up and looked at her brother. "This is insane. We came here for dinner, not to be a part of something that I don't understand. We should go, don't you think, Tyrrell?"

"No. I don't. I don't know this man, but I can tell that he's a good person. That's what I was told, anyway." She asked him if he'd known about this. "Yes, but not until after you were called and asked to come here to see me."

"You called me." He shook his head. "You did. I know your voice as well as my own. You told me to come here and we'd visit."

"That was a witch." Tanner cursed long and hard, and his mother popped him on the back of the head. Tyrrell continued with a laugh. "She called me after talking to you to tell me what she'd done. How she'd arranged for you to come and see me. And that Tanner was here. So I thought, for you to be happy — one of us to be happy anyway — you'd come here and get married, and we'd get to visit as well."

"You knew this, and you didn't tell me." She looked around the room at the people there. "Welcoming me to the family because of some sick idea that I'm going to just let this man, this man that has no use for me, take my hand in marriage and be my mate? You're all sick fucks."

"There ain't no need for you to get your panties in an uproar. We meant well. And you'd have met anyway, the way I'm thinking." She told James that she didn't trust any of them. "No, I can see that you don't. But you're here now and he's got your scent, so that'll make things better for you."

"Better how? So that I can be with a man that, for all I know, could be just like Rogan or worse?" She turned to Tanner. "Thank you for the invite, but I think I'll go back home now. And I do mean my home."

"I'll have to go with you." She stared at him until Tanner spoke again. "We've met and touched. While we've not bonded or mated, I'm still going to need to be with you. If not, then I'll be a monster. Not just to humans, but to my family as well. I'll have to be put away."

"Why should that be my concern?" He said that he didn't know, he was just telling her. "I see. You're trying to make me feel guilty for you going insane? It won't work. I've been blamed for a great many things, but as you can tell, I bounce back from it."

She made her way out of the house before she started crying. Getting into the limo again, she asked the man to take her home. She didn't know if he'd take her or not until Tanner came out and got into the car with her. As she moved to the other side of the car away from him, the car started to move.

~~~

Tanner watched her on the drive back to the B&B. He wasn't sure what to say to her, but her tears were making him hurt in ways that he never had before. Even his wolf was angry at the way things were working out. He decided to talk to her; whether she listened or not was up to her.

"Chris Bentley is a grand witch. I really have a limited idea of what that means, but basically, she governs and rules all the witches in the world. Hell, for all I know, there could be some on other planets that she rules too." The joke fell flat. "Anyway, she's very powerful, and she has helped us out on a few things—things that saved our lives—and she also gave us some magic. The moment you touched me, you received some of it. I don't know how—"

"What sort of magic? Not that I believe you, but what would you have given me when all we did was hold hands for a moment?" He told her. "I don't want to be an immortal. You have her take it back right now. I like my life the way it is. And the thought of being this alone forever isn't my idea of a good time. Not that I want to spend it with you either."

"I can't do that. Neither can she. Or so she's told me." Giyanna looked out the window again. "Anyway, I was going to tell you what she did to help us. Do you want to know?"

No answer, but he didn't care. It was a way to fill in the uncomfortable silence. A way for him to get her to turn and look at him before he reached out and took her hair from the braid that went down her back. He wanted to see if it was as silky as it looked. As curly as the little pieces of her hair were. Her skin, he knew, would be soft, the delicate kind of softness that only a true red head would have. Tanner's fingers burned to just touch her once more. He remembered that he was going to talk to her, and told her a story of how Chris came to help them.

"There was this she-devil that decided that my brother, Sterl, could father a bunch of monsters for her. She killed a lot of his friends, and hurt him badly when she decided that he was an alpha. He could be, but he's not a practicing one." She turned and looked at him. "In the she-devil's fight to take him

35

from us, almost killing him in the process, Chris came and helped us by summoning a demon by the name of Richard."

"Richard? What sort of demon name is Richard." Tanner told her that he'd thought the same thing. "What did a demon, I'm assuming from the underworld, have to do with this she-devil thing? And I don't even want to guess what that is."

"Her parents created her, I've heard. And in doing so, they called upon this demon to make their child the strongest being there is. And it sort of went to her head. Anyway, she was taken away because Sterl hit her in the face and drew first blood. Honestly, that's a very shortened version of the way it happened, but that's what it was." She leaned back on the seat now and was no longer looking out the window. "Chris and her family became friends with my family, and her and Myra have been helping—Myra is about the strangest and most colorful woman you could meet. And by colorful, I mean just that. She's very colorful. But Myra has been hanging around with all of us and fixing our homes with the help of magic. She's one of the nicest people you'll meet too. If a little odd."

"I don't believe in magic. It's a fairy tale, told to children to make them believe in something other than the suffering that they're going through. At least that's my thoughts on it." He nodded. "You're not going to try and convince me otherwise?"

"No. But if you'll allow it, I can prove to you that there's magic. We're going right by my house. And if you don't trust me to be in it with you, you go on in and I'll wait out here for you." She was curious, he could tell, and since she didn't tell him no, he knocked on the window between them and the driver and told him to take them to his home. "You'll be able to go in and once inside, have a look around at the way my house looks. I can almost guarantee you that it won't look like it did when I left today."

"You're trying to tell me that your house changes, and that'll I'll be able to see it." Tanner told her it was subtler than that. "Sure it is. And if you think I'm going to fall for your horse shit, you're stupider than Rogan. And I'm assuming that you know just how stupid he is."

"He is pretty stupid. Did you hear that he shit in the bed that he shared with Bridgett, and then laid in it?" Giyanna tried not to laugh, but she finally did. He nodded as he continued. "Once he was arrested for making a public nuisance of himself, they had to call a tailor in to have a jumpsuit made for him. It took three of them sewn together to get what he has on now."

"Rogan never learned how to push away from the table like a normal person. If there was food left on anyone's plate when they were done, he'd sit there and eat it like he was afraid that someone was going to get more than him." When she looked at him, he could see the sadness in her eyes. "I don't hate him, but I don't want anything to do with him either. He's a mean bastard that I would just as soon rot where he is than to talk to him. The things he would do and say to Tyrrell and me when we were kids was abusive and sadistic. Rogan has no sense of other people's feelings, especially if they differ from his own."

"I'm sorry." She nodded and asked him about his house. "I bought it some time ago. Not long, but I've been starting projects then leaving them go. I hated my job working as an attorney in a big firm, so quit it one day and started working for Noah. He's a vampire." She quirked a brow at him, but he moved on. "The house, I was putting it off, but when I found out that you were coming, I called out to Myra and asked her to finish it for me. She said that all she could do for now was to finish the projects and to inject a little magic in the house. And what I mean by it not looking like it did when I left today, I mean that. The house will go into your mind and find out what you want in a house, and fix it to match it."

"I don't believe you." The car came to a stop, and before she could reach for the handle, if that was what she was going for, the door opened and there stood the driver. "You just expect me to believe you, like I'm stupid or something?"

"No, I know that you're not stupid. Not even close. But in order to show you that I'm not lying to you, go in and try to think of something that you want in the living room. It's to the left as you walk in." He watched the indecision on her face. "Once you see it for what it is, then you come out here and we can talk, or you can go back to the B&B. All right?"

"I'll do it, but I don't believe you." Giyanna got out of the limo and he did too. But instead of following her, Tanner leaned against the car and watched her. As she got to the steps, she turned and looked at him. "You'll come with me. But if you try anything or hurt me in any way, I'll make you regret even being born. I'm not joking on this. I don't care if you are some kind of wolf, I will hurt you in ways that your own mother won't recognize you when I'm done."

"All right. While I do understand your need to make sure that you're safe, I want you to know that I would never, even under threat of death, harm you in any way. Nor will my family, any of them." She nodded, for some reason believing him. "Shall we go in?"

He walked up the steps with her, careful not to touch her again. She was on edge enough, and he didn't want her to feel like he was pressuring her into anything. As soon as she opened the door, she turned to look at him, asking about locking his house.

"I did lock it. It knows who you are." She tsked at him, but went into the house. As soon as he entered the entrance hall, he knew that it had taken her thoughts and changed things. Christ, the house was beautiful. "I have to say, you have excellent taste."

"I want to see the living room." He nodded and moved with her to the left after the entrance. The parquet flooring was beautiful, but he loved the grand staircase more. The stained-glass window at the top with all its silver and golds was shining light down on them like a beacon. "You're going to tell me that it didn't look like this when you left here today, aren't you? That all this magically appeared because of what I thought of in a house."

"It didn't, and yes I am." Tanner moved into the big room and looked around. "When I left, I had a couch that I didn't care for, as well as a card table that I had a lamp on." She told him she didn't believe him. "All right. Let's try this. Close your eyes and think of this room again. But this time you make it something...like your living room at your house. I promise you, you'll be a believer after that."

The furniture morphed into something else. The couch was gone, and in its place was a large overstuffed chair that looked like it was well used. The fireplace disappeared too, and he was saddened by that, but nearly laughed at the paintings on the wall. Most of them, he'd bet, had been painted by her when she'd been a child. There was a homemade quilt on the bed that he could see in the corner. A table and chairs that were also old but solidly made. When he took her hand away, she stared at him for several seconds before she turned and looked at the room. Tanner caught her before she fell on her ass.

Picking her up in his arms, he sat her on the couch as the room started to change again. It was as it had been before. The soft looking furniture that was new but didn't have that feel to it. He asked her if she was all right when a man appeared in the room with them. He bowed before introducing himself.

"My name is Ruben. I was asked to come and work for you sir, my lady. I am a good friend to the witch Myra, and she said that you would need my skills. Would you like something to eat? A glass of juice or tea?" He told him to bring the lady a glass of tea and also a plate of scones if he had them. "I have whatever you wish, sir."

His hands were filled with a large silver tray. Tanner was glad that Giyanna hadn't seen it appear—she seemed to be close to the edge right now. When she drank down the tea, he laughed when she watched the glass refill, and she set it down on the table in front of them. Her hands were shaking badly by then, and he wondered what was going on in her head at that moment. When she looked at him, he had a pretty good idea.

"I'm overwhelmed." He nodded. "Don't just nod, damn it. Say something, like this is a dream, or I've died, and this is where I'm going to spend eternity. Something other than just nodding your head like a puppy dog in a window. I'm freaking the fuck out here."

"I'm sorry, I am. But should you like, you could spend an eternity here. It's a lovely home. As I said before, you have excellent taste." She growled at him and he laughed again. "You need to practice more. When you growl, it needs to come more from your belly and then roll up through your throat. Want me to show you?"

"I need to get the fuck out of here." But she didn't move. When she looked at him, he could see the fear again and his wolf moved along his skin. "Did this really just happen? The room changed because I wanted it to look like this? I'm calming down some, but I really need for you to tell me that this isn't a dream and that I'm not going nuts. Well, nuttier."

"It's not a dream, nor are you nuts. It really did happen because the house is magical. You might not believe in magic, but that's okay. The house believes in you." He moved a strand of hair from her cheek and put it behind her ear. "I don't want you to be overwhelmed, but the rest of the house is the same." Nodding, she looked around again and then back at him. "I'm sorry, but I didn't know any other way to show you that I'm not lying to you."

"I need a minute." He started to stand up, to give her some time. "Where are you going? I only need a minute. Don't leave me in here alone. What if the house starts to change me into whatever it is that you want? It can change things for you too, I'm guessing. I don't know what you want, but I'm sure it will figure it out."

"No, it won't change you." She asked him if he was sure. "Yes. To me—and I can't believe I'm saying this after telling anyone that would listen that I don't want a mate—to me, you're about as perfect as they come. Welcome to the family, Giyanna."

41

Chapter 3

Rogan sat where he was told and his hands were chained to the table, then his ankles to the large circle on the floor. He hated the way they were treating him. Like he was some kind of deviant or something. He had his rights and they weren't meeting them. Rogan looked at the man who came in with his sister.

"Well, well, well. Lookee at what the cat dragged in. Why the hell haven't you bailed me out, Giyanna? I know that you've more than likely got enough money to do it. When you were a kid, you were forever hiding a stash of cash from me. But I found it all, didn't I? Get your skinny ass out of here and get me the fuck out of this place." The fist that slammed down on the table startled him, and he looked at the man. "What's up your ass?"

"You're to talk to her with respect or we'll both leave here, and you'll be represented by a court appointed lawyer. And that might be difficult after what you did to the last man

43

that was here." He looked at his sister and noticed that she was afraid of him, but she was trying really hard not to show it. Good, that was the way he wanted it. "Did you hear me? Behave or we walk."

"I heard you, but she didn't answer my question. Why hasn't she bailed me out yet?" The man answered him instead of Giyanna. "What do you mean, there ain't no bail set for me? There is always bail for someone like me. Didn't Ty take care of that? He told me that I had no bail, but I thought for sure that he'd do right by me and get that fixed. I want the fuck out of here, damn it."

"Well, lucky for us, this time, it's in the world's favor that you're not getting any bail set. Now, we're here to talk to you about a plea." He said that he'd done nothing wrong. All the man did was take out a bunch of pictures of his house that he and Bridgett had lived in and lay them out before him. "So? The government has money for that kind of damage. Just have them fix it up again and get over themselves. I don't have time to be in here. Besides, they won't give me more to eat. And my bed broke, and now they're making me sleep on a fucking air mattress that ain't all that comfortable. I want to be out of here now. There ain't no reason for me to be caught up in this when it was Bridgett that ran off with my kids. All I did was get pissy about it."

The man sat down and Giyanna stood near the wall. He wanted her close, close enough that he could pop her a good one. He'd not been able to do that in too many years. When the man started talking while pulling out a notebook and a pen that he didn't lay down, Rogan looked at him again.

"My name is Tanner Calhoun. I'm working with your

brother and sister to get the charges against you reduced."
Rogan told him he wanted them all to go away. "That isn't
going to work, no matter what we try to bargain. You're going
to serve some serious jail time, if not prison, and how much
depends on what you have to say for yourself. Or how much
you piss everyone off while you're in here. These people talk
to judges, and they'll tell them how much you moan and
groan about petty stuff. So I want that to stop right now."

"My wife, she took my kids. I want her to come back here
and bring them back. That ain't fair that she gets to run off
like she could just up and leave me. She better know that she's
going to get a beating, too. I don't stand for the way she's
been getting uppity lately about the food card and the house."
Calhoun told him that she wasn't going to come back unless
she had to testify against him. "She can't testify against me.
I'm her husband. I know the laws too."

"Then you know that since she put a restraining order out
against you, as soon as you broke it, and then hurt her, she
has all the rights that she wanted. And she's filing for divorce
as well. With your track record, then—"

"No. No siree bob, that isn't going to happen. She married
me for better or worse, and I want her to come on back and
start cleaning up the mess I made. Them people told me that
I can't live in those government houses because I don't have
a family. So she has to come back so then I have a place to
rest up. I need my house back. Then she's gonna drop these
charges against me or suffer my fist." Calhoun said nothing
but stared at him. "You don't seem to be getting the whole
picture here, Calhoun. I want things, and you're not doing a
damned thing to get them. You see, I'm used to people getting

up and doing what I tell them. Ain't that right, Giyanna?"

Rogan laughed at her when she paled. This was a lot more fun than his brother coming in to see him. Tyrrell was real brave so long as he had these chains on. But he hadn't gotten it through his head yet that Rogan was going to be free soon enough. When she turned her back on him, he thought she was gonna cry and he was all ready to make fun of her. Then she turned and looked at him, and the change in her sort of scared him a little. Not that she'd be able to hurt him, but he was afraid of what she might know about him and tell people. That wasn't going to set well with him.

"You haven't changed one bit, have you, Rogan? Still the bully. Do you still steal from houses? Shoplift when the mood strikes you and you're low on cash? Have you beaten anyone lately? Oh, I nearly forgot, you're in jail chained to the floor like the animal that you are. I have to say, I'm glad to see you here, groveling for your meals to be bigger, complaining about your mattress. Poor Rogan, nobody likes him and he's all mad about it." He told her to shut up. "I won't. I've been quiet about you for long enough. I'm going to do everything in my power to make sure that you never see those kids or Bridgett again. So, they can live a normal life without you there knocking them around all the time like you did me and Tyrrell. You've made your bed, now you can fucking lie in it, you fat fuck."

"You begged for me to hit you. Same with Ty. If you had just done what I'd told you—" She cut him off, asking him how that had worked. "Hiding all your money away from me like you was gonna use it on something special. I'm the special one, Giyanna. You should have learned that a long time ago. Then you and him, you go and leave me there all by myself. That weren't fair at all, you know that. How was I supposed to have you clean up after me if you and him were off doing things without me saying you could? I could have teached you how to be like me, living off the land and shit."

"The only thing I learned from you was to be better at keeping myself safe and to hide my money better. And there wasn't any reason to clean up after you, as you tried to make us do. You would just come right in behind us and break everything and throw it to the floor. You didn't want it clean, Rogan, you wanted it neat, so you could break things easier." He told her to bail him out. "No, I would never do that even if there was a way to do it. Even if it was only a buck, I'd not do it. I like you right where you are. In jail behind bars, where you can't hurt anyone else."

"Then what good are you to me? Am I supposed to believe that you're going to work really hard at getting me out of here? You won't, and we both know it. I might as well put in a change of address card now, because this is where you'll leave me. After all the shit I did for you, you're going to be ungrateful and leave me to rot in here." Rogan tried to stand up, but the chains held him down. "Get out of here. And don't you be coming back. You're nothing but a fucking cunt, and I hate the ground you walk on."

When she left them there, he looked over at Calhoun. He was putting his things away as well. He asked him where he thought he was going. He'd not told him he could go yet.

"I told you to not talk to her that way. And you're very lucky that you're in here, McGowan, because if we were in an outside setting, I'd rip your throat out and feast on your blood." He took his briefcase in his hand and went to the door. "You have a change of heart, then you have them call me. But until you apologize to Giyanna, you're on your own."

"You can't make me do shit." Calhoun knocked on the window and Rogan felt his temper shoot up another notch or two. "Get your ass back here. I got me a court date in a couple of days, and I want to know how you're getting me out of here. This is all trumped up charges that they got me in here for. And as soon as Bridgett comes back here and brings my kids, then things will be just like they was before. Go and get her and see if they aren't."

"I'm not going to get you out of here. Like Giyanna, I like you right here. Chained up is like a bonus for me. Good day to you. Like I said, you tell your sister and brother that you're sorry, then I'll consider working for you. Otherwise, you're fucked. Because the way it stands right now, you'll be lucky if you don't get life plus."

Calhoun left him there, and all he could do was to try and break the chains so that he could go after him. And when Rogan flipped the table over, feeling satisfaction for about a minute, he found himself on his head, with the table holding him up while his legs were still chained to the floor. The fucking police laughed at him for ten minutes or more before they got around to helping him. They were going to regret laughing at him, he'd make sure of it. Just as soon as somebody got up off their asses and got him the fuck out of there.

~~~

Tanner wasn't sure where she had gone and asked the officer at the desk near the cells. He told him that Giyanna had gone to the bathroom and she didn't look well. Going in the direction that he was shown, he found himself wanting to go back down to the cell that Rogan would be in by now and kill him. No more conversation, just murder him where he stood. His wolf agreed with him, even going so far as to run along his skin like he was just waiting for the opportunity to do so.

He knocked on the door when she didn't come out by calling her name. At her "Go away," he knew she had her temper back, but he still wanted to see her. Going into the neutral gender bathroom, he stood by the sink where she was and asked her if she was all right.

"No, I don't think I'll ever be all right so long as he's around. The day before we left home, he beat Tyrrell and I up. Not just a little, but bad enough that we both ended up in the emergency room needing x-rays and stitches." He didn't say anything but held onto his wolf. "He was gone when I went back to get my money and my clothing. Tyrrell had to stay in the hospital overnight. I talked one of the nurses into letting me sign myself out so that I could get some things together for us to run. She knew who had hurt us and let me go. It took everything that I had in me to go back to that house. I was terrified that he'd be there, waiting for me. Or worse, that he'd have a gun or something to shoot me with."

"Was he there waiting on you?" She told him that he wasn't waiting on her, but he came in while she was there. Lucky for her, she'd already taken her things out of the house and had come back in to have another look around. But Rogan took the opportunity to knock her around some more. "Why didn't the police help you?"

"No one would help us. We were related to Rogan, and to help us would surely get them into deep shit with him. He was about as scary as they came. But the police, they were just as bad as he was. I noticed that there is a new chief in town. Back then they would just as soon rob you as much as he did. Then they'd put you in a cell right with him so that he could have his little fun while they watched." He remembered what it had been like and asked her to go on. "As soon as I got what I could, I got out of the house and never looked back. My parents were gone again, nothing unusual about that. And if you're going to ask me what they thought of Rogan doing this, they were almost as bad as he was. They would throw knives at each other when they were fighting. And for the most part, they ignored the fact that they had kids even when they were home. Which really wasn't all that often."

"You had a terrible young life. I wish I could have known you then. I could have helped you in some way, I think" She snorted at him, and he watched her as she got up on the counter and continued. "I had no idea it was that bad between the two of you. Nor what sort of person he was. We never walked in the same circles or I might have known more about him. Does Tyrrell know?"

"No. And I don't want him to either. Not to say that he doesn't have his own secrets. I'm sure that Rogan cornered him as much as he did me. And he'd try to pit us against one another. It didn't work, and that would piss him off too." Tanner said he wouldn't tell him. "And don't tell me that I should share that sort of information either. The shrink that I was seeing said the same thing. That I needed closure."

"Tell me the rest of the story. I want to hear it." She nodded but only sat there. He noticed two things about her then. She wasn't as fragile as she looked, and she wasn't just mad, but spitting mad. "You're very beautiful. Your cheeks are all rosy, and your hair is falling down around your shoulders. You look sexy too."

"Cut the horseshit. I know what I look like. And sexy isn't a word that anyone has ever used about me before, so don't do that." Tanner smiled but said nothing as she continued. "This is something that I've never told anyone. Not ever. But I was on my way out of the house when I saw him in the living room. He was there with a woman, but I didn't know her. He was naked, and she was as well, but she looked more like he'd torn her clothing off of her than just taking them off to have sex. He was taking her from behind, brutally, and she was screaming for him to let her go."

"Christ." He moved toward her and took her into his arms. When she didn't fight him, he held her and told her to finish please. "You need to tell me this as much as I want to hear it."

"She saw me, though I don't know how — her face looked like he'd taken a belt to it. Both her eyes were bloodied, her left eye was swollen nearly shut. She screamed for me to help her, which alerted Rogan that he wasn't alone with her any longer." She took a deep breath and let it out slowly. Tanner didn't know what she was going to say next, but he was barely holding onto his wolf as it was. "He didn't stop. He kept taunting me as he took her, slapping her on her back and legs with the hard end of the belt he had in his hand. And when he was finished, he never took his eyes off me and pulled her body to him and snapped her neck. Just murdered

51

her where she was right in front of me, like it was nothing for him to do something like that. Before he could come after me, I ran. I ran as if my life depended on it, and I was sure that it did. To this day, I can still see her face and the way that he murdered her. I've often wondered if he'd done something like that before. Had he murdered someone else along the line and we didn't know about it."

"Why did you come home? Why did you even bother with coming here to try to get him off?" She sobbed then, and he held her to his chest. "I'm sorry, love. I really am. I didn't mean to hurt you with that. I only wanted to know how you could stand to be in the same room with him. I'd have killed him had I known. I still might."

She cried holding onto him. He wanted to tell her to wait while he took care of Rogan, just went down the hall that the cells were in and tore him apart. Tanner was reasonably sure that anyone in the station house might help him, turning off the cameras there as well as unlocking his door for him.

"He just dropped her like she was nothing at all. And I suppose to him she wasn't." Tanner now wanted to go down the hall and kill Rogan over and over again. Cause him to suffer in ways that would make Tanner's wolf very happy. "I called my aunt the next day and told her what had happened. I told her all of it except for him killing the woman, and she told me to come to her. She wired me enough money to buy a ticket, and I went to her the next week, leaving my brother all the cash I had on me so that he could make a clean break as well. We had a party in the little room we were in before I left. I could have told him then, but we were so hurt by all of what Rogan did to us that I only told him that Rogan was gone and that I'd gotten my things. He moved in with a cousin, and was with them when my parents came home. I don't know what happened to the woman, only that there was never a news report about her missing, nor that her body had been found. For all I know my parents helped him clean up the mess and then acted like nothing had happened at all. They were good at that, it seemed, ignoring what they didn't like and treating Rogan like he really was the boss of all of us."

When she pulled away, he let her. One thing he had learned from her story was, she had been battered in more than just her body. And she was the bravest person he knew. Telling her that would piss her off, he knew that, so he kept it to himself. The fact that she'd gone to a different country to get away from her brother was brave enough, but to have sat in the room with him earlier was more than he could have done if all this had happened to him.

"I don't want you to come here anymore." She just looked at him. "I'm not trying to tell you what to do, but this can't be easy on you, and I hate to see you hurting over him. And no matter what you tell yourself, you're hurting, aren't you?"

"Yes. This is the reason that I can't be a part of your life, Tanner. He's going to drag us down, Tyrrell and I, and there isn't any point in you being brought down as well."

He could have told her that he didn't care but he did, about her and her brother Tyrrell. Instead of saying anything that might come out wrong, he pulled her back into his arms and kissed her. It was all he could do to not have his wolf go and kill her brother.

He didn't deepen the kiss, for as much as he wanted to, he didn't want her to be mad at him. Tanner didn't doubt that she would be, but he was going to take what he could while he could. Pulling back from her, he looked down at her face and could see more freckles than he'd thought she had earlier. They were the cutest things he'd ever seen, the way that they danced across her nose and onto her cheeks.

"You kissed me." He said that he was glad that she'd noticed. "You shouldn't have done that. You know as well as I that it only leads to trouble. And I don't know if you're aware of this or not, but we have enough trouble going on as it is."

"I'm willing to take my chances. How do you feel right now? Well enough for me to kiss you again?" Giyanna glared at him, but didn't pull out of his arms. "You have the prettiest eyes. I guess I knew that red heads had green eyes, most of them anyway, but yours are the greenest emerald color that I've ever seen. And the softest skin. I find myself waxing poetic about it in my mind."

This time, she did pull away. "I need to get back to the place we're staying and tell my brother what happened. And that you and Rogan didn't get along any better than we did." He nodded. "Then we have to figure out what we're going to do about this. I can't be around him. Not now."

"No, and I don't want you to be. If you'd allow us to, Tyrrell and I can do the trial and you can help my sister-in-law, Chloe, find the missing woman. Someone would have reported her by now." Giyanna said that she'd go to jail. "No, you won't. She'll be so glad to help you out that she'd be willing to overlook the fact that you didn't report it. Not to mention, she knew all about the station house well before we did. And now it's a good place to be. Just help Chloe, and I'm thinking between the two of you, not only will you find the woman, but also if there are any more of them."

He reached out to Chloe and Joe to tell him what he was doing. And what Rogan had done too. When he was finished neither of them said anything, but he knew they were upset. It wasn't until he had her in the car and they were on their way back to town that Joe spoke.

I can look for her in the missing person reports that are on the computer. There is bound to be something there. There will more than likely be a picture. Do you think she'd remember what she looked like to make an identification? Chloe said that if the other department had done any of the paperwork, then maybe, but there was a good possibility that they'd not. *Perhaps we'll get lucky and one of your relatives remembers someone that came up missing about then. They would have heard about it, no doubt. If there isn't a report, we'll go that route.*

I never thought of asking them. I'm worried about Giyanna. She's gone through a great deal today, and we haven't even gone to trial yet. Joe said that they should come to their house for dinner tonight. *I don't know. Last night didn't go over so well.*

It'll just be the four of us. Then she can go to dinner at someone else's house and so on until she meets us all slowly. I know from when I first met you all in one room, it can be a bit overwhelming to say the least. He liked that idea and told Joe that. *Good. Tell her that I'll have some information on her lady before then, and if I need any more information, I'll ask her when she gets here. This is going to be so helpful, Tanner. Not just in keeping the man in jail but making it so that he doesn't get out anytime soon. With what they have on him now, the most he'd do is a few years, probably no more than ten or so.*

55

Chloe spoke then, each of them lending support for Giyanna as he knew that they would. *And I'll see what I have here. There are some new files that are being uploaded onto the computers now. The feds aren't going to give us back the other ones until after everyone has had their trial. That could be a very long time.* Tanner asked Chloe if Anastasia might have some information. *She might. If we have a name, she can maybe ask the earth to help her find her. That might be all we need for us to look for her. Under the pretense of a water main break or something.*

Tanner decided that he wasn't going to hold information from Giyanna, and told her everything that he'd done so far. She nodded but didn't say much on the way back to where she was staying, and he asked her if she'd join him for dinner at Trent and Joe's home.

"I don't know. I don't do well with people in large groups. I have to puke before each trial that I have back home. Like I said before, I didn't care much for being an attorney, but it paid well, and I was good at it." He told her he knew that feeling before working for Noah. "It'll just be them? The four of us?"

"Yes, they promised to do this slowly this time. I should have known it would be too much for you. I mean, they're too much for me sometimes." She nodded and asked if her brother could come as well. "Of course. We'll ask him when I take you upstairs."

She was quiet the rest of the drive, but he could tell that she was nervous about something. Instead of talking about it or telling her that he was here, he decided that he really wasn't going to push things. He would let her come to him. His wolf, surprisingly, seemed to be all right with it as well.

56

As soon as they pulled into the parking lot behind the big house, she turned to him.

"Your family, they're not just wolves, are they?" He shook his head. "I was too scared last night to figure it out, but I think that Joe is something more too. And she's sort of old world, isn't she? Not just non-human, but she gives you an air that she's very old and very smart."

"She's thousands of years old. When she was much younger, Noah, a vampire friend of the family, saved her from being killed. Joe worked for him as his day watcher, doing things for him like investing his money and so on." She nodded. "All of us, you included, are more than the average wolf or human. As I told you before, you're an immortal now. But there is more too. Magic is yours for the taking and for you to use whenever you wish."

"And that means what?" He told her that she'd live forever. "There has to be some kind of catch to that. Like, I don't know, beheading or being stabbed in the heart. How do we die?"

"We don't. And we have the ability to not have our heads removed, and nothing can harm our hearts nor any other part of our body that might kill us. We can be hurt, but we'll not die from anything." She nodded, and he laughed. She asked him what was so funny. "You're taking this surprisingly well for someone that is new to all of it. And for someone that didn't believe in magic at all. Though I have to wonder what you thought happened when a shifter turned into his other half."

"I'm not freaking out, you mean. And I never really thought about it before today. It was just something that they could do, and that was the end of my thoughts about it."

He nodded at her then. "Yes, well, I'm trying my best to be opened minded about all this. I'm not saying that I'm going to stick around, but I think that I should have a better handle on this before things get out of control. Don't you? I mean, what if you get funky or whatever and decide to change yourself? I don't want to stand there screaming like a ninny when there is danger about."

Tanner laughed. He just couldn't help it. She had gone from someone that seemed to be defeated to this woman—a strong person who had been knocked around and down more than most. And to top that off, it was her own flesh and blood too. He really was growing to admire her for her spirit and her wit.

Giyanna went in to get her brother and asked Tanner to wait, telling him that she needed to go back to his house. She didn't say why, but he was willing to have her go anywhere with him. When she came out with her brother, he let Joe know that Tyrrell was joining them. She told him that was great. The more the merrier.

As soon as he pulled into the driveway to his home, he knew that something more had happened. There hadn't been a third floor to his home, and now there was. Tanner knew that he had to talk to Giyanna about his inability to have children, and having more empty bedrooms hurt him in ways that he couldn't imagine. To have a little red headed daughter like her mom would be the best thing he could think of.

Giyanna told Tyrrell all about the house as they got out of the car. "You should have seen it when I did. It was my place at home. Even the pictures on the wall were the same. And it even smelled like it. I'm telling you right now, I would never have believed it had I not seen it with my own eyes."

"Okay." Tyrrell was a little disbelieving, but he was going in with an open mind, he thought. More open than he might have been, he supposed. "And you said that it's the way you want it now? Even the little rugs in the hall?"

"Yes. I can hear in your voice that you think I'm off my rocker, but I assure you that it's right. I know, I saw it happening when I thought of the house like I wanted this one to be. We'll do the same for you that he did when we got here. Think of your home." She looked at Tanner. "Will it work for him, you think?"

"I don't know. I suppose you could ask the house to give him this. Then for it to change it back when he's convinced. I love the way you have it decorated with all the warm colors." She laughed, and he did as well. Tanner thought that he could get used to having her laugh all the time.

Giyanna turned to the house and yelled at it to allow Tyrrell to change the living room to look like what was in his mind.

"Okay. Now remember, this is the only time you can do this." Tyrrell looked at him, skepticism all over his face. But he was being a good guy about it and letting her lead him into the house. As soon as he heard Tyrrell shout, he knew that the house had let him change it.

She held onto him and Tanner helped him go to the couch. It was ugly, the couch and the chair, but he didn't care. In a few minutes, as soon as he was convinced, then it would go back to what Giyanna had liked. The way that he'd liked it as well.

"This is my living room." Giyanna asked him if he was

color blind, because that had been his first thought as well when he entered the room. "No, I'm not. I just love color. The office that I have in the firm that I work for, they don't allow anything but gray in all their decorations. And you can't have anything hanging on the walls that isn't business related. So, at home, I have color. It makes me feel good and it's fun. We never had much fun, and I love this."

"Tyrrell, this shit is ugly." They all laughed, and he said that he knew it was but that wasn't the point. He just wanted to have something that wasn't drab. "Yes, I can understand that, but it's really ugly. Couldn't you have gone with, I don't know, colors in different areas of your room? I mean, this is really, really ugly."

"You've said that. Several times now. I know that." They were still laughing as they teased each other about the furniture. Before they were settled with a glass of tea and more scones from Ruben, the room and furnishings were back to the way that Giyanna had wanted it. "This is very nice. And you have pops of color all over the place."

"You should try it. Pops of it, not every color of every pattern all over the place."

Before they got into another argument about the color of his things, Tanner told Tyrrell what had happened at the jail. Not all of it. Giyanna would have to tell Tyrrell herself if she wanted him to know about the story she'd told Tanner in the bathroom.

"I'm going to be his lawyer. He's not going to be able to get to your sister again, not if I can help it. And if you'll second with me, then I think we can get him a reduced sentence. He thinks that he's going to get off, but that's not going to happen." Tyrrell said he'd do it, but he wasn't sure how Rogan was going to take it. "Frankly, I hope he fires us. Then he'll get who he gets and that'll be the end of it. And that way, we can hope that he gets someone that is very green and has him in prison in no time."

They sat and talked until it was time to go to his brothers' home. He had spoken to Joe and Chloe twice while they'd been at his house, and they had some pictures that he was going to see if Giyanna could look at. If she could identify the woman, it would add a murder charge onto Rogan's sentence. And that would take him off the case permanently. He wasn't a lawyer that dealt in murder cases. Tyrrell said that he wasn't either.

While they were going there, walking this time, he held Giyanna's hand. Tanner was enjoying the quietness of the evening, and was happy that she didn't put up a fuss when he took her hand into his. The walk was fun, the night was cool, and Tanner wondered what all his fussing had been about in taking a mate.

He was already in love with her. And she had made his house a home. Not only that, but it was something that they had in common, their love of warm colors, soft sturdy furniture, and family pictures on the walls. He would have to make sure that, somehow, he got a few pictures of Tyrrell to hang up as well.

Chapter 4

Noelle was just putting the finishing touches on the planter that she'd just gotten in when she felt the tightening of her belly. It was hard to stand up when it hit her, and sitting on the floor, she noticed that she was sitting in liquid. It took her befuddled mind a few minutes to realize that her water had broken, and she knew that it was time. Calling for Marty, she was as calm as she could be when she told her what had happened.

"Really? You're in labor now?" She said that she wasn't hurting, but her water had broken. "That's the start. I've been reading up on this since I started working here. All right. We have to make some calls. You contact Elijah and I'll get Sterl. He's been working upstairs to be close in case we needed him."

When she was alone again, Noelle reached for Elijah and told him that her water had broken. He was as calm as she'd been, and she was glad for it. They'd been planning to go in tomorrow for her to be induced, and he said this was so much better.

I'm on my way. She thanked him. *I'm letting everyone else know too. So, you be prepared for the invasion.*

I don't hurt at all. I mean, I've had this backache since I got up, but I did move all that stuff into the babies' room last night. He had told her then and again now that she should have waited on him. *I wanted to surprise you.*

Well, you did at that. He told her again that he was coming, and she felt better knowing that he was on his way.

Sterl came downstairs, lifted her up off the floor, and took her to the office, telling Marty to lock up. As soon as she was in her office, the pain started. It hurt badly now, and she could hardly breathe around it. When she was lifted again, she saw that Elijah had her and she asked him where he was taking her.

"To the hospital. You don't want to have the babies on the floor, do you?" Noelle was hurting too badly now to joke around, and she told him she thought she just might. "Hang on, baby. We'll be there soon."

They weren't going to make it. As soon as she was put in the back seat of the car, she felt the urge to push. And it hurt so bad that she screamed with it.

Noelle could see that there were others around her, some she could make out and others she didn't even care. When one of them told her to breathe, she looked around at her and wondered where she'd come from. And for that matter where she was.

"It's Giyanna. I've done this before, delivered a baby. And thankfully we're not on a busy highway in rush hour traffic when I do it this time. You just keep breathing and we'll be fine." She told her that she hurt. "I know, honey, and I wish I could give you something for it, but I don't think your antique shop has morphine in it. We're going to get through this, you and I, and when it's all over, you'll have your baby."

It seemed like forever since this started, but Giyanna kept telling her that she was doing fine, great as a matter of fact. And when the urge to push came over her this time, there was no denying it. Noelle pushed as hard as she could while Giyanna told her to breathe between contractions.

"I'm breathing, damn it. This fucking hurts." Giyanna told her that she could see the head. "Really? It's coming? I want to hold them. Hurry this along, Giyanna, I need to hold my children, so I can forget all this pain."

"You will. And honey, it's the baby, not me, that's taking its time. We'll get it in your arms. Just one more push like that last one and I'll have your baby for you." She heard her father-in-law say there was twins. "Oh. Well, I'll have baby number one for you in just a minute now."

Noelle could hear sirens. She didn't know if it was her screaming, really, or the police. They were going to arrest her, she just knew it. Waking the dead with her screams had to be breaking some law, she thought hysterically. Giyanna told her that there wasn't a person in the world that would arrest her, not so long as she was with her, and Noelle believed her.

She was told to push again, and Noelle felt the first baby leave her body. For a few moments she was in heaven. Nothing hurt, but she wasn't sure that she could do it again. It was then that she noticed that Elijah was behind her, holding her up like the chair did at practice. They'd been to all their

65

classes, and she was glad for it. Then the first baby screamed.

It was possibly the best sound that she'd ever heard. But before she could hold her little boy, she had the urge to push again. This time she pushed once and expelled her little girl. Noelle couldn't help it, she fell unconscious before she could ask if they were both all right.

Noelle woke to someone talking. And when she opened one eye she realized that she was in a real bed in the hospital. Elijah was on his cell phone, talking quietly, when she saw where he was standing. There was a large crib in front of him, and he was talking while looking down at it. Noelle said his name.

"I have to go, Chris. Yes, I'll tell her what you said, and we'll see you tomorrow." He told her that he was happy, then put his phone away. "How you doing, Momma? You feel like holding one of your children? You fell asleep so quickly after they were born you scared me a little. But my mom told me that you'd done more labor than most and needed it. Which one do you want to hold first?"

"Both of them." He laughed and told her that he'd help her. "Are they all right, Elijah? Do they have all their fingers and toes? Did you make sure that they were healthy and not hurt from me having them at the shop?"

"Honey, they couldn't be more perfect. They have ten of each. I counted them before you were brought here. And they're very healthy. Our son is full wolf, and our daughter is human. I'm so happy that I have to keep pinching myself to make sure that I'm not dreaming." She took the first bundle from him and held her son. "We still haven't picked out a name yet. We don't have any more time now."

"I know, but it's so hard. They'll have it for the rest of their lives." He said that was the plan. "You know what I mean. They'll be labeled if the name is too silly or strange. And they'll be made fun of if it's easy to shorten it into something dirty or even funny to say. I don't want that for them. They need to have a name that will be perfect for this clan. A name worthy of being a Calhoun."

"All right. Then what would you like to call our son?" She knew what she wanted to call him, but was afraid that he'd think it was too much. "Noelle, just tell me, love, before they all come in demanding names. And you know as well as I do that they'll start making suggestions, and that will be all she wrote. What were you thinking for our son?"

"Elijah James Anthony Calhoun." He smiled, and she felt like that was the perfect thing to call him. "We can do as your father has done and call him E.J. for short. Then for our daughter? Let me think."

She traded him babies and held their daughter for the first time. She was simply perfect, just as E.J. was. She thought of how she had ended up with them here. How a near stranger yet family had come to save them all.

"Christine Jasmine Giyanna Calhoun. For the two people in the world that I think the most of. And the woman who made it so they were brought into the world safely." He kissed her on the mouth and told her she was wonderful. "You don't think it's too much for her? I know what I said about them being made fun of, but she needs a powerful name, don't you think?"

"You couldn't have picked any names, all three of them, more powerful. I love them both." With another kiss, he told her to be prepared, they were coming in. And almost as soon as he finished speaking, the door opened, and the family crowded in.

Noelle loved this family of hers. They were kind and bossy, generous and very nosey. But she loved them as her own. And when Elijah held his son so that they could all see him, she laid her little girl on the bed and unwrapped her.

"My goodness, what a pretty little thing." Noelle looked up at Mom and smiled. "And you, just look at how happy you are. Motherhood suits you. Can I hold her now?"

"Absolutely." Handing her Chrissy, she smiled at her. "We've got names for them both. Would you like to know what hers is?"

"Oh my, yes, I need to know what to call this precious little bundle." She told her the name and also what she thought they should call her. "You named her after me? You did that for me?"

"Yes. Being that she's a human, she needed a strong name. Something that would empower her as she got older. I don't know of any other women that I could have named her after and been happy with it." Mom wiped at the tears that were on her cheeks. Then when Sterl brought his little boy to them, she held him while the others passed hers and Elijah's babies around. Life was suddenly very fulfilling for her. And she was as happy as she'd ever been before.

Benson, Sterl's son, was getting so big now. He was a happy little fellow, despite the fact that he'd lost both his parents in such a short time. Sterl and Marty were raising him to know that he was adopted, and hoped that someday he'd want to take over the gallery that his father left for Sterl so that it would be in his family again. This family was forever thinking of the other person when they made plans. Noelle thought that was why she loved them so much.

Everyone seemed so pleased with the names that they'd picked out. And each of them liked the idea of calling them E.J. and her daughter Chrissy. It would keep the confusion down as well as help them when they were older. All the Trents in the family got confusing when a stranger would call the house asking for him.

She was exhausted again when they were getting ready to leave, but she had to talk to Giyanna and thank her for helping her bring her little babies into the world. Her shyness had Noelle warming to her more, and she held her hand as she spoke to her.

"You did something for me that I cannot repay you for." Giyanna said that it had been her pleasure, but not to make a habit of it. "No, I won't. I don't know what I would have done had you not been there for us."

"You would have done just fine. Women have been having babies for a very long time. It was easy really. I mean for me, not you so much." They both laughed. "I want to thank you for naming your daughter after me. You didn't have to do that. I'm just as happy as I can be that everyone is safe and sound. You did a great job there, Momma, and you should be very proud of yourself."

"I wanted her to be strong. It's so hard in this world to be something different. And while she is wholly human, she'll have magic that will set her apart from the rest. Besides, you're going to be my sister-in-law, right?" She just looked over at Tanner but didn't answer. "He's a good man. All the Calhoun men are. But Tanner has always been someone special to me. Others too. He's like the big brother that I never had. And he's a smart, good guy to have around."

"I know that, but I'm not exactly what he would be dating." She asked her why not. "I don't know. I have a lot of baggage. More than most, I would imagine. I mean, Rogan alone is enough to make a lesser man run for the hills."

"You have no idea how much baggage we women brought when we joined this family. And a great deal of it was something that our families had brought down on us. Even Joe—she had things in her life that she had settled just the way she wanted. Living her life the way she wanted. But now that she has Trent, they're as happy, both of them, as I've ever seen a couple." Giyanna said that her brother was causing trouble. "Yes. And we'll get through it. Like a family. All of us will be at your back, your side, or wherever you need us. That's the way they do things around here. You'll see what I mean when things start to fall apart—these people will hold you together."

"You're very sweet, but I think this is well beyond what they've been dealing with." She told her about Sterl and his she-devil, and the demon that came to get him. Also about the demon Richard. "Tanner mentioned that, and it seems unreal, don't you think? But now that I think on it, maybe my troubles are not so bad. At least I hope not."

They both laughed, and when Giyanna told her that she was glad they were going to be friends, Noelle thanked her again. It was getting harder and harder to keep her eyes open. And as she was drifting off, no longer able to fight it, she felt the kiss to her forehead and knew that it was Elijah. She loved that man more than she thought possible.

~~~

Tanner was in his office when Giyanna came to see him. He'd been working on the things for the trial when she sat down across from him. Looking at her, he could tell that she was upset about something, but he let her take the lead. Instead of asking her about it, he told her what he was working on.

"There isn't any way that he's going to get out of most of this. I've tried to explain it to him, but he just doesn't believe that he's been doing anything wrong. Not even beating his wife and kids." She nodded, and he knew that she wasn't really paying attention to him, so he had some fun with her. "Then there is the fact that he dances naked in his cell nightly, and had rituals that involve him taking little snips of his hair and using them for chewing gum."

"I found out who the woman is." He told her that was good. "Yes, and now that they know her name, Joe can ask the earth to help her find where he buried her. I'm not at all sure how that works, but I'm guessing that she can do it and do it well."

"Yes, she can, and that's good, right? Trent has a way to make sure that the prosecuting attorney can figure it out and bring those charges against him as well. He told me that he has a foolproof plan in regard to that." She nodded. "What else is it? Did someone say something to you?"

"The woman that Rogan killed was a nice person with a family. Not a whore at all like I had thought at the time. I think in my mind it was a way for me to deal with what he'd done. Not that she deserved to die like she had, but I was only a teenager and couldn't deal with it any other way." Tanner told her that he might have done the same. "No, you wouldn't have. You'd have been outraged and done something about it. Don't patronize me."

"I wasn't. And I'm not nearly as strong as you seem to think I am. I want you to take a deep breath and let it out slowly and tell me why you have a burr up your ass today." She just stared at him—he could see that she was really pissed now. "Or you could come over here, sit on my desk, and let me have my way with you."

"Do you ever think of anything but sex?" He told her plenty, but he was making a joke. "I'm not in the mood."

"I can tell."

She got up to pace, and he reached for Chloe to find out what happened. *She's tense and upset. Can you tell me what the hell happened? I've never seen her like this before.*

Tanner, we couldn't have ever found this woman had she not helped us. It was good of her to tell me, and to help us close this for the family. He asked about the woman. *Her name was Margaret Penny, and she was a mother of four and married to a very nice man who has been grieving for his wife since she disappeared over ten years ago. The children are nearly grown now, of course, but they still remember her and miss her daily. When Giyanna figured that out, she cried for an hour. I think this has been harder on her than even her brother has been. She's been holding onto this knowledge about the death, and I think that it's been eating at her more than even she realized.*

After thanking her, he got up to sit on the edge of his desk, waiting for Giyanna to come back his way so that he could talk to her. When he reached out to touch her, it was as if that had been all she was waiting on and she burst into tears, clinging to him as she told him what Chloe had.

"She had children that missed her. He killed her for no other reason than to prove a point to me, I guess. It was lost on me then, and even now, why he had to murder someone like he did. Was it to frighten me? I was already afraid of him. I don't understand why he thought it was all right to kill anyone, but this woman had a family. She was a good person. People have been looking for her since she was killed."

He held her, listening to her disjointed conversation. When she started to calm a little, he picked her up in his arms and took her to the couch that was in his office. There he sat with her, just holding her as she cried again.

He'd never been good around crying women. He knew that there were a few of them that thought that was the way to get him to do whatever it was they wanted. But he was more turned off about that than he was if they whined. And Tanner hated a whiner. But this was different. She wasn't asking him for anything but support. Nor was she trying to get anything from him.

"Chloe said that you were helpful in the search. Had you not then they would never have found her to help the family." She laid her head on his shoulder but didn't say anything. "I'm sorry that I was joking around with you. I had no way of knowing that you were that upset or why."

"I shouldn't have snapped at you. I'm not used to people being...well, being kind to me, I guess. I'm new to this kind of feelings for someone." He asked her who had been mean to her. "I only just realized that I became an attorney for all the wrong reasons."

"I'm sure that you're just upset." She told him she was,

but that wasn't it. "Then tell me why you think they were the wrong reasons."

"I wanted to see justice for that woman. And I thought if I was this great attorney that I could have my brother arrested and taken to jail, and I could come home again. I missed my brother, Tyrrell, the weather here, believe it or not, and the way people are here. They're not as nice sometimes as they are where I was, but here was home to me. But I couldn't return even after I got my law degree because I was afraid of Rogan and what he might do to me even then." Tanner told her that he was someone to be afraid of. "Yes, well, a woman never got the proper burial, and her family didn't get the closure that they needed because I was afraid of him. But they will now, damn it, even if I have to pay for it all by myself."

"I'm so very sorry." She didn't move but stayed on his lap with her head resting on his chest now. "Rogan wants to see you. He's going to tell you that he's sorry, or so he told me. He goes to court tomorrow morning. I told him that I'd not go to bat for him unless he told you how sorry he was. I don't think it'll be all that sincere, but he is going to say it to you."

"I don't want him near me." He nodded and adjusted her on his lap so that his erection could get a little relief. She sat up and looked at him. "You're very hard, aren't you?"

"I am. And I've been in a constant state of arousal since I met you. You have no idea how hard I've been since I've met you." She looked at his mouth, then at his eyes. "You're very beautiful, Giyanna. And I'd like nothing more than to kiss you again. But I want you to realize that I want you very badly, and have since I touched you the first time."

"It's inevitable, isn't it?" He asked her what she meant.

"That you and I come together. That we have a relationship that will be based on DNA rather than love."

"I do love you." She started to move, and he held her. "No, wait, let me finish. I do love you. And perhaps, yes, it's DNA that makes me love you after such a short time. I don't really care how it worked out. You're my other half, the woman that was to make me a whole person, and you did. More than that, you gave me something that I didn't realize I was missing, and that is calmness. Loving you is nothing that I ever expected to happen. Not the way that I do. I knew that you were coming. With the rest of my family mated and happy, I knew that it was only a matter of time before I was as well. However, I never thought that I could be like my brothers in their relationships. I thought, and this was before I met you, that I wasn't going to have time to have you changing me. I liked me the way I am. But you came into my life, and it's like I've been waiting my entire life for you to be there with me. My home is that, a home now, when before it was just a house, a place where I slept and ate leftovers from someone's house that I ate at the night before. My life seemed to be going along like it should. But it was far from perfect, as it is now with you here. I'm more relaxed, happy with the turn of events, and I couldn't love you any more than I do right now. I'd die for you."

"Why?" Tanner asked her what she meant. "What is it about me that you love? I'm not much like the women you more than likely dated before I came along."

"You're very different than they were. When I dated, which really wasn't all that much, I'd go out with a friend of a friend. A sister to one of the women that my brothers were trying to woo. It wasn't that I didn't have fun, I really did, but it wasn't all that exciting to me." She asked him if he thought she was exciting. "You are. And funny. You have this calmness about you that brings me in too. Makes me feel relaxed, and I can think better. And sometimes you make me feel more like a man than I have before."

"I don't know how to be the woman that you might need. I'm just me." He asked her again what she meant by that. "You know, pretty and bright. I have opinions and ideas, and I'm not afraid to voice them."

"You think that I'd not allow you to have an opinion?" She shook her head. "Then we can mark that off the list. All right. Ideas. Yes, you should have them. And act upon them if you want to see them work. The fact that you had no trouble going to see Chloe and helping her makes me believe that you have a sense of justice. That you wanted to help, and you did so. I'm happy for you in that. Happy for all the people involved in you coming forward and finding out who this woman was."

"She could have been buried a long time ago. With her family knowing what had happened." He nodded but waited for her to say more. "I should have done this much sooner, before leaving. Maybe gone to another police station or called them with a tip. Of course, I had no idea what her name was, nor where he might have buried her."

"You could have, certainly. What do you think would have happened back then?" Giyanna asked him what he meant. "You know that the force was corrupt and that they had their own set of rules. Do you think they would have brought your brother in? Put him in jail? Or would they have gone after you? A young pretty woman that tells on her own family? I shudder to think what might have happened to you had you done either of those things. And, as you said, you had no idea where she might have been, nor her name. They would have marked you as a crackhead and jailed you for fun or sent you back home to Rogan."

"They would have brought me in, like you said, and jailed me. Perhaps sent me home with him too. I would have been unable to get away when I did." He nodded. "My brother would have come to get me, and no matter what I had told them that Rogan had done, they still would have given me over to him, and I would have been killed by him too. And probably even buried next to the young woman, where my body would never be found."

"Yes, he would have." He held her tighter and she laid on his chest again. "I never would have met you. I would have been a lonely man for the rest of my life, wondering what had happened to my other half. And your poor brother, he would have been killed as well. There wasn't going to be any way that anyone would be able to think it was anyone but Rogan that had done it."

She got up then and stood in front of him. He wasn't sure what she was thinking, but the smile that she had on her face brought out his own. Tanner would have given everything that he had to know that he'd been responsible for such a look, but for now, he'd take whatever he could get from her.

"I want to go shopping." He said all right. "I need some clothing and some other shoes. I know that I can make them. I can, right?"

"I don't know how that will work for you." She closed her

eyes and he thought even her concentration was beautiful. When she was suddenly in a pair of shorts and a T-shirt, he laughed. "I guess it does work for you. All right then, what are we shopping for? The reason I ask is, we have to find the perfect store."

"I want to go and see Second Time Around. I heard that Noelle and Marty have the nicest things in there." He took her hand when it was offered. "Also, your grandda was telling me about the buildings that are being renovated. I'd like to see those as well. Show me our town, Tanner. I want to see it all."

She had said our town, but he didn't get his hopes up yet. They had a lot of things to work out, the two of them. And he wanted to get a start on those things right away. But not today. Today was for fun. He was going to show her the entire town, take her to lunch, then he was going to take her shopping anywhere she wanted to go. Tanner was nearly skipping when they left the house.

Giyanna was telling him about her home, the one that had been left to her in Ireland. And that she wanted to keep it so that she could go and visit sometimes. It was a place that was near to her heart simply because it was the first one that she'd ever owned. He agreed with her, telling her that at one time, he thought his family had owned a few houses there. His grandparents liked to travel, but they hated hotels.

"We'll have to find out how close we are to some of their homes." He told her they were going to his parents' house for dinner tonight. "Okay, I'll be better at handling them now, I think. You're all very big guys, aren't you? I mean, Rogan is big, but he's sloppy fat. And someday I bet it will be his downfall. But you guys are tall and muscled."

"And yet my mom and dad still call us their boys. And if we do something wrong, when she's nearby, Mom will pop us in the back of the head like she did when we were younger. And let me tell you, I didn't get hit nearly as many times as the others did. I was the baby, and special to her."

They were still laughing about it when he pulled up in front of the antique shop. Taking her hand when they got out, Tanner kissed her again. Today was going to be a good day.

Chapter 5

Rogan looked over the pants and shirt he'd been brought to wear today. He wasn't able to fit the pants on himself, but the shirt did all right. He'd had to think when he'd gotten so fat over the last few days. Like it had snuck up on him or something. He supposed that he should have been more careful of his weight, but there were so many foods out there that he just couldn't help himself. When he heard the door open and close, he didn't bother looking up. It would be someone coming to take him to the shower.

"You ready?" The man there had a gun on him, and there were two other men behind him. "Come on, Rogan. You have things to do today. And having a shower is going to top that list. No more putting it off."

"I hate that shower stall. I don't fit in it. Can't I just go like I am? I'll wear a lot of deodorant." He told him that wouldn't work, that his hair was nasty, and he stunk. "But the hot water doesn't last as long as I want it to. I think you guys are cutting me off before I'm ready. You're all out to get me, and as soon as I'm free from here, and I will be, I'm going to tell my governor about your ill treatment of me and that you locked me up for no reason at all."

"We want you as clean as you can get. Coming down here to just give you your tray of food is enough to make us sick. Get up and let's get this done. The van will be here soon to pick you up. And if you miss it, you'll not get a second chance at going there today."

He didn't want to be humiliated again. They had all had a good laugh at him when he could only reach in and turn the water on but not shove his fat body into the stall. It was then that he realized just how monstrous he'd gotten.

As he walked to the stalls, he thought of how pissed off he was that he was this fat. He could have blamed it on the diner that he ate at once a day, or the fast food shit that he picked up when he was out and about, but it was all him in this.

Rogan didn't remember the last time he'd seen his feet, much less his dick. And even when he was feeling horny, there wasn't shit he could do about it, not like he was. So, he'd just watch women. And that had even become no fun for him until he got to kill them.

He could still kill, and he supposed that was what he really liked to do anyway. The sex was just something that he did to have the women screaming and begging for their lives. Like that was going to happen. The last time he'd killed someone he'd had to just leave the body on the ground. There wasn't any way for him to dig a hole, not without joining the dead woman in the grave too. Rogan knew that he should have thought about his size then, but it never occurred to him.

He just thought he was really out of shape.

The shower was the same as before—too little, and the tile was cold against his body as he tried to reach the soap and shit that they gave him. But this time there wasn't a crowd in the room with him. He just tore his clothing off; unbuttoning it and trying to pull it off was too much effort. And anyway, he was going to go home today, so it mattered little what he did with this orange suit that made him look like a giant pumpkin at Halloween. He wasn't going to have to come back here to put the stupid thing on, so fuck it.

Rogan had been working on a plan for when he got out. The first thing he was going to do was gather up his family. He knew that they'd have some cash on them. Both of them. The way that his sister was dressed, she had to have more than Tyrrell did. Plus, she'd just come here from someplace far away too. Tyrrell hadn't told him where she was, only that it would take her at least a day and a half to fly in. That sounded to him like she had money to burn. And if she was going to do that, spend it on clothing and girl stuff, she could damn well give it to him.

And Tyrrell being a lawyer, he'd have cash too. Or some credit cards with really high limits. He didn't care for them himself; credit cards were hard in his pocket, and people usually wanted to see some kind of ID with them. Not to mention that stupid machine. It was made, he knew, for people like him to look stupid when they didn't know how to work them.

He thought of his little sister and smiled. Giyanna had always hated him, he knew that, and thought it was funny that she would think that he even cared. But she'd help him

83

out of this, and when it was over, he'd find her, take what she had, then kill her. She had seen things that he wished now that he'd not shown her. The woman—she'd seen him kill her. Rogan knew as soon as he'd done it that it was going to come back and bite him in the ass, and if she talked, he wasn't getting out of here for a long time.

It wasn't as if he had tried to hide what he did. Rogan had been fucking the woman like he liked it, hard and mean. Then he saw his sister. She'd been so shocked, and he could still see the horror on her face as he broke the woman's neck. Going after her, he was going to kill her that night, but she'd been faster than him and he couldn't find her when she ran off. After that, he'd not seen her again. But he did worry once in a while about her.

Weeks afterward he still worried about who she might have told. Not that the cops back then would have done anything to him. He was their go to guy when they wanted some drugs or whatever. Not that he ever used the money that he charged them for it to pay for the drugs, but killed the dealer and took all that he had. Sometimes he could go weeks without having to kill anyone for cash; he usually could get plenty from one drop. But that had dried up too when that woman had taken over for his crew. Damn it, women were the ruination of everything that he had loved.

After he was dressed, he was shoved into the back of the van. There was another reason for him to hate that he'd let himself go so badly. Four men had to help him shove his fat ass into the back of the van that he'd have to ride in, and then he could feel every bump in the road as they drove down the road with his fat ass on the floor because the seats wouldn't hold him. He was going to have to do something about this soon or he'd be pushing up daisies before his time. And what was he going to do when he got back home with his wife and kids? They'd need to stand close to him and stay there, or he'd never catch them again.

Chained and brought into the courthouse, he asked if he could take a piss. They, of course, told him he should have taken care of that when he had time. Besides, one of them told him, the stalls were the regular size and he'd not fit in them. He said that he didn't have to shit, just piss, and they told him that it was a genderless bathroom, whatever the fuck that meant.

He was taken in the courtroom not long after that, and seated at the long table where his brother and that Calhoun guy were. He didn't care for him, but after he told his sister that he was sorry yesterday, Calhoun told him what his plans were for today. He claimed there wasn't any way that he was going to get off. But he knew better. His family wouldn't let him rot in there, or he'd make them see reason. He was going to anyway, but they didn't have to know that until he was released. Then, by damn, they'd know what the fuck it was like to be caged up.

As soon as the judge was in, he was able to relax a little. This would be over soon enough, and he'd be home. There was shit going on there that he wanted to take care of. And all the missed opportunities as well. Rogan needed to make himself a trap or two to keep his sister in. He wasn't even above killing her on the street just to show her that he always got what he wanted. And he wanted her dead in the worst kind of way. She'd been a burr in his ass for a long time, and it was time he took care of her.

He wasn't even sure why he hated her so much. Rogan had hated her from the moment that she'd come home from the hospital. Her and Tyrrell had been disliked by their parents for all their lives, and they'd been left without, so he knew that wasn't it. They got better grades than he did in school, but it didn't matter to his mom and dad. Not that he really cared about that part, but he did hate that they thought themselves to be better than him.

Rogan supposed it was the way that Giyanna had always looked at him, like she knew something that he didn't. Which wasn't possible, since he was older and had seen it all. But she would stare at him with those big green eyes, and he'd want to take a knife to them and peel them out of her head. It was a dream of his to take her eyes out and make her eat them.

As soon as he was old enough, he'd dropped out of school. Their parents didn't care. They were seldom home anyway, and they'd leave him in charge. That was another thing that she did that pissed him off—Giyanna never was around when he was in charge. It was like she knew that something was going to come up and she'd disappear, taking Ty with her when she did. And he would look for her too. Wherever she was hiding, it was a better place than he could find. Rogan had become an expert of sorts in finding her money and stuff, but when he was to be her boss, she never came around so he could beat on her.

"Are you paying attention?" He looked at his brother and told him he wasn't. "Well, you'd better. They found something on the land out where you used to live, and they're asking for a continuance."

"What does that mean?" He told him how he'd have to come back when they were done looking into whatever it was they found. "Oh, hell no. I'm not going to come back here. You tell them that."

"Keep your voice down." He was going to knock Calhoun's head off when he was freed too. He was nasty mean, and was never afraid of him. Well, he'd make him afraid, even if he had to kill him to do it. "You'll have to go back to jail. The judge said that there is enough evidence on whatever they found to want to investigate it more thoroughly."

"No." Calhoun just cocked a brow at him. "You tell them it's too late to be making me go back because they can't get their shit together and do this today. I got no reason to be in jail in the first place. So what? I did something wrong. It's not like you wouldn't do something too if you got the chance to. I ain't perfect, and as much as that bothers me to say it, you tell them that, so I can get home."

"I would never do the things that you've done. Not even on a bet. I'm reasonably sure that I didn't trash my home, and wouldn't threaten the police if they came to arrest me. Or beat my wife and kids and then act like nothing happened." He told him all that was his business. "No, it's not. Especially when it's government housing and your wife pressed charges against you so that you'd keep away from her. Also, you were to stay one thousand yards from her and the kids at all times. You didn't do that either. Now shut up so that I can figure out what is going on."

He wanted to slap the shit right out of him. What did it matter if he had done those things? It had been his house, wasn't it? Besides, the government had all kinds of money to fix things up that he'd done. That's what they were there for, to make sure that he had safe housing. There hadn't been anyone around when he'd done it, so he wondered how they got to pin that shit on him. And the police were pussies if they thought he'd been threatening them. He'd been promising them that he was going to kill them, not threatening them. A threat was worthless if you didn't ever follow through.

When he was lifted up and the police told him to come on, he looked at the judge and asked him what the hell was going on. Calhoun told him to be quiet, that he'd explain later, but he wanted someone that had smarts to tell him, not this pretty boy that didn't know shit. And he was beginning to think that he'd gotten the worst lawyer in the whole state — hell, even the entire world — in having Calhoun at his table.

"Mr. McGowan, you've been told three times, that I'm aware of, to shut up. If I were you, I'd do that. I'm in no mood for you to be loud in my courtroom. You'll have everything explained to you by your attorn—"

"He's an asshole. I don't care for the way he talks down to me either. I might not be the sharpest tool in the box, but I'm far from stupid. And I don't want to go back to the jail. I want to go to my house and wait for my wife and kids to come back. They will, too, when I have a little talk with Bridgett." He slammed his fist into his hand, making sure that the judge could understand how he was going to get her to behave. "There ain't no reason for me to be taken back there. All this shit they have on me, it's not right that I should have to sit in the cell all day when I could be out having me some fun. You tell them whatever else they've found out, it's too late for that shit and for them to just let me go. I had plans to go on home

88

today. I'm guessing that they got my house—"

"They found a body, Mr. McGowan. In your yard. It was wrapped up in a shower curtain that had been in your home." He asked how they knew that. "DNA was all over it. And if that wasn't enough, the cadaver dogs have been brought out, and they think that there might be as many as three more. That's what the delay is. And you should know, if this turns out to be your handiwork, that there is no statute of limitations on murder. We just want to make sure that we arrest or have arrested the right person for the murders. And for now, since we have you right where you can't take off, we'll leave you right there."

"I don't know nothing about them. So that should be enough for you to let me go home. I don't know what you're snooping around my yard for anyway. I can't even get someone to come out and fix the toilet when it's stopped up." He told him that he didn't have a home to go to. "Yeah, I do. That one there on Meadow Lane. I've been living there off and on for most of my married life. And that ain't gonna change because I'm in here. You can't kick a man when he's down, no matter how many bodies are in the yard. I'm not saying I had anything to do with them being there. You should ask the neighbor—he don't like me none either. You can't hold me on something like that."

"Oh, but I can hold you on just about anything I want. I'm the judge, and that's what I do best, is judge people. Additionally, you've been barred from the home on Meadow Lane and any other house that the government owns. The restraining order that your wife had on you has made it so you weren't to live there any longer with her or the children.

Then there is the fact that you did several thousand dollars' worth of damage to the house. How do you propose you are going to pay for that?"

"Me? Ain't my fault that they have shitty workmanship." He grinned. "You and I both know that the government has all kinds of stashed away money for stuff like that. You just call up some of them, have it fixed up, and I won't bother anyone again about it. Except for getting my wife home. She ran off with my kids and that queer brother of hers. No telling what sort of things he's doing to them. I'm going to take care of him too, see if I don't. He's a pervert."

"Mr. McGowan, you are a piece of work, aren't you?" He nodded, thinking that it was nice to have someone notice. "I'm not giving you a compliment, but telling you that I cannot believe the stuff that is falling from your mouth. I'd say that your brain needs a rest, but I think that's what it's been doing for most of your life, resting. You'll be going back to jail, right now as a matter of fact. And you should prepare yourself for a lot longer stay this time. I might take me a little vacation and leave you in there indefinitely."

Rogan wasn't sure how it happened, but in no time he was back in the van on his way to the jail again. Nobody was talking to him either. As soon as they took the chains off him so that he could move around, he asked to speak to his attorney and his family. He wanted them there right now. And by God, they'd better have a damned good reason for him being here again. Rogan had quit this place, and to be here again went against the grain.

"There won't be any visitors tonight, Rogan. You'll have to wait until tomorrow. The judge has said that you can't have your family here until then. Though why they'd want to be around you at all is lost on me." He'd not have anyone talk to him this way and told the man to come over there so he could bop him a couple of times. "Do you really expect me to just walk over there and let you hit me? You're dumber than I thought you were. And that is saying a lot."

This was all his fault, that Calhoun guy. He should have told that judge that he didn't need to be put back in his cell. He wasn't going nowhere. Of course, if he was loose, he'd go and hit his family, especially his sister, up for some cash, then take off to find his wife and kids. But nobody had to know that but him.

~~~

Giyanna wasn't sure what to do with herself. Tanner was in court, and she was all alone at his house. Their house, he told her several times, and she could change it any way that she wished. That had been fun for about ten minutes, but now she was bored, and she needed something to occupy her time. Going out onto the lawn in the front of the house, she was startled when the women from the family got out of the big van that had just pulled in.

"We've come to get you." She didn't even ask, but got into the van with the rest of them. Joe laughed as she continued. "I'm guessing that you needed a break. I've never been one that liked to be in my own company either. I have scary thoughts, and then I can't rest at all."

"I was about to leave anyway. I had no idea where I was going to go, but I needed to get out of the house for a little while." Chloe said she could understand that. She'd been bored too. "I'm guessing not much happens in a town this small. Not that it's a bad thing, but I could use some excitement now and again. And please don't take that as a challenge, Chloe."

She liked these women, and the fact that she could joke around with them as if she'd known them her entire life. And the best part was, they didn't treat her like she was the sister of a murdering asshole, but instead like a friend to them.

"Nothing much happens here, not really. Oh, we have our trouble, like most towns do, but since I've taken over, things are a little less hectic and dishonest. You remember this place when you lived here?" She said that she did, and was glad that the police station was a safe place to go. "I am too. Anyway, we're going to the mall to do some shopping for the upcoming auction. We have several gift cards that were given to us to buy something huge with them. Also, we're picking up things that have been donated."

"What's the auction for?" Marty told her it was for school backpacks that were filled. "Wow, what I wouldn't have given for something like that when I was a kid. I barely had lunch money most of the time, much less the things for class. And I know that the families that get them are very happy too."

"It's getting better around here since we have new places that are hiring. The economy is also going up. People are getting out more, and thankfully starting to be friendly neighbors again. Which is what most of the people had missed a great deal." She said that she noticed that as well. "The day after tomorrow, we have two businesses that are coming here to see if the land we have is suited for their manufacturing plant. One of them is distribution, the other is manufacturing. Together they'll hire on about a thousand employees when they're up and running. This is what this town needs, an influx of money coming in and a place to spend it. Thus, the new shops that are going in. Keeping it home is the motto that we've come up with."

She could hear the pride in Laney's voice when she talked about the businesses. Like all the women, she was active in the town's growth, and whatever it needed to make it safe as well. That's what she wanted to do, to be a part of something that was going to make a difference to someone else.

"I've been rethinking my life." Christine asked her what she'd come up with. "Not as much as I would have hoped, really. I know that I hated being an attorney, and its only just occurred to me that I did it for all the wrong reasons. But I'm done with it. I've given my notice of not returning to my boss, and he seemed to be relieved about it. He told me that things were not as good as he had hoped they'd be right now, and that he was going to have to lay off a couple more people. That's so sad to me. Some of those people I worked with had worked for his dad. But with the Internet a lot of people are doing everything they can, like wills and such, online. It hurts attorneys when they do something like that. Not that I blame them, but it's that trickledown theory at work again."

"Yes, I can bet that was the bread and butter for a small office. But back to what you were saying. So, you've taken steps to get your life in order. Tell me what it is that you want to do, not what you think you should do." Honestly, she told her, she really didn't know. "Well, it's not like you don't have plenty of time to try new things. You were told that you're an immortal, weren't you?"

"Yes. But I wasn't sure how that worked since Tanner and

I are working things out between us." Jas nodded too, like she could understand what she was going through. "I like him, a great deal more than I thought I would after such a short time, but I don't love him. He tells me that he loves me all the time, but I'm not sure what I think about that."

"He loves you, you can bank on that." She nodded at Christine, but still wasn't sure. "Tanner is my baby. But even when he was little, he had his head on straight and knew just what he was going to do when he grew up. Be an attorney for the downtrodden. Did you know that he took more pro-bono cases than he did paid ones when he worked for that law firm? It's the way he likes to do things. He said that it balances him. And he gives them the best that he has, just as he does the ones that pay him. Tanner is a good man."

"Not to mention that twice a week, when he has the time, he goes to the shelter and sees what sort of things he can do for people there. He's helped some of the people there set up accounts so that they could have their social security checks sent to them instead of their kids getting them. There was a time when he helped one of the women down on her luck not just get a job, but to work in one that made her safe. She still works for him, doesn't she, Christine?" Christine nodded at Jas's question. "All the boys are working hard to make sure that there are businesses that they can be proud of. When Trent took over as alpha of the pack, he did more for them in the first few months than had been done for years when Casey was in charge. They have a medical team on site now. There are better schools too, with more teachers."

"I'm not saying that I don't admire him. As you said, he's a good man and he works hard. I just don't know what

kind of fit I am to him. He's so very different than I am."
Jas asked her what she meant. "He's so...he is wonderfully
patient with everyone, including Rogan. He took the case so
that my brother didn't have to. And so that I didn't have to
be subjected to his mouth and fists. Rogan would hit me if he
could, of that I have no doubt."

"Honey, he took that case all for you. Your brother
would have done it, but Tanner didn't want him to have to
be subjected to Rogan either. And since Tyrrell hadn't tried
a case like this, Tanner is helping him so that you don't have
to." She asked if she was serious. "Oh, I know that I'm right.
Just ask him. And by the way, you can talk to him without
being in the same room, did he tell you that? If you exchanged
blood or any other personal things."

"You mean a kiss?" They all laughed and said that would
do it too, but Giyanna thought that she had missed something,
something important, but didn't know what it was. And
wasn't entirely sure that she wanted to know. "How do I do
this? I'd like to ask him something about the house."

"Just think of him, and then you talk to him like with
thoughts. After you get really good at it, you can send him
pictures or visual thoughts that you have as well." Joe leaned
toward her to whisper the rest. "You can see through each
other's eyes too. But I'll show you how to do that. It's not
for the faint of heart. You see whatever he's seeing, and
sometimes it can be a little disconcerting."

She decided to try that later. While it sounded fun, she was
sure there were drawbacks to it as well. Thinking of Tanner,
she felt like she could dance when she heard his laughter in
her head.

You've been talking to someone in my family, I'm thinking. I'm glad that they told you about us being able to talk to each other. I completely forget about it when we're together. Giyanna told him where she was. *Oh yeah, I forgot about that. I have a few donations at the house. If, when they bring you back, you could give it to them, I'd appreciate it.*

I will. How did the trial go? Is he getting out like he thinks? Tanner told her what had happened, every detail of it. Even what the judge had said to her brother before he'd been taken away. *So, he's still thinking that he should get out anyway. That sounds just like him, to think that everyone around him is too stupid in thinking he could be anything but an upstanding guy.*

Yes. He certainly isn't making any friends of the court system. There is something else that you can do, honey; you can read the mind of a person that you've had contact with. I tried to see what he was thinking, your brother, but we've never exchanged much more than a handshake, and that wasn't enough to make it work. She asked him if he wanted her to read Rogan's mind. *I do, but be careful. He might not know what it is if you're poking around, but if you go too hard, then you'll hurt him. If you'd like to wait until I get home, I can be there for you should you need me.*

You think that he's going to be thinking of things that are going to upset me. He said that he was sure of it, and that they'd more than likely be about her demise. *Then I'll wait until you get home. I don't know if I'd like to do that alone if he was thinking of killing me.*

Tanner said nothing, and instead of asking him what he was thinking, she moved on to asking him about the house. She wasn't sure about poking into Rogan's head. Giyanna didn't want to know what sort of plans he had for her.

The rooms do enlarge, but I've never been standing in it when it did it. It's sort of freaky, isn't it? She laughed and told him that it was more than that, it was dizzying too. *Well, what room is it? That way I can be impressed at the size of it when I see it.*

The dining room. The table is larger as well. I was thinking that should we have your family over, there'd not be any room for everyone to sit down. Also, the table was too small. Now it's not. She laughed again. *You might also notice that the china cabinets are larger, with more dishes in them. I think we could feed an army should we want to. There are glasses and silverware that goes with it all. I have never seen so many forks in my life.*

Good, because feeding my family is a great deal like an army. She told him that she had needed to talk to him, but didn't realize it. *I needed you a few times today too, but since I forgot to mention this part of our being mates to you, I didn't want to freak you out when I started talking. It's been known to happen a few times.*

It would have too, I think. They were pulling up in front of the mall when she told him she had to go. *And I'm ready to talk to you about this relationship that we aren't having. I don't know what the next level is, but I'm willing to talk to you about it.*

I'd love that as well. And remind my mom for me that I gave her some of the cards that are ready for you. They're from the bank, and spend whatever you want — we can well afford it. She told him that she had money and a credit card. *I know that. But since we're mates, no matter what level we're on at the moment, you are still my mate, and I want you to never have to worry about money again.*

Thank you. She supposed she could have gotten pissy about it, but it would serve no purpose. As she'd been told, he was a nice man and a good person. He gave her the cards simply because he wanted her to have them, not to rub in her face that she was his to rule over.

As they were getting out of the van, all of them laughing about how they'd fit things in there when they were finished shopping, she realized something. She was in love with Tanner. She didn't just like him a great deal, but she actually loved him. Staggering a little, she wasn't surprised that Chloe caught her. When she smiled at her, Giyanna blurted out what she'd just realized.

"I know. It's kind of nice, isn't it?" She nodded at the other woman. "And the sex is fantastic, if you need to know that. You'll think you're going to die one minute, and the next you'll feel the earth move under you. It's that good. Even better when you're all alone in the woods at dusk. Yummy."

Moving into the mall with them, it was a long time before she let herself think of anything but how good the sex was going to be. It was then that she decided to buy herself something sexy, to tempt the beast, she supposed. Yes, she was very happy that they were going to go to the next level. Perhaps all the way to the top, if she could convince him that she was ready.

Chapter 6

Tyrrell waited in the large room for his brother to be brought out to him. Rogan had requested for him to come and see him, for what was anyone's guess. But he came to see if he'd had a change of mind and was going to realize that he wasn't getting out of prison. Ever, if Tyrrell could manage it.

Rogan had gotten huge. And the fact that he was wearing a jumpsuit did nothing to hide the fact that he was sloppy too. When he was chained to the table between them, he picked up the phone when his brother did.

"I got me some trouble." He asked him what sort of trouble. "You mean other than me being in here? Plenty. That judge, he told me that they found a body on my property and that they're thinking that there might be a few more."

"Yes, I've heard that too. Four so far. What did you do, Rogan?" He knew that they were being recorded—the sign was right in front of them. He also pointed to it for Rogan to see. "They're recording every word we say, so you might want to think about that when you open your mouth."

"I don't give a shit about that. It's only a scare tactic when they say they're recording you. I know that they don't have time to man those things. But I need for you to go over to the station house and confess that you did all the killing. That way I can get out of here sooner and get Bridgett's ass back here so she can cook and shit for me. It's not like you have a life, Ty. Just do it." Tyrrell looked at the officer that was in the room with his brother, then back at Rogan. "Just tell them that you did it, so I can get out of here. I don't want to be in here no more, Ty. You do this for me and I'll owe you for the rest of my life. I might even not hit you anymore when you get in here. You'd be better at being in this place than I am anyway. You're used to being alone all the time. I got me a bunch of buddies that are missing me too."

"Are you kidding me? You want me to go and confess to the murders? I'm not going to do that, Rogan. I can't even believe you'd ask me to." He said he wasn't asking but telling him to do it. "No. I'm not going to do it. And I'm not a child that you can order around anymore. There isn't any way that anyone would believe me if I was to do that, which I most certainly am not."

"Ty, I'm not joking around here. They're going to try and pin them on me, and I'll never get out of here. I am not going to spend any more time in this jail than I have to. Just go over there and tell them that you did it all. And maybe you can tell them that you were the one that tore up the house too. They'll be nicer to you because you're a sap." Rogan nodded at him, like he wanted him to agree with him. "What does it matter to you if you're in prison? It's not like you have a woman or anything. And you know as well as I that Giyanna will come to see you. She will for a bit anyway. She and I have some unfinished business too. Also, before you do that, I want you to go to your bank and take all the money out of your accounts. I'm going to need that to find Bridgett and my kids. See if you can hit Giyanna up for hers as well. No credit cards, I hate them things."

"You're insane. Positively insane if you think I'd even consider doing that for you. Again, I'm not, but you cannot be serious in thinking that anyone would." He said that he was as sane as the next person; his temper sounded like it was coming through the phone. "I'm not going to do any of those things. I'm especially not going to confess to something that I haven't done. I can't believe that you'd even ask me to do such a thing. Christ, do you have any idea what they'd do to me if it ever came out that I'd had any part in your scheme? They'd disbar me, and I like being an attorney."

"I'm not asking you, damn it. I said to do it before I come out there and show you who's boss, like I did when you were a kid. There ain't not one reason that you shouldn't be doing this for me. I'm older than you, much smarter, and I have some shit that I have to take care of. You got nothing. And you will have an easier time than I would."

Tyrrell hung up the phone and stood up. Listening to Rogan was making him ill to his belly. Even through the glass, he could hear his brother screaming at him to pick it back up.

As he stood there, the police officer came up behind Rogan and told him to settle down, and that only seemed to make him angrier. Before he was able to step away from the phone where he'd been seated, Rogan was being pulled away by five officers. Tyrrell sat back down, his knees just too weak to hold him up at the moment.

Rogan had really expected him to just confess to murder. To say that he'd killed not only the woman whose body they'd found, but any other body they found as well. And even say that he'd been the one that had messed up the house. Tyrrell wasn't even around there when that happened, and the police would know that.

Tyrrell didn't know how he made it out to his car, but he found himself sitting in the driver's seat like he'd been there for a while. Looking at his watch, he figured that he'd been there for a little over an hour. His mind had never shut down, just kept swirling around with the same thing. *My brother wants me to confess to murders, and he thinks that I should be fine with it because that's what he wants.*

He wasn't sure that he could safely drive home, so he rolled down the window and let the breeze filter though his car. He needed to clear his head and to think about what he needed to do. No matter how he tried to spin what was said to him, he knew that Rogan was insane. No one could be sane and think that someone would do what he told him to do.

Picking up his phone with shaking fingers, he called the only person that he could think of. He wanted to call his sister, but he knew that she'd be as upset as he was. Instead, he called Tanner and told him what was going on.

"You said you told him he was being recorded?" Yes, he told him, and then told him what Rogan had said. "I'll get a copy of the transcript. They do record those. I've used them before. Are you all right? I'm sure that you're not, but do you want me to come and get you? I don't mind, I'm out and about anyway."

"You'd do that? Just drop everything and come here?" Tanner told him he was on his way now. "I don't...I'm so glad that you and my sister are going to be together. You're a good man. I'm sure you get told that all the time, but I wanted to tell you again. I like you, Tanner, and am glad that we're going to be related, even though its only through marriage."

"I don't hear it as often as I'd like to." Tanner laughed. "I'm joking. My mother would blister my butt but good if she thought that I'd left you stranded anyway. She raised us better than that. And I like you too. I'm glad to have someone to talk to about the law and such, and someone that doesn't mind calling me when he knows that he's in trouble with driving. You're a smart man, Tyrrell."

Tyrrell thought it was more than that, but told him he was thankful that he was coming for him. When he looked at the prison that his brother had been transferred to today, not jail but an actual prison, he asked Tanner why that had happened.

"They can't accommodate someone of his size locally. I guess there was some trouble in the shower stall and he put up a big stink about it. And the fact that they don't have suits to fit him. Out there, they're used to men his size and bigger. Also, they have a hospital right there should he get himself hurt." He asked him if he thought he would. "No, but you have to know that he's carrying around the extra weight, and it's going to come and bite him in the ass sooner or later."

"Hopefully sooner. But I learned to live with disappointment at an early age. I keep coming back to him thinking that I should do just what he told me. I'm at a loss as to why he'd think I would." Tanner said nothing, but Tyrrell realized that he really did hope that—that his brother would die and leave them alone. "Giyanna quit her job, did you know that? She's going to be living here, I'm assuming with you."

"Yes, she told me. I don't know about the living with me part; she goes between our house and the hotel once in a while." Tyrrell knew that they weren't sleeping together. He thought that if they were, both of them would be a lot more relaxed. "I'm pulling in now, Ty. And I've talked to the warden about your car. He's a wolf too. He said it would be all right for a couple of days if you need to leave it."

Hanging up when he saw the other man's car, he got out and locked his. This was beyond anything anyone had ever done for him in his hometown. Just getting someone to come help him when he broke his leg two summers ago was like pulling teeth.

Getting in the car with Tanner, he thanked him again. "I'm thinking of doing what Giyanna is doing. Not quitting my job, but I've had enough of corporate America. I think I'd like to go into practice here—that is, if you'll take me on as a partner." Tanner asked him if he was serious. "I am. I miss my sister, and my work has me traveling nearly all the time. I want to have a little fun before I'm too old or too cranky to enjoy it. And please, don't feel obligated to say yes because of my sister, either. If you don't take me on as a partner, I'll just hang out my own sign and be your competition."

"No, I don't do business that way. But I was actually thinking of asking you if you'd come work with me when this was all over." He smiled and Ty smiled back. "This will be great. I have the offices that I work from in town. I only have the one client, and I love working for Noah, but you could take on anyone and I could work with you. It might be the best of both worlds for us both."

"Yes, I know about Noah. I've not met him as yet, but I'm looking forward to it. Joe can't say enough good things about him. And he's done a lot for the town too, I've heard." He put out his hand and they shook on it. "Now I just have to move my household here and find a place to live. Easy, right?"

"Do you want a house or an apartment? The reason that I ask is, there is a really nice pool house on our land. They must have moved the pool closer to the house, because the pool house now is set back from the house. It can be converted into two bedrooms, and we can add on if you'd like. Giyanna would love having you that close, I think." He said that he'd talk to her; she might be sick of him. "I doubt it. She's having a good time with you being so close. And we're closing her house in Ireland in a couple of weeks. She's decided that she wants to keep it in case she wants to go back for a visit or two. I would love that, but that is all up to her."

By the time they were back at Tanner's home, Ty was ready to move in. Giyanna met them both at the door when they got to the house, and he hugged her and was glad to see her kissing Tanner. He understood her need to take things slowly, but they were in love, anyone could see that. He told her what they'd talked about, skipping over him talking to Rogan.

"That would be wonderful. You'd be so close that I could talk to you anytime I wanted. And I have a job. I'm going to work with Jas on the projects that she has going. I'm

105

organized, and she said that's what she needed." Tanner said that his grandma wasn't organized at all. "Yes, she told me. Oh, you have company. We've been talking since she arrived. It's Chris and Myra."

Tyrrell had yet to meet these women, and was looking forward to it. Giyanna invited him to stay for dinner and he told her that he would. Things were moving along now, and as soon as this deal with Rogan was finished, he was going to start living. He'd not been able to do that before, not because of his brother, not directly, but because he was so afraid. He was sick of feeling that way.

"Your home is all ready for you, young man." He asked the brightly colored woman what she meant when she spoke. "You were going to move into the pool house, correct? It's ready for you."

"Yes. But there were some renovations that need to be done first. Tanner said that there was a bathroom but no shower." Myra, she told him her name was, said it had one now. And that the basement was finished too. "There's a basement?"

"There is now. Oh, and it will have the same magic that is here in this house. If you've not been made aware of it, you should talk to your sister. I believe that she's been having some fun with it. There is also a cook for you; his name is Gibson, and he's a witch of some considerable age. You'll love him." He said he wasn't sure he needed a cook. "Everyone does. Come, sit beside me and we'll get to know each other." Tyrrell looked at Tanner for some help.

"You might as well just say thank you and enjoy it. She's already done it, and I've found that it's easier to just let her than to try and talk her out of whatever she's done." They were all laughing when they sat down, and Ruben brought them all drinks and a platter of fruit. "Now, did you see the babies?"

"Oh yes. My goodness, they're beautiful, aren't they?" Chris took a bunch of grapes, and Tyrrell noticed that they didn't disappear from the platter but replenished themselves. "You'll get used to us, Ty. We're a very magical group of beings. But I know how you feel. The first few times my magic became stronger, I was as freaked out as you are now."

"So I've noticed." He sort of wished for a scone; he loved the fruit filled ones. As he was reaching for one of the bunches of grapes, his hand was filled with a scone. He looked back at Chris when she laughed. "I'm going to have to get used to this, I think, like you said. It might take some time, but I love that food just comes to you. It might turn out to be bad when I'm as big as a house, but I'll try and curb it."

"You will, and then wonder how you worked without it. The house that you'll be living in, it too will help you out. The rooms will enlarge should you need them to. Furniture will adjust itself to suit you rather than what was put in there. Also, the house is protected. No one will ever be able to enter that has ill will in their heart. All the homes have that." He nodded and thanked Chris. "No reason to thank me, Tyrrell. We're just happy that you're now, and forever will be, a part of this family."

"I'm sure that I missed something in that statement, but I'm a little on edge right now. Tanner had to come and get me at the prison today. It was...it was enlightening, if you want to know the truth." He looked at Giyanna. "Rogan is nuts."

"I knew that. What sort of man beats his family and thinks it's all right? But what happened? Tell us what he said to you so I can beat his ass." He laughed as he hugged her.

Finally, he had to tell them what had happened at the prison. "He went on about how I was to take the blame for it because he wanted out of prison. Like that would have even worked. And the fact that he was warned that the place was recording him didn't even faze him." Giyanna shivered as he continued. "I'm sorry, honey. I didn't mean to upset you more."

"You didn't. I mean, I'm upset, but that's not the only reason. I heard from Chloe a little while ago, and they've found eight bodies so far. And there was one lying on top of the ground, like he had gotten it to the yard and it was too much for him to go on." Chris said that was just what had happened. "You knew that they were going to find bodies there?"

"Yes, there is yet one more that will be found on that property. And I know what you're all thinking, how did he get this by Bridgett and the kids. It was easy really. She worked, and while she was gone, he would take them out back and bury them. When he was less heavy, it was easier for him. But now that he's put on that extra weight, he can't do it as well. There are more women that he's killed that are buried elsewhere. And once they have his DNA, they'll attach him to other murders too." She looked at him and Tanner. "You'll excuse yourself from the rest of the trial. And tomorrow if you can. There isn't any reason why you need to be a part of this now that he's going down for a great many murders."

"What do I tell the judge about not being able to help

Rogan anymore? Neither one of us have ever tried a murder case, but I don't think that'll be enough, do you?"

"Tell him that you're marrying his sister and you cannot, because of the new charges, be a part of him any longer." Tanner nodded, but Tyrrell wasn't so convinced. He asked her why she knew this. "I'm a very powerful witch. The grand witch of all witches. And in that, I have the power to see into the future. While I can't make any adjustments to it, I can tell you what you should do. I have some very strict rules that I can bend a little but not break. I try to help those that are willing to help themselves, but sometimes people are just too stubborn to listen to me. And it gets them hurt, or sometimes killed."

"Can you tell what's going to happen?"

Chris told him to a point, she could. "Sometimes things happen for a reason. I'm sorry, but I cannot warn people that they are going to perish. And if I do, then the fates will find other ways for those set to die to die." He asked her if he was set to die at Rogan's hand. "You're an immortal, Tyrrell, just as the rest of the Calhouns are. Even if you were injured, you'd not be killed. But there is no reason for you to be harmed either. I promise you this, that once the dust is cleared, you'll be fine."

"My brother wants me to go and see him." Chris said that Giyanna should see him. "I don't want to. I know that I should, just to tell him to fuck off, but I don't want him to say things to me that I'd just as soon not hear."

"You're a very brave and strong young woman. You have within you a lioness that will keep you safe and bring out the part of you that will win against him." Giyanna nodded, but didn't comment. "I must be going. Myra will be around should you need her. It is always a pleasure to see you, Tanner. You do what I suggested, and things will go better for your lovely mate here."

"I will."

After she was gone, Tyrrell couldn't shake the feeling that he was missing something in what she'd said. No matter how many times he went over it, he was sure that he should have paid more attention. Oh well, he thought, he'd sleep on it and then it would come to him. If it didn't, then it might not have been as important as he had thought.

~~~

Tanner was heading up the stairs when he saw Giyanna. She was standing at the top of them staring down at him. He wondered if she was sleep walking, but when he got to the top, she came to him and wrapped her arms around him. He held her tightly and inhaled her scent for himself.

"We're going to have sex, and a great deal of it." His heart skipped several beats before she spoke again. "I'm not going to wait on you hand and foot, so get that out of your head right now. I'm not going to jump when you tell me to either. I have things I want to do as well, so if you're thinking I'm going to be at your beck and call, then you can just forget this."

"I'm not sure what this is about, but I'd never expect you to do any of those things." She nodded and let him go. The warmth of her body being gone made his chill to the bone. "Can you tell me what brought this on?"

"Yes. I've not been myself since I've been here. I'm not a nice person." He wisely kept his mouth shut. "I'm a fiery red

110

head that is bitchy and has a temper. I've been so worried about what my brother was going to do that I became someone that I didn't like. This is me and all that I am."

"All right. Why now? I mean, you have a reason for letting your inner self go, right?" She told him damn right she did. "Well, can I hear it?"

"Chris." He asked her what she had to do with it. "I've been thinking about what she said, that I should go and see Rogan. I'm going to go, but not like I did before, where he had me cowering in the corner like a small child. I'm a fucking adult. And it's high time that he began to realize that. Also, I'm not going to take him abusing me verbally either. I'm done with his shit."

"Yes, you are." She continued telling him what she was. He liked this version of her. She was spicy and hot. The freckles on her face were more visible. Tanner realized that she was waiting on him to reply to something she'd said, but he missed it. "I was thinking about how beautiful you are right now, and not paying as close attention as I should have been. Will you forgive me and repeat it please?"

The low growl had him nearly laughing, but the look on her face told him that he'd be hurt badly if he did. So, asking her what she had said again, he waited while she had an entire conversation with herself about men and how they listen. Then she stopped and stared at him.

"I told you that I love you." He was stunned into silence. "Did you hear me that time? Or do I need to say it again until you get it? If this is how you're going to listen to me, or not listen to me, in the future, we're going to have some issues, you and I."

"I heard you this time. I'm letting it settle into my heart so that I can keep it forever. You love me. You really love me." She smiled at him, and then came toward him again. "Not that I'm complaining, mind you, but what brought this on?"

"I was thinking about you after we head talked today. And I thought of how kind you were and how you made me feel even when I was being childish and letting my heart rule my head. Rogan is never going to change. He's never going to be a brother that anyone can count on. He's a monster, a killer, and he just doesn't care how he gets his way, or who he hurts to get it, so long as things benefit him." Tanner agreed with her. "I guess coming here, I think in a small way, I was hoping that he'd changed. And with that change, I'd have the brother that I never had. But what I got was so much worse that I couldn't even think beyond how disappointed I was. But now I have had a good talk with myself, and I'm ready to take him on. With gloves on too. He's nasty."

Tanner laughed with her this time. "I'm so sorry that you had to have this happen to get that." She nodded and wrapped her arms around him. "So, thinking of your brother made you realize that you loved me?"

Laughing, she shook her head. "No, it was how you rescued me. Gave me time and space to love you like you knew that I would. You never once rushed me into anything, and for that I'm so happy. You just let me come to love you in my own way at my own pace, and that was what I needed." He told her that he loved her. "And I love you, Tanner Calhoun. With all my heart."

Picking her up in his arms, he carried her to the bedroom that she'd been sleeping in. Laying her on the big bed, he looked down at her. She was perfection, he thought, and all his. He wanted this to be perfect, as perfect as she was for him.

"When this thing with your brother is over, I would like to have you marry me." She nodded and said so long as it was a small ceremony. "You have met my mom and grandma, right? I think their version of small is going to be vastly different than yours. But I'll try. Just so long as you're my wife at the end, I don't care how we do it."

Her giggle made him feel like a king. And when he pulled his shirt off and dropped it to the floor, she sat up on the bed. As her hands traced over his chest and muscles, Tanner could only think about what he wanted to do to her. How he wanted to make love to her. And when she kissed him, wrapping her arms and body around his, he crawled onto the bed with her wrapped round him.

Kissing her, he could taste the slight taste of lemon. He knew that she loved the lemon scones that Ruben made. He could almost taste the sunshine too from when she'd been outside earlier. Everything about her was erotic and sexy, also appealing and charming.

"I need you." He laughed, thinking that she didn't know the meaning of need. "I've thought of nothing but having you here with me all day. The way that you will fill me up and make love to me."

"I need to tell you something." She asked him if it was important. "Yes—well, sort of. Christ, I want you. I can't father children." That had her pause and she looked up at him. "I was in a car accident when I was a teenager, and I hit my head and took a hard blow to my testicles. By the time I was conscious again, the damage had been done. I can't father children. The reason that I bring that up now is that you're in heat, and it made me remember."

"Do you love me?" Tanner told her that he loved her with everything he was. "Then we'll work something out. It's sad that you won't be able to have a child of your own, but we can bring them into our hearts and be better parents then they might have had. So long as we can be together, we can adopt as many children as we want."

"I love you, so very much, Giyanna."

He ripped off her clothing, not even caring that it might have been expensive. Or one of a kind. The need to have her was overruling his head, and when he took her breast into his mouth, Tanner knew that she was his.

Tanner moved down her body, tasting wherever he could touch. His fingers massaged her tight muscles, his mouth soothed any hurt that he might have caused her. Running his tongue into her navel, tasting more of her there, he moaned when she moved her leg to rub against his cock.

"You keep that up and this is going to be very one sided." She told him she didn't care so long as he loved her. "I do at that, forever. But you need to slow down so I can show you how much I love you and your luscious body."

Her scent perfumed the air around them. He could smell her need, that she was wet and ready for him. But he needed to taste her cream, have it fill his mouth and belly so that he'd know everything about her.

Touching his finger to her clit, he grinned when she cried out. When he suckled it into his mouth and bit down gently, she screamed out his name. No longer able to wait, he buried his mouth over her and slid his fingers deep inside her, and was rewarded with all of her cream from coming again and again.

He ate her for as long as she would let him. Everything about her was delicious. When she begged him to stop, he moved up her body again, still taking small bites, still marking her as his. And when his cock was there, where he wanted to fill her, she looked up at him and told him once again that she loved him. Tanner slid hard inside of her and felt like he'd come home.

Giyanna screamed with her release. She held him to her, her mouth so close to his throat that all he could think about was her biting him, her taking a part of him into herself as he'd done to her. And when he felt his release riding him hard, he cupped the back of her head and told her to bite him.

"Do it, Giyanna. Bite me hard and drink from me."

She licked the path from his throat to his pulse. He was going to come the moment that she sank her teeth into him. And when she did, he not only came with her, but saw stars and unicorns, as well as all sorts of other creatures as he released a second time.

Dropping atop her, he knew that he should roll over but wasn't sure that he had the strength. Finally, when she squirmed a little, he rolled, taking her with him. Closing his eyes, Tanner thought of her large with a child, and let himself fall asleep with that image in his head.

Chapter 7

The dream came to Tanner slowly. The children running around the house. The swing set in the back yard. His family, ever present in his life, sitting under the big tree that he'd thought was dead. As they laughed and talked, he found himself looking outside himself, his body moving above those around him. Tanner had heard of out of body experiences, but had never had one before. Then he saw her.

The little girl was no more than seven or eight. She sat on his dad's lap talking to him about her day, the same red hair of her mother gleaming in the afternoon sun, her happiness a bright spot to his day. Dad looked around when he was close enough, and told her that they'd be fishing in the morning. That Grandda and Great Grandda had a spot picked out just for them.

Myra was there, dressed in red, white, and blue, her hair the same colors, and she had a sparkler on the top of her head. Tanner surmised that it was the Fourth of July, and that was

117

the reason for the celebrations. But he'd yet to see the one person that he needed more than he'd ever known he could. Giyanna had yet to make an appearance. And needing her to be there with this going on, he was afraid for her.

Tyrrell was there, with a child on his lap as well, a beautiful woman sitting next to him holding his hand. He was happy for the man. So glad that he was able to find himself some happiness after all the time he'd been alone.

His brothers were there too, not looking a day older than they did today. He had no idea how much time had lapsed with this dream, but he had a feeling that it had been years. All of them would live forever, he knew, but he'd thought that they'd age some. He moved to the house to find his wife.

There were children going in and out of the house. The pool was being used by them, as were the other toys that lined the yard. Moving into his home, he found food on the counters, and on the extra table that was there to use. Ruben was directing faeries into what to take out next. All he could think about was how happy they all seemed as he moved through the living room.

He found her there, nursing a small baby. The expression on her face was that of tranquility, happiness, and love. The way she looked down at the child, he knew her to be his mother, but wasn't sure how that was to work. When she glanced up, seemingly smiling at him, he turned to look and found himself, his true self, walking in the door, coming to sit by their lovely bride. Because that was what she'd be to him, a bride, no matter how long a time they'd been wed.

"I've come for a kiss." They kissed, the two of them, and Tanner could almost feel it on his own mouth. He loved this woman with all that he was, and was so glad that they were so happy in whatever future this was. "How's my little guy today? Having himself a nice lunch while the rest of us are waiting?"

"Hungry like his father. Did you make sure that Rachel doesn't get too much sun? She'll burn easily, you know." He nodded at Giyanna and took the little boy. Tanner, as the spirit—he had no other name for himself—looked down into the face that was his. This child was his, and he still had no idea how that had come to be.

It was then that he felt himself pulling away, coming back to the real world and all its problems. He didn't want to wake just yet. He wanted to go and see his son and daughter. He needed to listen to his wife and hear her sweet voice telling him about their son. Sitting up in the bed, he wanted to cry.

"Are you all right?" He pulled Giyanna to him and held her tightly. "Tanner, are you all right? You were talking strangely in your sleep. I've never slept with you before, but I don't think that's the norm for you, is it?"

"No, no. I'm all right. Just an odd dream."

As he lay there, the dream or whatever it was began to fade from his memory. The children's faces were the first to go. Closing his eyes, trying his best to capture the dream again, he felt the small intrusion of someone needing to talk to him. Now wasn't the time, he wanted to tell them.

Go away. I'm exhausted. The laughter brought a smile to his face, and he asked Myra want she wanted. *You should know that it's really late, and whatever you want, you should invest in a watch.*

Watches are for people who have schedules to keep. I go with the flow, young man. He said that he'd figured that out about her. *I forgot to tell you something about your home.*

And this couldn't have waited until morning? She laughed again, and told him it wouldn't. *All right. If you're going to tell me that the house is going back to the way it was, I'm going to be very disappointed. Giyanna is having so much fun playing around with it, and I enjoy hearing her laughter when she does.*

Never that. It's perfect for you and your family. No, you asked me to fix your home, do you remember? You said for me to fix everything for you? He said that he did, but frowned when she laughed again. *Well, you were in the house too. I fixed you as well.*

Thank you. And what was broken on me that you needed to tell me now that you fixed me? As far as I can remember, I've not been hurt lately, and I've never been sick. She told him he could father children. *No. I can't. I was just having a lovely dream about that, but I can't have them. I did wonder how it happened, but it was that, only a dream.*

Yes, you can. I fixed you. And the child that you created tonight, it will be magical beyond your wildest dreams. Tanner opened his eyes, almost afraid to believe what she was saying to him. *Believe me, my dear boy. I couldn't let you go through life without children of your own. You're much to special to Chris and me to let that happen.*

"We created a child tonight?" Tanner realized that he'd spoken out loud when Giyanna sat up in the bed too. Tanner looked over at her. "We're going to have a baby. You and I, we made a baby tonight."

She looked at him as if she thought he was having a bad dream or something. After telling her what had happened, how he had talked to Myra, she looked down at her belly, then back at him. They were both laughing and crying as what was going to happen to them finally hit them both.

It took them both a while to calm down again. When Giyanna was asleep, he laid there thinking of the dream and wondering why he'd not told her about it. It wasn't a secret, he knew, but there was a part of him that wanted to keep this for himself. Perhaps only for a little while, but he wanted to savor the feeling of being a father like he had been in the dream.

Tanner finally got up when he realized that he wasn't going to sleep anymore tonight. Going down to his office, he thought about the trial and what it might mean for his family. Nothing really. It would affect Giyanna and Tyrrell more than him, but in that, he'd be hurting for them. Pulling up the names of the dead women that he'd been given by Chloe— only three had been identified so far—he wondered what sort of lives these women had, and how their families would deal with this once they were notified.

Noah had given him some things that he wanted done, and he was working on them when he realized that he was no longer alone. Looking up, he wasn't really surprised to find the man himself sitting in the chair across from him. Tanner grinned at him.

"Do you ever rest?" He told the old vampire that he was a slave driver of a boss and that he couldn't. "Yes, and I'm sure you believe that. I have a favor or two to ask of you. It involves one of the buildings on Main Street. I believe that it's up for sale. It was at one time called the Bakers Building."

"Yes, well, it's for sale, but they're hoping to sell the other building that is there as well. It's nice—not as nice as the Baker

121

Building, but it does have potential." He asked him why they were selling them together. "It's the last two buildings on that street, and they couldn't get anyone else to buy them. If you're planning to make any improvements on them and perhaps hire one or two people to work there, I can get them for you for nothing, or close to it."

"You don't say. And these free buildings, what will they cost for me to completely renovate into a working building? So long as I can have the lower levels for myself." He pulled up the specs on the buildings and told him what they had and the last work that had been done on them. "I was there tonight, and the one has some homeless people in it. Do you know what will happen to them when renovations start?"

"They'll be either taken or directed to the shelter. From there, I don't know." Noah asked him if he could find out. "I can. Are you more interested in the homeless people or the building?"

"Both. But mostly the homeless. There is a young woman there with an older man. I believe him to be her father or grandfather. I took a little taste of him tonight and found that he isn't long for this world. The young woman with him is aware. When he started to cough while I was there, she asked him to go to the doctor. I had a feeling that it was a constant question that goes unanswered."

"So you want to buy the buildings and do what with them? And how much did it cost you to heal the man?" Noah glared at him then stood up. He looked to the doorway, unsure of what made him, move when Giyanna came into the room with them. "Noah, I'd like for you to meet my wife to be. Giyanna, this is the man I was telling you about, Noah

Stark. I work for him."

"It is a pleasure to meet you, my dear. You have a lovely home here, and the best mate that you could ever want." She told him that she knew that already. "So you would. I've come on an important matter, and young Tanner here has agreed to help me."

Noah sat down when Giyanna did, and told Tanner that he wanted to hire the homeless man to run a little shop for him. A place that would cater to men such as himself.

"You mean vampires?" He smiled at Giyanna and showed her his fangs. "Are you trying to scare me or impress me? I'm in too good of a mood for either of them. What do you think the building could be used for?"

Noah looked at him, then back at Giyanna. "You are a pistol, aren't you?" She said that she was working on it. "Good for you. I cannot wait for you to come into your own. All right. What I meant was, men who are older and aren't used to wearing today's fashion. It would be a clothing store, dealing in mid eighteen hundred apparel. Suits and hats. Some specialty canes as well."

"So there would be others like you coming into town." Tanner just leaned back and let her deal with Noah. It was funny to him to see the man squirm under her questions. "Will they be coming for a meal as well as their new duds, or just the food? I'm not going to be very happy if they come here just for a quick meal."

"No one will ever feed from anyone here unless it's compensated." Giyanna asked him how that worked. "When I feed from someone around here, I leave them money or sometimes something that they might need. Sometimes it's a little, only about a hundred or so dollars, but if I forget myself and take even a drop too much, they are paid handsomely for their troubles. I will expect no less from the people who come here. Of this, I can promise you."

"And if they take more than they should and don't pay them? Or perhaps go on a killing spree that will devastate this town?"

Noah put out his hand to her and told her that he would end them. "I promise you that is the way it will be. I'm a very old and very powerful vampire, and if anyone loses control, I don't care if they are someone that I've known for a great number of years, I will tear them from limb to limb and drain them." He put his hand closer to her. "And if I do not, for any reason, I will tell you how you can kill me and allow you to do so."

"I believe you." They shook on it and she looked at Tanner. "I'm going to see Rogan today. I'm going to tell him some things that he's neither going to like nor want to hear. But I'm tired of being afraid of my own shadow where he is concerned."

"Good. Would you like for me to go with you?" She told him no, but to be close when she got home. "I'll be around wherever you need me."

When she left them to get dressed, Noah laughed. "She's wonderful. And I so love the red hair. She is as feisty as she is beautiful, young Tanner, and you are a lucky man." Tanner told him that he was aware of that, but thanked him anyway. "I was thinking of going on a trip, but I think that I might hang around for a bit longer. Just to see this little girl go toe to toe with her own monsters. And I have a feeling that her brother won't know what hit him when she's finished with him. Yes, I think this might just be more fun than not."

~~~

Giyanna was waiting for them to get done inspecting her purse when she thought of all that she wanted to say to Rogan. First and foremost, she was going to make sure that he understood that he was never leaving this place unless it was in a body bag. Giyanna was also going to tell him how much she hated him. It had occurred to her while she was getting dressed to come here that she did hate him. And more than likely always had.

She was led to a row of chairs sitting by a petitioned off area. She'd been at a prison before and knew how this worked. Giyanna had already asked them to please make sure they recorded this conversation, and she asked for a copy of the one that had transpired when Tyrrell had been here.

"Yes, ma'am, we can get that for you. And if you will tell Tanner I said congratulations on finding you, I'd appreciate it." She asked him how he knew. "You have his scent. I'm a shifter too. Puma. And Tanner and I have been friends since we were kids. He's a good man."

"He's the best there is." The man nodded and told her that he'd get them for her before she left today. Taking a deep breath when she saw Rogan come through the door, she let it out slowly. This was going to free her, she knew it.

He didn't pick up the phone that would give them access to speak. She didn't either. It was a contest between them, and she was determined to win this round. When he finally reached for it, nearly jerking it off the wall, she saw Rogan get talked to by the guard on the other side of the glass.

"You come here to bail me out? If not, then I've nothing to say to you." She told him she had plenty to say to him. "Like I care what you have to say to me. And you'd better watch yourself. When Ty does what I tell him to do, then you'll be hurting, and bad."

"You mean when you told him to confess? That's never going to happen." He just laughed. "You think I'm joking with you, Rogan? He is currently closing down his house and moving his things closer to me. I'm getting married soon."

"You think he's not going to do what I told him, then you're stupider than I thought you was. And that was pretty stupid. Also, you ain't getting married either. When I get out of here, you're going to do your duty by me and clean my house. Then when I get my kids back, you'll make sure that they're taken care of." She asked him what sort of duty she had to do for him. "I just told you, you're going to take care of my kids."

"What about Bridgett?" He said she wasn't long for this world. "Rogan, you do know that you're being recorded, don't you? I mean the sign is right there where you can read it."

"I know what that says. I also know that they can barely keep us in line around here. They ain't got nobody to be recording this shit. And besides, after I get out of here, then it'll be nothing. You'll see. And when I do get out, you're going to tow the line too, sister." She asked him what that meant. "Just you wait and see. I'm not going to have you acting like you know more than me. You don't."

"I came here to tell you two things, Rogan." He told her that he didn't care what she had to say. "Regardless, I'm going to say them anyway. You're never getting out of here. They've enough on you right now to convict you of several homicides, as well as the attempted murder of Bridgett and her brother Phillip."

"That queer? He's better off dead anyway. And they got nothing on me. They'll have even less when Ty does what I told him." She didn't even bother telling him again that he wasn't going to do it. "The world will be thinking I did them all a favor when I get him in a head lock and break his faggot neck."

"I never realized until today how much I hate you. That's the second thing I planned to tell you. I really hate you." He laughed. "Yes, you think it's funny, but for a long time after I saw you murder Margaret Penny, I thought you were sick in the head. But that's not it. You just don't give a shit about anybody but yourself. You remember her, don't you? You took her from her car and then raped her. Then when I saw what you were doing, you snapped her neck like it was nothing to you. She had children that missed her. A man that has been grieving for his poor wife for ten years. Don't you care?"

"Boo hoo. No, Giyanna, I don't care. Not at all. If she hadn't of wanted me to take her, she should have locked her doors against me. She was begging for it anyway. Besides, you think she was the first? Or even the last? I only killed her like that to show you what a powerful man I am. And that I could and probably will do the same to you when I'm out of here." Rogan had just threatened her. And confessed. "If you ain't got nothing more to tell me, then get out of here. And you tell Ty what I said. He'd better be making up his will, cause I'm gonna kill him too. As soon as I'm out of here."

"How do you think you're going to manage that? If he does what you say he's going to do for you, he'll be here instead of you." He told her that he had connections. "I'm sure you don't, but you go on living in that fantasy world of yours. I'm finished with you."

"You thinking that is going to break my heart, Giyanna? I don't give a fuck about you or Ty. You were just somebody for me to knock around when I didn't have anyone out there that I could murder. Yeah, I said it. I like to murder. There is so much fun in it for me, that I find I just come all over the place." Her belly lurched up and she knew she was going to be sick. "When I get out of here, and I will, you'll get a firsthand look at what I do."

Hanging up the phone, she could still hear his laughter. Standing up cost her more than she thought it would, and the woman guard that had brought her in grabbed her by the arm and took her to the ladies' room. There Giyanna threw up several times, her belly not able to handle what a vile person her brother really was.

"You all right, honey?" She said that she didn't think she would ever be again. "I don't blame you none. And so you know, we didn't stop him from getting angry at you so that he'd talk. I knew he was a sick bastard, but I didn't know just how bad."

"I didn't either."

After flushing the commode, she came out of the stall and washed up. After rinsing her mouth out several times, she looked at the other woman. "He killed those people, and had not a care in the world who they might have left behind or who would be looking for them."

When she felt like she could drive home, she took the copies of the transcripts and thought about Rogan. He would have killed her, given the chance, and Tyrrell too. The man had no remorse about what he had done either.

Instead of going directly home, she went to Jas and James's house. They were the sweetest couple she knew. As soon as she pulled into the driveway, however, she knew they had plans. And there wasn't any way she was going to allow them to change them because she showed up.

"Nonsense. You come right on in the house and we'll have us a nice cup of tea. James was just going to run into the hardware store, and he can well do that on his own." James kissed his wife then pecked Giyanna a small kiss on the cheek when he left. "Now, Tanner told me that you were going to see your brother. Did that go as badly as it looks?"

"Worse." Giyanna started sobbing about what he'd said to her and the things that he was going to do to her and Tyrrell when he was released. "And he didn't even care that he was being recorded. He said that they'd not have the time to watch the tapes. But they did, and he is going away for a long time."

"Good." She laughed and nodded at the older woman. "You know as well as I that if he was to be freed, the old turd would be out causing mayhem all over the place. Not to mention that poor wife of his and the children. I heard that she's filed for divorce."

"Yes. Tanner is taking care of it for her. He doesn't foresee any issues with it, especially after he's convicted of the crimes he's committed. And for everything that they find on him, two more things pop up." Jas said that she'd heard that as well. "Rogan told Tyrrell that he was to confess to the crimes so that Rogan could get out of prison. Then he said that he was going to kill us both. Just like that. It was no big deal for him to just say, 'I'm going to kill you both when I get out.'"

"The man needs to be taken care of." Giyanna laughed, she was so shocked. "Yes, that's what I said. And he needs to be buried in a deep hole where no one will ever find him. Nasty man, that brother of yours. I can't believe that something so sweet as you is related to him. Where are your parents in all this?"

"You know, I don't know." She thought about the last time she'd heard from them. "I can't remember the last time I talked to them. It's been years. We were never a very close family. Our parents would have just as soon not had us, I think. They left us alone in Rogan's care when we were smaller. And as you can well imagine, that went over badly for us. Do you suppose he might have killed them too?"

"Oh my goodness. That's a thought. I know that.... We should have someone find them. Joe can do that better than anyone." She nodded, as if it was something she was going to do. "To change the subject, are you still coming to work with me? I'm so excited to have a real place to call our own that I can hardly stand it. James is going to let us have one of the buildings downtown so that we can have an office. We'll need storage areas too, for all the donations. I think that this year's toy event will be the best yet. What with all the adults working more and new houses being built. Did you see the little homes that are going up along Route Forty? They're the cutest little things."

"I saw that they've started on the wing for the library too.

It's going to really add on some more space for them." Jas told her that they were going to have a place they could hold meetings, as well as an area for play time for the children's activities. "I volunteered to go to the school with the others too. I'm going to teach them how to write a check and balance a checkbook."

They talked for a bit more and Giyanna felt better. She'd had a blow to her heart, and Jas had mended it for her in one afternoon. By the time she left, she was feeling better about herself. Rogan, she knew, was never going to hurt anyone again. And that was a very good thing.

Going home now, she read the note from Tanner telling her that he was doing some things for Noah, and that if she wanted to give him a call, they could meet for lunch. Reaching out to him, they made plans to have lunch before he finished up for the day.

Chapter 8

Tanner made a bid on the buildings downtown twenty minutes before the closing. He didn't have any idea if there were other bids, but was told to wait for a few minutes and that they'd get back to him. He sat on one of the benches just outside the offices and pulled out his cell. Tanner was happy now that he'd made sure that he could get to his email through his phone.

Half an hour later, he was called into the office. Chloe was there, as well as the mayor, and he had his envelope in his hand. Not sure what was going on, Chloe winked at him and he felt better. Then the mayor spoke.

"You were the only bid on the building. And I'm sure that you're aware that it was to be both the buildings, the one to the right of it as well." Tanner said that it was. "I'm glad that he's getting them, Tanner, but I don't suppose you can tell me what Mr. Noah is going to do with them. It would help me to know that there is some kind of development going in. We're doing so much now to the area, and I'm very pleased with it."

"I can tell you that he plans to hire as many as ten people to start, and all the construction will be local." Smiling, the mayor nodded. "Also, once the second building is started on, I believe that too will hire as many as a dozen people. He has plans for both of them."

"Good, that's what I like to hear. Growth is going on, and we'll just keep adding to it every week and we'll be a viable town again. I heard that your brother is expanding his pack too." He nodded, and told him that the pack had purchased seven hundred more acres to use and were building homes. "I don't know what we'd do without the Calhouns around. You all are good people, and good to the town."

"Thank you very much. I'll tell my grandparents and parents what you said. They're very proud of the way things are going too." He still wasn't sure what this was about until he was handed the envelope. "It's my bid. And it's been marked out."

"Yes, well, I had a little talk with Chloe here, and we decided that since no one else bid on the building that you could take it off the city's hands for a buck. Which you can pay as you leave. With him hiring twenty or so people, that'll make it easier on a lot of the local shelters, as well as food banks." Tanner thanked them both. "No worries on that. I'm just glad to have it off our books. I know that with the income of taxes and things we're doing better, but you can never have enough so far as I'm concerned."

When the mayor left, Chloe asked him if he had a minute. He followed her to her office and sat down when she asked him to. This was going to be bad, he just knew it.

"Your wife went to see Rogan today." He said that he was aware that she had. "He confessed to everything. Including trying to kill his wife, as well as her and Tyrrell. And if one more body turns up—and from what I'm to understand, it will—then he'll get life without the chance for parole."

"I can't say that I'm not happy about that. I've not heard from Giyanna yet. Did she have a hard time of it?" Chloe told him how she'd ended up at his grandma's. "They have a special bond. I noticed that right away. I didn't hear from her, so I assumed that she was either still there or it went all right. What else is going on?"

Chloe sat down and pulled a photo out of a file. He noticed right away that the file was thin, and was worried either that it was just the beginning of an investigation or the end of one on a missing child. She handed him the picture of a couple.

"This is their parents. I think that Giyanna looks a great deal like her mother, and Rogan looks like his father. Tyrrell is a cross between the two of them." He asked her to stop beating around the bush. "They're dead. Both of them. Their bodies were found, along with three others, on the back end of pack property."

"Rogan." Even though it wasn't a question, she said that he'd done it. "What happened, do you know?"

"They're running an autopsy on them both. The women, they're in the same shape as the ones on the property where they all lived. This man is a sick pervert, in case you didn't know that. The things that were done to these women is sadistic." He asked about the parents, her thoughts. "They were both robbed. The father still had his wallet, about the only way we were able to identify him. His head had been

135

bashed in by a mallet. The mother had her neck broken. Her purse was with her body, but it was devoid of anything other than a set of car keys. We're still looking for more of its contents. Joe has a system that beats anything I could use."

"Who knows about this?" He said he did. "You okay with me telling Giyanna? I mean, I can do that for you. I think she has an idea that they're gone anyway."

"I figured as much too. She had to know something was up when she asked me if I could find them." He'd not known that, but she had been out as much as he'd been lately. "She said she thought that the last time she spoke to either of them was about four or five years ago. I'm only married into this family, and I can't go ten minutes without talking to one of you. But I can understand it too. The coroner says it's been about five years give or take, so that fits."

"What's going to happen now? I mean with Rogan. You said that he confessed to the murders." She said yes, as well as the plans of murdering his sister and brother. "Yes, that scares me like you cannot believe."

"He has a court date in two days. I'm not sure who will be working on his side of the table. I'm to understand you have taken yourself off the list?" He told her what he'd told the judge. The family ties were just too great. "I don't blame you a bit for this. Rogan seems to think that someone is going to bail him out, or that Tyrrell is going to confess. That part confuses me, but then this entire case does. He's been living here all his life, getting away with murder, and we had no idea. Or, and this is more than likely it, people were afraid of him and the police force here was shit."

"I think a combination of both, if you ask me. He does

make a good argument for leaving him the fuck alone." Chloe laughed when he did. "I'll talk to Giyanna when she gets home tonight. And then Tyrrell is coming over for dinner too. I'll tell them both what we've found out."

"They'll be able to bury them, if they want in, about a month. We'll keep them in the morgue for that long in the event that there are questions about their murders when this thing goes to trial." He nodded and stood up. "You going by your buildings?"

"Yes. Noah said that there is a man, and he believes his daughter, living in it. He wants me to get them housing, money, and then he's offering the man a job. He has spoken to them, I guess." She walked out with him into the wonderful sunshine. He needed it after that conversation. "Do you have the transcripts or does Giyanna still have them?"

"I have a faxed copy of them. I guess she gave them my number when she left. My buddy up there said she was sick afterwards. He suggested that she not return." He said that was her plan. "If you get a chance, bring her copies to me, please. It would be nice to have a good copy to give to the judge when it goes to court."

He walked to the building from her office and saw that it did have a great deal of potential. The front curved glass was still intact, and he thought that the display shelves behind the counter were perfect for what Noah had in mind. He went up the stairs, calling for not just the man but the woman as well. They met him at the top of the staircase with a ball bat.

"Noah sent me." The man nodded but didn't put it down. "I'm to get you housing and money. He said that he talked to you about working for him."

137

"He did something to me, didn't he? I haven't felt this good in ten years or more." Tanner told him what Noah had told him. "Yes, I was dying. And I lost all I had when this doctor told me that he had this cure for me. Wasn't nothing but sugar pills, I found out too late. Mortgaged my home and just about everything else I had."

"I'm sorry about that. Do you think you could put the bat down?" He flushed red, and Tanner would bet that he'd forgotten he had it. "My name is Tanner Calhoun. And he told me your first names but nothing more."

"I'm Rich Farley, and this is my granddaughter, Jenny. Jenny and I have been staying up here since just after Christmas. We were doing all right but for the fact that it's been cold. But we managed." He congratulated him on not getting sicker. "Yes, well, it wasn't like we had much in the way of choices. What is it that he wants us to do?"

"He wants me to find you both housing. There are several that you can take; Noah owns a few properties here and about anyway. There is furniture in one of them, that's the one he suggests that you take, and if it doesn't suit you, then he'll fill the house that you do want." Rich asked why this man would do that for strangers. "He's a very nice man, but he doesn't want that to get around. And as you know, he's a vampire. A very old and powerful one. Sometimes, as one might when they've seen it all, he gets bored and needs to stretch his mind a little."

"And if he gets bored with this shop that I'm supposed to run, then what do I do? I need to take care of Jenny here."

Tanner nodded and looked at the young woman. She looked familiar, but he wasn't sure from where.

"When he makes a commitment to something, he sticks to it until the end. Not the end of it, but the end of it being useful to him. This place that you're going to run, it's primarily for other men like him. Older gentlemen that like a certain kind of dress. He'll supply all that you need to make it work." Rich asked him if he'd be doing the tailoring. "I'm not sure. Do you know how to do that?"

"I do. I've been a tailor for a great many years, up until my son and his wife were killed. I've been caring for my granddaughter since. I don't think she needs this old man anymore, but she keeps me going." They hugged, and he could see the love and respect between them. "I can't go out of here without her."

"No, and you won't have to. There's a house, as I said, and the one that he wants you to look at first, it's three bedrooms and three baths. He thinks you might need the extra room." Rich and Jenny followed him out of the building. "Noah owns this building now, and he'll begin work on it today if possible. That's why I've been told to come by and see that you're settled, and that you have everything that you need."

They chose the house that Noah had thought they would. It was a very nice house, and had a big yard. As he was leaving, Jenny followed him out to the sidewalk. He knew that he'd seen her someplace before, but just couldn't place it.

"I'm looking for a job as well. If you hear of any, I'd like to apply for it. I can do most anything." He asked her how she felt about plants. "Plants? They're all right. You mean work in the greenhouse? I'd love that."

When he left them, Tanner felt good. He'd won the bid on the buildings, and the couple there was now housed and working. The only thing left for him to do was to talk to Tyrrell and Giyanna. And that would be the hardest thing he thought he'd ever done.

~~~

Tyrrell had already figured that his parents were both gone. But what he'd not thought of was how they had died. While Tanner didn't give them much in the way of details, Tyrrell knew that it had been Rogan, and he'd not been quick about it. He looked over at his sister as she sat next to Tanner. He asked him if he had any questions.

"Did Rogan do it?" He nodded, and he felt like he'd been sucker punched. Lying back on the couch, he let that settle over him. "If I ask you how he did it, will you tell me?"

"Yes, if you wish, but I'm sure you don't want to know." He nodded and told him that he did. "All right. According to Chloe, who was there when they were found, your father's face would have been unrecognizable. They believe that he was killed with the mallet that they found, along with the shovel that had dug their graves. Your mother's suffering was shorter—her neck was broken. But there is an autopsy being performed now, and it'll show more than what she has now on them."

"What else did you find there?" He looked at Giyanna when she spoke. "Were there others with them? Other women?"

"Yes." When she nodded that she understood, Tyrrell was glad that Tanner didn't tell them anything else. "There was a wallet found with your father. Your mom only had her purse, and it was empty except for a set of car keys."

"She wouldn't have had anything in it." Tanner asked

140

him if he knew why. "I don't know. She'd take Dad's wallet when he was driving and put it in the purse. The only thing she ever carried in there that I can remember is a package of tissues and car keys. We never understood why she even bothered."

"That'll help Chloe in not searching for any more contents for it. There was a car too, we suppose. Do either of you know where it might be?" Giyanna looked at him, then at Tanner. "We're searching for it now, but not having much luck. The last license plates were renewed about ten or so years ago."

Giyanna said she might know. "It should be in the parking garage that the housing development used. It's the one that Bridgett used too, to keep a bunch of cars off the yard. Rogan, as far as I know, never had his driver's license. Not to say that he didn't drive, but the last time I knew that's where the car was." Tanner said he'd have someone look at it. She told him the make and the model. "That's going to really be helpful. Anything else that you can think of? The state has a good solid case against him; he'll be in prison for a very long time, if not forever. But anything that you can think of, that'll go a long way in helping them have all the information at once."

Tyrrell didn't want to think about anything anymore. It was too much, all this information that was going around and around in his head. Rogan had been a murderer, and he could have killed them too. And he'd killed his mom and dad. That alone made him want to go to Rogan and ask him why he'd do such a thing.

Tanner and Giyanna talked softly on the couch, so Tyrrell closed his eyes and let the day just wash over him. It was the way he'd been dealing with stress since he'd had a slight heart attack when he'd been only twenty-two years old. Not only was it a wakeup call for him, but it also made him realize how much he hated Rogan. All he could get his mind to center on, however, was what had happened one day when he'd been about ten.

"You're going to go and help me with something." Tyrrell had told him no, he had homework to do. "It's not like it's going to do you a shit load of good, Ty. You're not going to need it soon enough. Besides, look at what I've gotten, and I'm only fifteen. You won't need it. Trust me."

He didn't have any idea what his brother was talking about, and argued again that he was going to do it and not go with him. In the end, Rogan hit Tyrrell in the head hard enough to knock him off his seat. He also had to get a dozen stitches in his head after his parents had returned. But he'd never forget his brother when he came home before Mom and Dad had.

Rogan was covered in blood. His face looked like it had rained down on him—his hair was matted into knots too. The white shirt that he had on when he'd left looked pink now, with big splotches of a darker pink. Even his pants were nasty, and Tyrrell was afraid.

"What are you looking at?" He said nothing to Rogan. "You damned right you don't. And if you breathe a word about this, to anybody, I'll do that same to you that I did to her. You hear me?"

"Yes."

After his brother left him in the kitchen, he sat there staring at nothing for a long time. When Rogan came back through and went out the door, cleaned up this time, Tyrrell heard the car start in the yard and his brother left.

Tyrrell had waited until he counted to fifty before getting up from his chair. He'd gone to his brother's room and looked around. He wasn't sure how much time he had, but he wanted to find something that he could show someone. Anything at all. Stepping into the closet, thinking he was not going to find anything, he found one of the floorboards moved. Pulling it up, he found more than he was looking for.

"Tanner, I just thought of something that might help." He nodded. "Tell Chloe that I give her permission to go through our old house. I had to pay the back taxes a few years ago. I didn't know whether or not it should have been sold or not, so I've been keeping up on them now. As far as I know, there hasn't been anyone living in the house in years. Rogan was in jail for something else when I was contacted about it."

"What is it, Tyrrell? You said it would help the case—what is she going to find there?"

Tyrrell felt his belly churn up while he remembered what he'd found that day. And until that moment, he'd not thought of it at all.

"Souvenirs." Giyanna asked him what he'd said. Tyrrell raised his voice a little more. "Souvenirs from women, I think. Hair and jewelry. Pictures. He has it in a cigar box under the floorboard in the back bedroom, in front of the closet, at our old house. He more than likely has one where he's living now. I don't know how you can check there."

Tanner left them, saying that he was going to make the call. Giyanna came to sit next to Tyrrell, and he was glad, for now, that she didn't touch him. All of a sudden, he felt dirty. She asked him when he'd found it.

"You were at a school thing. I don't remember what now. He wanted me to go with him. Told me that I didn't have to do my homework because something was going to happen to me so it mattered little. Then a couple hours later, I was still at the table when he came in the house. Covered from head to toe in blood." She put her hand over her mouth as he continued. "When he left the second time, I went to find the clothing that he'd worn, to see if I could make Mom and Dad believe us when we told him that he was mean to us. But I found that instead. I never thought of it again until just now."

"Oh, Tyrrell, it must have been horrible for you. and you should have told me." He asked her what she might have done if he had. "I don't know, but I could have helped in some way."

"It would have gotten us both killed if he had found out. Seeing it in there, hidden away like that, all I could think about was what I'd seen on the television the night before. That television show that Rogan used to watch, remember it?" She told him she did. "He more than likely watched it to get ideas or something. I don't know. But don't you think he'd do it again if he was still killing?"

Tanner came into the room, and he looked grim. Tyrrell felt his pain and thought perhaps he might not sleep well tonight. He sat down across from them and told him what Chloe had said.

"She wants me to go too? Why?" He told him. "Okay, I guess I can see where she'd have to have me on camera saying that I gave her permission. The house—I want it leveled after this is done. I don't care if you use it for the fire department or what, it needs to be gone."

144

"I agree." Tanner said that Chloe was on her way with her crew, and that Noah was going to go to the other house to have a sniff around for her. "You'll need to be there at both houses, I'm afraid. I told Chloe that I didn't think you'd want to be there when they took it out, and she agreed."

"Thank you for that. No, I'd just as soon not be there." Tyrrell thought of what he would have done if he'd been older back then. "I wanted to follow him the next time. But going through my mind was the things that he'd taken, all the stuff that was there. Then I wondered if he would have put anything of Giyanna's and mine in there when he murdered us. I was so sure that he was going to kill us after that, I took to putting bells on the door so I'd hear it when he tried to come in."

"That's why you did that." Giyanna smiled at him, but it was not a happy one. "I wondered about that for years when I thought about it. I thought you just liked the sound of them. Oh, Tyrrell, the things that we had to endure just to survive."

"If you don't mind me asking, why did you two separate when you left the house?" Tyrrell looked at his sister before answering Tanner. "I mean, if it's too painful, I understand."

"When we decided to leave, we both wrote out what we had seen and things that we knew. Neither of us read the others, but I had hers and she had mine. If either of us were to come up missing, we were to mail it to the newspaper." Tyrrell continued when he drank the tea that was just brought into the room for them. "Being separate meant to us that it would have been harder for him to kill us both. This way, one of us, either of us, would have been able to avenge the other one. We were only just kids then. I think now that our logic

145

was a little screwy."

Tanner spoke just as the sirens sounded in his driveway. "I think that you two are the bravest people I know. Hands down. And the fact that you turned out to be upstanding citizens is a miracle in and of itself. You should be very proud of yourselves. I know that I am."

Tyrrell didn't feel that he should be proud of himself. He had let a killer go on for years, over a decade, without telling anyone. The way he felt, he should be in prison right alongside his brother.

Chapter 9

Tanner was there to mark and seal up the evidence. And there was quite a bit of it too. Giyanna had elected to stay outside while Tyrrell and he went in with the police to look around. The house held bad memories for them both, and he'd not want to be there either if he could help it.

"The floorboard there is the one that I found it on." The recorder was running when Tyrrell got down on his hands and knees to show them the place. "There was a box in there. An old cigar box that was closed up with a rubber band. I don't know how many pieces were in it, but it seemed like a lot to a ten-year-old kid."

When Tyrrell was asked to move back, Chloe went to the place and put a crowbar in the slit in the floor. It wasn't necessary — the board came up out of its resting place without any trouble. The camera zoomed into the place when Chloe put her flashlight right over it. Then everyone backed away.

"I can see the boxes." Tanner asked if she had said boxes,

147

as in plural. "Yes, I can see three on the top of the wood that's in there. I don't know how many more until we start pulling them out."

One by one the boxes were taken out, and Tanner watched the inventory of them. There was so much of it that Chloe had to have one of her officers go back to the stationhouse and bring more evidence kits. He ended up bringing back a case of them. As each piece was removed from the boxes, Tanner would sign off on it with Chloe across the seal. It was a long and tedious process.

They pulled out seven of the boxes, all of them cigar boxes, and all sealed up with a rubber band. There were pictures in each one of them. Chloe thought they went with the people that he'd taken the things from. She had a picture of each body that they'd been able to find but one.

"It's of Giyanna." He looked at the little girl in the picture when she handed it to him in the evidence bag. "You think his plan was to kill her and add something of hers to this box? Tanner, there is even a picture of his parents in these things. What a cold and heartless bastard."

"You're not going to be any happier either." Noah appeared in the room with them. "I've been to the McGowan house, and have found three hiding places that you'll need to go to. The reason that I was able to find them is that he was sloppy on a few of them, and I could smell blood. I'm afraid that those pictures aren't going to be that easy to identify."

"Did you look at them?" He said that he'd only looked into the first one he'd found, to make sure that was what it was. Chloe thanked him for his help. "You're a good man to have around, Noah. I don't think we tell you that often enough."

"Thank you, my lady. Coming from you, that's a high compliment indeed." Noah asked to speak to Tanner, and he met him in the front room. "What did you find out?"

"I'm sorry, Noah. With all this going on, I forgot to tell you." He told him he completely understood. "You got both buildings for a grand total of a buck. I paid it already, and all you need to do is show some kind of improvement in the next six months. If not, then they take it back and sell it again. That's the way we've done all ours down in that area."

"Much better than I had hoped. And the people there — have you spoken to them?" He told him what he'd learned as well as where they were staying. "Good. Thank you. Now, I'm going to go and see them again. The young woman, she's his granddaughter then?"

"Yes, her name is Jenny. I think she's taking care of him. He sort of raised her, I guess, when her parents were killed." Noah nodded and asked him if he could get the crew started for him, that he had plans drawn up already. "Yes, Benny brought them by my office this morning before I went to the courthouse. I think it was in the bag that you got them."

"Giyanna, she's all right?" Tanner told him that he didn't think so, not yet at any rate. "When this is over, you should take her on a long trip. I have a great many houses that the two of you can stay in, and I know that Joe would want you to look at hers as well. Take a few months off and see the world with your lovely bride."

"I think I will." He nodded and said that he'd be at the other home when they were ready, for him to call for him. "I will. And thank you, Noah, for everything."

"You are so very welcome, young Tanner. I will have a word or two with your mate, then I shall go and take care of my needs until you need me."

Tanner watched him walk into the yard and go to Giyanna. When they embraced tightly, he felt like he needed a hug too. But duty called, and he was trying to make sure that when this went to court in the morning, it would only be a matter of how long Rogan was going to be gone rather than if he was going to prison.

When everything in both houses was cataloged and put into the box, it too was sealed up, and then he put his name over it as well as Chloe did hers. They both stood there for several minutes, neither of them speaking. All he could think about was how many pieces were in the box. How many lives were torn apart because of one man.

"Take her out to dinner." He said that he was going to do that. "Then take her home, make love to her all night, and help her forget. That's what I'm going to do."

"I've talked to Scott several times. He didn't want to bother you, but he could feel that you were upset." She said that she had spoken to him too. "He's taking you out as well. Why don't we double up? Have some laughs and enjoy the fact that we're living."

"I can do that." She looked in the bedroom that had been stripped of all the furniture earlier this week. The entire house was devoid of anything that made it a home. "I'm going to talk to the city about having this house dozed, and then not have anything else put here. Perhaps a garden in memory of those that lost their lives."

"I'll help." She said she figured that he would want to.

"Chloe, will he get the death penalty for this? I mean, it's no less than he deserves."

"Doubtful that we'd be that lucky and someone take him out for us. Sadly. But I have a plan. I'm not going to tell you what it is, but Noah is going to help me." He nodded and said that he understood. "Good. I'll call you after I get a shower and burn these clothes. I don't ever want to wear them again."

They left after that, and Tanner held Giyanna's hand as he drove them home. She was quiet, and he knew that he should say something. But what?

As soon as he got them home, Ruben met them at the front door with a silver tray in his hand. Giyanna said she was going to get started on her shower and went up the stairs.

"Sir, there is a message for you from the lady queen." He asked which one. "The faerie queen. She wishes to have a minute or two of your time. She said it would only take that little time from you."

"All right but tell her that we're taking a shower and then going to dinner with my brother and his wife. We need to... today was difficult on us, and we need something different." He said that he'd tell her. "Ruben, could you do me a favor? Could you ask the lady queen for some flowers for my wife? Just whatever she can gather up for her. I'd like them to be in the house when we return from dinner."

"I'm sure that she can come up with something. She has a romantic heart too." He nodded and wondered what the fuck he was doing now; his mind was a fog. "Shower, sir, then dinner. I shall see you when you come down."

He went up the stairs wishing now that he'd not made plans. But the moment that he saw Giyanna standing in the

151

bathroom without anything on, he knew that he could at least fulfill one of the things Chloe had told him to do.

"You need a massage." Giyanna turned and looked at him. She'd been crying again. "Oh honey, I'm so sorry you had to go through that today. I'd not wish that on anyone ever. I love you, Giyanna. So very much."

"Make love to me."

He nodded and kissed her tenderly on her mouth. When she wrapped her arms around his shoulders, he held her to him. She was chilled, her skin cool to his touch.

"I need to warm you up first." When she smiled at him, he sat her on the counter. "First thing I have to do is massage your arms for you, get your blood flowing."

Taking her hands into his, he rubbed them until they felt warmer. Then moving up her arm, he made sure that he touched her breast whenever he could, made her nipple peak to a hard tip. Leaning down, he took the tiny nub into his mouth and suckled just the tip until she jerked his head up by his hair.

"I need hard and dirty." He stared at her. "Take me like this is the last time you'll get to fuck me and you want me to remember."

That he could do. Turning her around so that her ass was to him, Tanner willed his clothing away and slammed his cock into her pussy from behind. When she cried out, he took a handful of her hair and jerked her back so that she was watching him fuck her. Her breasts bounced with each stroke, and it made him want to take her harder just to see them move. And when her hands came up and filled with them, he didn't know if he wanted to beg her to tweak her nipples or watch her play.

"Harder, Tanner. I want you to make me yours." He leaned her back down now, holding onto her ass with both hands. As he fucked her, Tanner leaned over her and licked her back, her shoulder, then her neck just under her hair. "Bite me, I want to come."

His wolf took him a little then and he felt his teeth shift in his mouth. Snarling at her when she begged him again, he bit down into her shoulder hard and knew that he'd touched bone. Her screams were of both pleasure and pain, he could tell when she told him she was coming. And when she slid her fingers over his cock as he took her, Tanner felt his own climax not just take him, but explode over his entire being. Even his wolf whimpered a little.

He couldn't move, which he supposed was a good thing. Had he taken but one step, he would have fallen on his ass, bringing her with him, he was so weak. Laying his head on her back, he felt when she started to giggle.

"You think nearly killing me is funny?" He smacked her hard on the ass. "I'll have you know my wolf is now afraid of the bathroom."

"I'm so glad that you found me." He let her up, and she turned in his arms and he held her. "I want to take a shower. Will you scrub my back?"

"I will." They had the water on in minutes and they were both under the spray. "When I took a shower here this morning, I could have sworn that there was a single jet and it didn't come from the top."

"I love this more." He did too, and washed her back with the loofa that was in there. "We're having dinner with Chloe and Scott tonight?"

"Yes. I think we're having something like steak or perhaps pizza. It depends on what you want." She said that she could eat either, and was starving. "Yes, draining me like you did, that would make you hungry."

They made love again in the shower, this time slower but no less wonderful. When they got out, he dried her back and she did the same for him. Dressing for himself, he looked over at Giyanna to see what she was wearing. Tanner was pleased that she had on jeans and a T-shirt, because that was what he wanted to wear after being in a suit and tie all day.

When they exited the bathroom, Giyanna in front of him, he ran into her when she stopped moving. He started to ask her what was wrong when he looked around. The entire room was filled with flowers.

There were vases of them, baskets with violets as well as small periwinkles. He could see roses in taller vases of every color he'd ever seen. And some that he hadn't. On the bed there were chocolates too. Big boxes of them that looked expensive and imported. When she moved deeper into the room, he followed. Everywhere he looked there was more to see, more color and more flowers.

"You did this for me?" He told her how he'd asked the faerie queen to bring her some flowers. "They're beautiful. No one has ever gotten me flowers before."

"I would have thought men would have been trying to ply you with them for all your life." She turned and hugged him before squealing and heading to the chocolate. She had three pieces of the darker chocolates before he could even choose one.

When they went downstairs, there were more flowers there. But these were plants, not cut flowers. There was a basket of herbs for the garden. Perennials as well as annuals. He was blown away by how much she had done for him, Tanner knew that he would owe her a great deal. And it would be worth every bit of whatever she wanted, just to see the look on Giyanna's face as she darted from place to place.

When they sat in the living room with the queen, Tanner thanked her as many times as Giyanna did; she had made her and him very happy. When she smiled at him when he asked what boon he would owe her, he knew that he was in deep trouble.

~~~

Giyanna loved the restaurant and the company. After making love as they had done, the flowers in the house, and now this, she was feeling much better. Chloe was good company for when the men were talking, and they spoke about all sorts of things. From going to see the twins soon to what they were going to do for the Fourth. It was a huge holiday for the pack, as well as the Calhouns.

"I guess they roast this huge hog, and people come from all over with covered dishes and desserts. I've never been to one, but I've seen pictures of it. It's an all-day event." Giyanna said she was looking forward to it as well. Chloe told her that she was bringing something that their cook had made. "I don't cook at all. Do you?"

"A little. I've been working at getting my life together so much that I sort of worked all hours, even when home, and never bothered with a good meal." Chloe told her that she'd not be able to skip meals now that she was going to have a

155

baby. "Does everyone know?"

"We can smell the difference on you. It's nice that you are. The next time that I ovulate, we're going to have one too. I can't wait." She asked her what kind of cop she'd been. "Beat for a while, then undercover. That's how I ended up here. Best thing that has ever happened to me, finding this family."

"That's what I was telling Tanner before we left." She thought of the boon that the faerie had asked for. It wasn't much, not for what she'd done for her. "We're going to put in a garden of just flowers. And the faeries are going to help with the greenhouse all year round."

"They're wonderful, aren't they? Having this little person around that you can just talk to and not have to worry about him or her judging you. There are a lot of them at the house, and a couple at the police station." Giyanna said that they were staffed at the house. "You should ask one of them to be your assistant. They're very helpful with things. Big or small, they can help a great deal."

"I will."

By the time the pizzas arrived they were well into their third pitcher of tea. She'd never drank it without sugar before, but it was really good once she got used to the taste.

Just as they were piling their plates full of the wonderful food, Chloe's phone rang and she stepped away to answer it.

Giyanna looked at Scott. "Is everything all right?"

"She's always on duty, being the chief. But I think this was some results that she was waiting on. I don't want to bring you down or anything, but they took the car in and were running tests on it." She nodded and thought of what that might mean. "It's all for the case to make it stronger, Giyanna.

She wants this as rock solid as she can get it. And the fact that it could well be over tomorrow is going to be good for a lot of people."

When Chloe came back, Giyanna asked her what was going on, if it had anything to do with the case. She nodded and smiled, and that made her breathe easier. Something was going right. Not that it hadn't been from the start, but to have something else to keep him locked away was very good.

"There is enough DNA in the car that it looks as if he carried about six of the victims in it. His fingerprints, as well as your father's, are all over the car. No one else. And trust me, they looked." She looked at her. "This is going to finish him off as far as him ever getting out. He'll get life plus if I know my judge."

Giyanna started crying, and Chloe told her she was sorry to have sounded so happy. Trying to tell her that wasn't it, she hugged her and tried again. She was just so happy.

"You guys went to bat for us from the very start. There wasn't any kind of hesitation on your part—you just jumped right in with both feet and hit the road running. I know that's a lot of clichés, but you understand me." They said that they did. "I love you guys. You're the best thing that has ever happened to me, and I can't thank you enough for all that you've done."

She was a sobby mess but knew that this was the right thing. Rogan would be put away and not be able to hurt anyone else. And that was her biggest fear besides him hurting her brother and her. That he would get out of prison and exact revenge on them for all that was held against him.

After dinner they sat and talked some more. It had been

so very long since she'd had the kind of relationship with a person where she enjoyed their company. They really didn't talk about anything that was life changing or was going to save the world. Just two couples getting together to enjoy themselves.

"I heard that you're going to work for Jas. She's hell on wheels if you don't mind me saying so." Giyanna told her that she was especially looking forward to trying to get donations for the upcoming charity auction they were getting together. "What's the cause? I might have some things at the station house that we're cleaning out. Some old holsters and stuff like that. People collect them, I think."

"Oh yes. That would be wonderful. And kids like those sorts of things as well. But the cause is for more money to put into the fund for Christmas food. I never realized that you'd have to start so early in getting ready for that." Chloe told her that usually Jas started in January. "She told me she's a tad behind this year. And Christine has said that she'd help too if I were to help her with the backpacks that they'll put together."

"We all work on those." She looked at Scott when he spoke. "Last year we put together enough backpacks to give one to each and every child at the elementary school. It certainly helps when parents are stretching every cent they can to make it. I'm hoping that this year will be a little better, however. With a lot more of the town working, we'll have less worry that someone will go without."

"Sterling is going to donate a painting for us to auction off. And he's called in some of the patrons of the gallery to come and bid on it. And the other things too." Tanner told her a little about his paintings. "He's been working hard, I've noticed, for the upcoming show that he thinks is going to be a dud."

They all laughed. Apparently Sterling thought that of every show. Giyanna had seen some of his work when she'd been by his studio, and she thought while very dark, it was the best that she'd ever seen.

As they made their way home, she thought about the trial in the morning. She knew that Rogan was going to be there; he'd been warned by the judge to keep his mouth shut or he'd send him back to jail. She had a feeling that Rogan thought the judge meant if he kept his mouth he wouldn't have to go back. Her brother Tyrrell had decided that he was going to go and sit with her. Tanner was going to be there, as well as the rest of the family. They might be the only ones there, she thought with a laugh. The Calhouns alone would fill the small courtroom.

Giyanna was exhausted when they got to the house. It had been a very stressful day, and she knew that tomorrow was going to be just as bad if not worse. Tanner told her that they'd get themselves a hot tub about the time that Ruben came in to bring them warm scones and tea. It was the perfect ending to the day.

"There is one on the back deck, sir." Tanner asked Ruben what was on the back deck. "The hot tub. The house again. But I think it might have put it in earlier today. When you returned from the house. It's a lovely item and it's ready to go. I have taken the liberty of putting towels in the cabinet that is out there as well."

"Thank you."

They walked out onto the big deck and found the hot tub behind the trellis that was hanging full of wisteria. The smell alone was enough to have her melting. It was perhaps her favorite flower for the out of doors. Tickled, she turned to Tanner. "This is a bit of heaven if you ask me."

"I agree. And the fact that it's all warmed up for us is like a bonus too." He stripped off his clothing and slid into the water. "Christ, this is heaven, and I'm never leaving here. Come on and join me, love. This is wonderful."

After all the times they'd had sex, and it was a great deal, she was still shy about being naked in front of him. So when she was naked, she hurried to get into the water so she'd not be too exposed. He laughed when she moaned.

"You are the oddest little thing." She smacked at him, splashing warm water over his head. "I'm seriously thinking that this is something I could enjoy all year round. And in the winter, it'll be even better. Don't you think?"

"They had one at the gym where I would work out once in a while. I never used it. I don't know, but I didn't know the people that had used it before me, and had no idea what sort of things they might have done in the water." He made a face at her. "See, we have our own germs in ours."

"I wanted to tell you something before I fall asleep. I have moved a couple of people into the house on Silliman Street, and was wondering if you could go by there sometime and welcome them to the neighborhood, as well as show them around. The name of the granddaughter to the man who will be working for Noah is Jenny. The man's name is Rich. They're the Farleys."

"I can do that. It'll be fun." Tanner nodded, but she could

tell that he was going to fall asleep. "It's been a long day, perhaps we should go inside."

"In a minute." Laughing, she got out and dried off. Waking him up was like waking the dead, she thought. He didn't want to get out of the warm tub. "Will you join me here tomorrow night and we'll break it in? Then you can add that to your list of germs."

They were both laughing when they went up to bed. Tomorrow wasn't going to be any better, she thought, but at least she'd have a good night's sleep tonight. Almost as soon as her head hit the pillow, she was sound asleep.

Chapter 10

Rogan rode to the courthouse in the big van, but this time he just sat on the floor. There wasn't any point in getting tossed around again, and the men in there with him didn't seem to care where he sat down. He looked at the chains on his ankles and wrists.

He'd be rid of them today. There wasn't any doubt that his brother was going to come through for him. Ty was a pussy and afraid of him. He might have to work on Giyanna a little more, but then in the end, she'd be dead too. Things had gone on too long with her, and he wanted her out of his life. The nerve of her telling him he wasn't going to get out. He knew better.

The courthouse wasn't all that fancy, but he supposed he didn't expect much from this town. They'd let him get by with so much that he knew that they were a lazy lot. When he was inside the filled-up room, he wondered if something was going on after he was released from jail. There sure seemed to be a lot of people around for his trial if they were all here for that.

The judge was calling things to order when this little lady in a cop's uniform asked to talk to him. Whatever was going on, it didn't affect Rogan so he didn't pay any attention. Turning around, he looked for his brother. The sooner he got his shit together, the sooner he'd be out of here. Ty had better come through, that's all he knew.

"Your honor, this evidence has only just come to light, and that's why you're getting it right now." Rogan glanced up front when he heard his attorney talking to the woman who had just spoken. "I'm aware of that, but as I said, this has just been found, and I'd like to have it used as evidence."

"I'll have to have a look at it." She said that she hoped that he'd say that. "All right. I'll need an hour recess. There is no point in taking Mr. McGowan away. I won't be that long."

His attorney came back to the table, but only gathered up his files and a pen. Rogan asked him what was going on, he had shit to do, and Rogan told him that he needed to talk to his brother too.

"You'll have to wait a bit longer, Rogan. There is new evidence against you, and the judge wants us all to be there while he reviews it." He asked him what sort of evidence, and again said that he needed to talk to Ty. "I'll be back."

That pissed him off, but he knew that if he opened his mouth, they would send him back to the jail. He knew that today was his big day, and decided to work on his list of things that he wanted to do. Like first off, he was going to put it out there that his wife was missing and he wanted her back at all costs. Then he was going to kill Giyanna.

He wasn't just going to kill her, he was going to make her suffer too. No breaking her neck until he'd broken all the other bones in her body. Rogan didn't want it quick; no, he wanted her to suffer for every day he'd been in this place.

Rogan looked around again and finally spotted Ty. He motioned for him to come to him, but he wasn't doing what he wanted. Finally, he stood up as much as he could and yelled for him to come up. The officer that had been in the back of the room came to his table and told him to sit down and shut up.

"I need to talk to my brother. He's going to do something for me." He was told again to sit down and shut his mouth. "You're going to be sorry when this day is over. That I can tell you."

When he wasn't able to get Ty to come to him, he stared at Giyanna. Christ oh mighty, she was a stuck-up bitch, he thought. Dressed up on her pretty clothing, she looked like she didn't shit anything but gold bricks. And the man next to her, he knew him, he thought. Tanner something. He looked like he would have done anything to have her under him. He didn't want his sister that way, but he didn't want anyone else to have her either. When she finally looked at him, as if she knew that she was being looked at, she flipped him the finger then smiled at him.

"What the hell is wrong with you?" The cop came back and told him it was his final warning. "She flipped me off, and I can't do it back to her? What kind of idiot do you take me for that I can't retaliate when I need to? You should go and tell her to shut up and behave. I didn't do nothing wrong to her. Not yet anyways."

"If I have to come up here one more time, I'm going to load you into the van myself and take you back to your cell. And the only way that you're going to hear your verdict is when I get around to getting back to your cell to tell you." He stood up, showing off that he could stand upright, no doubt. "Shut up and behave."

He didn't look at her again. She was just trying to get him into trouble so he'd go away. Well, he wasn't going back to that place. Not so long as he could get his brother to do his duty to him. And Ty would, or he'd regret being born. Today was his big day, and he had fucking plans.

The hour stretched out before him into the next one. By the time he was ready to tell them he'd had enough, that he needed some food and relief to piss, his attorney came out of the little doorway and sat down. Whatever had happened, he sure looked pale about it. Before he could ask him what the hell was taking so long, the judge came back in the room and stood at his special table. The cop was sworn in and seated at the left of the judge.

"What the fuck is she doing up there? You said that you'd make it so I didn't have to have a trial. And did you talk to Ty? He's going to confess for me." He shook his head and then leaned over to him, asking him once again to change his plea. "You mean to guilty? I ain't done nothing wrong, and as soon as Ty clears this up for me, then I'll be able to prove it to everybody that I'm not going to prison."

"Chief Calhoun, I'm to understand that you wish to add some evidence to this trial. I'm allowing this because the attorney for Mr. McGowan has agreed to it. Tell us what you found when you searched the house of Tyrrell McGowan. He took it when he paid the back taxes. I have the deed here, as well as a letter from the bank stating how it occurred."

What the hell were they doing in his house, he wondered? When she started to talk about how she'd been informed about some hidden boxes, Rogan stood up as best he could. The judge told him to sit down.

"They ain't got no cause to be going through my house. Whatever they found out there, I didn't give them any kind of permission to go into my house." He looked around, then back at her. "Girl, you're barking up the wrong tree right now. If you know what's good for you, you might want to go on back home and start your day over."

"Are you threatening me?" He told the woman cop that he was just saying it like it was. "Well, sir, that's exactly what I'm doing here. Saying it like it is. But we didn't need your permission to go through the family home. Your name isn't on the deed. It belongs to a Tyrrell McGowan."

"He's my brother, and if you ask him, whatever you found there, he did it. And he's going to confess to whatever else you think you found there too." He smiled at her. "I didn't do a damned thing, and once Ty comes up here and tells you, then we'll see who was threatening who."

Ty was asked to come forward. And when he was about two feet from where he sat, Rogan tried to reach out to him, to make him understand that he'd better do as he told him. But he jerked away from him, and Rogan was left holding nothing but air when his brother started talking.

"I talked to Rogan while he was in jail, and he tried to convince me that I needed to take blame for all the murders. He also told me that I had to do my duty by him, your honor." He asked him if he had done anything to warrant him confessing. "No, sir, I haven't. I've not lived in this area for a long time, so it wouldn't have been possible for me to have murdered as many people as you've found."

"What the hell is wrong with you? Ty, you'd better do what I tell you. It ain't going to go well for you if you don't." Ty just looked at him, and he could see something there that he'd never thought to see on his face. He wasn't afraid of him. And he hated him.

The latter, he didn't care about. He hated both him and Giyanna too, but to see the lack of fear made his belly twist up. Rogan had counted on him being just afraid enough of him that he'd do what he was told to do. Ty looked at the judge again.

"Your honor, I'm here to testify against my brother Rogan McGowan. He's been a terror to this town and the people in it since I was a small child. I left home too young when it became evident to me and my sister that he was going to kill us the first chance he got. I found those boxes, at least some of them, when I was snooping around in his room. He had come home from someplace covered in blood, and when I went to find evidence against him, to get the police to help us, I found the stash of souvenirs." The judge asked him how long ago that had been. "I was just shy of my tenth birthday."

"You went in my room? You were looking for evidence against your own flesh and blood? What kind of brother are you? You traitor." Rogan didn't like where this was heading. "You have to make him do what I told him to do. I ain't going back to that prison. That is not a place where I think I should be."

"And where is it you think you should be, Mr. McGowan? Your wife took your children and left town to assume a better life for herself and the kids. Your own family has turned against you. For reasons that I can understand. We have more bodies that we can pin on you for murder, as well as your own parents. I have you recorded not only confessing to the crimes that you are on trial for, but also the threat of your sister and brother that you plan to kill. Where should I put a man like you?" He told the judge that Ty had done it all, that he was going to confess. "Are you, Tyrrell? Are you going to say that you committed these heinous crimes? That you went out, searched for people to kill, then did it, hiding the bodies so that no one would find them?"

"No, sir, I am not." Rogan tried to stand up; he was going to knock some sense into his brother. And failing that, he was going to kill him. But he was chained down like a fucking animal. "In fact, sir, if at all possible, I'd like to be there if he's given life. It would make me feel a great deal better about things."

"I'm not going to get life, you moron. You're going to do this for me, or so help me, Ty, I'm going to kill you too. Tell them you did this, or else I'm going to snap your neck like I did them others. You tell them, damn it. Right now." He looked around when no one was speaking. The room was as silent as a tomb. "What the fuck is wrong now? He's going to do this. I told him to, and he'd better fucking do what he's told."

"What do you mean, you're going to snap his neck like you did the others?" He asked the judge what he ament. "You just said that. That you were going to snap his neck. What are

169

you referencing this to? Not that it matters — we have you on a recording telling us what you've done. But I'd like to hear it from your mouth. Did you kill those other women, and now want your little brother to take the blame so you can get out?"

"I don't know what you mean." He didn't either. Rogan was confused as to what he was asking him. "I told him that he had to take the blame for this. I don't know what else it is you need to know. Ty killed those woman and our parents, and he's going to say that he did or I'm going to hurt him."

"No, you're not. Mr. McGowan, I hereby sentence you to state prison to await the trial in the deaths of fourteen women, as well as three men. And in that time, you'll be put in solitary confinement so that you don't hurt anyone else while you're there."

As he was being dragged away by his arms and legs, he was screaming at Ty. The fucking little shit had done him wrong.

"You tell them, or so help me, Ty, I'm going to murder you too. Do you hear me? I don't belong in jail, and I'm not going. Let me go." He tried his best to jerk from the cops that held him, but between holding him like they were and the chains getting all tangled up on him, he was falling all over the place. "Let me the fuck go. I have to find my wife and kids. She's going to pay for leaving me. Just like them others. Ty, you'd better make this right."

They shoved him in the back of the van again, and this time the other cops weren't with him. These fuckers were going to pay for this. And he was going to start with his brother. After him, then Giyanna. There wasn't any reason that either of them should not have confessed to get him out

170

of here, and he was going to make sure they knew it. He just had to figure out what the hell was going on. And the fact that they'd gone through his things — well, that shit was going to get taken care of too.

"Hello, Rogan." He turned and looked at the man he'd not seen before. He was dressed in a dark suit, and that was probably it. He asked him if he was there to get him out of this mess. "In a way, I suppose I am. I've come here to make sure that you don't have to spend the rest of your life in prison, just as you wanted."

"It's about fucking time someone did what they was supposed to. You gonna confess? I got me some shit I have to do, and being in prison ain't gonna help me." The man smiled, and he could see the gleam in his eyes, like one of them dogs that was running around his property that eyes shone up at night. "What are you going to do?"

"Kill you."

He didn't even get a chance to tell the man that wasn't right. He felt his throat being sliced open just like one of them canned hams that he got himself sometimes. Trying to stop the bleeding, he put his hand as close to his neck as he could, but all the blood did was pool in his hand. Rogan was getting weaker with every handful of blood he lost. Falling back, he closed his eyes.

"Well if this isn't wrong, I don't know what is?" Then nothing.

~~~

Tanner knew that he was supposed to be working, but for the life of him, all he wanted to do was find Giyanna and go out on a picnic. Today was bright and sunny, and she'd been

171

working so hard since the trial. He could understand it; he was shocked by it too. Standing up, he sat back down when Noah joined him in the room.

"How is that lovely wife of yours today?" He told him that she was acting as if nothing had happened. "That's probably the way she's been handling her brother for years. I just spoke to young Ty. He's going to be helping you in your practice. I hope you don't mind, but he needed something to occupy his mind too."

"No, that's fine. I was going to talk to you about it anyway—he and I already spoke about it. But thank you." He nodded. "What else are you here for? I know you well enough to know that you don't come out during the day just to tell me things like that."

"No, I'm here for something else. And I will get to it. But for now, I'd like to ask you what you think about working for me." He asked him what he meant. "You seem like you might be bored with working for me. And I will remind you that at one time, you wished to be my watcher. What do you think of your job now?"

"I love working for you. It's afforded me more time to do things that I want to. Hang out with my family more, and to be with Giyanna whenever I want. She should have been mentioned first, by the way." Noah nodded and smiled. "Are you thinking of firing me?"

"Oh no, never that. But I do have something that I'd like for you to do. Did you know that the current mayor is stepping down at the end of his term? I have it on good authority that he will regardless of whether there is someone to take his place. He is ill, you see, and wants to spend his final days with his family."

"No, I didn't know that. You want the job? You'd be good at it." He said that he did not want it. Too many daylight hours. "Okay, that's right. I never thought of that. Who did you have in mind?"

"Giyanna." Tanner just stared at him. "She would make a good mayor. With your sister-in-law already in place as the chief of police, and your older brother running the pack, I can see her making a good showing in the polls. And she knows the law as well as anyone."

"I think she's happy where she is helping my grandma." He nodded. "You think she'd take it? And now that you mention it, what does that have to do with me and this job?"

"She would be great for many things, that wife of yours. I wouldn't be surprised if she were to make it all the way to the White House with you in her corner." He asked if he was serious. "Oh yes, very much so. And she'd be just as good at that as she would be anything she sets her mind to, don't you think?"

"Yes. I mean, she's smart and very good at making people believe in themselves. The other day she was talking to a couple of the elderly. In no time she had them up and working the loom that Mom brought over, and weaving things like they'd done it all their lives." Noah told him that was just a drop in the bucket for her. "You really think she'd go for being mayor?"

"I do." Noah got up and moved around his office. Not touching things but still talking about Giyanna. "She's much stronger than even you think. And I believe that you have a good understanding of her strengths. The fact that she handled her brother well—both, as a matter of fact—that makes me think that she'd be a whiz at managing Congress, or any other branch that has to report to her."

"Are you going to ask her?" Noah just looked at him. "Ah, so this is a ploy to make me ask her about running. You old devil you. But you're right. She would be very good at being mayor. As for the rest, I don't know. I'll tell her what you think, but I don't know how she'll take to it."

"She adores me." That she did, he told Noah. "And she loves the fact that I make her smile. No matter her mood, I have something about me that makes her smile."

"I was told it was your old-world class. Which reminds me, the shop renovations are coming along nicely. The wallpaper is spot on to what you wanted." Noah agreed with him. "Jenny is doing a great job with the faeries at the greenhouse too. I think they want her to be their boss now that she's proven herself with them."

"It would be good for her as well." Tanner said that Giyanna was going out to see her today, to see if she needed anything. "It will be good for them to see her. Her brother might like to meet her as well."

It hit Tanner right then. He knew how he knew the woman. She was the one holding the baby next to Tyrrell in his dream. Holy Christ, they were mates, or whatever humans called falling in love. He looked at Noah when he laughed.

"You knew too." He said that he had a little inkling about it. "They'll be happy together then? Tyrrell has been sort of down lately. I think he's feeling like a failure about his life, and the things that has happened with his brother."

"Rogan is gone, and once Tyrrell figures out that he could

174

no more have stopped his brother from killing than I could have, then he'll be all right. The love of a good woman, that's what he needs. But you mustn't tell anyone what you know. Just let it flow like it did for you and Giyanna."

"No, I'd not do that. Things, I've learned, have a way of working themselves out." Noah agreed. "But when Giyanna goes to see Jenny today, I'll have her take her brother out. It'll be good for him to get out of the house for a little while."

"Good idea." Noah sat back down after that and stared at him for several seconds. "Benny and I are going on a long trip. We'll return, but not for a while. He has yet to see anything more than this state, and I have a need to go away for a little while. You and Giyanna are still planning to go and see to my homes, aren't you?"

"Yes, we leave on Monday. It was very generous of you to let us use your plane. In all the time that I've known you, I had no idea that you had one." He said that he had plenty of secrets that he didn't know. "I'm sure you do. A man as old as you, you'd have a great many tales to tell as well. You should write a book on them."

"I may yet, you never know. What shall I say about you, young Tanner? That you were a man of men, or that you let your wife rule the roost and enjoyed life to the fullest?" He told him that he could be both. "So you shall then. I must be going. Let me know when you arrive at the houses, and I may join you for a day or two. I might enjoy that more than I can say."

After Noah left, Tanner felt better about working. When Giyanna came into his offices at around one, she told him she was going to see Jenny. He asked her to take Tyrrell with her, just to get him out of the house.

"He has been cooped up for a while now. I was with him yesterday when the old house was burned to the ground. I never thought that I'd say this, but I think I might miss it a little. Not that I want to go back there, but Tyrrell and I, we had fun with each other there." Tanner told her that he was sorry about it. "I'm not. My Aunt Bea told me that I could let the past rule me or I could rule it. It wasn't until I had to plan for Rogan's funeral that I understood what she meant. I broke off with Rogan years ago, in my heart anyway. But not my head. Doing that for me meant nothing, the same as he'd become to me. Nothing more than a nuisance. Now that he is dead, I feel like I can live, for the first time in my life."

"I'm glad that I can and will be a part of that living part." He smiled when she did. "Also, Noah thinks that you should be mayor of this town when the new elections come up. He seems to think you'd be very good at it."

"Really?" He told her also about her going to the White House someday. "I'd be good at that too, don't you think? I mean, running the country can't be much harder than working with your grandma and mom. They're two of the most dangerous people when they're together. I should be able to handle just about anything."

"I agree. And so you know, Mom thinks the same thing about you and Grandma. I guess she said that you two team tag in the teasing part." Giyanna laughed with him. "I love you, my dear. With all that I have."

"And I love you. I'm going to go and get Ty and bully him into going with me. Then we'll have lunch. It's time for him to get out of his funk and have fun with his sister, don't you think?" He told her if anyone could do it, it would be her. "Damned right I can do it. I can do just about anything I set my mind to."

He was still laughing when she left him a short time later. Tanner really did have a lot of work to get done, and it wasn't going to if he kept sitting here like a knot on a log. He was working on investments today, and was adding his name to the same deals that Joe had told Noah to use. If he did what she told Noah every day, he might be a trillionaire when he was ready to retire.

Chapter 11

Chris sat at her desk reading over the problems that had come to her last night. There would forever be someone that was taking things just a little too far, and she was glad for the distraction for a moment. When Myra appeared in the chair across from her, Chris carefully laid the paperwork down and asked her what she'd found out.

"All the bodies have been accounted for, and everyone has been identified. I'm glad now that you gave me the name of the last woman. Her family is most grateful for the closure, as you can imagine. You did a wonderful job with this." Chris thanked her for that. "Now I need something else to do. The plan with Ty meeting his own mate will come to fruition, by the way. They've not met as yet, but things will be looking up for the two of them. Jenny is going to be good for the young man, just as you said." Chris told her that she didn't know, but was glad that it worked out. "Also, Tanner and his wife are leaving on Monday to take their honeymoon in looking

179

at all the homes of Noah the vampire. I would have thought they'd put it off for some time yet, but I think they need to get away now as the papers are having a good time with all the speculation about the murders. I think that's what bothers her the most about all this. Not Rogan's death."

"I know that it does, and this is a good thing on their part. We did send flowers to the two of them, so they know that we care. I think that you're right in the honeymoon they're taking. I know that we're going to meet up with them at some point, so I'm glad that they're on their way." Myra nodded. "Where on earth did you see that pattern you have on?"

The colors were very muted, very unlike the witch. If there was a pattern to the colors, she certainly didn't see it. The fact that it was so drab in the way the colors came together was beautiful to her, but very unlike the witch, who made it her job to have the brightest colors ever made.

"I was in the Market Place yesterday and this woman was selling quilts. They were quite lovely, and very well done. I saw this pattern and it made me happy. I even bought the blanket from her. I put it in your room so that you could have it." Chris thanked her. "You're very welcome. I may make a habit of going there weekly. There is always something new to look at, and I have found a good place for a few of the herbs that I'm forever looking for. You should go yourself."

"I might yet. I've been so busy lately that I've had little time to do much more than guide new witches on the right path. There is so much to distract them nowadays that I forever worry that they're going to turn to the dark side before I have a chance to get to know them." Myra agreed. "Also, you should have seen the look on their faces when I showed up at their last meeting. You'd think that I was bringing the world down around them. It was fun to watch them, and to know that I was that way at first."

"You are a little bit hard to be around when they're afraid of you. Not afraid—no, that's the wrong term. In awe of you. And people really are. I knew you would be great the first time I saw you." And she had too, guiding her along the right path. "You've used your young faerie again, haven't you? Daegan, he's been a good man to have around, and he's a bit smitten with you. But, he has been rewarded again for his part in the death of Rogan? I have to tell you, I'm so very glad that he's gone. That was a monster that we could all have done without."

"Yes, he said that he enjoys playing a vampire. And I did tell him that I might have need of his services again. But he was ready to slay the dragon, so to speak, in this man. I only needed to tell him a little and he knew all about him. Daegan said that he still has a deep connection to the earth, and he had known about the deaths of so many, but not who had done it." She leaned back in her chair and watched the older witch. "What's on your mind today? You seem a little too happy to have been out with the humans, as I know you were."

"I am very happy, all the time. But I was thinking of the Calhouns and all that they've been through of late. It's always surprising to me that anyone with only the magic they had at the beginning could have done so well." Chris had thought of nothing else but the family for some time now. "Do you suppose that a hundred years from now they'll look back on this and think that they were guided along their paths, or that it was the fates as they believe?"

Chris said nothing, because they both knew that the fates had left that particular family up to her. "I think they will believe that they are very lucky to have found each other, and nothing more. And if they do think of us, and perhaps know that we might have meddled a little, they'll know that we had the best of intentions." Myra nodded, but didn't look convinced. "Don't you think so? They're all very happy. They have family around them all the time, and that's good for them. And they have all that they need in the way of magic and friendship."

"I know that I have fallen in love with them. As, I think, you have as well." She said that she had, especially Tanner. "He is what I've come to talk to you about. That poor young man could use some happiness, don't you think?"

"I wasn't aware that he was unhappy." Myra just waved her off, as if she might know better. "What do you have in mind, to make him have a happy ending to all this? He is full of magic, some of it yet untouched. He has a lovely mate, that I believe you picked out for him. And as I said, his family is nearby and he's living a good life. What more is there we can do for him to make his happier?"

"His wife is running for mayor. Did you know that?" Chris hadn't, but it didn't surprise her. She was very smart and well received. "I think someone is putting those thoughts in her head."

Chris laughed. "You don't like the idea of her being mayor, or is it that you didn't give her the idea and that's what bothers you?" Myra said it was the last one. "I see. So, you know who this monster is that is making her into something that we can be proud of?"

"Noah. The vampire. He's meddling where I want to meddle." Chris figured it was him. He was as bad as her in wanting the best for the family. "He and that young man that is working for him, Benny, they're going on a trip soon. Perhaps while he's away I'll work on her for even greater things."

"I don't know what you're planning, but I do hope whatever it is, you tell me about it first." She said that she would. "Good. And while you're there talking to her, would you please tell her that we'll be seeing them for Christmas, as was planned?"

"I can do that. I think she would make a great president, don't you think? I could be her advisor. I would certainly be memorable. And while she's there, perhaps I can get her to add some color to the House itself." Chris told her that one could never forget her. "I thought as much."

"But I do believe that it's called the White House for a reason. You don't want to mess with that. It'll just confuse people." Myra nodded but smiled, so Chris had a feeling that if Giyanna did make it to the grand house, there would be little doubt to anyone that her advisor was a little on the color-blind side.

When Myra was gone, Chris picked up the paperwork again. There was much to do in her job, and sometimes she had the worst of it. There was always something going on somewhere that needed her attention. Like this that she had in front of her. The killing of a young witch for her magic. It broke her heart to hear of such things.

After she helped the family of the young victim deal with their overwhelming grief, Chris went in search of her mate.

They had things to do today, and she was going to see if she could talk him into chasing her in the woods first with his cat. The man was a wonderment with his body and tongue.

~~~

Tyrrell wasn't enjoying the trip to the greenhouse. In fact, he wasn't enjoying being out of his house at all lately. He was broken hearted. Not for the death of his brother, but because he couldn't bring himself to care that he was gone. Not even a small tear at the loss. There had to be something wrong with him, was all he could think about. He had no heart, or something much worse. And when Giyanna bullied him into going with her, he'd had no choice but to go. She said she'd turn him into a frog if he didn't get up and get going. Tyrrell wasn't sure that she could do that, but the things he'd seen lately made him not want to take chances.

"Where are we going again?" She told him that he knew. "Yes, I know, but why am I going too? You do know that I'm older than you."

"Yes, by a whole fourteen minutes. Hush now, and enjoy the day. And look at all the greenery. You know, this time tomorrow, all this will be sold. The Market Place is doing very well this year, and I'm very proud of it." He stopped to look at the pretty roses that were tied up with a trellis. He had something similar in his yard, but he didn't know the color as yet. "Tyrrell, you have to come around to being happy. I can't stand it when you're not."

"How do you feel about Rogan being dead?" He hadn't meant to ask her, but now that he had, he really wanted to know. "I feel nothing. Not even a little remorse that he's gone. I even went to his grave the other day, and it could have been

184

a perfect stranger for all the emotion that I felt standing over it.

"I don't think about him, if I can help it. But when I do, all I can remember is your face when you told the courtroom that you'd found the boxes one day when he'd come home covered in blood. I wish you had told me. I might have been your lookout or something, and we could have gotten him arrested." He said that it wouldn't have worked. "Why not?"

"The police back then. You remember how they were. They weren't any better than Rogan was. And the one and only time that we did go to them about him, they called him up and had him come and get us. Do you remember what he did to us that day?" He rubbed the scars on his arms that were forever a reminder of how violent Rogan could be to them. "No, going to them would have gotten us killed."

"Why do you have to feel anything for him? I mean, yes, he was our brother, but only because we had the same parents. There was never a time when he was good to us. Never do I remember him saying anything kind to either one of us. And there is also the fact that he had planned to kill me." He shivered when he thought of knowing that her picture had been among the things that Rogan had collected from the dead. "Like I said, he's gone, and you and I have come together again. That is the only thing that he ever did for us. And even that was done for selfish reasons because he needed an attorney."

"I think that Mom was afraid of him as well." Giyanna asked him why he thought that. "She would never be alone with him. When they were in the house together, don't you remember she'd make one of us or both sit in the kitchen with

185

her. Even as a young child, I could see the look in her eyes. Do you suppose they knew what he was doing all that time?"

"Yes, I think they did. And they too were afraid of the police not doing anything." He'd not thought of that. He asked her how she felt about their parents being with the other dead. "Now that you mention about Mom being afraid of him, I wonder if that was why they were gone so much. To keep him from hurting them. I mean, that doesn't make it fair for us to have been left behind, but I can see it."

They were quiet as they looked for Jenny. Giyanna needed to give her a message from one of the brothers, and that was why he'd come along with her. Not that there would be trouble, but she did want him there when she was able to give her the good news.

His own job was something that he was looking forward to. Tyrrell hadn't liked being an attorney for some time now, but he thought that he'd enjoy working with Tanner. He was a good man, and a great person to have as a future brother-in-law. He just hoped that he could live up to the high standards that he had. Tanner was an amazing attorney.

Giyanna was talking to a young woman, and he had to get closer to her. Her eyes, he thought, were beautiful. Yet the closer he got to her, the more he noticed about her. She was stunning and had a lovely voice too.

"Jenny, I'd like for you to meet my brother Tyrrell. Tyrrell, this is Jenny Farley. She's just been promoted to manager of the greenhouse. The faeries are very happy with her promotion too." He took her hand in his, and was surprised at how tiny it was. And how warm. "She's living with her grandfather, who is working for Noah too."

"Grandda is having so much fun getting the little shop fixed up. And some of the boxes of clothing came in yesterday. I think he wanted me to try one on so that he could work his magic on it. I wonder how Noah knew that he'd been a tailor at one time?"

Giyanna said something, but Tyrrell was mesmerized by the movement of Jenny's mouth, the way she used her hands when she spoke. Tyrrell almost missed it when she asked him a question.

"No, I've never had a suit tailored before. I just never found that it was all that necessary." Jenny told him how Grandda would disagree. "I bet he would. Would you go out with me?"

He had no idea where that question had come from, but he was glad that his brain was working with his mouth. When she smiled at him and said yes, he could have danced a jig, as Noah was so fond of saying.

"Your name is very formal, isn't it?" Tyrrell asked her what she meant, loving that she'd said yes to going out with him. "I don't mean anything by it, but my name is Jennifer and everyone just calls me Jenny. Do you go by anything shorter? Like Ty?"

He hadn't wanted anyone to call him a shortened version of his name since he'd been smaller and Rogan had called him that. But it sounded so much better when it came from her that Tyrrell told her that he'd be very happy if she called him that.

They walked around the greenhouse, her pointing out the names of the faeries that were there, or the name of a flower when he asked. It smelled good in here as well, and he found himself bending to smell each one that she showed him. When they got to the roses, he told her about the one he had in his yard, and how it had no blooms on it as this one did.

"You have either a late bloomer or one that only blooms every other year. I didn't know there was such a flower until the faeries told me." She showed him the one that was in the last line of bushes. "Does it have this kind of leaf, or this one here?"

She showed him the two different ones, and he had to focus on what she was saying. The movement of her hands had him distracted again. Jenny laughed when he told her that he'd not really looked at the leaves.

"I didn't either before working here." He followed her, and all Ty could think about was kissing her. Taking her into his arms and kissing the daylights out of her. "Are you all right, Ty? You look like something has upset you."

"Honestly?" She nodded at him, and he felt like he could talk to her in ways he couldn't even with his sister. "I'd like to take you right here. Not just to kiss you, but I need you in a way that I could never have thought of before with a woman. I'm not a virgin or anything like that, but sex had come to mean as little to me as my life did. But with you, the simple things that you say and do, it makes me want you in my life."

"You make me feel the same way." He nodded, and wrapped his arm around her waist and pulled her closer to him. "I think this is going to be an epic relationship, don't you?"

He said that he thought so too and kissed her. Christ, it was like kissing a hot volcano, her body was so warm and supple. When she wrapped her arms around his neck, Ty had no choice but to deepen the kiss. Not because of what she'd done, but because it was the most natural thing in the world for him to do. And when she moaned, her body shuddered against his and he felt his cock thicken and stretch. It was as if he'd been awakened.

Love. He knew that it was much too soon to say it aloud, but he could feel it. Like she'd caressed his heart and woke it to hers. Lifting his head, he looked down at her smiling face. She was looking at him in a way that he knew no one else had ever looked at him before. Kissing her again, this time with as much hunger but not for as long, he held her to him and tried to get his mind and body to think of anything but taking her to his house and having his way with her over and over.

"You and I, we're mates." He nodded, not sure what to say about that; he was only human and told her that. "So am I, but I can feel that we're to be together, can't you?"

"Hell yes." Her laughter was like a balm to his heart, a lifting of his spirits. "I'm sorry. Was that a little loud?"

Ty laughed with her. This was something that he could get used to, this Utopian feeling of being in love. As he hugged her to him again, he saw his sister staring at him. And when she gave him the thumbs up and walked away, he could have kissed her. She had done this for him.

Not really, but her bullying had paid off. Her need to nurture and to love him. Walking around the greenhouse with Jenny, he listened this time, wanting to know whatever she was telling him in the event that she wanted him to work with her.

~~~

Giyanna reached for Tanner to tell him the good news.

Tyrrell is in love. They both laughed. It was strange to see him this happy after he'd been so down lately. He asked her who the lucky girl was. *Jenny Farley. I was only gone for a few minutes, and when I came back, they were kissing and holding onto each other.*

Yes, well, that's the way it works when you find your other half. I'm so happy for them both. There couldn't have been a better matching than them. Other than us, of course. She laughed again. *By the way, have I told you today how much I love you?*

You have, but only a few dozen times. Giyanna was in love with the man of her dreams and then some. *I'm coming to see you in a little while. We'll have lunch, then ravish each other in the back room. You think you could do that?*

I can suffer through it for you, my dear. She wanted to skip and giggle. Things that she'd never done before. And all because of one man and his family.

She was in the office when she thought of her brother, Rogan. She knew how he had died. Tyrrell didn't yet. She wasn't sure that she'd ever tell him. The papers put it down as a massive stroke brought on by his weight, which was a big factor, and the stress of the trial. But she had known that he wasn't long for this world, and Chris Bentley had come to her to let her know.

"He would have continued on his task to kill anyone that he could." Giyanna had nodded and told her that she believed it too. "When I put someone out to cause his death, it was only speeding up the process, not messing with the events. He would have died, but not soon enough for seven more people that would feel his wrath. And you and your brother would never have been as happy as you are now."

190

"It was always going to be there in the back of my mind, whether or not he was going to be freed." Chris nodded. "I thank you for what you've done for me. And for my family. I wouldn't have been able to go on knowing that he was there, killing a captive group of people."

"I'm sorry, my dear, but you're very brave. And I'm very happy that you took Tanner to your heart." She asked her what she meant. "That you love him so much."

"He is the one that should be thanked. Without him, I'm not sure where I'd be in my life. Certainly not here. Not with Tyrrell and the rest of them. I'd not be having a child that I plan to love and cherish for the rest of my days. Without Tanner, there would be no me. I'm sure of it." Chris had hugged her then, and she'd felt a little tingle along her skin. When she asked her what that was, the woman only laughed.

Going home, she thought of all the things that were going on right now. Her life was full, so was her heart. Giyanna decided to stop by the marked plot that her brother Rogan was in, and sat on the ground next to the plain memorial to a sadistic man.

"This will be the one and only time that I come to see you, Rogan. I wanted you to know that you got just what you deserved, and that I think it should have happened long ago." She looked around the area and thought it a fitting place for a man such as him. "You were cruel and mean, you never let anyone be happy, and I think that's the saddest thing ever."

There was a couple near a new grave. She wondered if it was one of the women that had been found, and her heart broke for them. They put flowers on the newly turned earth and sat on a pretty bench by the marker, each of them holding

191

onto the other as they grieved for their loved one.

"You did that to so many people. Broke them with your need to kill. I haven't any idea what sort of thoughts went through your head all the time, but I'm glad that you're gone, that you're no longer a threat to anyone that I know and love. Nor to the strangers that can now walk safely out and about." She laid the single flower on his grave; it was dead, shriveled up, and black. "This is what your heart was like. And a reminder to you that you aren't going to do this to my heart ever again."

Heading home again, she felt lighter than she had before. And she knew that she'd never think of her brother again. As far as she was concerned, he'd never been and never would be again. As she pulled into the drive, there was Tanner, standing on the deck waiting for her. Yes, her heart thought, this is love.

Chapter 12

James sat on the flowery bench and thought of what they were doing there today. It was time. He and his lovely mate Jas had talked it over, and they were ready to move on to the next phase. A move that was breaking his heart with every beat of it. But they'd been around for a very long time now; they were chasing two hundred years old, and it was too much for them.

"You're sure this is what you wish? I cannot change it back once I'm finished." He nodded and so did Jas when Chris spoke to them. "I thought you were so happy to be alive with all your family. I'm sad to see that you wish to no longer be a part of their lives."

"We're tired. And we've been here far longer than we should have been. It's time." Jas nodded and held his hand as he continued. "There are so many of them now, so many children of the children, that we can no longer keep them straight. And when they come to visit us, we're too far behind

193

in what they're doing in their lives for us to keep up. Oh, I suppose that we could have, but we are just going through the motions of life, and that's not the way that it should be."

"We loved being able to meet them all. The children of our son are something that we were blessed to see. And their children have been such a joy to us both. But as my James said, we're tired. And want to follow on with the family and friends that we've outlived for far too long." Jas looked at him, and James just fell in love with her again, as he did every day of his life with this woman. "We've seen too much in our time. Deaths of friends. Our family ever expanding. It's time for us to take this next step, the step that we both want, and to end our lives."

"What does your family say about this? I'm sure that they're as upset as I am." Jas shook her head, tears falling down her cheeks, as did his own. "Jas, I'm so sorry to make you cry."

"No, no, you didn't. I was thinking of the first grandchild that I held in my hands. Trent was such a lovely baby, chubby and so good. And then his brothers being born and coming into my heart. It was more than any woman could ever hope for, to see my child have children. He was our dream for TJ and Christine. The dream of having someone to love so unconditionally that it could only make your heart beat faster and better." James kissed her then, holding her to him as he had a million times a day. "When I told them that we were ready, they seemed to be sad at first. But then we told them, just as we have you, that we're tired. Not of life or love, but just tired. We were old before we were given such a gift, and it didn't get any better for us, just longer. And I think, in a way, they understood that better than we could have told them."

"You are the nicest people that I have ever had the pleasure of knowing. You know that, don't you?" James had been a little in love with Chris since she'd come to his home to help his grandson, Sterling, with the she-devil so long ago. James nodded at her, and told her that he didn't know anyone else that could have helped them with this or they wouldn't have broken her heart over it. "I thank you for that. As I said, you are the best."

"We've said our goodbyes today and yesterday. They are broken up about it—they are, but they understand. I couldn't have asked for a better family than that. And when we told them that we was going to you today, they had us a party. A celebration of our life and all the things that we have done together." Chris nodded, wiping her own tears away from her cheeks. "We're ready anytime that you are."

The celebration had been wonderful too. And as he sat at the party, he'd thought of each of his grandchildren and what they were about now. Nothing in this world could have made him prouder than his grandchildren.

Trent, the oldest and by far the one who was into most things, he and Joe took care that the town was prosperous and safe. They had set up more programs for the people that lived there than most whole states had for their citizens. They were also good to the children that came into their lives. And there was now a sixth Trent James—a seventh and the eighth were on their way. Joe, from time to time, would look over the investments that he had and have him tweak them. He'd left all their money to her to distribute where it was needed.

Elijah was still making the family money. Not that there

was any need for more of it, but they not only donated a great deal to the causes and programs that Trent had going, but they also worked at the school, teaching the kids the value of money. Noelle did more for the children than anyone did. She had a special place in her heart for every one of them. Not that he blamed her, not the way that she'd been raised.

Scott had gone back to teaching people how to have sex. He supposed that was the wrong way to put it, but it mattered little. He was happy again, and as far as he could see, that was what he'd want for them all. Chloe was still running the town's police station. She was good at it too — they'd not had a robbery or a murder in decades. Well, there was that time that a bunch of kids decided to rob mailboxes, but she nipped that in the bud right away. A night in jail scared them boys on the right path, it surely did.

Sterling. He loved that boy more than the others. Of course, he'd never say that. But Sterling had been through more than the others in his lifetime. Probably more than a couple of them. When that she-devil had tried to kill his Sterling, James had been so afraid for him. His art hadn't changed, though. It was still dark and scary, but he couldn't keep a painting without someone wanting to buy it before the paint even dried. His and Marty's little boy that they adopted when his parents were killed, Benson, took over the running of the gallery and did as good a job as his daddy ever did. That Marty, she hadn't changed a bit either. Still a pistol, and a mouth on her that made him blush sometimes.

Randal didn't teach as much as he used to. But he did run a lot of after school programs for the kids. There was a time when he had food in his room for all the kids that didn't have much to eat. Also, there was gloves and hats. Now they had a room that was dedicated to the children with everything they could want, from good food to eat, to boots for the cold months, to having backpacks filled with enough supplies to get them through the year at school and to take home to do homework. He loved his kids, he called them all. Laney had made up with her daddy after a time, and he still spent time with them, but he didn't think she'd ever be as close to him as she was to his son, TJ.

Then there was his boy Tanner. He'd had a rough time of it when Giyanna had been in a car accident after their second child was born. She'd been pregnant with another little boy, but he had been taken from them. James thought for sure that it was going to break them both, they took it so hard. But when after their second child, a little boy, started talking, they seemed to come out of it. He'd never been so happy in his life when Giyanna announced the very next year that she was having another baby. Sure did his heart good to see them happy and living again.

Yes, sir. His grandkids had done him proud, and James didn't think there was a grandda happier with their growing up and become fathers themselves as he was of them. He was sure gonna miss them.

He knew that he was asking a great deal of the witch. But James and his lovely mate had never been asked if they wanted this. Not that he wasn't glad for the time that they'd had, but they were ready now. Perhaps if they'd been a little younger, they might have been all right with things. But they weren't, and now they needed to get to the stepping off place, as his momma had called it.

"If you could give me an hour, I'll have the place ready where you can rest. Or have you taken care of that?" Jas told her that they had a marker all picked out, but, no, they'd assumed after all this time they'd just turn to dust. "Not quite, but we'll take care that you have a very nice spot, close to the family so that they can visit you. I'll call on the lady of the earth now and have it arranged."

"How would we get there, if you don't mind me asking?" James couldn't seem to let go of Jas's hand. "I mean, traveling here wasn't any hardship on us, but we'd really like to be close to the children."

"Yes, of course. I can arrange that."

She left them there, and he looked at his wife of just under two hundred years.

"You've been my rock and foundation our whole life together. I couldn't have made it in this life without you and this family. You know that, don't you?" Jas nodded and laid her head on his shoulder. "I don't know what I'd have done had you not been there at that hospital when I woke up. Seeing you there, so pretty, like you are right now."

"Oh, go on with you. You know as well as I that I was just a little bitty thing. To think, having my daddy bringing me to work like that, and what do you think happened? I find my other half being worked on by him." James remembered it like yesterday. "You were so afraid of him, I think now. You wanted to impress him that you'd be a good man."

"He didn't much care for me, I'm thinking." She laughed, and he did as well. "Then it only took us another ten years before you became my other half, my wife for all time."

They rocked on the bench, taking in the sights that were

all around them. They'd been doing that a great deal over the last months and days here on this earth. Taking in the sights so that they'd have something to comfort them when they were ready to go on. That was where the first conversation had come about, when they'd been taking a long walk one night after supper.

"I remember you being large with our TJ. Best sight I ever seen was when you handed him up to me from that bed. You said, 'Here you go. Now raise him to be as good a man as you are.' And I think between us, we did a good job." She told him they had. "Then he did the same for his sons. Six strapping boys he had, and I couldn't have been prouder of them than if they'd been ours."

"Christine loves them all so much. It's like those girls were born to her too...she loves them as her own. Like it should have been." James knew that too. And he loved them as if they were his granddaughters as well. "James, I'm going to miss them, I am, but I'm so ready for this."

"I am too, love. I surely am." He rocked them some more, watching the deer in the field beyond playing with their newborn. "All I can think about is how much I love you. And how I know this is the right thing to do."

"Yes, myself as well. I'm so tired all the time, James, and I'm sorry for that." She started crying and he held her. James couldn't have stopped his own tears from falling under threat of death. He told her that there was nothing to be sorry for. "Like you said, had we been younger, we might have been better."

"Better? Oh darling, we were the best there was, I'm thinking." He pulled out the envelope that he'd gotten from

Trent last night. He took half the pictures and handed her the other half. "This is why I know that we were the best. Just look at them faces. And the smiles on all of them children. We did that. We started this long line of happy faces. You remember that."

"I will. You, I'll remember your face as well." He looked at her again, and she traced her fingers over all of him. His face, like hers, wasn't like it used to be, but to him, she was still the loveliest creature ever born. "I love you, Trent James Calhoun the third. Forever and a day, I shall forever cherish our time we had together, and all the memories that we made."

He was just about to cry again; his heart was so full. They'd been telling each other they loved the other since they were wee children. And now, all these decades later, they were still saying it. James held his wife until Chris came back to tell them that it was all set up.

"Good. That's right kind of you, Chris. It is." She nodded, then asked him if they'd changed their mind. "No, we haven't, have we love?"

"No, we're ready as we'll ever be. But I do have a single request." Chris told them anything. "I should like to watch the sun setting while you do this. I'm not sure what all this entails, but the sun setting, like us setting into the earth, so I'd like to watch it once more."

"Of course. And as much as I'd like to tell you that it's easy, it won't be on me. I have come to love you two like my own grandparents. People that I've respected and needed in my life daily. I could not have asked for better friends." They both nodded. "All right then, you two just sit here and watch the sunset. It should be soon. And then just close your eyes

200

when you're ready."

"That's all?" Chris nodded and wiped again at her tears. "You tell that husband of yours, and them brothers of his, they'd better be good to you. You're something special too."

"Micah is good to me, and so are the others. I couldn't have been mated to anyone kinder and more supportive than him. And to have a family like I do—well, as you know, it doesn't get any better than this."

They rocked back and forth when she left them there, sitting on the front porch just swinging back and forth. They would remember something that would pop into their heads, talk about it for a bit, then watch the sun going down behind the mountain.

"It sure has been a good life, my love." She told him for her as well. "This is the best way to leave this earth. Sitting with someone you love, just rocking away the final minutes. Yes, if I could have picked a better ending, I'm not sure what it would have been. You and me, we sure had some adventures."

"Yes, and I'm betting that we'll have us a few more, wherever we end up." He nodded. "It's time, my love."

"Yes, it's time."

He turned to her then, kissing her while watching her eyes. And when the sun showed its final colors of the day, they both closed their eyes, much as they had done all their lives, when they were just too tired to go on.

~~~

Trent knew the final moment of his grandparent's death. His heart skipped a couple of beats as he watched the same sun going down over the same mountain as they were. And it

201

broke his heart in two knowing that he'd never speak to them or hug them again.

Chris had told him through their link that she was going to set them up a faerie garden that would be blessed by the queen of the earth, as well as the queen of faeries. He loved that idea, and his family did as well.

They had gathered together, his brothers and their wives, his parents and close friends, to sit together, remembering the couple who had been there forever. And when the time came for them to be no more, no one said a word or uttered a single sound for several long moments.

The faeries came to get them an hour later. The garden was finished. Gathering what they'd already decided to take to the garden, all of them went to the place that he'd picked out for them. His mom started to sob, and Dad held her while he too fought with the tears. Trent didn't care. He cried like his heart had been broken, because to him, it had.

"It has been an honor to do such a thing for you, Lord Trent. They were our favorite people in all the world, we think." Trent thanked the little blue faerie. "The White Witch said that you had things that you wished to lay with them. If you would do so now, we'll make sure that they are safe from harm forever as well."

Trent put his first dollar on the garden. "From my first sale that you talked me into. We made very little money that time, but it got me hooked in helping other businesses."

The next person to lay something in the circle was Elijah. He put upon the place of interment a shell and a fishing hook. "The first time we went fishing, not at all good at it by the way, all I caught was this shell and several times my skin. I'll miss you, old man."

Next was Scott. He put a small whip and they all laughed. "To my grandma. The only person that seemed to understand me more than most, and could embarrass me the best. I will miss you both so much."

Sterling set a small picture on the marker. It was a picture of the two of them that he had painted for this day. "My memories of the two of you are too great to have picked just one. So, I'll use this to remind you both of how much we're going to miss you."

"Randal? Your turn." He nodded and laid a book on the grave. Trent laughed hard, as did the rest of them. The tattered copy of *Moby Dick* was what they had read together each night until it was finished when he was a child.

"You are the reason that I teach. And the reason that I'm still doing it." He blew them a kiss. "For all the nights I begged you for just one more chapter."

Tanner was last, and he seemed to hesitate longer than Randal. But when he walked to the grave and put the small booties on the marker, he didn't need to say a word. The booties were for the son that he and Giyanna had lost when there had been a car accident several decades ago. The grandparents had stayed up with Tanner and Giyanna all night when they were heartbroken. No one else could comfort them as they had.

Next was Mom and Dad. Mom just laid her hand upon the marker, her tears staining the bronze stone. Then from her pocket she pulled out the handkerchief that Grandma had been using since they'd been kids. It had been forever tucked into her sleeve to use when she needed it.

Dad went to the circle alone. He didn't say anything, but they knew that he was heartbroken by the loss. He cleared his throat and then started to sing. His voice, even after all these years, was as clear and beautiful as it had ever been. And "Amazing Grace" had never sounded as good to him before.

Walking back to the house, he turned once and looked at the circle. The faeries were busy taking care that the items that they left were well preserved with their magic. Trent turned back to his family and walked the rest of the way in silence.

"He'd kick our collective bottoms if he was here." Trent asked his dad what he wanted them to do. "We go on living like we did before. Have fun with the children. Let's have a nice dinner and celebrate what we think of. Just anything."

"All right. I'll run into town and get some steaks. If you guys will have someone start on sides, I'll be back soon." Trent was warming to the idea. "I'll even see if I can find us a pie or three or four too."

By the time he returned they not only had the fire going and several side dishes, but the ice cream maker was going as well. There had been several pies at the store—not as good as homemade, but it was spur of the moment and they were good. Peach, apple, pineapple, as well as cherry. Grandda's favorite. Then he had picked up banana cream for Grandma.

The night wore on, and they ate better than he thought they had for a while now. The pies were eaten with gusto, and even the ice cream seemed to hit the spot. They were a family that had just lost two loved ones, and Dad was right; Grandda would have kicked their butts had he seen the way that they were mourning their deaths.

When Myra showed up a little after seven that night, he

welcomed her with open arms, as did the rest of the family.

"I've come to tell you that the Bentleys would like to open a scholarship fund in your grandparents' name. It will go to underprivileged shifters so that they might go to college a little easier. It'll be called the Trent James and Jasmine Calhoun Foundation." Trent and the others thanked her. Joe asked if they might put to it as well. "Yes, she said that she would welcome you to help the others."

"Will you stay and have some pie with us? We're having a sort of celebration." She declined, and that was when he noticed what she was wearing. Trent got a good laugh out of that. "Balloons, huh? I don't suppose there is a story that goes with that, is there?"

"As a matter of fact, there is. Your grandfather was a sneaky man. One day when I was around, he told me that he could use a glass of tea. I told him, since I was standing, that I'd make him some. But he insisted that I use what was in the ice box, as he called it. When I opened the door, two hundred or so balloons came out—scared ten decades off my life. And then you know what the old poop did? He and Jas sang me Happy Birthday. First time in more years than I could count that anyone had done that for me. I have never forgotten it."

They all laughed again, and he realized that they were much better now. Even Mom and Dad seemed to be in better spirits. He was glad now that Dad had suggested this. It was the perfect ending to the day.

Before You Go...

HELP AN AUTHOR

write a review

THANK YOU!

Share your voice and help guide other readers to these wonderful books. Even if it's only a line or two your reviews help readers discover the author's books so they can continue creating stories that you'll love. Login to your favorite retailer and leave a review. Thank you.

AWARD WINNING, BESTSELLING AUTHOR

Kathi Barton, winner of the Pinnacle Book Achievement award as well as a best-selling author on Amazon and All Romance books, lives in Nashport, Ohio with her husband Paul. When not creating new worlds and romance, Kathi and her husband enjoy camping and going to auctions. She can also be seen at county fairs with her husband who is an artist and potter.

Her muse, a cross between Jimmy Stewart and Hugh Jackman, brings her stories to life for her readers in a way that has them coming back time and again for more. Her favorite genre is paranormal romance with a great deal of spice. You can visit Kathi online and drop her an email if you'd like. She loves hearing from her fans. aaronskiss@gmail.com.

Follow Kathi on her blog: http://kathisbartonauthor.blogspot.com/

Printed in Great Britain
by Amazon